Moral
Values

Library of Conservative Thought

Volume 2 of Ethics

with a new introduction by
Andreas A.M. Kinneging

Moral
Values

Nicolai Hartmann

Transaction Publishers
New Brunswick (U.S.A.) and London (U.K.)

Library of Congress Catalog Number: 2002032029
ISBN: 0-7658-0962-1
Printed in the United States of America

Library of Congress Cataloging-in-Publication Data

Hartmann, Nicolai, 1882-1950.
  [Ethik. English]
  Moral values : volume two of Ethics / Nicolai Hartmann ; with a new introduction by Andreas A.M. Kinneging.
    p. cm.—(Library of conservative thought)
  Originally published: [S. 1.] : MacMillan Co., 1932.
  Includes bibliographical references and index.
  ISBN 0-7658-0962-1 (pbk. : alk. paper)
  1. Ethics. I. Title. II. Series.

B3279 .H23 E8813 2002
171' .2—dc21   2002032029

CONTENTS

PART II

THE REALM OF ETHICAL VALUES

(AXIOLOGY OF MORALS)

Section I

GENERAL ASPECTS OF THE TABLE OF VALUES

Section II

THE MOST GENERAL ANTITHESES

CONTENTS

Section V

SPECIAL MORAL VALUES
(FIRST GROUP)

Section VII

SPECIAL MORAL VALUES

(THIRD GROUP)

Section VIII

THE ORDER OF THE REALM OF VALUES

TRANSACTION INTRODUCTION

In 1926 Nicolai Hartmann (1882-1950) published his monumental treatise on ethics, simply entitled *Ethik*, in one fat volume of about 800 densely printed pages. In 1932 an authorized English translation appeared, in three separate volumes, adding up to slightly less than 1100 pages. It is this translation, entitled *Ethics*, that is now being republished by Transaction Publishers.

Why three volumes? Because the work consists of three parts, each of which constitutes a whole in itself. Part one is entitled "The Structure of the Ethical Phenomenon," part two "The Realm of Ethical Values," and part three "The Problem of the Freedom of the Will." All three parts have also been given a subtitle by the author, respectively "Phenomenology of Morals," "Axiology of Morals," and "The Metaphysics of Morals." In the translation these titles and subtitles have been retained—one will find them at the top of the table of contents of each volume—but on the cover of each volume different and shorter titles are introduced. Volume one is named *Moral Phenomena*, volume two *Moral Values*, and volume three *Moral Freedom*.

As has just been mentioned, each part/volume constitutes a whole in itself. That does not mean, however, that one can read the parts/volumes independently of the others. They are intimately connected, as each successive part/volume enlarges upon the ideas and themes set out in earlier ones. Hence, volume one, *Moral Phenomena*, provides the groundwork of the entire *Ethics*. There, Hartmann delineates the meaning he attaches to the concept that is fundamental to his approach of philosophical ethics: value. The central chapters of volume one—section V, "The Essence of Ethical Values," and section VI, "The Essence of the Ought"— provide an extensive analysis of this concept of value, and of some concepts closely related to it.[1] In the Introduction to the Transaction edition of volume one, which aims to give the reader an outline of Hartmann's thought *in toto*, the most important features of these concepts are discussed at some length.

The purpose of the present introduction is to prepare the way for the perusal of volume two of the *Ethics*: *Moral Values*. But since this volume builds on the ideas expounded in volume one, it is essential that one has at least some knowledge of these ideas. A short summary is therefore in order here. For a more extensive overview the reader is referred to the Introduction in the Transaction edition of volume one, *Moral Phenomena*.

I. Values, Being, and Man

The question of what we ought to do is not, *pace* Kant, the fundamental question of practical thought, including practical philosophy. The question of value is the question that practical thought must deal with first and foremost, according to Hartmann. What is valuable in life and in the world generally? After all, I can gauge what I ought to do only when I "see" what in general is valuable in life. Values are the *principia* of practical thought.

What is the foundation of values? Are they grounded in the nature of things, an aspect of the order of being, or are they the inventions of man himself, subjective and mutable, perhaps even founded on nothing but his desires? The moderns tend to believe the latter and see values as something added to the world by man, through his own free creativity. Hartmann's ethics is in essence an effort to discard this view and vindicate the pre-modern conception that values cannot be invented but can merely be found, and are therefore objective and absolute. They are not posited by us, but subsist independently of our desires and consciousness. Values have being in themselves (*Ansichsein*). They belong to a realm of being first discovered by Plato—the sphere of ideal being—a realm with its own structures, its own laws and order.

What is the sphere of ideal being? Hartmann argues that there are two different ways of being (*Seinsweisen*): real being (*reales Sein*) and ideal being (*ideales Sein*). Real being includes everything that is in or attached to the spatial-temporal world, including the incorporeal. The entities that partake of this kind come into existence and perish; they are impermanent, altering, and singular.

Real being consists of four different strata or layers (*Seinsschichten*), from the stratum of inorganic being at the bottom, through the strata of organic being and mental being, to spiritual being at the top. The categories of the inorganic and the organic are more or less self-evident, but what are mental and spiritual being? Mental being encompasses everything that exists within the individual soul, consciously or unconsciously. Mental being everyone has for himself. It is an inner, esoteric being of the individual that is not transferable. Animals, al least the higher animals, also seem to have a mental life. Spiritual being is built upon mental being, but it exceeds the mental. It is transferable, for every individual it is objective, and only man is a spiritual entity. "Culture" is a term that renders the meaning of spiritual being quite accurately, if one defines it as including language, morality, law, politics, historical consciousness, ideology, the arts, religion, and philosophy.

In contrast to real being, ideal being is timeless and not spatial. It consists of ideal entities, such as mathematical units and laws, the laws of logic, the essence (*Wesen*) of concrete, existing things, acts, and occurrences. And it includes values. The kind of being peculiar to an ideal being is that of an *ontós on*. It is that "through which" everything participating in it is just as it is. Ideal being manifests itself in real being, but it is not absorbed in it. It is the "ground" of the being of real beings.

The case of mathematical being is instructive. In the units and laws of mathematics man first discovered ideal being. Mathematical units and laws are beyond time and space, beyond genesis and disintegration, which are typical of everything in the real world. But although mathematical being differs fundamentally from real being, it pervades the latter. The principles of mathematics are the principles of reality. Things, acts, and occurrences in the real world necessarily comply with the principles of mathematics. It is possible, by eliminating or adding one or more axioms, to develop a mathematics that has little to do with the real world, but it is not possible for the real world to escape from the grip of mathematical principles. The real contains and is molded by the ideal.

There is, however, one fundamental difference between values and the other species of ideal being, such as mathematical units and laws. Unlike the latter, values do not categorically govern real being. They can, of course, be realized, but they can also remain unrealized. It does not lie in their essence as principles that the real must correspond to them. Values are not inviolable determinants to which everything real is subordinate.

This leads to the question: what—if any—is the relation between values as ideal entities and the real world? At this point Hartmann introduces the notion of "the ought." Values and the ought are indissolubly bound together. The ought is not principally an ought-to-do, but an ought-to-be. The ought-to-be is the mode of being of a value, and a value is the content of the ought. The ought-to-be of the values refers to the real world. When the ideal finds itself in opposition to the real, when it is unrealized, the ought-to-be becomes actual. The ideal "calls out" to be realized.

To be heard—and acted upon—Hartmann writes, there must be in the stream of real existence, i.e. in fluctuating reality itself, a point of support upon which the ought-to-be impinges. There must be something or other within the real course of the world that shares completely in the world's existential mode of coming into being and perishing. Yet it must at the same time be able to be a carrier of the imperishable, the ideal; it must in this one respect be more than the other entities, must be distinguished from all other reality by this essential feature. This point of support is man. He and only he is capable of grasping values and of acting upon them. He and only he can convert the ought-to-be into reality. The rest of existence is dull and dead to the call of the ideal. Man is the guardian of the ought in the world of real being. In man only the ought-to-be is transformed into the ought-to-do, and in man only the ought-to-do is transformed into a moral act.

Man, in Hartmann's view, has a double nature: he is both a "subject" and a "person." Man as a subject belongs to the stratum of mental being, man as a person is part of the stratum of spiritual being. Subjectivity is the precondition of personhood (*Personalität*).[2] Only a person is a moral subject, with the power or the freedom to take hold of a value or not and to place his acts in its service or not, and with the responsibility that goes with it.

How exactly does a person grasp values? Let us go back once more to mathematics, as the archetypical species of ideal being. The real world is suffused with mathematical principles. These cannot be observed empirically. The validity of mathematical principles is universal and stringent, whereas empirical observation can only render probable results. Therefore, knowledge of mathematical principles must be the product of a different kind of observation, a kind that is not empirical and can claim absolute validity. Plato called it an inner perception, a perception with the mind's eye, so to speak. Hartmann speaks of "a priori" knowledge as an inner grasping of a state of affairs that has immediate certainty and can claim generality and necessity. What goes for mathematics goes for all other types of ideal being as well, viz. for the laws of logic, for the essence of concrete, existing things, acts, and occurrences, and for values. All of these cannot be observed empirically, but are perceived a priori. Hence, our knowledge of these ideal entities is a priori knowledge.

As we have seen, however, values are not entirely on a par with the other classes of ideal being. The other classes have a categorical hold over the real world. Real being is wholly conditional on them. All real entities conform to them inexorably. That is not the case with values. Real being can, but need not, be in agreement with the values. It can be valuable or not. Due to the indissoluble bond between the real and the other classes of the ideal, it is possible in those cases to direct our thinking to the ideal through the real by bracketing the ephemeral in it. In the case of values, this is impossible. How then do we grasp a value?

Grasping a value is sensing it, or more precisely, being gripped by it (*Erfaßtsein von ihm*), writes Hartmann. The specific "organ" with which man perceives values is his sense of value (*Wertgefühl*).

This sense of value is neither a cognitive nor a conative, but an affective, an emotional capacity. It is a peculiar axiological sense, an "ordre de coeur" or "organe morale,"[3] a primary, pre-, or subconscious "response" to the presence of values.[4] It is this sense, and the conscious discernment of values (*Wertschau*) based on it, that enables us not only to recognize values, but also to intuit the ranking order between them.

Of course, the fact that one has the capacity to sense values does not mean that one actually senses them. The sense of value of concrete persons is often immature, deadened, or unevenly developed, and consequently they are blind to a part of the realm of values.[5] It is here just as it is with mathematical insight: not everyone has the eye, the ethical maturity, the spiritual level, for seeing the situation as it is. The universality, necessity, and objectivity of the valuational judgment hold good *in abstracto*, but this does not at all mean that everyone is capable of the valuational insight in question. It only means that whoever is capable of it, whoever spiritually gets hold of its meaning, must necessarily feel and judge thus and not otherwise. The sensing of values presupposes devotion and attentive listening. The realm of values needs to be lovingly and carefully hearkened to. Only to the attentive and patient does it reveal its secrets.

Thus far a short summary of the main contents of volume one of Hartmann's *Ethics*, *Moral Phenomena*.

II. Structure and Contents

Values are not posited by man, but are part of the nature of things. They cannot be invented or created, they can only be discovered. They have being-in-themselves, not real, i.e. spatial-temporal being, but ideal being. Together they make up an ideal realm of values. Volume two of the *Ethics*, entitled *Moral Values*, aims to describe this realm of values, in particular the region of moral values within it, with respect to both its content and its structure.

A comprehensive description should not be expected, however. Value research is still young and our survey casual and unsystematic, writes Hartmann. "Our knowledge of the structure and order of the realm of values is still in a rudimentary stage. We can look out upon the whole realm only through specific groups of values which happen to be accessible, but we cannot deductively determine particulars from a general view of the whole."[6] Indeed, it is uncertain whether we will ever have such a general view, because some parts of the realm of value may lie beyond the limits of what can be reflexively known.[7]

This lack of systematic knowledge of the realm of values, the need to proceed inductively, from the bottom up, stipulates the method of investigation. First, we must assemble a catalogue of values. In this way we acquire some insight into the contents of the realm of values. With this knowledge we can subsequently try to discover the structure inherent in this realm, i.e. to see how the various values are related and fit together. This is the plan of *Moral Values*. After the introductory section I, which deals with some important underlying questions, Hartmann plunges into an extensive investigation of the value contents of the realm of value that takes up two-thirds (sections II to VII) of the book. It is only in the final section VIII that the question of the structure governing the realm of values is returned to. Thus, the weight of the volume clearly falls on the former. *Moral Values* is first and foremost a detailed and profound phenomenological description of values, and of moral values in particular. It is possible to read these sections separately, because the analysis of the values presented there is largely independent of the more general structural analysis.[8]

Now, it is clear that there are several different, perhaps even an infinite variety of, species of value. There might even be species of value in the ideal realm of value that are not accessible to man. For being is much richer and more profound than that which can be made an object to man.[9] Moreover, of some species of value, such as the aesthetic for instance,[10] we are aware, but we can hardly be said to have much knowledge. Consequently, our inquiry is of necessity limited to those species of value we know something of. Since moral values are central to our concerns, they must stand at the heart of them, and it is a happy coincidence that they seem to be among the most accessible values in the whole realm of values.

However, moral values cannot be discussed in isolation. Other species of value, though themselves not moral values, but in some way or other foundations upon which moral values are built, cannot be left out of the inquiry. Thus Hartmann.

Three species of morally relevant values are singled out and discussed at length in *Moral Values*: "elementary values" (*elementarste Werte*), "subject-values" (*dem Subjekt anhaftenden Wertfundamente*), and "goods-values" (*Güterwerte*). Because the moral values are, in different ways, grounded on these values, they are discussed first. Before going into the contents of all these values, however, Hartmann discusses two issues that are at the heart of his ethical theory, and need to be understood first in order to grasp his description of the values and the concluding musings of the structure of the realm of value: first, the disparity between the intended value and the value of the intention, and second, the problem of conflicting values.

III. Intended Value and the Value of the Intention

"[W]herein would an honest man be superior to a thief, if the things purloined were not somehow of value? What one man can steal, what another can treasure as a possession, is not merely a thing but a good. Honesty, then, if it is a moral value, necessarily presupposes the positive value of goods. It is inherently dependent upon the latter. In the same way, chivalry, which secures an advantage to the weak, rests upon the value of the advantage; love for one's neighbour, which gives, or which takes upon itself another's burden, assumes the value of the things given and of the relief from the burden; not otherwise is veracity related to the value for the other person of the truth asserted. *In all these cases the value of the act is altogether different from that attributed to the external good, whether this be some simple material possession or some complex situation.*"[11] Only the act itself has a moral value (*sittlicher Wert*), not the external things realized by it. These merely have goods-value (*güterwert*).

Four important conclusions can be derived from this analysis. First, moral values are intrinsically higher than goods-values. (Why exactly this is the case will be shown *infra*.)

Second, moral values are necessarily affixed to man—primarily to his acts, but also to his person, which is shaped by and expressed in these acts. In the latter case, when values are inherent in a person, we speak of virtues. Moral values are always attached to acts or persons, never to things and the relation between them. Only acts or persons can be morally good or bad.

Third, *moral value appears "on the back of the act" (auf dem Rücken der Handlung),*[12] *not in the goal that is aimed at.* In being truthful one does not aim at veracity itself, but at giving the person being spoken to the possibility of learning the truth. "[L]ikewise, the object of the high-minded or loving person is not to be high-minded or loving, but that the other person, to whom something is given or whom he makes glad, may have the gift or the gladness. He gives out of love, but not for the sake of being a loving person. He is concerned not at all with his own moral being, but with the being of the other person, and indeed by no means only with that other person's moral, but with his whole being, bodily as well as mental, that is to say, with conditions (*Sachverhalte*) that are valuable for that person. But these conditions are valuable for him in so far as they embrace goods (i.e. goods-values, A.K.). The knowledge of a truth is as much a good (i.e. a goods-value, A.K.)—or surely intended as a good—as the gift bestowed or the gladness occasioned."[13]

Fourth, since, given the above, the moral value of an act does not depend on the value of what is intended (*intendierter Wert*), but on the value of the intention (*Intentionswert*), the moral value of an act does not depend on the success of the act, but merely on the value of its intention. Needless to say, this view derives from Kant.[14]

Do these conclusions imply that human action is completely determined by the goods-values aimed at? Are moral values nothing but side effects? The expression of moral value appearing "on the back of the act," not in the goal aimed at, seems to imply this. Such an inference, however, would be mistaken. The functioning of our conscience is crucial at this point. "[T]hat clearer or obscurer inward self-knowledge (*conscientia*) concerning the value

or disvalue of our own conduct, is by no means merely the condemnation after the deed, which one generally understands by it,
but equally an anticipatory prohibitive factor which is determinant, at least negatively, by its barring out of that which is immoral. It therefore makes itself felt, at least through selection, in
the choice of ends."[15]

Moreover, in some instances a moral value can be intended.
Otherwise, moral education, whether of oneself or of another, would
be impossible. But, "[e]ven where the end of the endeavor is the
moral value of a person (one's own or another's), it is never the
same as the moral value of the endeavor. If, for instance, the trend
of an educator is towards magnanimity or self-sacrifice in the pupil, this tendency is not on that account to be called either magnanimous or self-sacrificing. Just as little is it a tendency to be
honest or veracious, when the aim is honesty and veracity. Rather
there is attached to it another moral value, which may be difficult
enough to name precisely, but which without a name is plainly
enough seen as a moral value.'[16] Hence, even in these marginal
cases, the intended value differs from the moral value of the intention.

IV. MORAL CONFLICT AND THE GRADATION OF VALUES

Older moral thought tends to regard moral conflict as nothing but
the antagonism between moral and immoral, or even non-moral
impulses in man, between "duty" and "inclination," writes
Hartmann. "The 'natural man,' or even an inborn tendency to evil
in him, was made responsible for the immoral impulses. Antiquity
saw their origin in the desires; Christian ethics in a kind of passive
resistance, the 'weakness of the flesh.'"[17] All these views are to a
certain extent correct. There is a conflict between natural instinct
and the sense of values.

But there is also a moral conflict of another kind: the conflict
of moral values with one another. Certainly, not all moral values
are exclusive of others. On the contrary, many can be combined in
a certain harmony. "But among them there are some which contradict one another, which in concrete cases by their contents ex-

clude one another and which nevertheless, in one and the same situation, ought all to be realized. Here arises a conflict of another, evidently higher kind, not between moral and immoral, but between moral and moral. The alternative is here not that between wrong and right, but between wrong and wrong. Either way a value is violated and, again, either way a value is fulfilled. Whoever is entangled in such a conflict—and life continually places man in such situations—cannot escape from it without guilt."[18] Hence, man has to deal with two different types of moral conflict. How should he settle them? In both cases, the key to the answer lies in the gradation of values.

With regard to the first type of moral conflict, that between "duty" and "inclination," Hartmann argues that "[i]t is in the nature of human volition that it is never directed towards anything contrary to value as such. That was the never-to be-forgotten meaning of Socratic ethics: no one does evil for evil's sake, it is always a good (something valuable) that hovers before him."[19] So how can the desires, how can "weakness of the flesh," divert the will from the valuable, if the very nature of volition is to be able only to turn to the valuable?

The answer is that even the will that is diverted by desires and weakness of the flesh moves towards values, but it moves towards lower ones. It is captivated by the morally indifferent goods-values. It fails to select in accordance with the higher, moral values. "Their surrender to the individual's self-interest in the goods is a moral mistake. For this is precisely the peculiarity of moral values, that they come forward with a claim of more unconditional validity, and allow an interest in the lower values only within the limits of their own preservation by the person."[20]

As to the second type of moral conflict, that between different moral values, Hartmann contends that, although man cannot escape guilt here, he has to decide in a way that answers for his guilt. In that he can succeed only if he is able to chose the higher among the conflicting moral values. Hence, in this type of moral conflict too, choosing correctly is choosing according to the objective gradation of values. But that presupposes knowledge or at least an

awareness of that gradation. Here, however, not the gradation between goods-values and moral values is at issue, but the gradation
of moral values among themselves. And whereas the ranking of
goods-values in comparison with moral values is evident, according to Hartmann, the ranking of moral values in comparison with
each other is much less obvious. Hence, we must return to this,
once we have more insight into the contents of the realm of values.

V. ELEMENTARY VALUES

What do we know of the content of the realm of value and, more
specifically, of moral values? What values and what moral values
are there? We possess only a partial knowledge of them. "The
extent of the realm of values is greater not only than our philosophical consciousness of value, but also than our primary sense
of values."[21] Lacking knowledge of the whole, there is no prospect of attaining insight into moral values on the basis of a general theory of value. Therefore, a deductive approach is out of the
question. We have to proceed inductively, by the gathering and
putting together of scattered details. We have to resort to the accidental clues supplied by intellectual history, i.e. to the various
values that have been discovered and put forward at different times
and places.

As has already been said, Hartmann singles out four species of
values in *Ethics*: elementary values, subject-values, goods-values, and moral values. Though they are not moral values themselves, elementary values, subject-values, and goods-values are discussed at length, because they are morally relevant values. They are,
in different ways, the foundation upon which moral values are built.

The elementary values are the most basic values that can be
known. They are contained in all the higher values. The sphere of
these values has an inherently antinomic character: besides the
opposition between a positive and a negative, a value and the
opposite disvalue, that is obviously not antinomic, one finds oppositions between positive and positive, value and opposite value
here (*Wertgegensätze*). Since the elementary values are the foun-

dation of all other values, this is an ethically deeply significant fact, pointing out the pervasiveness and profundity of antinomies in moral life.

Each of the antinomies of elementary values is a dimension on which the various more specific values are located. Because there are several antinomies, it follows that the realm of values must be conceived of as a multi-dimensional intelligible "space" in which all the specific values have their particular position. The antinomies of elementary values provide us with the basic structure of the realm of values.[22] There are modal, relational, qualitative, and quantitative antinomies of elementary value.

The *modal antinomies* spring from the different modes of being of values.[23] Hartmann discusses two. First, there is an antinomy between *necessity and freedom*. First, values—the ought to be— are necessary, because they have (ideal) being independent from the possibility or impossibility of their realization. This necessity is itself a value, it is an aspect of the meaning of every value. "It gives the ideal being of the values that sublimity, in comparison with being of any other kind, that elevation above the relative, that inviolable subsistence, beyond (real, A.K.) being and not-being, for which language has no name, and in which the authority of these principles inheres. [...] The moral sense (i.e. the sense of value, A.K.), bowing before this incorruptible power, looks up to it as to the object of highest veneration, and rises inwardly towards it, and in the mere participation in it in his ethos he takes his greatest pride."[24]

This value of necessity has its counterpart in the value of freedom that is left to man. There is no compulsion in realizing the ought-to-be. If there were no such freedom, man would be an automaton, of necessity realizing the values. In that case, participation in the values would not be something sublime and distinctive. It is precisely the absence of compulsory force on the side of the values that is valuable, since it is precisely that which constitutes the moral subject, i.e. the person.

The second modal antinomy is one between *the value of the reality of a value, i.e. its having been realized, and the value of its not having been realized.* The value of the reality of a value is immediately evident, whenever or wherever that is the case. However, "[t]he non-reality of values also has a value. This becomes perceptible, as soon as we consider that active, intended realization is possible only where a value is non-existent, and that, in addition to that, it is active, intended realization, in which the higher, moral, species of value is realized."[25] Hence, the value of attainment here stands in opposition to the value of attempting the effort, even if the goal is not attained or not even attainable.

Relational antinomies between elementary values are antinomies springing from the relation between values and the moral subject, i.e. the person. Of these there are five, partially overlapping each other.

First, the antinomy between *the intended value and the value of the intention, i.e. the moral value.* What this means has already been set out above. The intended value is attached to the person who is the object of the act—the value of the intention—whereas moral value is attached to the person who acts.

Second, the antinomy between *activity and inertia (Trägheit).* Activity in the broadest sense, i.e. intentionality, constitutes the person, but his personhood is also dependent upon a measure of inertia: self-abandonment versus self-poise.

Third, the antinomy between *the height and the span of the values* intended by a person. A one-sided cultivation of a single or a few related values is valuable, Hartmann asserts. "Everything great and decisive in history may rest on the forcefulness of one-sided value-cultivation."[26] And yet, the development of the ethical being of a person in all directions is also valuable.

Fourth, the antinomy between *harmony and conflict of values.* Harmony is always an immediately perceived value, but so is conflict. It is from conflict that intention, decision, and action are born. Conflict keeps alert the sense and discernment of value, and opens up new vistas. Moral life in general is life in the midst of conflicts, seeking the right solutions to them.

Finally, there is a relational antinomy between *moral simplicity and complexity* in a person. Both are valuable. Moral simplicity in a person amounts to being straightforward, unequivocal, without doubts or second thoughts, uncomplicated. Moral complexity on the other hand is directed at the avoidance of injuring any value, the fitting moral response in every different situation, a many-sided interest, which presupposes a many-sided person.

The last antinomies of elementary values are the *qualitative and quantitative antinomies*. These are the most significant of this category of values, writes Hartmann. The first of these relates to the antinomy between *the value of universality or generality (Allgemeinheit) and the value of singularity or individuality*, the second to the antinomy between *the value of the totality (Allheit) and the value of the individual*.

The value of universality or generality comes to the fore most clearly in the idea of law, in so far as it is based on the equal treatment of all persons. Kant's categorical imperative is another example of an expression of this value. However, generalization is also schematization, impoverishment, indeed a sin against the richness of the values given. The axiological uniqueness of the ethos of each specific person, and of each specific community, is a value as well. On these all the special duties and claims are founded that a person has in addition to his general duties and claims.

The value of totality is distinct from and independent of the value of generality, just as the value of the individual is distinct and independent from the value of individuality. The antinomy between the totality and the individual is of a purely quantitative nature. In older conceptions of morality, the true moral task concerns the being of the totality, i.e. the community. In this view, life of the totality is more majestic than that of the individual, it is the carrier of greater aims and values. As a consequence, the individual takes a second place.

The value of the individual, on the other hand, has again and again called forth opposition against this conception of morality. This is justified, because only the individual has personhood, only the individual is a carrier of the highest values: moral values.

Hartmann's argument for this is highly interesting. "[P]recisely the highest values that can be realized in a community are not

properly communal, but individual. The legal and constitutional
order, public arrangements of every kind, of course inhere in the
community and not in the single man; he only has a share in them,
producing and profiting from them. But precisely as values such
assets are not the highest, for they are not moral values. Public
spirit, on the contrary, is a moral value, the civic and patriotic
spirit that bears such fruits. But this spirit is that of individuals,
the community as such has no such convictions."[27] Even a man,
sacrificing himself for the good of the community, realizes in himself the higher, moral value, and "thus in offering himself up he
preserves and enhances himself axiologically, he perfects himself
morally."[28]

Does this mean that the community has to yield to the individual? No. The community cannot exist without the individual.
And the latter is axiologically the higher being. But that does not
imply that the individual can ignore or repudiate the community.
The individual, taken by himself, is only an abstraction. He exists
only in a community, he is formed by it as by an infinitely stronger structure, he owes virtually everything to it. Hence, the individual must recognize the value of the community. Otherwise he
would negate himself.

Of course, strictly speaking, totality and community are synonymous only with regard to humanity as a whole. States, peoples,
and other collectivities are intermediate beings. These beings also
have value. They are the "individuals" of humanity. Every state,
for instance, has, in a sense, an individual life that moves according to its own laws of life, which are impossible to transfer, and
would be unnatural for any other state.

Then again, states (or other collectivities) are not persons, and
thus not carriers of moral values. In what then lies their value? In
their individuality. Humanity can do without national individuality as little as a state without personal individuality. "For not
only are temperament, spiritual type, morality, literature, and moral
education necessarily specific, with a national individuality, inimitable by other nations, but there is also a national calling, a
specific task within the whole of humanity and for its sake, a task,

which not humanity, but only a specifically endowed nation, with its particular gifts and in its unique position can fulfill. Herein lies the purpose of nations, their inner vocation."[29] Vintage Hegel!

VI . VALUES INTRINSIC TO THE SUBJECT

The realm of value might be an unbroken continuum, but we are not able to see it as such. Our present sense of value enables us to see only groups of value, between which whole areas of the intelligible "space" of the realm of values remain empty. Whether this is because these areas are impenetrable by the mind (*irreal*) or merely not yet discovered (*transobjektiv*), we do not know.

The first perceptible group after the one of the elementary values is the group Hartmann vaguely calls the values that condition contents (*inhaltlich bedingende Grundwerte*). These are the values inherent in the general configuration of real being. Like the elementary values, they are foundational for the moral values. Contrary to the first, however, they are not inherently antinomic. Here we are faced only with the simple opposition between values and corresponding disvalues. But antinomies between them are quite possible and in concrete situations often actual. Moreover, the values in the group are not equal in height—some are higher than others. There are two species within this genus: values intrinsic to the subject, and values intrinsic to the object. We have named them subject-values and goods-values above.

Hartmann distinguishes eight values intrinsic to the subject: life, consciousness, activity, suffering, strength, freedom of the will, foresight, and purposiveness.

The most elemental of values intrinsic to the subject is *life*. Without life, there would be no subject and hence no person. Life is the root that sustains the being of man as a subject and a person. Opposed to this value stands the disvalue of death, which not only destroys physical, but also mental, i.e. subjective being, as well as spiritual, i.e. personal being. "The matchless weight of this disvalue is elucidated by the enormity of the moral sin against life, murder. But also every injury to or enfeebling of life bears the same stamp of the disvaluable: for instance vital deterioration, decay, degeneration. A serious peril to life is all spirituality inimical to life, all excessive civilization and vital weakness, the failure of the firm instincts, the result of which is the symptomatic, disintegrating pessimism concerning life of those who are not fit for life and sickly."[30] The influence of Nietzsche at this point is obvious. But Hartmann is also critical of Nietzsche. Vitality, health, and strength are basic, but not more than that. One can also overestimate the value of life, turn it into the highest good. That, Hartmann contains, is a false ethical naturalism.

Consciousness is a value because it is the foundation of spiritual being. For only what is illuminated by consciousness becomes the spiritual property of man. What remains closed in the depth of the soul, man passes by without noticing. The value of consciousness increases with the degree of its development, i.e. with the depth of its penetration, with the extent of its participation in being. Consciousness is the mirror of the world, and the more it reflects of it, the more its mission is fulfilled: to be that being for which to exist gives everything real a meaning, which it does not have of itself.

Man's spiritual and moral being, his personhood, is built upon consciousness, as consciousness is upon life. His personhood has value of its own, higher than that of life and consciousness. It is a complex structure, of which activity, suffering, strength, freedom of the will, and foresight are the constitutive elements. In the characteristic of purposiveness these elements are all summed up.

To *activity*, not in the sense of a mere restless striving, but of taking a stand, of taking the initiative, and of commitment, also where it does not issue in overt action, moral values and disvalues adhere in the first place and most visibly. Opposed to it as a disvalue stands inertia, not in the sense particular to the elementary value discussed above, but of indifference against values, of *acedia*.

However, some values do not depend on activity. *Suffering* is such a value. A glance at the corresponding disvalue may be instructive. "It is the incapacity to suffer, the inability of bearing grief and misfortune, the collapse under its weight, an inner suc-

cumbing, sinking, the degradation of the human essence, its brittleness and inner inelasticity."[31] Those incapable of suffering are
disfigured and broken by it. In contrast, those capable of suffering
are strengthened by it. Their bearing power, humanity, and moral
being grow. As Aeschylus expressed it long ago: *pathei mathos*,
the lesson taught by suffering.

Of course, there is a limit to the capacity of suffering for everyone. "But within this limit, and the nearer to it, the more, suffering
to man means the awakening of his innermost moral nature, the
unlocking of the depth of his being, the liberation of his noblest
powers. Whoever has been tested in suffering is steeled and solid,
for him nothing is too difficult."[32] This new power "also brings
about the silent deepening of moral feeling and understanding.
Great pain is also a deepening, it opens up depths of which the
lightly treading untried has no suspicion. And not only the depth
of one's own heart, but also those of others, indeed the depth of
life in general and its inexhaustible circumstantial richness. The
whole attitude towards life changes. The perception of value of
the carefree stays on the colourful surface; the man matured in
suffering sees the same circumstances, conflicts, the same human
striving and wrestling more profoundly; he participates in it in a
different way, his perception of values has broadened and sharpened. Suffering has given him the organ for values that were hidden from him before. Indeed, perhaps it is not too much to say that
suffering is the true educator of the consciousness of value."[33]

Moral strength (*Kraft*) lies behind activity and suffering, and
both of these grow out of it. Its value is most visible in willpower,
determination, resolution, perseverance, the overcoming of opposition, indeed the thriving under it. A weak will is morally inferior,
even contemptuous, independently of the value or disvalue of its
aim. But beyond the sphere of action, the same holds good of all
inner intention. There is a strength of inclination, of love and
hate, of conviction, of belief, "that can remove mountains."[34]

A person differs from all other beings mostly in not being predetermined in his action. He retains his freedom vis-à-vis the principles that hold good for him: the values. This singular dignity

has always been described as *freedom of the will*. It may be that
such freedom does not exist. Whether it does or not is the subject
of volume three of the *Ethics, Moral Freedom*. Here that is not
relevant, since we are merely concerned with the value of the freedom of the will. Even if there were no carrier of this value, if there
were no persons, and hence no moral beings, the freedom of the will,
as an ideal being, would still be valuable, Hartmann contends.

However desperate the problem may look, however overwhelming all psychological insight may speak against the freedom of
the will, man cannot let himself be robbed of it. He struggles with
all his might to retain his belief in it. This is documented most force-
fully in the will to be responsible, indeed to bear the guilt for one's
own acts, and the aversion of the presumption of exculpation and
repudiation of guilt, that one comes across in moral life. "A guilty
man has the right to carry his guilt. He must refuse redemption from
without. To retain his guilt is valuable for him, despite its oppressive
load; it signifies for him the preservation of his personhood, the conservation and recognition of his freedom. With his guilt he would
lose a greater moral good: his humanity. In taking upon himself his
own deed and his guilt, in asserting his responsibility, in his sincere willingness to carry it, the moral pride of a free act expresses
itself, the majestic right to humanity, that grounds all moral being
and not-being. [...] The presumption of diminution of guilt, of ex-
emption, the admission of 'mitigating circumstance' is at bottom a
moral disenfranchisement and a degradation of man."[35] Again,
Hegel's presence is palpable.[36]

Foresight is the visionary element in man. It is the capacity to
look forward in time, to see future things, to prepare beforehand, it
raises human consciousness above the mere reflection of what is,
of reality. This is of great value, because in a sense only the future
belongs to man as a practical being. The future is his only field of
action. The past rests motionless forever and cannot be changed,
but neither can the present. Only that which still has to become
real can still be influenced and modified.

The negative opposite of foresight is clinging in thought to the
present and to the completed, being struck with blindness to what

is not yet real, drifting mindlessly in the stream of events, living obtusely from day to day, for which only looking back and regret remains.

Beyond freedom of the will and foresight lies *purposiveness*, which completes man's personhood. Man is the only being in which we find this teleological capability. It is the threefold ability to choose ends, to finds means towards their realization, and to guide the blind causal stream of events towards these ends. To this ability of predestination he owes his power in the world. Because ends are goods and goods are a specific species of values, man in this way performs his metaphysical role as mediator between the ideal realm of values and the real. He primarily realizes goods-values, but in so doing, on the back of the act, he also realizes the moral values.[37]

This capacity of predestination is the most powerful but also the most dangerous of all the gifts that have been given to man. It is a value only within the limits of his ability to handle it. Beyond that it is a disvalue. Man's whole practical life is nothing but a play with this dangerous gift: not because he wants to, but because he has to. There is no choice for him in that respect. As long as he breathes he cannot withdraw from it. Only how he shall play the game, how he shall use his gift, is up to him. And it happens that this power leads him astray, that he overlooks the limits of his strength, and is crushed.

VII. Values Intrinsic to the Object

Goods-values are values of things (*Sachen*) and situations (*Sachverhalte*) that are objects striven for. They are the ends of human action. They are morally relevant, because in our struggle to realize them, we realize the moral values. They differ from the subject-values in that they are not values *of* the subject, but values *for* the subject.

Hartmann distinguishes between basic or general goods on the one hand and the class of special goods on the other. In addition to these, there is a class of goods that have no value in themselves, but are pursued for the sake of other goods. These fall under the category of the useful.[38] There are four basic or general goods: existence *(Dasein)*, situatedness, power *(Macht)*, and happiness.

The *existence of the world*, real being as it is, with everything in it that can serve his ends, is valuable to the person, from natural resources like the earth, water, air, and light, to the special sources of nourishment and wealth. But this category of goods also includes, for instance, the causal determination of the world, for if it were causally undetermined, man's purposiveness would be of no use, and man could not consciously realize his end. One cannot modify the causal process if there is no such process.

The value of *situatedness* to man is twofold. First, concrete situations are man's field of action, the existential foundation of his personal and moral life. It is in the variety of concrete situations that his sense of value develops, that he faces his tasks, and that he has to take a stand.

On top of that, another value inheres in situatedness. A concrete situation can have its own moral significance, independent from the moral being of the *dramatis personae*. For example, a highly dramatic moral conflict can occur between morally insignificant persons. All the deeper human relationships are to some extent of this nature. Hence, situatedness is the catalyst of moral life.

Power, in the sense of being able, of having under control, is yet another goods-value. Rather than merely a means to other goals, it is, Hartmann believes, a goal in itself. Obviously, powerlessness is the corresponding disvalue.

Happiness can relate to the objective favorableness of the situation, but also to the subjective sense of happiness. Interestingly, the two are relatively independent from each other: the feeling of happiness is not a function of the goods of fortune, but of the capacity for feeling happy. Neither of them has any moral value.

The disvalue corresponding to happiness is unhappiness, of course, but happiness itself is not without its drawbacks: in happiness itself lurks a hidden disvalue. Anyone pampered by happiness becomes shallow. It is as if the proximity and obtrusiveness of the wealth of goods present pushes the higher, moral values out of sight. We can bear only a limited amount of happiness, without sinking morally. Precisely that what happiness lacks, suffering provides: the deepening and steeling of man, the sharpening of his perception of value.[39]

In addition to these four basic goods of existence, situatedness, power, and happiness, a variety of *specific goods* can be distinguished, all of which partake to a greater or lesser degree in the basic goods. The most elementary class of specific goods are the material goods: possession and property. After that comes communal life, from the family to the community of all humans. Then there is the class of spiritual goods, including the law, language, knowledge, education, et cetera. And finally, there is a category of goods dependent upon the moral conduct of one's fellow-men, such as the good reputation one enjoys, the honor one is paid, the trust bestowed by others, the friendship or love that is offered. Although these are obviously primarily moral values, they are goods-values to those who receive them as well.

VIII. FUNDAMENTAL MORAL VALUES

With this we have completed our overview of Hartmann's list of morally relevant virtues. We must now turn to that part of *Moral Values* that is devoted to the moral values themselves. J. N. Findlay, one of the few authors from the Anglo-Saxon world with a substantial knowledge of Hartmann's *Ethics*, has remarked that "[t]his part of the book has a richness and a truth to value-experience which renders it comparable to Aristotle's *Ethics* or Hegel's *Phenomenology of Spirit*."[40]

The description of the moral values themselves takes up almost half of this second volume of the *Ethics*. They are divided in four groups. First, there is a group of fundamental moral values, encompassing the good, the noble, richness of experience, and purity. Then there are three groups of what Hartmann calls special moral values. These he names "virtue-values" (*Tugendwerte*). The first of these groups of virtues comprises the virtues dis-

covered by the ancients, the second group roughly those discovered by Christianity, and the third group those discovered by the
moderns.

What is stressed in the virtues is their moral content. Little is
said about the ancient conviction that virtue is a moral quality of
a person (*habitus, hexis*) rather than an act. Presumably this is due
to Hartmann's focus, at least in this volume, on a description of
moral values as ideal beings and not on their realization in or by
man. From that point of view, the question whether an act can be
called virtuous only if it springs from a fixed and permanent disposition is not relevant.[41]

The enumeration lays no claims to being comprehensive.
Hartmann never tires of repeating that we do not possess comprehensive knowledge of the moral values. Other moral values can
probably be added to those mentioned. What is claimed by him,
however, is that the enumeration represents a set of objective and
absolute moral values, valid always and everywhere. If a person or
a group does not recognize the validity of some of these moral
values, that does not impinge on the validity of these values. It
merely proves the blindness of that person or group to those values.

That *the (morally A.K.) good (das Gute)* is the fundamental
moral value is undisputed. But what is it? To understand that, it is
necessary to return to the values intrinsic to the subject. Suppose
all these subject-values—life, consciousness, activity, suffering,
moral strength, freedom of the will, foresight, and purposiveness—
are realized in someone. Does that mean that he is a good person?
No, it does not. If all of these values are, at least to some extent,
realized in man, he is a person, which means that he is capable of
good (*Gut*) and evil (*Böse*). The value of personhood consists of
having moral capacity, of being able to act and be good as well as
evil. Personhood itself is not a moral virtue, it is still on this side
of good and evil (*diesseits von Gut und Böse*). A person can go
both ways; that is his freedom. "To be thus suspended, with both
perspectives continually before him, to be menaced at the depth
of his soul, and to be a menace to others, because of his highest

and proudest capacity, that is what it is to be a moral being, to be a man. Dangers outside themselves are also known to other creatures. But within himself, within his highest inner good (i.e. his personhood, A.K.), only man is in danger. He must be on guard against himself, must struggle against himself. The existence of a moral being is a journey along the edge of an abyss."[42] Thus, good and evil arise in the direction of the intention and the act of a person. Good is a direction towards values, evil a direction towards disvalues.

How is this possible if, as has been argued above, man cannot do evil for evil's sake? Man is not a satanic being. He is always directed towards a value. This Socratic insight still stands, Hartmann insists. So what does being directed at evil, at disvalues, mean? "The concrete situations of life are all of such a nature, that several values are involved in them at the same time. But the intention of the person who is in the situation cannot as a rule be directed towards all at once. It necessarily involves a decision in favor of one or a few of them, and at the same time a violation of others. Now, within such a constellation of values that are involved simultaneously, the good is always the direction towards the higher value, and the evil the direction towards the lower."[43]

Hartmann, uncharacteristically, is not very clear at this point. Presumably, "direction towards" (Richtung auf) should not be interpreted as "aiming at." For in that case moral values, which, as has been set out, in general appear "on the back of the act," and not in the goal aimed at, would carry no weight in the decision of what to do, and morality would depend merely on taking into account the relative height of the goods-values involved in a situation. That, however, is not Hartmann's position. Otherwise, he would have given much more thought to the ranking of goods-values than he in fact does in the Ethics. In fact, he explicitly states that "the interest of ethics in goods is a limited one."[44]

What Hartmann appears to hold—though, admittedly, some remarks point in a different direction—is that in every situation in which a choice has to be made, the good is not to violate the higher, moral value in favor of the lower, goods-value. Moral values,

as the highest values, should never be violated, in order to realize a
goods-value. But how then are they taken into account, considering that they are not aimed at? As has already been set out, this is
the crucial function of our conscience. Our conscience cannot tell
us what concrete goal to aim at, but it can tell us what moral
values not to violate in pursuing that goal.

Apparently, albeit he does not say so, the moral values Hartmann
has in mind with respect to the good are the lower moral values,
since he argues that "the good is a sort of fundamental moral demand,
expected of anyone. The ought-to-be in it is absolutely universal.
Heroism and moral greatness cannot be demanded from everybody,
but what can be demanded is that one is...'a good man.'"[45]

The fundamental moral value of *the noble* (*das Edle*) is very
different from the good. "The opposite of the noble is the common. This is far from identical with evil. It is not in the same sense
abject; it is merely the inferior and as such contemptible at most.
[...] Noble on the other hand is the spirit that is directed towards
the high, the ideal, turned away from everything small and lowly.
It is that which language designates as generous, magnanimous,
high-minded."[46]

The noble is not everyone's concern, as is the good. Its claims
always appeal only to the sense of value of the few, the *aristoi*.
The exceptional is of the essence of the noble. Thus, if the good is
concerned with the lower values, those that apply to all, the noble
seems to be concerned exclusively with the higher values.

The noble does not, in general, negate the good, but from among
good men it picks out those who from its point of view are the
best, and makes extra demands on them. However, to some extent
the noble and the good clash. The good can be common, and the
evil can, within limits, be noble. There is such a thing as banausic,
narrow-minded virtue, ignoble contentment and righteousness.
Conversely, who would deny that there is such a thing as noble
wrath, noble hatred, noble disdain, indeed noble revenge?[47]

In the third fundamental moral value, *richness of experience*
(*die Fülle*), yet another aspect of valuableness comes to the fore.
From this point of view, what counts is the breadth of the sense of

value, the understanding of and participation in all values, the axiological richness of the person, his moral span, so to speak. The corresponding disvalue is moral narrowness, the blind simplification of moral life, inner moral shriveling and one-sidedness.

In this ethos the teleological aspects of striving, intention, action are of secondary importance. What takes their place is the inner attitude of openness towards, participation in, and appreciating of everything. Evidently, it is in this respect opposite to the ethos of the noble: it is not exclusive, and not only does not bar out the lower values, but within certain limits not even, in a sense, what is contrary to value, because there is no other way to moral maturity and width than through the experience of evil. Hence, from this point of view, everything in moral life is valuable, even failure, deficiency, wrongdoing, and guilt.

Purity (*Reinheit*), finally, means untainted by evil. It is the principal Christian value. The greatest example of it is Jesus Christ, as depicted in the Gospels. He is pure who desires no wrong, who is not tempted to sin. He has no awareness of disvalues. He is innocent of evil, unspoilt.

It is peculiar to purity that it can neither be striven for, nor realized. One can lose one's purity, but one cannot regain it once it has been lost. Purity is not the result of fighting and conquering evil, it is an original state before all guilt, a *sancta simplicitas*. It is the virtue of a child, not earned, but of the highest moral value. Ignorance, simplemindedness, gullibility are values from this perspective. "One who is pure has nothing to hide; concealment, secretiveness is alien to him. He willingly lets others see himself, he lacks the shame of the guilty. He needs no covering, no mask, his nudity is not nakedness. The same goes for his directness in conduct. He takes hold of something without reflection, he makes straight for the matter at hand. He lacks both the occasion and the worldly wisdom for tricks. He has no need of deception."[48]

Purity and richness of experience are evidently antinomic. They wholly exclude each other. Yet, paradoxically, the ethos of richness of experience endorses the ethos of purity, and vice versa. "In the experienced person there is a yearning to return to the purity

which he has lost, the yearning of the morally mature, indeed of
the adult, for the original state of childlike innocence, simplicity,
and guilelessness. Similarly, there is a yearning of him who is still
pure for the fullness of experience, the yearning of a child for the
full, rich humanity of grown-ups."[49]

IX. ANCIENT VIRTUES

On the basis of these fundamental moral values arise three different groups of special moral values. As has been explained, these
Hartmann calls the virtues. The contents of these groups are much
richer and more manifold than his description of them, Hartmann
admits. However, comprehensiveness is not aspired to. To pick
out what is the quintessence of each group of values is the goal.

As has been said, the first group encompasses the virtues discovered by the ancients, the second roughly those discovered by
the Christians, and the third those discovered by the moderns.
Hartmann's analysis of these virtues is not exegetical, but phenomenological. He is not primarily interested in setting out what
exactly these virtues meant to the authors who discerned them
and passed them on to us, as in establishing what their ideal essence is. These authors are *auctores* to him, i.e. they have authority, but whenever Hartmann thinks they have overlooked or mis-
interpreted something, he feels free to take a different view.

Of the ancient virtues, making up the first group, the four Platonic virtues that have come to be known as the cardinal virtues—
justice, wisdom, courage, and self-control—are discussed, as well
as some of the aspects of the Aristotelean virtues, as discussed in
the *Nicomachean Ethics*.[50]

"The Platonic system of virtues culminated in *justice*
(*dikaiosunè*). It was a sort of crown to self-control, courage and
wisdom."[51] However, "among the virtues justice is not the highest, but rather the lowest value. That finds expression in the fact
that the ought-to-be in justice articulates not a maximum, but
evidently a minimum of moral demand. To begin with, its claim
upon a man's conduct is purely negative: not to do injustice, to
commit no transgression, not to encroach upon another's liberty,

not to injure another nor anything belonging to him."[52] Hence, in Hartmann's mind, justice is the minimum of morality, which precedes all the other specific moral values.

The Platonic *dictum* that it is better to suffer injustice than to commit injustice already sharply expresses the distinction between a goods-value and a moral value, as well as their hierarchical relation. To suffer injustice is merely the lack of a goods-value; to commit injustice is a positive moral evil. Equally, to enjoy justice is a great goods-value, but not more than that. To do justice, on the other hand, is a moral value and hence, a much more valuable, moral dignity of the person.

Wisdom (*sophia*) is not equal to theoretical insight and knowledge. These are instrumental elements within it, but they are remote from its essence. Wisdom is the outlook of man on life, both that of himself and of others. What it means is well indicated by the Latin translation of *sophia*, i.e. *sapientia*, that is derived from the verb *sapere*: to taste. Wisdom is moral taste, more specifically a subtle, differentiated, discriminating, cultivated taste, the refinement of the moral organ, that, directed towards the fullness of life, senses and affirms everything of value. A sense of the values inherent in reality, that is the secret of the wise man. To him, failing to notice this wealth of values is a sin against life. His heart is filled with pure joy, deep gratitude, and a reverential wonder at the moral richness of life.

Wisdom is the value of the leading element in man, *courage* (*andreia*), that of the executive element. The wisest outlook is morally impotent unless it is coupled with vigor, with preparedness to cope with obstacles. The most conspicuous form of courage is outward bravery, but it is much broader in scope. Courage is everywhere where there is self-conquest in the face of hazards, dangers, menaces, conflicts. Moral life requires courage at every turn: the courage to act, but also the courage to speak to one's own conviction and opinion, the courage to face the truth, to confess, the courage to think, to bear responsibility, to incur guilt, et cetera.

Negatively, *self-control* (*sóphrosunè, enkrateia*)[53] is directed against inner excess, lack of balance, inner dividedness. Positively, it is power over the affective impulses, the virtue of inner measure, the shaping of emotional life. It is a kind of inner order, inner justice, comparable to *dikaiosunè* in outer life. Like it, self-control is one of the lowest moral virtues, Hartmann declares, a minimum claim of man upon himself. On this virtue, as upon a foundation, arise the other, higher virtues.

Thus the four Platonic virtues. However, the table of virtues, as worked out by the ancients, contains more. "Especially Aristotle and the older Stoa have added quite a lot, that has proved to be of abiding value. The *Nicomachean Ethics* is still a veritable treasure house for the explorer of values," writes Hartmann.[54] In the subsequent discussion of the Aristotelian virtues, he concentrates on Aristotle's doctrine of virtue as a mean (*mesotès*) between two extremes (*akra*), the too-little (*elleipsis*) and the too-much (*huperbolè*), both of which are evils (*kakiai*). This doctrine was very fruitful, as it enabled Aristotle to discover several moral values and disvalues no one before him had seen. When applied to the Platonic virtues, little new insight is gained; but for the analysis of other virtues the doctrine is really helpful. Liberality (*eleutheriotès*) in regard to money is indeed pointedly characterized through the double contrast to penuriousness (*aneleutheria*) and prodigality (*asótia*). The same goes, with regard to anger, for gentleness (*praotès*), and its extremes of irascibility (*orgilotès*) and spiritlessness (*aorgèsia*); with regard to honor and dishonor, for greatness of soul (*megalopsuchia*), and its two extremes of vanity (*chaunotès*) and meanness of soul (*mikropsuchia*); and likewise for many others.[55]

Notwithstanding its heuristic usefulness in discovering moral values, Aristotle's doctrine of the mean has always been subjected to mockery, because of the seeming absurdity that after a point a further enhancement of a moral good should become a vice, whereas it appears to be evident that further augmentation can only increase the value of a virtue. Self-control, bravery, justice, and the other virtues do not have an upper limit at all. One cannot have too much of them. Axiologically, they are not means, but extremes. Countering this criticism, Hartmann develops an illuminating reinterpretation of the doctrine of the mean, to which we will return further on.

X. CHRISTIAN VIRTUES

"With the transformation that the ancient ethos underwent in Christianity, a new layer of moral values penetrated into consciousness. Whether this was in all respects a higher layer may be left open...but in its basic value, brotherly love (*agapè*)—as opposed to the basic virtue of antiquity, justice—it is indeed on a higher level."[56] On the other hand, Christianity has in some respects obscured the moral values discovered by the ancients. The idea of wisdom, for instance, was submerged in the new relationship between God and men, controlling everything. "For the foolishness of God is wiser than men," as Paul has it in 1 Corinthians 25. Similarly, *sóphrosunè* submerged in the religious idea of grace, and the ethos of courage and pride in the steadfastness of faith and the humility of the sinner. In brotherly love, however, nothing earlier is obscured. In it a new area of moral value is discovered.

Brotherly or neighborly love is not love as such, of which there are various kinds.[57] It is "primarily directed towards whoever is nearest, towards the other person, and it is a positive, affirmative bent, the transference of interest from the I to the Thou. The word 'love' is therefore misleading, in so far as it stresses the emotional side too much, while the essence of the matter lies in one's disposition, intention, and...conduct.... The modern, admittedly often misused, concept of altruism exactly expresses this fundamental meaning of it, as opposite to all egoism...."[58]

Like justice, brotherly love consists of an attitude towards others. But justice is only concerned with justified claims, the rights of others, not with their personal being. In fact, justice implies that decisions are made without respect of persons. The eyes of Lady Justice are bandaged. Brotherly love, on the contrary, takes interest in the person himself, for the sake of himself, without regard to rights, merits, and worth. It is a mysterious participation of the I in the spiritual and moral being of the other, reaching his hidden core, and recognizing from the slightest signs the most complex of inner conditions.

Brotherly love has to do primarily with the needy, those who are in want, the weak and oppressed. This had led to the idea that it is merely an aspect of pity. But that is incorrect. One pities a person *because of* his sickness and poverty, one loves him *in spite of* it; brotherly love perceives, behind the sickness and poverty, the person himself as someone valuable. Thus, Nietzsche's idea that neighborly love is love of such disvalues as sickness and poverty, and hence an expression of moral resentment, is fundamentally mistaken according to Hartmann.[59]

The discussion of brotherly love is followed by overviews of truthfulness or uprightness, trustworthiness and fidelity, trust and faith, modesty, humility, and aloofness, and finally, the values of social intercourse. Though classified as Christian virtues, this denomination should not be taken too literally, since most of these virtues were already well known and admired in antiquity, as Hartmann certainly knew. The most one can say is that with the coming of Christianity more emphasis was put on them. The last two mentioned, however, aloofness and the values of social intercourse, definitely do not belong in this category at all. They should have been included in the discussion of the ancient virtues. Their inclusion at this point is mystifying.

Truthfulness or uprightness primarily denotes the agreement of one's word with one's thought, beliefs or knowledge, but because words are not the only form of expressing one's ideas, there is also such a thing as truthfulness in conduct. One can lie by means of an act, a bearing, a pose. Lying is its negation, the disvalue associated with it. It is a stain, a degradation of oneself, often induced by cowardice. Sometimes, however, lies are committed for a good reason: love, for instance. Conversely, there can be something very unloving in a truthfulness.

Trustworthiness stands for the agreement between word and deed. It is thus complementary to truthfulness.[60] The trustworthy or reliable man is he whose promise is of value, whose will is fixed by his word, who will abide by it until he is discharged, however much his mind may have changed afterwards. He holds himself bound by his promise.

Now, "by far the greatest part of all existing ties and order in public and private life rest upon agreement, whether it was formally entered into, or arose according to custom and was tacitly recognized. But then it is evident that only a trustworthy man is capable of keeping to such ties and order, i.e. of living in a community."[61] This is the reason that in moral life trustworthiness, reliability, has such a decisive and dominating position. Universalized, it bears the lofty name of *fidelity (Treue)*, which goes much further than keeping one's promises. It is in essence the moral assiduousness of a person, and extends to everything to which the human will can commit itself: a goal, a cause, friends, a spouse, one's country, et cetera.

Unlike justice, for instance, which has a goods-value for anyone enjoying it, the goods-value of truthfulness and trustworthiness are dependent upon a certain corresponding disposition in those affected. They must have *trust or faith*, the latter of which Hartmann considers the foundation of the former. All human relations are based on trust and faith, from monetary loans to the highest forms of power in public life. All community depends on trust and faith. It binds individuals together in a more elementary and inclusive way than either justice or brotherly love, since it is less reflective than justice, and more universal than brotherly love.

Credulity is a moral fault, of course, but habitual distrust, an automatic scepticism as to all human intention, is a much more serious moral failure. A distrustful person sins against the trustworthy, and belittles the truthful and faithful. When distrust and lack of faith infect a whole community, it is lost. Distrust brings in its wake the breaking of all social bonds. Lack of faith in a cause or in men entails social disintegration.

Modesty and humility are counterpoints to the ancient virtues of justice, wisdom, bravery, and self-control. For these can turn into presumptuousness. They have a hidden propensity towards arrogance. Modesty and humility balance them out. The modest man looks up to those who stand on a higher moral level; the humble man measures his own moral being against the ideal, the perfect. Both are imbued by the awareness of falling short.

Aloofness (*Distanz*) is similar to modesty and humility in that it is also a counterpoint. Aloofness balances out the Christian virtues of brotherly love, truthfulness, trustworthiness, trust, *et alea*. For these virtues can become obtrusive, meddling, and disrespectful. Brotherly love, for example, can go hand in hand with curiosity and sensationalism, pity is often shameless and slighting. Aloofness, keeping a distance, is a moral sense of shame, not for oneself, as is the case with Aristotle's *aidós*, but for the other, whenever he is exposed and defenseless. Aloofness is reticence from a regard for the other person.[62]

The ethos of aloofness (*Ethos der Distanz*) leads us on to a group of values, which neither have Christian origins, nor are considered very important by Christianity. In fact, the Christian tradition has often been critical of them. These are the values or virtues of social intercourse.

Aristotle has included three of these virtues in the list of virtues presented in the *Nicomachean Ethics*. First, correct self-presentation (*aletheia*), with boastfulness (*aladzoneia*) as excess and self-depreciation (*eiróneia*) as deficiency. Second, friendliness (*philia*), with the excesses of obsequiousness (*areskeia*) and flattery (*kolakeia*), and the deficiencies of the quarrelsome (*duseris*) and gruffness (*duskolia*). And third, wittiness (*eutrapelia*), with the excess of buffoonery (*bómolochia*), and the deficiency of boorishness (*agroikia*).[63] Even more enlightening and much more extensive are Cicero's remarks on the virtue of *decorum*, made in *De Officiis*.[64]

Consideration, tact, modesty, kindness, politeness, good manners, a sense of propriety and fitness, judgement as to when to come forward and when to retire, and many others, all belong to this category of virtues. Superficial as they may seem, they are nevertheless, in Hartmann's opinion, "profoundly necessary to life, and anyone who violates them sins against his fellow men exactly as much as a person who is unjust or unloving. Indeed, by doing so, he is unjust and unloving, he is a 'criminal in miniature.'"[65] The peculiar form they take is of no consideration. They are always a manifestation of true moral values.

XI. MODERN VIRTUES

The third and last group of special moral values does not really constitute a group at all, Hartmann admits. Of the four values that are included in it, each has to be conceived of as itself constituting a group of moral values, for each lies in a separate valuational region. "There is no historical ethos corresponding precisely to them. Consequently, they have no name, like so much else that our sense of feeling knows quite well and differentiates."[66] Hartmann names them love of the remotest (*Fernstenliebe*), bestowing virtue (*schenkende Tugend*), personality (*Persönlichkeit*), and personal love (*persönliche Liebe*). Unknown to antiquity and to medieval Christianity, these virtues were discovered by the moderns. Hartmann refers to Nietzsche as a pioneer in articulating the first two virtues. The last two are clearly the upshot of the general modern responsiveness to individuality. To Hartmann, they all represent summits, at least as far as we can see, in the sphere of moral value.

Love of the remotest or, as Coit translates, love of the remote, is the moral value that comes to the fore in the idealism of creative man, that is directed towards a humankind more perfect, more encompassing, and spiritually richer than at present. This idealism is a "mean" between, on the one hand, spiritual inertia and absorption by what lies nearest, by what is most evident and at hand, and, on the other hand, an unpractical, daydreaming idealism, exhausting itself in perpetual yearnings and inevitable disappointments. True idealism presupposes genuine discernment of values and the possibility of their realization. Such an idealism manifests itself in life and history as a really creative force.

Love of the remote is not everyone's business. On the contrary, the vision of the ideal is always limited to a small minority. But these are the salt of the earth. "It is precisely in this inequality that a peculiar strength lies in the human race, its ability to advance. Only where among the many there are individuals who excel, who

as to some value or other are the 'best,' is upward evolution possible...."[67] Hence, love of the remote is a love that fosters that
which is best in the few who are the best with an eye to a future,
more perfect humankind.

Obviously, this love conflicts with both justice and brotherly
love. In the eyes of justice all men are equal, and in so far as they
are not, they ought to be; love of the remote not only accepts
inequality, but embraces it as a value. Brotherly love concentrates
on the here and now, and on the weak and needy; love of the
remote on the future and the far away, and on the best and bright-
est. Since love of the remote is the higher value, does this imply,
as Nietzsche thought, a transvaluation of justice and brotherly
love? Should they be considered disvalues? Hartmann denies it,
but he thinks that it does indicate that their value is restricted by
another, higher, value, and that they must, if necessary, yield to it.

A second high point in the sphere of moral values is *schenkende
Tugend*, the virtue that bestows. Coit translates radiant virtue. It
refers to the giving away, the sharing of spiritual goods, and it is
also a form of love. Giving away to others is the only attitude
proper to the spiritual goods one possesses. Unlike material goods,
one does not possess these goods exclusively. They belong to
everyone capable of comprehending them. Possession of them is a
mere participation in and guardianship of them. To keep them
from others is to treat them contrary to their nature. Such an attitude constitutes moral miserliness.

Brotherly love bestows upon the weak, the needy, the unfortunate; *schenkende Tugend* bestows upon everyone who knows how
to take, upon the appreciative, the open-minded. That is why the
Schenkende loves, not the just, the truthful, the faithful, but those
who are still capable of learning, the unripe and immature, those
who are still bendable. "He is the eternal *erastès* of youth."[68] And
to those who are open to him, communication with him shines a
mysterious ray of light on them, and is a blessing to their souls.

Personality (*Persönlichkeit*), in the sense of a uniqueness of
the individual human being, is something every man by nature
possesses. This is more than mere personhood (*Personalität*), which

is common to all. Personality is that which is distinct in each person. There is, however, another meaning to it as well. From factual personality must be distinguished the value of personality.

Personality as a value differs radically from all the values previously discussed, in that it is not a general value, whose content is the same for all. Its specific "ought" is applicable only to one particular person; only he ought to be "so." Thus, personality is concerned with the ideal ethos of the individual person. Empirical man inevitably falls short of this ideal, just as much as he falls short of the ought that inheres in the general moral values. In fact, it happens that a person deviates further and further from his personality, either because he imitates someone else, or because he is subject to the host of lower forces within him that cause him to fail his higher ethos, or again because the tyrannical dominance of one or some general moral values represses his personality.

Hartmann maintains that everyone has such a specific ideal ethos, though not all have one equally distinctive. The ethos of most men is rather common; they have "little personality." "Whoever really has a marked personality, carries his standards unequivocally within himself, and in following them he is faithful to himself. He has very definite and imperturbable sympathies and antipathies, for which he can give no other account than that which is to be found in their presence and felt necessity. He sees the world in his own light, unlike anybody else, in the light of his specific values, and he lives accordingly. He is a world for himself, in the true sense of the word."[69]

Where does this leave the general moral values (virtues), applicable to all, such as justice and brotherly love? It would be misguided to infer, Hartmann asserts, from the recognition of values specific to the individual personality, a general moral individualism. The value of personality may be higher, but the values of justice, brotherly love, et cetera are stronger. They come first, because they are more urgent and more basic to life.[70]

That does not justify a moral rigorism, however, which considers universal demands endangered whenever personality sets up its claims. Within the general framework of universal demands

there is sufficient room for differences in what individual personalities ought to be or do, because various different values stand
side by side on the same axiological level, without perceivable
difference in rank. When such values conflict with each other in
concrete situations, each can and should choose according to his
personality.

Everyone ought to "be" in accordance with his individual ethos.
Imitation of another person's personality is ridiculous. Following
the example of another person is sensible only with respect to
general moral values. There can be discipleship in justice, brotherly love, truthfulness, and the like, but not in personality. One
who imitates another's personality does not become a copy of that
personality, but a human ape.

How then do we know our individual ethos, how do we recognize the ought that is specific to us? Since it is specific to us as
individual persons, there are no general rules here, such as "Love
your neighbor like yourself." And imitation is out of the question.
This suggests that the conscious discernment of these values
(*Wertschau*) is often impossible. The values of one's personality
cannot always explicitly be stated, particularly when there is no
other person for whom they are valid. For such "private" values
there is no language. In such cases we have to fall back entirely on
the tacit knowledge, the knowing-how, of our sense of value
(*Wertgefühl*).

Personal love is the love of one personality for another. It is the
consciousness of and devotion to the value of that personality.
Personal love perceives the ideal ethos of an individual in his
empirical *persona*. Looking back from the ideal upon the imperfect carrier, it loves the empirical individual for the sake of his
personality, and helps him to become who he ideally is. "For,
ashamed not to be really what the lover sees in him, the beloved is
exalted above himself. But instead of feeling that he is misunderstood, he rather feels understood to a pre-eminent degree, and at
the same time obligated to be what the other sees in him."[71]

Personal love is the most positive of all human feelings. Using
the word "happiness" to describe it is misleading. "Happiness is

secondary in love. In truth, it always includes both suffering and joy. The peculiar eudaemonological phenomenon in it is rather that beyond a certain depth of feeling, pain and pleasure become indifferent to it, they become literally indistinguishable. The suffering of the lover can still be happy, his happiness can be painful. The specific emotional value of (personal, A.K.) love is beyond happiness and unhappiness."[72]

XII. Stratification and Foundation

With the discussion of personal love, which, in Hartmann's view, gives ultimate meaning to life, his overview of the contents of the realm of value is completed. In the final section of *Moral Values*, section VIII, Hartmann returns to the second aspect of his problem: the structure or order inherent in the realm of value, i.e. the relation between the different values. Conscious of the imperfectness and the incompleteness of his survey, he nevertheless asks himself the question: what can we learn from it as to the laws that govern the realm of values?

The answer is only within very modest limits in the affirmative, as Hartmann puts it. One should have no great expectations. Perhaps the greatest merit of the analysis of the content of the realm of values lies in having uncovered the great difficulty and complexity of the problem, since that is not self-evident. What we have is an initial orientation in the realm of value that can serve as a point of departure for further investigation. Having articulated this caveat, Hartmann proceeds to distinguish three pairs of laws of connection (*Zusammenhangsgesetze*) between values: laws of stratification and foundation, laws of opposition and complementation, and laws of height and strength.

The laws of stratification and foundation are concerned with the vertical, hierarchical relation between values. Hartmann commences with the laws of stratification. What do these denote? As has been set out, real being consists of four different strata or layers (*Seinsschichten*), from the stratum of inorganic being at the bottom, through the strata of organic being and mental being, to spiritual being at the top.[73] The lower strata are the ontological basis of higher strata. Higher strata are dependent on lower strata, in the sense that the lower strata are the matter out of which being at a higher stratum is formed. Many fundamental characteristics or, in Hartmann's idiom, categories (*Kategorien*) of being of the lower strata return in the higher strata. This is the law of recurrence. But they often recur in a different form. This is the law of modification. Also, in each stratum new categories are frequently added and others disappear: the law of novelty. Finally, there is not an unbroken continuity between strata, but a gap (*Distanz*): the law of stratum-distance.

These four laws of stratification reappear in the relation between lower and higher values in general, as well as, more specifically, between lower and higher moral values, though the relation between the various groups of value is much looser than that of the various strata in the real world. The elementary values recur throughout the hierarchy of values, and the four fundamental moral values reappear in a variety of modifications in the moral virtues. The subject-values and goods-values on the other hand disappear completely at the higher levels. Also, within the moral values themselves recurrence of lower in higher values is almost completely absent. The laws of modification, novelty, and distance predominate in the realm of value.

In addition to the laws of stratification, the realm of value obeys a law that has no equivalent in the real world: the law of foundation. This law refers to the relation between goods-values and moral values, which has already been set out more than once. Goods-values are the foundation of moral values, in the sense that the latter appear "on the back" of the goods-values, which are the goals of human intention and action. This is a unique relation, very different from a relation of stratification.

First, there is no recurrence at all of the lower value in the higher value. They are entirely different. Second, whereas in the real world the lower strata are the basis of higher strata, and the latter cannot exist without the former, here the realization of the higher value is possible without the realization of the lower. All that it takes for a moral value to be realized is the intention. Success is irrelevant. Third, in general where there is a relation of stratification between values, the height of the higher value varies with the height of the lower, conditioning value. The value of trust, for instance, rises with the value of strength and of courage; the value of *schenkende Tugend* rises with the value of the richness of experience one possesses. But in the relation between goods-values and moral values this relation is lacking. The moral value of justice is not smaller when small goods are involved instead of large, the moral value of neighborly love remains the same, whether it works great or small things in the life of one's neighbor.

XIII. Opposition and Complementation

The laws of opposition and complementation are concerned with polar relations between values. These are either antithetical or complementary.

There are two kinds of antithetical relations between values. On the one hand, the antithesis between value and disvalue, which is specific to and omnipresent in the realm of values. There is no counterpart of it in the real world. And on the other hand, the antithesis between value and value, which does have an equivalent in the real world.[74] This is, in Hartmann's verbiage, an antinomy. The antithesis between value and disvalue is a problem neither to ethical understanding, nor to moral life. We know we ought to choose the value. Moreover, we cannot even willfully choose a disvalue. Human intention is always directed towards values, to what one judges to be valuable.

The antithesis between value and value, however, presents a grave problem both to our understanding and to our lives, at least whenever they seem to be equally valuable. From a practical point of view, we cannot live with such antinomies. Whenever we act, we are compelled to "solve" them, simply because human action is by definition unitary. We cannot split ourselves in two halves. From a theoretical point of view, antinomies are also objectionable, at any rate as to moral values, because the universal synthesis of moral value, "the unity of virtue" as the Stoics had it, is inherent in the idea of moral value or of the Good. Thus, the problem of value-antinomies leads us on to the question of the possibilities of value-synthesis.

It is in this context that Hartmann returns to Aristotle's doctrine of the mean, in order to demonstrate that behind the Aristotelian virtues lie two antinomic virtues, and that consequently these virtues are not so much *mesotètes* as syntheses of value. "In juxtaposition to *sóphrosunè* stand *akolasia* (profligacy) and *anaisthèsia* (insensibility); only in contrast to the former is it properly self-control; in contrast to the latter it is the fully developed aptitude of reacting emotionally, of the affective life. In contrast to *deilia* (cowardice), courage is spirited endurance, in contrast to *thrasutès* (rashness) it is deliberate circumspection, cool presence of mind. Seen against *orgilotès* (irascibility), *praotès* is mildness, but seen against *aorgèsia* (lack of spirit) it is the capacity of righteous indignation. *Eleutheriotès* is liberality with regard to material values, and at the same time the capacity not to spend, the former in contrast to *aneleutheria* (meanness), the latter to *asótia* (prodigality). *Aidós* is the capacity to be ashamed of oneself, and at the same time it is the limitation of shame, the latter as opposed to the conduct of the *kataplex* (the bashful), the former to that of the *anaischuntos* (the shameless). Still clearer, if that is possible, is the relation in the case of the more complex virtues. Nemesis stands in contrast to *phthonos* (envy) as unenvious delight in another's happiness, but in contrast to *epichairekakia* (malice) as compassion in undeserved calamity. *Megalopsuchia* (greatness of soul) in particular is perhaps the purest example of such a decomposition, in its dual position with regard to *mikropsuchia* (smallness of soul) and *chaunotès* (vanity); in opposition to the former it is justified moral pride, self-respect, in opposition to the latter, the modest consciousness of the limitation of one's own moral being."[75] Hence, Aristotelian *aretè* (virtue) is a synthesis of two one-sided moral values.

Hartmann believes, though he acknowledges that it cannot be proved, that the principle of value-synthesis is a general, fundamental law (*allgemeines Grundgesetz*) of the sphere of moral value.

The fact that we often do not perceive the synthesis between two antinomic moral values does not prove that there is no synthesis. It merely proves that we cannot see it. We may once be able to see them, or they may be out of reach of human cognizance forever, but our uneasiness in the face of antinomies, and our permanent search for syntheses, shows the truth of what Aristotle so strongly felt, without being able to express it, that all moral values, taken in isolation, are barbed, that they are tyrannical, and that to be truly realized in man they need a counterweight. The moral ideal is the combination of justice *and* brotherly love, brotherly love *and* love of the remotest, justified moral pride *and* humility, purity *and* *Fülle*, and so on.

Besides antinomic relations between values, we also encounter complementary relations. It is particular to these relations that the one value requires the other and realizes its meaning in it, without losing its identity. We encounter this relation between goods-values—most goods are valuable only in combination with other goods—in the subject-values—for instance between activity and strength—and also between moral values. We see it in trust and trustworthiness, faith and fidelity, personality and personal love, kindness and gratitude, heroism and admiration, worthiness and esteem, et cetera.

There is, however, one important difference between the complementation of moral values and that of other values. The complementation of the former is interpersonal. This is of immeasurable significance to moral life, which comes to pass in concrete interpersonal situations. If complementary moral intention and action of different persons were dependent solely upon the creation of interpersonal syntheses between persons defending different and antinomic values, then moral conduct would be in a sorry plight, if only because we often do not have a clue as to what these syntheses might be.

XIV. Height and Strength

In deciding which value must prevail and which must yield, we must know their relative ranking in the realm of value. At first glance, that seems easily established. The choice should depend on the relative height of the values involved. But it is not that simple. As we have discovered, in the ranking of moral values more than one criterion must be allowed for. The rank of a moral value depends not only on its "height" (*Höhe*), but also on its "strength" (*Stärke*).[76] These two dimensions are not only different, but opposite to each other.

The higher value is commonly the weaker, and the lower the stronger value. "To sin against a lower (moral, A.K.) value is in general more grievous than to sin against a higher; but the realization of a higher is morally more valuable than that of a lower. Murder is held to be the most grievous crime, but respect for another's life is not on that account the highest moral state—not to be compared with friendship, love, trustworthiness. Property is an incomparably lower value than personal benevolence, but nonetheless a violation of property (theft) is much more reprehensible than mere malevolence. A sin against the lower (moral, A.K.) values is blameworthy, dishonorable, excites indignation, but their realization reaches only the level of propriety, without rising higher. The violation, on the other hand, of the higher (moral, A.K.) values has indeed the character of a moral lapse, but has nothing degrading in it, while the realization of these values can have something exalting in it, something liberating, indeed inspiring."[77] "Heroism deserves admiration, but the absence of it is neither despicable nor outrageous, and is at most to be bewailed as a human weakness; conversely, trustworthiness is merely commendable, or just a trifle more (since anyone can and ought to be trustworthy, not anyone can and ought to be heroic), but a breach of trust is despicable, indeed outrageous."[78]

How is this to be explained? Hartmann suggests that the higher moral value is always the more conditioned, the more dependent, and in this sense, the weaker, because its realization is meaningful only in so far as it builds upon the realization of the lower moral values. But the more unconditioned, the more elementary, and in this sense the stronger moral value is always the lower, because it is only the axiological base of moral life, not a realization of its meaning. "This is equivalent to saying: the most grievous transgressions are those against the lower (moral, A.K.) values, but the greatest moral desert attaches to the highest (moral, A.K.) values."[79]

The realization of the lower moral values thus takes precedence. They come first because they are more urgent. An offense against them is much more serious. That is because of their strength. But realizing them is not meritorious. It involves not so much the realization of values as the avoidance of disvalues. Hence, the lower moral values can assume the form of commandments. "Thou shalt be trustworthy" can be reasonably commanded; "thou shalt be heroic" cannot. And the more elementary these commandments are, the more they appear as prohibitions: thou shalt not steal, murder, commit adultery, bear false witness, and so on.

Clearly, the claims of these values on man boil down to what might be called a morality of duty. However, the sphere of moral values is Janus-faced. The realization of the higher moral values cannot be commanded, but it is the realization of these values only that is admirable and truly worthy of praise. Here there are no duties. These values are "beyond the call of duty." In contrast to the morality of duty, the moral claims on man pointed out here might be called a morality of aspiration.[80]

Man faces a twofold moral requirement, a twofold ought: not to violate the lower moral values, and to realize the higher moral values. Most historical moralities are one-sided. Some are pulled more towards the lower and stronger values, concerned above all with the avoidance of the more grievous transgressions, others are pulled more towards the realization of higher values, such as bravery, love, or moral greatness. But our sense of value seeks a synthesis between the two moralities, grasping that morality in the full and genuine sense is concerned with the entire ladder of moral values. "Amiss is a moral life that is turned exclusively towards the higher values and neglects the lower, as if it were possible to realize the former while they float in the air and have no foundation. But poor is a moral life that with all its aims is imprisoned in and absorbed by the lower values. A morality which culminates in self-control and justice easily becomes 'pharisaic.'"[81]

Postscript

Volume 2 of the *Ethics, Moral Values*, is a difficult book. Hartmann's ethical ideas are visionary and bold, profound, and complex. That alone does not make for easy reading. But on top of this comes the fact that words, sentences, and pages, which in German sound, if not beautiful and poetic, then at least normal and familiar, in English translation frequently appear outlandish, puzzling, and—above all—much too long. The result is a book that cannot be perused in a few days, but must be studied with great patience and care in order to penetrate it. But it is more than worth the trouble. Once one has broken trough the apparent opaqueness, an intellectual vista of immense wealth, vigor, and subtlety is opened up before one's eyes. Hopefully, this introduction has made that clear.

ANDREAS A.M. KINNEGING
University of Leiden, Faculty of Law

Notes

1. Sections I and II deal with some preliminary issues, sections III and IV criticize other approaches, and section VII elaborates on some central notions introduced in section VI.
2. Not to be confused with personality (*Persönlichkeit*), which Hartmann considers one of the highest moral values. Cf. *infra*.
3. *Ethics I*, p. 63. The notion of "ordre de coeur" comes from Pascal, *Pensées*, iv.283; Hartmann has adopted it from Scheler, *Formalismus in der Ethik*, 6th ed. Bern and Munich: Francke Verlag 1980, p. 259 ff., who has given it the specific meaning of axiological sense. Cf. "Transaction Introduction," in: *Ethics I, Moral Phenomena*, p. viii. Hartmann asserts that the word "Vernunft" (reason) might be applied to it, in so far as that notion refers to "vernehmen" (to hear).
4. *Ethics II*, pp. 57-58. The notion of "value-response" derives from Dietrich von Hildebrand. Cf. "Transaction Introduction," in: *Ethics I, Moral Phenomena*, p. xxxiv, note 60.
5. Cf. "Transaction Introduction," in: *Ethics I, Moral Phenomena*, pp. xviii-xxii.
6. *Ethics II*, p. 23. The wording of the Hartmann quotes in this introduction may differ from the wording in the text. In such cases, the present author has made his own translation from the German original.

7.   *Ethics II*, pp. 385-386, p. 472. The sentence on p. 386, "They lie beyond the limits of what can be known," is an overstatement and does not adequately represent Hartmann's views on this issue.

8.   Cf. O. F. Bollnow, "Die Behandlung der Tugenden bei Nicolai Hartmann," in: *Nicolai Hartmann, Der Denker und sein Werk*, Göttingen: Vandenhoeck & Ruprecht 1952, p. 84.

9.   Hartmann never went into the subject of "value modalities" systematically. Cf. Andreas Kinneging, "Realist Phenomenology and the Foundations of Natural Law," in: *The American Journal of Jurisprudence*, vol. 46, 2001, p. 270.

10.   Aesthetic values are named to underpin the idea that there are various different kinds of value, but they are not drawn into the analysis. The reason for this apparently is not the consideration that aesthetics is irrelevant to ethics, but that we know too little of aesthetic values. Cf. *Ethics II*, p. 23. On the relation of moral values with aesthetic values, cf. *Ethics II*, pp. 403-405.

11.   *Ethics II*, pp. 24-25. Emphasis added.

12.   The expression is taken from Scheler's *Formalismus in der Ethik*. Cf. note 3.

13.   *Ethics II*, p. 31.

14.   Cf. Kant, *Grundlegung zur Metaphysik der Sitten*, Erster Abschnitt, esp. the famous first sentence.

15.   *Ethics II*, p. 32; *Ethics I*, pp. 200-202

16.   *Ethics II*, pp. 36-37.

17.   *Ethics I*, p. 300. In general this may be true, but, as Aeschylus' *Oresteia*, Sophocles' *Antigone*, and many other Greek tragedies, in which we are confronted with a conflict between values, prove, there are important exceptions. Cf. *infra*.

18.   *Ethics I*, pp. 300-301; *Ethics II*, p. 76.

19.   *Ethics II*, p. 46.

20.   *Ethics II*, p. 47; pp. 54-57.

21.   *Ethics II*, p. 385.

22.   *Ethics II*, p. 78. To some extent the antinomies of elementary values are equivalent to the so-called elementary antinomic categories (*elementare Gegensatzkategorien*) basic to real being. Cf. N. Hartmann, *Der Aufbau der Realen Welt*, Berlin: Walter de Gruyter & Co. 1964 [1940], p. 200 ff.

23.   Cf. N. Hartmann, *Möglichkeit und Wirklichkeit*, Berlin: Walter de Gruyter & Co. 1966 [1938]. This book contains Hartmann's ideas on the modalities—possibility, reality, necessity—of being.

24.   *Ethics II*, p. 81.

25.   *Ethics II*, p. 84.

26.   *Ethics II*, p. 92.

27.   *Ethics II*, p. 108-109.

28.   *Ethics II*, p. 109-110. Hartmann adds: "The object for which the sacrifice is made (e.g. one's country, A.K.) must of course stand

higher that that which is sacrificed (e.g. one's life, A.K.). But the moral value of the sacrifice is not that of the thing sacrificed; it (the moral value, A.K.) is then by no means surrendered, but even realized in the surrender (of the thing sacrificed, A.K.)."

29. *Ethics II*, p. 121.
30. *Ethics II*, pp. 131-132.
31. *Ethics II*, p. 139.
32. *Ethics II*, p. 140.
33. *Ethics II*, pp. 140-141.
34. *Ethics II*, pp. 142-143.
35. *Ethics II*, pp. 143-147.
36. Cf. Hegel, *Grundlinien der Philosophie des Rechts*, § 100.
37. Cf. "Transaction Introduction," in: *Ethics I, Moral Phenomena*, pp. xxii-xxvii.
38. *Ethics II*, p. 164. Hartmann does not go into this class of goods any further.
39. *Ethics II*, pp. 160-162. Cf. *supra*.
40. Cf. J.N. Findlay, *Axiological Ethics*, London: MacMillan 1970, p. 77. Chapter 4 of Findlay's book discusses Scheler's and Hartmann's ethics. Although adequate as a first introduction, it does not sufficiently do justice to the richness and profundity of the ethical thought of either of these authors.
41. Cf. Aristotle, *Nicomachean Ethics*, 1105a34.
42. *Ethics II*, pp. 180-181.
43. *Ethics II*, p. 185. Emphasis added.
44. *Ethics II*, p. 163.
45. *Ethics II*, p. 190.
46. *Ethics II*, p. 192.
47. *Ethics II*, pp. 192-193; Cf. Nietzsche, *Jenseits von Gut und Böse*, and *Genealogie der Moral*, in which the ancient and aristocratic antithesis of "good vs. bad" is opposed to the Christian and democratic antithesis of "good vs. evil."
48. *Ethics II*, p. 213.
49. *Ethics II*, p. 220.
50. Cf. Plato, *Politeia*, bk.IV; Cicero, *De Officiis*; St.Ambrose, *De Officiis Ministrorum*. The last is the originator of the adjective "cardinal," which derives from the Latin *cardo*, hinge.
51. *Ethics II*, p. 228.
52. *Ethics II*, p. 231.
53. Contrary to Aristotle, *Nicomachean Ethics,* 1145a15 ff., Hartmann uses *sóphrosunè* and *enkrateia* as synonymous.
54. *Ethics II*, p. 253.
55. *Ethics II*, pp. 253-264. Cf. Aristotle, *Nicomachean Ethics*, 1107a30 ff. Here, Hartmann has interesting criticisms of Aristotle's treatment of righteous indignation (*nemesis*) and sense of shame (*aidós*).
56. *Ethics II*, p. 267.

57.   Cf. Anders Nygren, *Agape and Eros*, London: S.P.C.K. 1953.
58.   *Ethics II*, p. 268.
59.   *Ethics II*, pp. 272-274. Cf. Max Scheler, *Das Ressentiment im Aufbau der Moralen*, Frankfurt am Main: Vittorio Klostermann 1978 [1912].
60.   Obviously, trustworthiness is also used as a concept covering truthfulness. But it remains true that trustworthiness also applies to the agreement of word and deed, which is not the case with truthfulness.
61.   *Ethics II*, pp. 286-287.
62.   *Ethics II*, pp. 301-303. Cf. Aristotle, *Nicomachean Ethics*, 1128b10 ff.
63.   *Ethics II*, pp. 307-308; Cf. Aristotle, *Nicomachean Ethics*, 1108a10 ff. and 1126b11 ff.
64.   Cicero, *De Officiis*, I.93-151.
65.   *Ethics II*, p. 304.
66.   *Ethics II*, p. 311.
67.   *Ethics II*, p. 321.
68.   *Ethics II*, p. 338.
69.   *Ethics II*, p. 354.
70.   Cf. Section XIV of this introduction.
71.   *Ethics II*, p. 374.
72.   *Ethics II*, p. 376.
73.   The ontological structure of the real world is described *in extenso* in *Aufbau der realen Welt*. Cf. note 22.
74.   Cf. note 22.
75.   *Ethics II*, pp. 414-415.
76.   "Weight" would perhaps express the quality meant even better then "strength." In the sphere of the goods-values this antinomy returns. Cf. *Ethics II*, pp. 453-454.
77.   *Ethics II*, p. 53.
78.   *Ethics II*, p. 451.
79.   *Ethics II*, pp. 451-452.
80.   *Ethics II*, p. 449 ff. Cf. L. Fuller, *The Morality of Law*, rev. ed., New Haven and London: Yale University Press 1969, ch. I, entitled "The Two Moralities," from which the terms "morality of duty" and "morality of aspiration" are derived.
81.   *Ethics II*, p. 462.

PART II

THE REALM OF ETHICAL VALUES
(AXIOLOGY OF MORALS)

Section I

GENERAL ASPECTS OF THE TABLE OF VALUES

CHAPTER I (xxvi)[1]

THE PLACE OF MORAL VALUES AMONG VALUES IN GENERAL

(a) THE FIELD OF ETHICAL INQUIRY

IT is not only ethics that treats of values. The term is conspicuous in economics and has its origin there. Economics is the study of goods, in the first place of material, then of vital, social and mental goods of every kind. To the latter are closely related the values of moral, legal, political and artistic life. Research in this field is still young and our survey casual and unsystematic. There is a lack of comprehensive points of view; and previous attempts to attain them have too often been marked by a blind fumbling and uncertain groping.

So long as whole territories, like that of æsthetics, in spite of their dominant position, remain as good as unexplored, there is no remedy. Our knowledge of the structure and order of values is in a rudimentary stage. We can look out upon the whole realm only through special groups of values which happen to be accessible, but we cannot deductively determine particulars from a general view of the whole.

There is little prospect of our attaining any authoritative insight into moral values, as such, from the neighbouring fields or from a general theory. On the contrary, the domain of morality, as yet the most accessible among the more important fields, must itself furnish us with points of departure into general theory. In ethical research we cannot reckon upon guidance from outside.

How moral values differ from other kinds has in part been already explained (the two-sided relativity of persons)[2], but it

---

[1] In this volume, Chapters I–XXXIX represent Chapters XXVI–LXIV in the German edition, and the numbers in brackets (xxvi) are those of the chapters in that original.

[2] Cf. Chapter XV (d), (e), Vol. I.

cannot be more fully shown until we make a special analysis
of single values. So much, however, is easily seen, that not all
values which are ethically relevant, whether in the sense of
obligation or of participation, are on that account moral values.
The character of man is related to a multitude of values which
are not moral in their nature. Moral conduct is always conduct
towards persons, but never except in connection with other
kinds of values and counter-values. From this point of view
there was some reason for including, as the ancients did, the
theory of goods under ethics.

In a certain sense one may say that everything, which exists,
somehow falls practically under the category of values, that
everything in the world, even the most remote and indifferent,
is in the perspective of ethics either of positive or negative
worth. The same universe, which in its totality underlies
ontological phenomena, belongs also in precisely the same
totality to ethical phenomena. It is no less a world of goods and
evils than of things and their relations. At least it is as radically
the former as it is the latter.

(b) THE DEPENDENCE OF MORAL UPON NON-MORAL VALUES

This wider sphere, however, is not that of distinctively moral
values. These latter are affixed not to things and their relations,
but only to persons. Only acts of persons can be morally good
or bad. Nevertheless it is necessary to take the non-moral values
into consideration, even if not to study them in detail. Their
connection with the moral is not outward and not nullifiable
or even negligible. It is essential, inward, material. Moral values
presuppose other goods and the specific quality and worth
belonging to them.

In fact, wherein would an honest man be superior to a thief,
if the things purloined were not somehow of value? What one
man can steal, what another can treasure as a possession, is
not merely a thing but a good. Honesty, then, if it is a moral
value, necessarily presupposes the positive worth of material

goods. It is inherently dependent upon the latter. In the same way, chivalry which secures an advantage to the weak rests upon the worth of that advantage; love for one's neighbour, which gives, or which takes upon itself another's burden, assumes the worth of the things given and of the relief from the burden; not otherwise is veracity related to the worth (for the other person) of the truth asserted. In all these cases the value of the act is altogether different from that attributed to the external good, whether this be some simple material possession or some complex situation. And indeed the worth of an act is plainly of a higher kind, the character of which is seen in this, that its degree does not increase and decrease with the greatness of the non-moral good, but according to a standard of a totally different order. It nevertheless presupposes the value of goods not in themselves moral, and without them it could not itself exist.

A relation therefore of dependence holds between the wider and narrower spheres of values. It is an unequivocal, irreversible dependence of the higher upon the lower. But the dependence is purely material, not axiological. The lower is the stuff upon which the higher works; it is merely the *conditio sine qua non* of the latter. In every other sense the higher is independent of it; its specific quality, moral goodness, is something entirely new, something which was not represented in the lower value towards which it stands in complete indifference.

It is precisely the existence of the material stuff provided by the lower for the higher structural value, which makes this dependence necessary. Where moral values and their opposites appear in persons, there a world of positive goods must previously have been at hand, to which as objects of worth the persons react. But the converse is not true. The existence of the world of goods does not involve the emergence of a world of morality and immorality. The basis of the latter is provided only where a community of persons exists within one and the same world of goods. The content of the moral world lies on another plane; it is a structural novelty face to face with the

whole mass of values from other quarters. Hence the novelty of
its inherent quality. And indeed its pecularity—both material
and axiological—subsists without prejudice to the fact that the
moral conduct of the persons touched by it has, mediately and
dependently, the character of a "good."[1]

(c) OTHER KINDS OF DEPENDENCE

This relation of higher and lower is not universal. It by no
means holds good for the whole realm of values that the higher
is conditioned by the lower. Such dependence prevails indeed
over a wide area, but not everywhere, and it is itself not always
structurally the same.

It is the tritest commonplace that, for instance, spiritual
values can blossom only where the elementary biological values
are attained, that the cultural form of a higher kind can grow
only in a soil of prosperity and welfare of a certain grade. But
the same cannot be affirmed concerning the value of pleasure
and comfort, or even of happiness. Between these and culture
there exists no inner and necessary dependence, although the
former are lower in character than culture.

Between biological and spiritual values there is not the same
kind of dependence as between material goods and moral values.
The biological are only the ontological presupposition of the
spiritual, that is to say, their actuality is a condition for the
realization of the latter; their existence is only a means, only a
building-stone. But their value-quality is not a material condition for spiritual qualities. Non-moral possessions, on the other
hand, are in their specific value-quality a condition for those
of personal conduct—without prejudice to the axiological independence of the latter. Between the two there is only a relation
of a *conditio sine qua non*. But as regards the former the condition is merely external and ontological; for the latter it is a
structural, an internally axiological, organic relation of value-
entities as such, a fusion of the lower into the higher; in short,

[1] Cf. Chapter XV (c), Vol. I.

a purely constitutional relationship of values, or, more correctly, of the whole field of value as such, which is there before any actualization of value and which is independent thereof.

(d) SCHELER'S ATTEMPT TO ESTABLISH THE OPPOSITE THEORY

In place of the law that the higher fields rest upon the lower, Scheler maintained that the lower are dependent upon the higher.[1] According to him the lower can exist by right only in so far as the higher, to which they are related and in which they find their significance, exist. As an illustration he takes the relation between the value of the useful and that of the agreeable. To be useful "for something" is of the essence of utility; a thing cannot be useful in and of itself. Therefore, another, evidently a higher value is the axiological condition of the useful.

Against this argument, which is in itself unobjectionable, there is one thing to be said. Why must the basic value always be the agreeable? Rather is utility the value of means as such, and this is relative to an end already given. The end therefore must have a value of its own; but this need not necessarily be that of the agreeable. A thing can very well be useful for life and prosperity, for social and mental values of every kind. When one in this sense widens Scheler's theory it is undoubtedly, as regards utility, well founded.

But then the question arises: Does the same relation of dependence hold in the case of other orders of value? Is it true that biological values are based upon spiritual values, or that these rest upon some highest religious value? It is true that life gains a decidedly higher significance from spiritual values. But that fact is simply due to their place in the scale of values itself. May one, on the other hand, go so far as to say that the value of life would lapse, if it were not linked up with that of spiritual existence, in which the consciousness of bio-logical value is enclosed?

That would in truth deny the value peculiar to life itself;

[1] Scheler, *Der Formalismus in der Ethik*, second edition, p. 92 ff.

and the gravity of the moral crime involved in the destruction of mere life—even where there are scarcely any spiritual values worth mentioning—would be absolutely incomprehensible. It is likewise in contradiction to our sense of value and especially to our moral sense, when one makes the spiritual values (including the moral worth of action) dependent upon some absolute other-worldly value of a religious nature. The characteristic feature of spiritual values—for example, the æsthetic—is their self-evident autonomy, their perfect self-sufficiency and their independence of all wider perspectives.

The same holds good of moral values. To found them upon a higher value is evidently mere metaphysical speculation, conceived as a support for religio-philosophical theses which as such do not throw any light upon æsthetic or ethical reality. This entire notion that the lower depends upon the higher is at bottom a teleological prejudice; as a universal formula, it would read: lower structures are always dependent upon higher ones as ends, for the sake of which they exist and in which alone they find significance.

Such a teleological law would presuppose a thorough-going teleological gradation of values and a teleological structure of the realm of values, and would affirm something not only altogether unverifiable, but something which goes counter to those categorial laws of dependence which are violated in metaphysical personalism.[1]

Against this it must be maintained that all grades of values, genuine in their own right, possess their peculiar autonomy, which can be diminished by no kind of dependence upon anything above. The whole meaning of the realm of values, so far as it is a world of ideal self-maintaining entities, stands or falls with this foundation-principle. But especially is it the spiritual values, even down to their ultimate details, which by their constitution reveal this autonomy. What is beautiful is beautiful for its own sake; what is comical is comical in itself; what is noble or lovable is noble or lovable

[1] Cf. Chapter XXV, Vol. I.

intrinsically. All reference back to something else for the sake of which it is what it is, is fantastic speculation.

The citation of utility is therefore the worst imaginable. For in itself utility is not a value on its own account. By its very nature it can only be the value of a means to something valuable in itself.

Of an entirely different kind is the basing of the higher value upon the lower, as it is here set forth. It implies for the higher values no surrender of their autonomy; for it does not touch the valuational character of the latter, but throughout attaches only to some specific structural elements of their contents, so far as these already must have such a character of their own. The higher value is never conditioned completely by the lower. Its dependence is not axiological, not to mention teleological, but only material or, as in most cases, only modal. It gives us indeed a certain insight into the realm of value, but it by no means applies to the whole range.

Dependencies naturally can very well exist in a kingdom of autonomous entities; only they must not be total and constitutional dependencies, for such would destroy the autonomy of the members. On the other hand, the basing, axiologically and teleologically, of the lower upon the higher constitutes a total and essential dependence of the quality of worth as such. The basing of the higher upon the lower materially is, on the contrary, only a partial dependence of particular structural elements.

MORAL VALUE AND THE END OF ACTION

(a) THE MISUNDERSTANDING OF MORAL VALUES
IN THE ETHICS OF ENDS

BESIDES all its methodological consequences, our theory of
dependence leads us to a still more important point of view, one
which is decisive even for the understanding of moral acts.

The Kantian ethics shows the meaning of moral principles
solely in their character of Ought. The commandment, the
imperative, the claim upon man, was the moral law. If this
idea were applied to values, the meaning of morality would
needs begin and end in this, that man's will would have to be
directed to moral values as the highest ends. He alone would be
the morally good man who in all his actions sought to be morally
good, who spoke the truth in order to be truthful, who loved
in order to be loving, who practised magnanimity so as to be
magnanimous. The Kantian rigorism speaks out pointedly and
universally: only that action has moral worth which is done
"for the sake of the law"; it is not enough that it be in accordance
with the law, the law must further be the single motive and its
fulfilment the final end.

That this rigid rigorism leads to preposterous results is
evident and has often been shown. But here we are concerned
not directly with it, for it is only an outgrowth of the ethics
of ends. What shall we say of the ethics of ends? Is it true that
moral values constitute the supreme ends of moral action, of
that action whose valuational quality they produce? Is it true
that the morally good man ultimately has himself in view,
himself distinguished by the value of his action, that in his aim
by anticipation he sees his own picture in a mirror—the
picture of himself as he ought to be? Is the picturing of oneself
in the looking-glass the meaning of goodness, love, magnanimity,
straightforwardness?

That is an evident falsification of the facts contained in a moral act. The end of straightforwardness is not to be straightforward oneself, but that the man to whom one speaks may learn the truth; likewise the object of the high-minded or loving man is not to be high-minded or loving, but that the other person upon whom the gift or the gladness is bestowed may have the gift or the gladness. A man gives of course from love, but not for the sake of love. He is concerned not at all with his own moral being, but with the being of the other person, and indeed by no means only with that other person's moral, but with his whole, existence, bodily as well as mental, that is to say, with his actual situations whatever they are, so far as they have value for him. But these situations are valuable for him in so far as they embrace goods. The knowledge of a truth is as much a good—or surely is at least so regarded—as the gift bestowed or the gladness occasioned.

Herein is shown, in its bearing upon conduct, the significance of basing the moral values upon the non-moral. An act is of course morally valuable through its end, but not in so far as the content of the end is the moral worth of the act, and not simply in so far as it has goods as its content, but in so far as its content is a definite relation of goods to persons.

The end of an act is a situational value; its moral quality, on the contrary, is an actional and thereby personal value. Moral qualities characterize a person's conduct, but not the object of the intention in which his conduct subsists. According to Scheler's phrase, they appear "on the back of the deed," but not in the goal it aims at. The ethics of ends involves a fundamental misunderstanding of moral values, in its false identification of these with the value of the situation striven for.

(b) THE LIMITS OF THE OUGHT-TO-DO IN THE REALM OF VALUES

At first glance it seems to follow that moral values are not at all determinant factors in the moral conduct of persons, in effort, volition, precept and action.

This inference would be a great mistake. What we call conscience, that clearer or obscurer inward self-knowledge (*conscientia*) concerning the worth or worthlessness of our own conduct, is by no means merely the condemnation after the deed, which one generally understands by it, but is equally an anticipatory prohibitive factor which is determinant, at least negatively, by its barring out of that which is immoral. It therefore works, at least selectively, in the choice of ends. And as there is necessarily an Either-Or in the polar opposition of value and anti-value, this formally negative inrush into reality is after all positive.

Situational values, the actualization of which is alone the concern of effort, volition and outward conduct, are always subjected to a selection through the moral feeling—and in proportion to the mass and strength of the latter. This type of worth, when it is decisive, has a positive character, even where no effect is produced but an abstention from doing. In morality even a leaving-undone is a deed. The situation from which a person acts always bears the character of a challenge to him to make a decision. The mere shrinking from a sin is always a positive decision.

Another weighty question arises here. If the morality of an act never coincides with the content of the thing aimed at, does it not follow that moral values as such cannot be actualized at all? Can a striving, a volition, be directed towards them? And finally, if this must be denied, is there any sense at all in speaking of the Ought of these values? Is not every proper Ought limited to situational values, that is, to the disposal of goods in relation to persons? In a word, is man condemned to concentrate his efforts solely upon the lower kinds of value and not to strive for the finest and distinctively moral kind?

This question has more than one meaning. If it refers to realization it means one thing, if to striving, another, if to the Ought, still another; and it is to be answered differently according to the meaning.

As regards the Ought, the question does not apply to the pure Ought-to-Be of values, whether ideal or actual. The morally Good ought to be; and, since it can only be a quality of moral acts in which the reality of other values is involved, this means that this valuational intention of the acts should be so constituted, or the contents so selected, that the moral qualities inhere in the acts. That is by no means contrary to common sense. Likewise, where the intention does not accord with this requirement, the act necessarily will not be as it ought to be; the Ought-to-Be therefore will be something actual. This also does not contradict what was said above; "Ought-to-Be-so" does not mean: one ought "to strive" to be so.

It is quite otherwise with the Ought-to-Do, with the demand, directed to the person, to aim in the act itself at the unfulfilled value, in one's own person to have in view its realization. Here is the limit of the ethics of the Ought; for here evidently arises a contradiction to the law that the moral worth of a deed cannot at the same time be the value aimed at as the end in view. It is the Ought-to-Do which cannot be directed upon moral values. So at least it appears provisionally, but even this proposition must be qualified.

In any case it holds true in general that the ethics of Ought —whereby is always meant primarily Ought-to-Do—attaches not to the moral values of persons but to the lower grades, to situational values, and, in so far as these refer to goods, to the values of goods.

But thus much must be maintained, that the limit of the Ought-to-Do is not the limit of the Ought in general. The imperative character therefore of moral commandments, which are concerned with conduct as such, is not affected by this limit; still less is the imperativeness of moral prohibitions impaired, for instance those of the Decalogue, the positive and edifying sense of which shines through their outwardly negative form.

(c) THE LIMIT WITHIN WHICH MORAL VALUES MAY BE STRIVEN FOR

Since the Ought-to-Do is valid only where at least a possibility of effort corresponds to it in the person concerned, the limit of the Ought-to-Do turns out to be at the same time the limit of rational endeavour. What is true of endeavour holds good also of the Will, of resolution, design, decision, indeed of the objectively intentional contents of the disposition itself. That cannot of course mean that every Will to be morally good is a foolish or impossible volition. It means only that the volition in a morally good action is not a willing to be good, but the willing of another good, and of a good in another sense, namely, of a situation which in itself is good.

Now the question is: Does this limitation really signify what Scheler's ethics[1] infers from it, that every direction of a will or action towards the moral values of conduct clashes with the moral character of this Will?

If one replies in the affirmative, it follows that attainability by effort must decrease with the height of the value, and that personal values, which as specifically moral are the highest, cannot be striven for. Effort here = o, for it finds its absolute boundary this side of the moral values.

Personalism supports this theory by the proposition that a person as such, with all that pertains to him (his acts and qualities), can never in essence be objective—a proposition (as was shown in our criticism of personalism) which rests upon a misunderstanding of the categorial relation between subject and person. This sort of argument we may here regard as disposed of. Metaphysically there is nothing in the constitution of a personality to prevent it and its acts from being aimed at as an object either of knowing or striving.

Nevertheless the other proposition remains true, that in striving, values of situations and not of personality are commonly intended, that the higher a value is, the less it is striven

[1] Scheler, 527 f.

for, and that striving reaches its natural minimum in regard to the personal values which are the highest. Yet it does not follow from this, that the minimum ever equals zero or that personal values cannot at all be practically striven for.

The reason of such a diminution in effort is not due to the nature of personality and its acts, but singly and solely to the nature of moral values, namely, to the fact that they are not those of the contents striven for but are the qualities of the striving itself. What actually constitutes the limit to striving is an entirely different relation: the necessary non-identity between value and value—namely, between that of an act and that of the contents striven for in the act. But that the object of an act cannot be a structure of the same order, that is, not an act, not an attitude, not a striving intention—whether of oneself or of another person—this is not at all involved in the facts of the relation concerned. Consequently it does not follow that qualities of acts of the same rank cannot be intended. For it is not at all implied that with reference to any given action it is necessarily the same quality of value which must be in the intended object and in the morality which is realized in the doer —and that alone is excluded according to the laws of value.

In fact, how could there be such a thing as moral education —whether of oneself or another—if there were no striving to be morally good! It is by no means necessary to think here of pedagogically defective means—exhortation, instruction or one's own conscious example. There are many methods and means, and even if they should one and all be double-edged, the significance of their aiming at moral goodness remains valid beyond all doubt.

The defectiveness of the means is only a question as to success; but the strenuous intention stands to success in no assignable relation. In itself the capability of being striven for remains; it is a fact, a demonstrable phenomenon of the moral life.

Of course it is only a limiting phenomenon and it has therein its limit; that is to say, one may not universalize the ability to strive for moral values, one may not conclude that in all moral effort moral values are the thing striven for. Nothing of the sort follows from this phenomenon. But one must not refuse to an educator, to a father or to anyone who feels himself morally responsible for others, the right to take moral values as a goal. In like manner one may not refuse this right to the morally mature man in regard to himself or others. On the contrary, it is evident that in such striving the highest point of moral conduct may be discerned, despite the danger of mirroring oneself (which is always at hand). The reverse side of this phenomenon is the universal joint responsibility of each for each and for all, and especially for their moral being as such—a responsibility which Scheler thrusts into the centre of ethics, but which with him nevertheless floats in the air. Along with this there is, for instance, the consciousness of one's own moral example, good or bad, which everyone unavoidably gives in all his behaviour. From the same moral tendency arises the shrinking from giving a bad example, as also the desire, not incompatible with a becoming modesty, to give a good example.

Only a man who subjects moral phenomena to an arbitrary choice under the influence of preconceived metaphysical theories, can deny this group of phenomena. Either to deny them or to generalize them is to falsify the facts.

Now these phenomena contradict metaphysical personalism —or rather this personalism contradicts them and thereby destroys itself—but they do not contradict the law of the non-identity of the value striven for and the value of the striving. Rather is the non-identity preserved in them perfectly. Even where the end of the endeavour is really the moral worth of a personality (one's own or another's), it is never the same as the moral worth of the endeavour. If, for instance, the trend of an educator is toward magnanimity or self-sacrifice in the pupil, this tendency is not on that account to be called either magnanimous or self-sacrificing. Just as little is it a tendency to be honest or straightforward, when the aim is honesty and straightforwardness. Rather there is attached to it another moral value, which may be difficult enough to name precisely, but which without a name is plainly enough seen as a moral value. Perhaps it is a specific quality, not further analysable—the conscious willingness to be responsible for the moral being of another person; perhaps also it may be subsumed under "wisdom" (somewhat in the sense of the ancient σοφία) or under love—be it personal or universal. At least no one will challenge the moral worth of moral solicitude for another. But so much is clear: it is something else than what is aimed at in this solicitude.

There are many other proofs of this circumstance. One of the most cogent is the relation between pattern and imitation. To imitate means to emulate a marked type of moral being, that is, to strive to be like the pattern. And as it is here a matter of indifference whether the pattern be a real person or only an ideal, there is connected herewith a long chain of further phenomena which all show the same kind of striving directed to moral values as such. Under this head come the gradations of ideal ethical forms—so far at least as the ideals do not remain mere idle dreams but react determinantly upon one's own or another's conduct. But in all such cases the moral worth of the emulation is clearly something else than that of the ideal emulated.

This complex fact is in no wise contradicted by the law that moral values, and the values aimed at in volition, effort and action, are not identical. On the contrary, one can draw from this the lesson that it is not to the point to describe the value aimed at as a situational value. It can be also a personal value—at least in limiting cases. Here the object pursued is conduct, and indeed the moral conduct of a person. Yet this likewise must not by any means be generalized. It still remains a limiting case; commonly the values striven for are situational values. In spite of everything, a characterization of effort, will and conduct would be too narrow, which considered only the realization of situations as the object of intention. On principle one must include personal values—a clear proof that personal

Being and personal value are not less objective than the existence and value of things.

Taken universally, the proposition that moral values cannot be striven for is false. The truth contained in it is simply the difference between an intended value and the value of the intention. From this it follows that the limit of attainability by effort does not lie upon the boundary line between situational value and moral value, but plainly very much higher. Whether all moral values should be included in the sphere of things that can be striven for is not to be decided on general grounds. The real impossibility of striving would first manifest itself where the value of the thing striven for coincided with that of the striving. But whether this circumstance ever actually occurs is not to be settled before the values themselves have been analysed.

All the same it is very possible that there are some moral values which, in accordance with the nature of their contents, do not permit of being aimed at, not to mention of being realized—one simply has them or does not have them. Here one naturally thinks of the rich group of values peculiar to individual personality. But to explain why this exclusive relation to endeavour is characteristic of them, and why with them attainability by effort reaches an absolute limit, belongs to another group of questions.

(d) The Relation of Striving to Attaining

It is otherwise with the actualization of moral values. At first glance one would think that it was in a more unfavourable position than striving; much can be striven for, which cannot be attained; but what can be attained, so it is thought, must at least be capable of being striven for. Then the limit of attainability would need to be placed lower in the realm of values than that of the possibility of being striven for. We might accordingly think this limit would correspond with the dividing line between moral and situational values. Only the latter, then, would be attainable, while the former would also be capable generally of being striven for.

The implicit presupposition in this is that attainment by striving is the same as attainment in general, that the latter is conditioned by striving, but that striving is not conditioned by attainability. This is evidently a false assumption. Valuable things can come into being without any intention being directed towards them. Actualization does not need to be willed, purposed or pursued as an end. Goods and valuable situations come into existence without the assistance of someone willing them; they come either in a "natural" way or as the result of human action, but without their being the conscious goal of the action. Even the evil Will can bring forth good, against its own purpose. What becomes real is an affair of success; but success stands in no determined relation to purpose.

It follows that through actions much can be attained which was not striven for in them. The realization of a value therefore is not conditioned by its being striven for, also not by its capability of being striven for.[1] The sphere of what may be realized is not confined to what may be striven for. And the limit of what may be striven for is definitely not a limit pre-established in what may be realized.

If one remembers this in connection with moral values, one sees that their actualization in man is not conditioned at all by their being striven for. Here, too, there is more scope for actualization than for striving; and this fact is highly significant for the moral Being of a person. For moral values can be striven for (as we have seen) within narrow bounds only. Were they also realizable only to so small a degree, a man would be practically

[1] On the other hand, the possibility of being striven for is not necessarily conditioned by attainability. Otherwise there would be no such thing as an ineffectual striving. Realizability and endeavour stand in no fixed relation to each other, but they are not on that account indifferent to each other. Striving is constitutionally directed to realization, but the prevision of the one who strives is limited. His knowledge of attainability is not commensurate with the actual possibilities of realization.

debarred from almost all moral worth. In other words, if in his own Being a person could actualize values only through striving after them, he would be almost entirely incapable of attaining them.

Obviously this contradicts the facts of the moral life. In every just dealing, in all loving behaviour, in every good-will, a person actualizes true moral values in his own being. His intentions, however, are in no way directed toward these values, nor toward his own moral estate, but, outwards, toward the existence of others, or, more exactly, toward the circumstances which concern them.

Such is the nature of a man's moral worth that without aiming at it and by entire preoccupation with what is outside himself, he none the less actualizes it.[1] In general the proposition holds good that the more the intention of acts is directed outwards, the richer become the moral values in the innermost Being of the agent.

The paradox in this proposition is rooted in the essence of values themselves and especially in the dependence of moral upon situational values. As the moral value is that of the act itself, and therefore cannot appear in the object aimed at but only in the act as its own quality, so the actualization of the moral worth necessarily depends not upon aiming at it but upon aiming at situational values. Yet, as all intention presses towards the actualization of the thing striven for, there are necessarily two levels in all striving, willing and doing, in all practical conduct. The one is striven for, the other is not intended but simply takes place—and it takes place whether the intended actualization is attained or not. For the moral worth of an act does not depend on the success of the act, but on the direction of its intention. The unintended actualization of a moral value therefore does not first appear after the situation is actualized but arises in the mere intention, in the striving itself. One may therefore very well say that a person actualizes his own moral value "in" his striving, even "through" his

[1] This formulation is given in agreement with Scheler, p. 528.

striving. But rightly understood, he does not actualize it either through the actualization of the thing striven for or through the striving for his own moral value, but only through striving for other values (generally not moral), upon which the moral values are based.

This fundamental relation not only adheres to the particular striving, willing and doing, but, *mutatis mutandis*, generally to all acts which particularly aim at values, to every disposition, to all the behaviour of a person, even to that which seems purely inactive. For irrespective of differences in form, the whole practical conduct of a person moves, directly or indirectly, from a given position intentionally towards situational values. The manifestation of this depends upon actualizing the thing intended, not on the intention itself. But the actualization of what was not intended (the moral value) does not depend upon the actualization of the thing aimed at but on the intention as such. Something else than that which was intended is realized through the mere intention as such.

(e) LIMIT TO THE POSSIBILITY OF ACTUALIZING MORAL VALUES

It might seem from this as though unintended actualization had no limits, or at least no fundamental ones rising out of its relationship to the values. Here we must of course disregard the manifold empirical and external limitations to fulfilment in any individual case.

But in fact this is not so. Other obstacles than the intention can stand in the way of fulfilment.

Some goods by their very nature can never become actual, because actualization itself—even unintended—cannot be directed towards them, or because there is a process that moves away from them, but none that moves towards them. There are goods which one may indeed lose when one has them, but cannot gain when one has never had them, or has lost them. Of this kind are youth, ingenuousness, harmlessness; and closely related to these are certain forms of happiness, such as a cheerful disposition, healthy light-heartedness, also —up to a point—beauty, charm, natural grace and many related things. On the other hand, the fact that one may to a certain extent cultivate and develop fortunate gifts, plays a subordinate part—at least within a single human life; and, in the case of the first-mentioned examples, even this possibility does not exist at all.

In the realm of moral values also it is quite possible that there should be materials of such a nature, that realization could not be directed toward them. First of all one calls to mind those same values of individual personality, of which it was said that they could not be striven for. But the limit of what can be striven for is not the same as the limit of that which can be actualized. Nor do they coincide. The values of personality cannot be striven after, for this reason, among others, that, while they may indeed be felt, their structure can scarcely be grasped and an effort cannot be directed specifically towards them. But this is not necessary for their realization, because they do not need to be striven for. A person whose individual moral Idea is a power in him, actualizes it incidentally in all his dealings, no matter what he may be intentionally trying to bring about. He steadily builds, so to speak, out of his own distinctive moral Being, in so far as in all his strivings and dealings the intended situational values, besides being selected according to general moral standards, are also selected by the unique norms of his personal ethos. But he does not need to have a valuational consciousness of this building process, nor any consciousness at all. In short, the values of individuality are realized in exactly the same way as all other personal values: not by aiming at them but in striving after other, outer, values.

Actualization, then, meets with no limit in the medium of the values of personality. But there is quite another group of moral values which are highly individual, yet the substance of which cannot be actualized, only because their structure forbids and not because their position is axiologically higher in the scale of values. The representative examples of this group are innocence and purity. They stand in exactly the same position as do youth, ingenuousness and harmlessness among goods; the last two, by the way, stand on the border between moral values and goods. Innocence and purity one may lose, but cannot retrieve if they are once lost. A person may yearn to have them back, but there is no circumstance either willed or unwilled under which they can be regained. They come to men only as gifts from heaven—be it from nature with the first entrance into human life, when one is still a stranger to all moral conflict, or as a real gift of grace from the Godhead, through a sin and an atoning act, as the faith of the pious always hopes. But in neither case is the realization brought about through the conduct of the person, not even in the sense in which the unintended is actualized.

The group of values which are at the limit of attainability increases considerably, if one takes into account not attainability in general but that of any given individual. Thus for the coward by nature courage is utterly unattainable; in its place a substitute can at best be installed through reflection, self-control and habit, a kind of inner discipline. Likewise it is morally impossible for the phlegmatic and indolent to become energetic and ambitious, for the passive to become active, the tyrannical at heart truly sensitive, the servile and undignified knightly and proud. On all sides attainability finds in such cases its limitations independently of what can be striven for. Each one can realize in himself only what lies within the range of his individual ethos. Not every moral claim, however universal in itself, can be applied to everybody.

There is, then, a limit to what can be realized, as much as there is a limit to what can be striven for and what ought to be done. But it is a different limit and is differently conditioned. It lies in the essence of certain values—whether absolute or relative to a special human ethos—whilst the limit of what can be striven for lies in the essence of striving, which, when directed towards moral values, stands in its own way.

CHAPTER III (xxviii)

THE GRADATION OF VALUES

(a) THE METHODOLOGICAL DIFFICULTY IN THE PRINCIPLE OF GRADATION

WE have spoken continually of higher and lower values. The thought of a gradation in the realm of values has been tacitly presupposed.

To this no objection can be taken, for it is impossible to construct any interrelation of values without making this presupposition. But the right to do this is not on that account proved, nor is its meaning made clear. Now it would also be a false demand to wish to fix a gradation before the values have been elaborated; evidently a grading can be given only after there has been a more exact analysis—so far at least as this is possible. But the principle of gradation itself demands an exposition precedent to the analysis, even if it be merely to settle why only the phenomenology of specific values can furnish a sketch of a scale of value.

The methodological difficulty here consists in this, that one can bring the manifoldness of values not otherwise to view than in a series, and that the tendency arises quite of itself to suggest, at least generally, a gradation in such a series. The relation of interdependence between the two classes of value by its importance alone involves such a tendency.

If in the order of rank it were a question only as to the general relation of goods to personal values, our decision would be relatively simple and would from the first permit of being deduced. But the question is not concerning this alone. It refers to a thorough articulation of the ethical realm of value, not only of the realm of things and their reactions, but also of that of persons and their behaviour. And here one cannot otherwise proceed than by implicitly presupposing the gradation which can first come to light in the course of the analysis.

Even this subsequent result is to be understood only *cum grano salis*. Even the detailed analysis at best does not achieve a really thorough ranking of values. One must not forget that we stand at the beginnings of our inquiry, and that no proper and special investigations have been made. Accordingly one may not expect assured results. All that can be shown is the existence of certain more or less evidently connected groups, which cluster about single dominant and fundamental values, but the positions of these relatively to one another cannot by any means be shown to be permanently connected. The type as such is indeed clear, but from it no unifying principle of gradation can be drawn, let alone a principle wherewith to fill out the gaps between the groups.

The whole method is still in a state of seeking and groping. We may not speak of an a priori view. The fragments, which are becoming visible, of an incontrovertible, consistent and unified scale are evidently accidental merely, conditioned by the human attitude and by temporary partiality.

We must try to grasp the values where and how we can. For one group the leading point of view is a "systematic" one, inhering in the general nature of value and the Ought; for another it is drawn from the historically accidental development of the ethos; for a third it is in direct opposition to such a development and is conceived in contrast to it. It is evident that unity in such a case is lacking. Nevertheless, no one of these disparate points of view may be neglected. They are our given landmarks.

Thus our procedure must necessarily be of a loose and tentative character. We must see whether or not this method leads to a more strictly unifying point of view.

(*b*) CONSCIOUSNESS OF VALUE AND CONSCIOUSNESS OF ITS GRADATIONS

We must not on account of this unfortunate condition of the problem fail to appreciate how important, even how central,

the question is which we are here considering. Without knowledge of their relationships to one another all knowledge of
values themselves remains abstract. In all ethical situations,
however, manifold values participate at the same time; and for
the man who is confronted with the situation the task is to
determine his conduct from his consciousness of the situation
—a consciousness which weighs value against value. His feeling
for values, therefore, can really guide him only when there is at
the same time a feeling of their relative rank. Naturally this
feeling must be primal, not attained first through reflection.
Immediately with the feeling for the value there must be a
feeling for its place in the scale.

It is in the nature of human volition that it never is directed
towards anything contrary to value as such. That was the
never-to-be-forgotten meaning of the Socratic ethics: no one
does evil for evil's sake, it is always a good (something valuable),
which hovers before him. We have shown how Christian ethics
brings into consideration another determining factor, which in
human nature goes counter to the knowledge of the good,
the factor of weakness, the being under the spell of lower
powers.

But is the confusion in human craving hereby explained?
The difficulty is just this: how can weakness, how can feeling,
divert the will from the valuable, if the very nature of the will
is to be able to turn only to the valuable? The confusion cannot
be due to the fact that the will or craving is drawn to what is
opposed to value as such and on its own account. This kind of
swerving does not exist in man. A satanic being may be able
to will evil for evil's sake. But man is not a satanic being; his
craving is always unequivocally for the positive side of the
series of values, the side to which the good in a wide sense is
bound.

The answer must run otherwise: even the will which is
diverted by feeling moves towards values, only it moves towards
lower ones. It is diverted through outward, through morally
indifferent, goods; in it there is a failure to select according

to the higher, that is, the moral values. And even where this selection is not lacking in it, where perhaps a higher feeling of value whispers its claim, there it is overborne by the insistent strength of the lower values.

The solution of the problem is thereby found in the relative rank of values. In every concrete situation through the mere juxtaposition of persons interested in the same goods a condition is so given, that every act, even every inner attitude, falls at the same time under moral points of view. And these are the higher points of view. Their surrender to the individual's self-interest in the goods is moral confusion. For this is precisely the peculiarity of moral values, that they come forward with a claim of more unconditional validity, and allow an interest in the lower values only within the limits of their own preservation by the person. The consciousness of their being higher is utterly decisive. Every morally selective consciousness of values is necessarily a consciousness of the scale of values.

(c) "HIGHER" AND "LOWER," THEIR MEANING AXIOLOGICALLY IRREDUCIBLE

If one keeps this general situation in mind, one can scarcely doubt that behind moral conflict, as the situations of life produce it in various forms, there always stands the opposition of value against value in some form, not the opposition of value against anti-value.

The conflict has not the form of a logically contradictory alternative, but always that of an opposition which is positive (in the valuational sense) on both sides. Over against this, on the other hand, stands the fact, that the real conduct of a person cannot possibly decide at the same time for both sides of the opposition; of the two values at stake it can pursue only one and must violate the other. The decision of the will therefore cannot escape from treating the axiologically contrary opposition as if it were a contradictory one. Herein lie the absolute bounds of every human decision of the will. Everything which a man can do is confined to the tendency to give a preference to one value over another, and indeed a preference to which the value objectively has a claim. The scope of what one can do is wide enough to embrace the fulness of every moral For and Against. But within this boundary every positive decision depends on a question of valuational preference, of height in a scale, and it is a function of the consciousness of an order of precedence.

What is exactly the meaning of "higher" and "lower" in this order of precedence causes no difficulty to the sense of values, but it is scarcely to be given with conceptual strictness. The scale of valuational height constitutes a dimension *sui generis*. It is in no way to be traced back to dimensions of valuational variability which are otherwise articulated. This causes it to be utterly indefinable. It is, for example, wrong to see a foothold for the degree of value in the categorial structure of the valuational contents, perhaps in the opposition between simplicity and complexity. Even if it should be proved that in general the higher axiological position belongs to the more highly complex structure, one could educe no principle therefrom. For numerous individual cases manifest the opposite.

The common mistake which one meets lies in the other direction: men think they recognize the highest in the most comprehensive values, the lowest in the most specific (the individual values). But undeniably the most general have the simplest, the most specific have the most complex material structure. What misleads one here is primarily the analogy of logical concepts; in the place of the axiological relation of degrees of value, one substitutes, without noticing it, the relation of structural dependence in the sense of formal subsumption. There is naturally also in the realm of values a logical dependence; the more general and elementary values present themselves actually again and again as the structural elements of the more complex. But the latter are not on that account lower; they are for the most part precisely the higher. That dependence, therefore, without prejudice to its existence in the realm of value, is in any case no measure of rank in the scale of values.

Many types of philosophical ethics, however, have committed this mistake, of seeing the relation of valuational rank in the material relation of subsumption. Here belong all the theories which search for an ultimate fundamental value from which all lower ones can be traced. A logical relation of deduction unintentionally haunts such a tracing; we even surrender to the belief that in this way a system of ethical values can be derived. But even in this, we are yearning for an ultimate oneness of value. For example, in Kant's doctrine of the categorical imperative such a thought unmistakably lies hidden; for the unity of the moral law meant the universal standard of all possible "maxims." It is not to be wondered at that Kant's successors in the ethics of Ought—pre-eminently Fichte—were victims of the same suggestion as to the possibility of subsuming all values under a principle. But even in Plato's Idea of the Good there already lurked something of this prejudice. It was otherwise, however, with Aristotle and Hegel, whose teleological metaphysics, conversely, always sees the structurally more complex form in the higher telos. Here, however, the standard of height is by no means autonomously axiological.

Despite all the failures of such a construction, the tendency to be misled by the analogy to a system of concepts continues unabated. Philosophy seems unable to escape from casting the valuational system (so far as it attains thereto) into the form of a system of valuational concepts. The latter kind of system cannot be changed. For this reason, that prejudice can never be successfully coped with by mere criticism, but only by the introduction of a positive outlook, otherwise conditioned.

Now such an outlook, as already said, cannot be arbitrarily set up, but must be derived from progressive analysis of value itself. Here, however, the presupposition is that the phenomena of the sensing of the values which are to be analysed—that sense being the single assured landmark which we have—

contain implicitly in themselves the total phenomenon of a scale of values.

(d) The Multiple Dimensionality of the Realm of Values

A further prejudice which slips into the thought of an ordered gradation is the notion of a simple valuational scale which ascends in a single series.

Such a single dimensionality would be an advantage from the point of view of a survey. But this advantage—which would exist only "for us"—should make one hesitate. For instance, how does it agree with the relation of subsumption, which unquestionably exists in the realm of values (even if it does not concern their degree)? This relation presupposes the co-ordination of the commonly subsumed values. Besides, the mere co-existence of two heterogeneous orders of relationship in one realm (that of higher and lower and that of subsumption) would alone be enough to convince anyone of the fact of a plural dimensional order.

But there are other and stronger proofs of this fact. In the first place it is clear to anyone who has gained insight into the valuational realm, that the manifoldness of values is too great to embrace in a linear arrangement the intervals corresponding to the differences of content. The values would need to overflow continually into one another, which by no means corresponds to their actual and often very abrupt articulation, that is, to their difference given in the sense of value.

But in the second place, it is evident that the qualitative difference of values as such, which varies with their contents, signifies something quite other than a different valuational grade, and that consequently there is no necessity that values differing in content should have totally different rank in the scale. Rather does it issue unquestionably from the heterogeneity of valuational grade and of valuational structure, that both can quite well vary independently of each other, and that different valuational materials may be of the same valuational grade.

Hence it follows that "perpendicularly" to the scale of valuational rank, a relation of co-ordination among the different values exists upon the same level. At least on principle nothing stands in the way of such a relation. That does not in the least interfere with the thoroughgoing fixed co-ordination of every value on a given level. The order of gradation is thereby simply shown to be at the same time differentiated "laterally." But this means that the system of values has more than one dimension, and that only one of its dimensions is that of higher and lower.

This view does not here allow of being more exactly proved through phenomena. Proofs can first be given in the special analysis of values. There are valuational groups within which differences of higher and lower level can scarcely be pointed out, or which stand in no relation to very striking differences of content. In the domain of goods this fact is moreover very well known. "Who has the choice, he has the torment," is the content of a popular saying; axiologically expressed the thought is: two totally different goods can very well be of equal value. The same is without further ado to be expected of the moral values; and, within the limits of human opinion, which is not mathematically exact, it also can be proved to be there for the scale of values.

The significance of this phenomenon, again, is of great importance. For it is easy to see that where values of the same grade are at stake in one and the same situation, so that the doer can be just only to one of them, there the moral conflict must become a conflict of values.

(e) STRENGTH AND HEIGHT OF VALUES—SIN AND FULFILMENT

Closely allied is the error of thinking that the higher the grade of a value the more unconditional its validity, in a word, the nearer its proximity to absoluteness. In that case a lower value would, in comparison, be more contingent, more conditional. This is a confusion of thought. If values in general have an ideal existence in themselves, their validity is throughout of an absolute kind, incapable of being relative in any way. Validity cannot in this respect be graduated.

This conception finds apparent support in the fact that the Ought-to-Be of moral values is more unconditioned than that of goods; the realization of a goods-value can never, for example, justify its claim against a moral value, but vice versa. Only here one forgets two things. In the first place, the Ought-to-Be of a value is not identical with its validity, with the existence of the value of the content itself. Where the importance of the Ought-to-Be is graduated in many ways, the value of the specific matter can still be unconditionally absolute. But in the second place, the relation of goods to moral values is of a unique kind—a material relation of dependence *sui generis*— which by no means allows of being universalized, and in any case does not reappear within both classes of value. The gradation of higher and lower, on the other hand, permeates uninterruptedly the whole series of values. It is therefore at all events a different relation.

There is nevertheless an aspect of the order of rank which is related to this conception: the aspect of the strength, or of the power, in some manner or other, to determine one's judgment of values. In this respect, values, including among them those that are moral, are of very different quality.

Difference of strength, however, is not difference of rank. It might rather be affirmed that the two kinds of gradation are opposed to each other: the higher value may be precisely the weaker, the lower the stronger. Within certain limits this indirect proportionality of height and strength may well agree; the higher values are generally for the most part the more complex structures, the lower are the more elemental. But in strength the elemental is always the superior. In this point therefore there would be a return of the fundamental categorial law in the domain of value—the law that the lower categories are the stronger and more independent, while the weaker and more conditioned are the higher and more complex. Ontologically this law is manifest in the graduated relation of the categories. But we do not shut our eyes to the stratification of values. Values are not categories of existence, and their relation is not discernible in concrete reality.

One may easily be convinced that in general the reverse relation holds between height and strength. To sin against a lower value is in general more grievous than to sin against a higher; but the fulfilment of a higher is morally more valuable than that of a lower. Murder is held to be the most grievous crime, but respect for another's life is not on that account the highest moral state—not to be compared with friendship, love, trustworthiness. Property is an incomparably lower value than personal benevolence, but none the less a violation of property (theft) is much more reprehensible than mere malevolence. A sin against the lower values is blameworthy, is dishonourable, excites indignation, but their fulfilment reaches only the level of propriety, without rising higher. The violation, on the other hand, of the higher values has indeed the character of a moral defect, but has nothing degrading in it, while the realization of these values can have something exalting in it, something liberating, indeed inspiring.

There is no gainsaying this phenomenon, taken in such generality. What follows from it is a question by itself. Thus much in it can be seen with certainty, that height of value is something different from strength of value. But if one should wish to conclude further, that in this an indirect measure of the height of a value is furnished, one would at least be walking on insecure ground. For the categorial law is exactly fulfilled in the categories only. For values it holds but approximately; still holding distinctly with the larger differences of grade, it fades away and finally fails altogether before the finer discriminations of rank. And these latter are alone of importance. The relative level of roughly conceived extremes is evident to everyone.

THE CRITERIA OF THE GRADE OF A VALUE

(a) Five Tests of Rank in the Scale of Values

INVOLVED in the question of rank is the question as to the possibility of knowing the rank. This is part of the general problem concerning the knowledge of values, and partakes of its difficulties.

Are there any criteria of the height of a value? And what are these? As there is a consciousness of height, as well as of value in general, we cannot escape the assumption that some distinguishing mark is present. But this might be deeply hidden in the feeling for values and remain inaccessible to any analysis.

Scheler made a deliberate attempt to elaborate a system of distinguishing marks.[1] It is not based upon the ethical values as such in their relation to one another, but upon the whole realm, in which differences of height are naturally greater and more conspicuous. But that of itself would not exclude the transference of the criteria to the inwardly ethical differences of gradation. These marks must therefore be examined.

1. Values are relatively higher the more enduring they are; one might rather say, the more timeless they are. Not the durability of the carrier is meant (for perishability increases rather than diminishes with the height), but the super-temporality of the value-quality itself. Pleasantness is bound to the persistence of a given sensibility, goods to that of a given situation. Spiritual values have a hold superior to everything empirical; they persist above the transitoriness of disposition and situation. Moral values do not stand or fall with the act in which they inhere; love has meaning only *sub specie quadam æterni.*

---

[1] Scheler, op. cit., p. 88 ff.

2. Values are so much the higher, the less the quality of their carrier increases with its extension and decreases with its division. Material goods admit of being shared among persons only in as much as we divide them. Their value for the individual diminishes progressively with each division. Spiritual values are not in themselves capable of being divided; they are indifferent to the number of those participating in them. That the social conflict of interests depends upon material goods and not on spiritual, rests not in the nature of the interest directed towards them (not, as it were, in the greater intensity of this), but in the nature of the values. Material goods separate the persons who share them; spiritual goods unite men in a common possession. That moral values in a pre-eminent sense are unifying and scorn all distribution is self-evident. Their mode of Being is a Being for all and each, just because their self-existence is not relative to anyone's participation in them.

3. In the third place Scheler introduces the above-mentioned[1] relation of dependence. If the lower values are based upon the higher, such dependence is naturally a distinguishing mark of rank. Even in so far as this relation is shown to be wrongly conceived, and instead of it the opposite holds good,[2] the principle that dependence is a mark of height retains its force. The basic material value is, then, as the more self-sufficient and independent, at the same time the lower and more elementary, while the value which is dependent is the higher.

4. There exists an essential relation between height and the "depth of satisfaction" which accompanies the consciousness of fulfilment of value. The satisfaction in material goods may be ever so intense, but it still remains spiritually superficial; satisfaction in the enjoyment of art may be ever so elusive, but it still remains a deep experience. The "depth" of satisfaction has nothing to do with its strength. The whole quality of the emotional tone differs according to the height of the value

[1] Cf. Chapter I (c), Vol. II.   [2] Ibid. (a).

experienced; and in this gradation the inwardness, the identification with one's selfhood, is the characteristic feature. One's central spiritual nature reacts to the highest values. The meaning of stoical indifference in regard to outward fortune and misfortune is the inward concentration, the quiet imperturbable life in the depth of feeling for the highest values. Indifference to lower values is only the reverse side of this fundamental attitude.

5. Finally, an indication of worth-level consists in the degree of relativity to some specific value-sense. Values of pleasure and enjoyment have meaning only for a sensuously emotional disposition, biological values only for an organic sensitiveness; but moral values do not thus preserve their significance simply for a moral disposition; they are self-subsistent personal qualities with no relativity to the value-sense of anyone. As values of another sphere they are "absolute" in another sense. And accordingly in the feeling for values there exists an immediate consciousness of this absoluteness, however obscure; and, although it may only be felt, it is a consciousness in which the higher autonomy of these manifests itself.

(b) THE EVALUATION OF THESE CRITERIA

One thing is perfectly clear: If anyone wished quite seriously to determine the grade by such distinguishing marks, he would not get beyond the most general outlines. Each one of these criteria is enough to show that moral are higher than biological values. But this is quite evident without any of them: it does not need them. The finer differences of grade within the great groups do not become visible in this way. For them the criteria are altogether too crude, the indication of value-level is merely summary. For ethics everything depends upon a finer discrimination within the classes and groups. Such tests are of no use to it. For all moral values proper, super-temporality, indivisibility, dependence and axiological absoluteness are one and the same; these four features evidently constitute marks common to the whole class. Depth of satisfaction is the test most likely to help in further discrimination. For example, if one reviews a series of such values as honesty, truthfulness, goodwill to all and self-sacrifice, an increasing depth of inner assent seems to accompany the review. Depth, then, might be a point of attachment.

One plainly notes, however, that it is not simply depth of satisfaction which comes into consideration. The kind of satisfaction varies qualitatively also. The sense of values reacts in a totally different way to different values, and this differentiation penetrates much farther into specific qualities than do the other distinguishing marks.

By way of these qualitative discriminations a much finer perception of gradations can be attained.

(c) HILDEBRAND'S THEORY OF VALUATIONAL RESPONSE

Dietrich von Hildebrand's theory of specific response furnishes an easy approach to an investigation of this kind.[1]

For each value there is one, and only one, attitude corresponding to its nature, only one emotional reaction, the response suited to it. No one can find one and the same thing both "very neat" and "inspiring." The latter may apply to a great work of art, the former to a witty remark. The appropriateness of a specific response to a specific value can by no means be transposed at will. Who finds an inspiring thing "neat" shows merely that he has not understood; his response is not only out of place; it has in truth no meaning. The connection between a mental attitude and a value is something fixed in the nature of things. And, indeed, this constant uniformity holds in regard to negative as well as to positive values; also to every disvalue a specific kind of attitude corresponds, both as regards quantity and quality.

This law, correctly understood, would undoubtedly furnish

[1] D. von Hildebrand, *Die Idee der sittlichen Handlung, Jahrbuch f. Philos. u. phän. Forschung*, III, 1916, p. 162 ff.

us with a basis for the phenomenology of grades in a scale of
values, and not only for the larger intervals in a whole group,
but for the finer and often imponderable gradations of moral
values among themselves. Still the variety of response is
extraordinarily great, and is by no means exhausted within
the narrow limits of spoken language. The shades of value,
for which there are no names, must be described somehow
by circumlocutions. Hildebrand himself has not elaborated his
thought in this direction. But it must permit of being done.
Here is a definite task in ethical investigation which needs
developing.

(d) The Valuational Predicates of the Nicomachean Ethics

It is an interesting fact that this task finds an illustration in
antiquity—in the Nicomachean Ethics.

The series of "virtues" which Aristotle develops is not
meant as a variety of equal worth, but is evidently graduated
according to rank in a moral scale, although the sequence in
which they are cited only corresponds partly. A plain indication of this gradation is the differentiation of the valuational
predicates, which Aristotle applies to the single virtues. Without
forcing, one can arrange them in an ascending series:[1]

Not bad—worthy of praise (ἐπαινετόν); beautiful (καλόν);
worthy of honour (τιμητόν); lovable (φιλμτόν); admirable
(θαυμαστόν); superb (μακαριστόν).

The corresponding series of negative predicates is:—

Defective (ἡμαρτημένον); not beautiful (μὴ καλόν); blameworthy (ψεκτόν); disgraceful (ἐπονείδιστον); hateful (μισητόν).

Each series is further differentiated by an abundance of finer
shades. Behind these predicates, as the words show, is hidden
a graduated series, quantitative and qualitative, of acts which

[1] See M. v. Kohoutek, *Die Differenzierung des ἀνθρώπινον ἀγαθόν,
eine Studie zur Werttafel der Nikomachischen Ethik*, Marburg, 1923
(not in print), p. 21 ff. and 184.

assign or withhold values: to praise—to blame, to love—to hate, to honour—to defame, to admire—to scorn, to treasure —to despise. Here is unmistakably a double gradation of emotional reactions, that is, of valuational responses.

What makes Aristotle's procedure especially instructive is the circumstance that his differentiation of grades concerns not only general outlines but finer shades among moral values in the narrower sense. It gives the attitudes (ἕξεις) of the person himself, of which the valuational height is distinguished.

We may regard Aristotle's discriminations as only more or less felicitous; a first historical attempt cannot be perfect. But that does not matter. The Nicomachean table of values is by no means exhaustive; yet the attempt is a model for us. For in so far as the problem can be surveyed to-day, there is no other possible way of finding out the differences in the scale of values. Difference of response and the difference of predicates which runs parallel with it constitute the only means of access. And, we may add, the only natural access. If we look more closely to the efforts of ethical investigators, we find that, where they approach the problem of grade—and most of them do this in one form or another—they unintentionally pursue the method adopted by Aristotle. In many cases, of course, there is direct historical dependence upon him.

The problem deepens, as soon as we inquire into the inner ground of this phenomenon and into the justification for this procedure. The predicates and the responses are ultimately only outward manifestations of an existing inner connection between grade and the kind of valuational feeling. It is not otherwise possible; there must be a primal feeling of difference of rank, which corresponds with the types of response. And, indeed, this must be as original as the feeling itself, which discriminates qualitatively. In other words, the feeling of relation of height among values must adhere to the primal feeling for value in such a way that when two values are given the height of each is given. Indeed, it follows that a consciousness limited to one single value is only an abstraction, and that in all concrete feeling the sense of height in a scale of values is primary.

This would not imply by any means that the whole scale were known beforehand, but only that certain members were known together, or only a certain section of them. All discernment directed to a focus would then be drawn from the background of a continuum of grades discerned at the same time, even though partially. The complete absence of reflection in the responses to grade gives support to this interpretation. If we consider that in all the concrete situations of life a decisive preference is made between value and value—for a bad act is directed to values, only to lower ones—this inference cannot be avoided.

(e) SCHELER'S LAWS OF PREFERENCE AND THE ABSOLUTENESS OF THE IDEAL GRADATION

From this circumstance there follows not the presentation but the objective existence of gradation. In all, even the most unsophisticated, discernment of values, the presentation of a relative height, although seen only in a section, proves that there is a fixed, pervading gradation of rank, which is inseparable from the essence of values and has the same mode of existence as they, the same ideal self-existence. It is as little in the power of man to change this gradation, as it is in his power to gainsay the character of a discerned value. That in certain phenomena, as for instance in resentment, such a gainsaying takes place, does not overthrow the fundamental fact; here the point in question is the doing of violence to the sense of value itself, the habitual untruthfulness, manifested as a falsification in the evil conscience of the resentful man.

The absoluteness of the ideal self-existent gradation does not at all mean a corresponding and equally ideal consciousness of the gradation. Precisely on this point the limitation of all human consciousness of values is characteristic. If we further consider what in this case limitation exactly means, it becomes plain that the historically and individually variable notion of the gradation, for instance, its subjective relativity, in no way contradicts its objective absoluteness. From the limitation it follows that the gradational relations also are discerned only in a fragmentary way, and that, at any given time, what is accounted higher within the discerned fragment is seen to be higher. With a wider outlook it can be discovered to be lower in the scale. That the criticism, which is passed upon a subjectively valid gradation, is generally a thoughtful beginning, implies the existence of an objective independent gradation. The historical relativity of valuational appreciations is not a disproof, but on the contrary a confirmation, of its existence.

Scheler's ethics was the first to bring out this fundamental discrimination. He also pointed out the significance of "preference" in the finding out of the relation between the human consciousness of values and their self-existent scale.

A "preference," as a basic type of the acts which show the height of a value, is by no means found only in decisions of the will, but in all judgments as to values, in all taking of sides. It is not an act of judgment upon values, but is a primary element in the immediate sensing of them. All differentiation in valuational answers and predicates rests upon it, and at the same time upon its inherence in the feeling for values. This thought can be entirely detached from the five distinguishing marks of gradation which were discussed above, although it is true that in them also there are evidences of the laws of preference. Only they are not exhaustive for the phenomenon of preference. It goes farther, even to the finer and finest differences of grade. Whether there be a possibility of bringing into the light of philosophical consciousness the essence of this concealed and irreducible function in the objectively discerned categorial structures, must remain highly questionable. For ethics the important point is not so much this as the assurance of the existence of such a function. But the assurance needed to be in fact given in some such way as Scheler has done in terms of the phenomenon.

The central point here is not so much the relation of preference to height of value, as the difference, fixed by all such relations, between the thing related and that with which it is connected. For this perception of the height is clearly not exhausted in the fact that there is a preference; it never coincides with that. "For even if the height of a value is given in the preference, the height is nevertheless a relation inhering in the nature of the values concerned. Therefore the gradation of values is itself something absolutely invariable, while in history the rules of preferences are variable (a variation which differs greatly with the perception of new values)."[1]

Equally evident is it that the act of preference is not limited to cases where a number of values is given explicitly. There is also a mere suggestion of the related value in a specific consciousness of a direction upwards or downwards, which from the beginning accompanies the discernment of a special value. Likewise in preference the fact can be present that "here a higher value exists than the one sensed"—and, indeed, without this higher value itself being in the content of the feeling.[2]

Herein we have the confirmation of what was suggested above as to the ground of Aristotle's procedure, namely, that every concrete sense of value is primarily related to a scale of values, and that a strictly isolated, specifically focussed discernment of one value exists only *in abstracto*. Every living valuational feeling comes under laws of preference, which on their side are embedded in the order of valuational essences; there is throughout no specific sense of values, but one that is complex and relational. And this relationality of feeling does not resolve itself into any haphazard relations—primary or derived—of the realm of values, not into any formally subsumptive relation, not into the stages of absoluteness and dependence, not into the relations of basis and superstructure, whether of contents or of mode, or of any other kind—which may all be given limitlessly in the domain of values—but precisely into the relation of higher and lower as such. We

[1] Scheler, p. 85 f.   [2] Ibid.

might call these laws of preference, which are unerringly dominant in the depth of feeling for values and which resist outer influence, the "axiological perception of heights." It is the perception of an ideal scale *sui generis*, which cannot be compared with any other and which in extent coincides with no other.

Scheler rightly applies to this perception of height Pascal's phrase *ordre du cœur*. Closely related to it is Hemsterhuis's concept of an *organe morale*. And with still greater justification perhaps the strict meaning of the word "Vernunft" might be applied to it, in so far as in it is found the clairaudience of an inner "vernehmen." What here is discriminated to the finest degree is the system of intervals between intelligible tones, the chords of which make up the harmony of the ideal self-existent sphere.

Finally, with overpowering certainty it follows that there can be no derivation of any kind for the scale of values. That in it a supreme unifying principle may prevail is not to be denied, but we may deny that it can be known as such, and that it can be known before the discernment of specific values. Yet this would be required for every kind of derivation from a principle.

Our discernment of value is not based upon the unified structure of the sphere, but exclusively upon its contents in detail and upon the particular relation of these. In the phenomenon of preference we have an accompanying knowledge of the relative height of the value; but this accompanying knowledge has not the form of a criterion; it is not an ever-ready standard of unity by which we can measure and test. The phenomenon of preference is itself not apprehensible without a momentary deepening, a devotion and a most attentive listening. It is fleeting, it can be injured by rough handling, it wants to be lovingly and carefully hearkened to in its faintest whispers. Only thus to the attentive and patient does it reveal its secret—the ideal scale of values, to which it is the witness in man.

This circumstance no human need of unity and no philosophical need of system can change. We must accept it, consciously make it our own, and seek to discover by it as much of the scale of values as it is willing to disclose. That is the reason why the scale of values must remain for us necessarily fragmentary—a piece-work to a still higher degree than the philosophical knowledge of value.

THE PROBLEM OF THE SUPREME VALUE

(a) DEMAND FOR A UNIFYING ETHICAL PRINCIPLE

Now if all positive morality rests upon genuine discernment, and if all discernment of values is itself an aprioristic perception of valuational essences, the historical relativity of morals cannot rest upon that of values, but only upon that of discernment. Every current morality is acquainted only with certain values, or even only with one, which it then emphasizes, in order to relate everything else to it. Every current morality, therefore, has a substance of truth in it, however one-sided it may be. For a fragment of true valuational knowledge is in every one of them, however much each seems to contradict the others.

It becomes a task for ethics to resolve such contradictions —so far as they may be resolved—that is, so far as they are not due to an original antinomic in values themselves. So far as the latter is the case, ethics must not attempt synthesis; but it cannot disregard the demand for a unified survey. This belongs to its very nature. It must also select its point of view according to the phenomena, not the phenomena according to its point of view, even at the risk of comprehensibility. It must concede validity even to the incomprehensible; it must allow contradictories to coexist. For under all circumstances one thing must be kept open: scope for all ethical phenomena; therefore scope for all current moralities.

Hence it appears that in its principles ethics must always allow for an incurable pluralism as regards contents. But then not only does its own unity become very questionable, but also that of practical guidance in human life. Could it lie in the nature of ethics to prove that to be illusory which one rightly expects of it: the unity of the moral claim? An Ought has meaning only if it is unequivocal and does not annul itself by an inner contradiction—that is, it has meaning for a striving to which prescriptively or selectively it points the way. Striving must have unity, otherwise it disintegrates and destroys itself. A man cannot walk in two directions at the same time. No one can serve two masters.

Hence it is evident why every current morality has the form of a monism. It cannot be otherwise without making itself equivocal. Where no unifying principle presents itself, current morality forces such a principle upon the diversity of discerned values. It seizes hold of one single, clearly discerned value and sets it up above the rest, and subordinates them to it. Hence arise one-sidedness, narrowness, vulnerability, indeed the partial falsification of the scale of values. The transitoriness of every current morality is not so much a consequence of a restricted view of values, as of arbitrariness in regard to a unifying principle.

(b) THE UNKNOWABLENESS OF THE CONTENT OF THE "GOOD"

Obscurely conscious of the weakness of such a procedure, philosophical ethics has not seldom pursued the opposite course, in order to attain the required unity. If none of the discernible values is supreme, one must assume and postulate a supreme value over them all, and in contrast to all of them; one must unequivocally describe it as unknown, but on account of its mere position of superiority allow it to gain currency.

Such is the Platonic "Idea of the Good," the peculiarity of which is that it lacks all distinctive marks, that in content it remains simply indefinite. What man cannot discern may for all that exist in itself. In this sense one cannot deny that Plato's thought is justifiable.

The disadvantage in it is simply that the idea of the supreme value remains empty for our sense of values. With such a principle nothing but a postulate is set up; no valuational insight is gained. If we recall that the task of ethics is to disclose what the good is, we see that in this way the task is in no wise advanced. The principle gives no hint as to the direction in which the good is even to be looked for: the variety of possibilities, which existed without the principle, continues unreduced with the principle. Complete anarchy reigns.[1]

This situation is characteristic for the problem. It is agreed that somehow the good is the central ethical value; but that settles nothing. And nothing in the realm of values is more concealed than just this central principle, which is assumed by all morality as self-evident, but which in truth is everywhere differently understood. It was Plotinus who gave the formula for this situation: the good is "beyond the power of thought." But that means: the good is irrational.

Neither of the two ways which can be pursued leads to the goal. What remains for the investigation of values to do? Must it permit the open pluralism to continue, with the risk of surrendering the actuality of the Ought and the unity of striving? Or is there some commanding view of unity, which is conceivable, whatever the facts are as regards content?

At the same time the question arises: In what sense is the problem actual? If it exists only as a philosophical question of system, it is not important; but if it is a practical question as to the conduct of life itself, it has quite another import. The latter, however, would be the case only in so far as a plurality without a unifying value must be self-contradictory. But that cannot be unconditionally asserted. Much rather is it possible that a systematic co-ordination of diverse values could exist without culminating in one supreme point. In the domain of existential categories it is not otherwise. Even there the ultimate which can be discerned is not a single ruling principle, but a whole stratum of principles, each one of which is self-

---

[1] With all this it should not be overlooked that Plato's "Idea of the Good" receives a certain definite content from the four virtues, over which it presides. But this definiteness is not its own, but that of the virtues, and exists without it. The unifying principle in fact adds nothing. It is different with the metaphysical, cosmic meaning of the "Idea of the Good." But that again is not an ethical meaning.

dependent and conditions the others. We should accordingly expect the same in the realm of values, even if other grounds did not suggest it.

Now, in fact, it is impossible to set forth a single supreme value, as regards content; and in so far as the morality of all times has understood by the "good" a unifying value, this "good" has not been a discerned and full valuational substance, but an empty concept. To give it a general content is, of course, easy enough, for in it all the special values of the whole realm have somehow a place, and they touch upon it with a certain right. But such a bestowing of content is one-sided. The further one looks into this situation, so much the more does one become convinced by it, that in the obscure concept of the "good" somehow a universal relativity within the whole sphere must lie concealed, and perhaps, indeed, a principle of its structure, an order and an organic law.

This is confirmed from another side. For if one looks at the final discernible elements of value, one becomes easily convinced, that a unifying value lying beyond them can neither be seen nor inferred from them, but that the connection of these valuational groups is conceivable and evident. Unity of system, then, might still be existent. Unity of system is plainly in no wise dependent upon the focal unity, the one value, that was sought.

(c) Possible Types of Monism in the Given Pluralism of Values

We must free ourselves from the deep-seated prejudice which in all departments gives a preference to monism. In the domain of theory as well as of practice all monisms are of a purely constructive nature. They spring from a logical craving for unity, not from the constitution of the phenomena. In this way the doctrine of the categories has always suffered the most serious damage. The doctrine of value runs the same risk, unless it will profit by the damage done in other fields of thought. Naturally we must search for unity, since, in case it exists, it must be disclosed. But the customary assumption of unity is an entirely different matter. On this point what was said above holds good here in a higher degree: in the domain of values nothing can be anticipated, deduced, or proved universally; we must follow the phenomena of the valuational consciousness step by step. And at the very best the comprehensive unity could only be the keystone.

All that can be done, prior to any analysis of values, is a discussion of the question itself. First, the question whether there exists a supreme value must be separated from the question whether it could be discerned in case it existed. If the latter is to be negatived, the former could always be affirmed.

But, secondly, the question arises: in what general direction should one seek for the supreme value, in case there is such a thing? Here there are at least two possibilities. It could lie in the direction of the simplest and most elementary values, and indeed be capable of being exhibited beyond the last; but it could also lie in the opposite direction, in that of the most complex and concrete, and be recognizable beyond these. In the first case, by the supreme value is meant the strongest and most elementary (also the most general), but in the second, the axiologically highest.

These two cases are not manufactured *in abstracto*. All historical moralities clearly show either the one or the other type of search for unity. The ethics of pleasure, of happiness, of self-preservation, the Kantian ethics of universality, Fichte's doctrine of activity, seek for the supreme value in the sense of the most elementary and general. In the opposite direction, the morality of justice, of love for one's neighbour, of universal love, of personality, seeks for the axiologically highest value. That there are also mixed types, indeed that even those named are mixed, does not affect the matter. Both directions have a certain justification. For even the most elementary value has the position of the greatest range of validity and control; but the most complex and most limited in range of validity has the position of the highest standard. It might come about that the two unifying values of opposite type would co-exist in the same realm. As such they would not exclude each other. The monism sought for would thereby be again at the mercy of a primal dualism, which would no more satisfy the need for unity than the existing pluralism has satisfied it.

But even here the possibilities are not exhausted. For ultimately the question is whether the desired unity of values must after all be a value, whether it could not consist of a highest principle which was not a valuational principle. Even this question cannot be decided beforehand. Just as the principle of motion need not itself be a motion, of life not itself life, just as the principles of knowledge are evidently far from being knowledge, so the universally ruling principle of the domain of value could very well be something else than a value.

This thought has most to say for itself, so far as the problem is at all debatable a priori. At all events it meets the fact that our sense of values is bound to their fixed gradation. For if there should be a thorough harmony in the gradational order (even if it were inaccessible to thought), it would have the form of a unifying principle of the sphere, of a system of values. But such a principle would merely determine the categorial structure of the sphere; it would not constitute the quality as such of the values embraced by it.

We need not think of the connection of such a principle with values, as necessarily rent by a chasm. It might be that the quality of values would diminish in the direction of the simplest content, and would perhaps, farther on, beyond the limit of visibility vanish altogether. Then the "supreme value" as the limiting value of this evanescence would no longer be a value, it would be axiologically the lower limit of the realm of values. This meets the circumstance that the most general oppositions of value in fact exhibit only a very pale quality, so that we can detect the quality only from the more concrete values.[1] But even this thought justifies no inferences.

[1] Cf. the following section.

(d) THE MONISM OF ETHICS IN THE PLURALISM OF VALUES

Ethics must leave these problems unsolved. But because it cannot solve them, it must so adapt its own attitude as to leave the above mentioned possibilities open. It must reserve a place for a supreme value, and indeed in both the directions which come in question. At the same time it must not be influenced thereby in its analysis of values. That is possible only if the investigator never forgets how sporadic every view of values is, and how fragmentary in the most favourable circumstance every table of values, which can be constructed, must remain.

But more positive than this tendency is that towards a unity of scale of values. Although we do not know any supreme unified value, still the multiplicity of values must be joined together. Their unitary quality as such is a guarantee for that. Our view of them must be based upon their relations to one another: the relations of subsumption and foundation, of kinship and discrepancy, of structure and content, of height and interpenetration of the spheres of validity. It must allow for oppositions and conflicts as well as for harmonies—at the risk of coming upon valuational antinomies which for the sense of value remain insoluble. The desired unity must not become a postulate of harmony: such a postulate would deny antinomies (perhaps genuine), and thereby miss a problem which exists in the phenomena. It must not commit itself to a monism of value in the given multiplicity of morals; but it must hold by a monism of ethics in the multiplicity of values. For such a monism leaves the question open, whether the unity of the whole is a value or some other principle. An ideal table of values then must be unitary and absolute, above the manifoldness of the historical scale of values.

Hegel's thought, that in every philosophical system there is a portion of eternal truth, and that it is the task of philosophy to gather these fragments of one absolute truth into an ideal system, must be fruitful, *mutatis mutandis*, for ethics. In this search of unity, the ideal system of values must also hover before us as the task of possible and historical systems, and that, regardless of how near or how far we may be from the goal. To overcome "isms" is here a conceivable task.

Section II

THE MOST GENERAL ANTITHESES

CHAPTER VI (xxxi)

THE ANTINOMIC OF VALUES

(a) Positive Opposition as a Peculiarity of the Most Elementary Values

THERE is a group of values which the analysis of value and the Ought has already disclosed. It exceeds other discernible groups in elementariness and generality. The reverse side of this is its poverty of content and the low grade of its value. It is not on this account perhaps the "first" in the sense of being the most elementary, but is only the first that can be known; still more elementary ones may very well lie beyond them. These elements, which are contained in all the higher values, appear to the observation of the investigator to be on the boundary of his domain. They, therefore, show only a minimum of contents; they are scarcely perceptible to the sense of value. As regards discernibility, they are values in a state of evanescence. For the difficulty of all valuational analysis is this: only the content ever properly allows of being described, indeed even of being named; the character and quality do not admit of being recaptured. As for the contents, we can only induce the valuational feeling to set itself upon them, entering where every denotation fails. But if the feeling also fails, if it does not allow itself to be induced or set up, every effort to render the values visible is in vain. Now, with a minimum of procurable content, this group of values shows a correspondingly pale, a scarcely perceptible, quality. That is the reason there is need of approaching by way of the categorial factors.

This group has also the peculiarity that in it not simply the relation of the polar series of values, in which only a disvalue stands over against a value, holds, but also another kind of opposition: that of value against value. To be sure, there exist here the corresponding disvalues also, and in so far the general law of bipolarity is not interrupted. But it plays here a merely subordinate rôle. The distinguishing mark of this group is, that along with the relation of positive and negative the opposition of positive to positive subsists. This, of course, occasionally occurs elsewhere. But here it comes universally to the foreground. On this account we have here a sphere of positive opposites. And the dimensions between the opposites are throughout positive continuities, in which no neutral point is passed through, no negative part of the series continues the positive. And all the more special qualities, which inhere in these dimensional continua, are exclusively positive values, and thus are no disvalues. The corresponding disvalues are harboured in just such purely negative disvaluational dimensions. The sphere of these values has an antinomic character, which for ethics is a deeply significant fact.

(b) MORAL CONFLICT AND THE VALUATIONAL ANTINOMIES

It was shown above[1] how in life there is, besides the conflict between moral and anti-moral impulses (between duty and inclination), also a conflict between moral and moral. The structure of the former is not purely ethical in the inward sense; that of the latter touches the essence of ethical situations proper. Where in any situation value stands over against value, there no guiltless escape is possible. For a man cannot abstain from making a decision. He must choose either so or so, and even to do nothing is a positive decision. He may stay where he was, but he must choose at any cost. In the real world a man is continually confronted with the necessity of settling conflicts of value, of so deciding that he can be answerable for his obligation. It is his destiny not to be able to escape the obligation.

This constitution of the moral conflict cannot be discovered simply from the very general oppositions between values and

[1] Chapter XXII (c), Vol. I.

values, which are here considered. In them there is only a first reverberation of this difficult problem. Later, when we consider the oppositions in detail, it will become more distinct. Also the contrasting structure of these values is not all equally marked everywhere. Yet already we see the root of the conflict. And to have that before our eyes from the beginning is important for all that follows.

In general, oppositions between values have not necessarily the character of contradictions. They also need not be primary conflicts existing in the ideal realm. But even where value and value do not antagonize each other, the concrete situations bring it about, that only one can be fulfilled and the other must be violated. In practice, then, the values clash. For instance, whoever places personal regard above law, gives preference to love and violates justice, although in themselves justice and love do not exclude each other. Here the conflict first arises with the situation in the connection of the valuational contrast. The situation is a constituent element in the conflict.

Now so far as the oppositions are genuine antinomies, the antagonism is between the values themselves. In themselves these antinomies are insoluble. The antinomic character of the most general opposites, however, varies greatly. Some are almost in agreement, others are far apart and show no tendency to coalesce. In regard to these latter, the unifying tendency of the rational consciousness becomes most effective. Perhaps a solution of the discrepancy lies in a higher valuational region, of which we have no comprehension. It is also conceivable that, without absolute unity, the diversities, continued beyond the limit of cognition, may converge.

Then the antinomic character of opposites would be due only to consciousness (to the sensing of values), and our limitations would be the cause of our inability to reconcile them. But it is also possible that the system, pursued further, would not converge or would even diverge, and, if our vision could transcend its limit, must manifest ever bolder discrepancies.

In this case we should not be dealing with antinomies of "reason," but with antinomies of the ideal self-existent itself. The realm of values would then contain the antithesis in itself, and in the antinomics of the most generally discernible values we should have proof of the categorial structure of the whole sphere.

As we otherwise know little enough of this structure, such a proof would be of the greatest value in our investigation. As to-day the investigation is only beginning, little would be gained by it. We could draw no inferences from it.

But here it must never be forgotten that there is another way of settling valuational conflicts, that they are settled by men in each case in every actual situation (however full of conflict it be). Men cannot do otherwise than make decisions from case to case, according to their scale of values and their sense of the degree to which the various values enter into their consciousness of a situation. However biased or wrong their decisions may be, they nevertheless are and remain decisions, and indeed axiological decisions. But this means that from case to case there are new attempts to put an end to conflicts.

(c) THE DIMENSIONAL SYSTEM OF OPPOSITES AS AN IDEAL "VALUATIONAL SPACE"

Now, valuational opposites, like the great categorial opposites of Being, constitute a system of possible diversities, with more than one dimension. Each contrast is in itself a dimension, and indeed a completely positive continuum. As the more special values fall at the same time into different dimensions, it is clear that these penetrate one another, cross and constitute a dimensional system. Thus in the realm of values there is something like an ideal positional system of possible values, a sort of intelligible space. In it the specific values have their intelligible places.

One might feel tempted, from this point of view, to undertake an a priori derivation of values; a general law seems to be conceivable, and such a law is the condition for any possible derivation. But here one forgets that in definiteness of content this law is far from equal to filling the empty spaces—just as little as the law of mathematical space is adequate for the material filling of it. There exists nothing but a certain structure, which, indeed, if filled from some other quarter, is determinant for concrete values. An anticipation of the content is not to be thought of.

We shall, indeed, find later on that even concrete discernment, directed upon individual values, is very far from being able to fill all the places of valuational space. What this falling short of discernible values in their manifoldness, as compared with what might be expected a priori, signifies, is a question by itself. Perhaps it is possible that what is here felt is only the limit of human perception, that in the ideal self-existent realm the whole valuational space is filled and that only the narrowness of our sense of values prevents us from discerning the fulness. But it is possible and quite conceivable, that even in the ideal self-existent realm not all intelligible places are filled, indeed that they are perhaps as indifferent to such fulness as the places of physical space are as to whether they be filled or not.

To this ever-present possibility corresponds the chasm which divides any group of opposites from the nearest discernible group, from any group of concrete values. We are far removed from any continuous survey of the valuational realm; the discernible groups constitute only accidental sections, and how far the distance between the groups can be known—that is, how far the discontinuity is due to ourselves and how far to the values—cannot be judged from the structure of what is really discernible.

As was said, the analysis of value and the Ought furnishes the occasion for the development of the opposites. It is evident that many essential features, disclosed by this analysis, have themselves a valuational character—although with some it is

very slight. The last of the contrasts (the quantitative) undoubtedly shows a different aspect. It is only half within the
group of opposites, and only its evidently oppositional structure betrays that it belongs to the group. It is possible that in
it we have already a limiting member.

Further, it is not without interest to note, that the traditional viewpoint of the ontological realm of categories—quantity, quality, relation, modality—reappears unsought in the
contrasted pairs, although with a different degree of distinctness. That might, of course, be only an external pressure of
customary forms of thought. On this account no great importance should be attributed to the reappearance. It corresponds
only to the contents, not to values themselves. The mere
correspondence is also only a symptom. On the threshold of
the realm of values the meagreness of the valuational quality,
the approximation to the categorial form, is not an accident.

MODAL OPPOSITIONS

(a) THE ANTINOMY OF NECESSITY AND FREEDOM

OUR modal analysis of the Ought has shown that a kind of necessity inheres in the mode of existence peculiar to what ought to be—therefore peculiar to values. This necessity, unlike the ontological, subsists independently of possibility. Hence values are not dependent upon the real realm of Being and Not-being. It is a necessity which is "absolute" (literally: detached), free, bound to nothing outside of itself.[1]

Now this absolute necessity, so far as it pertains to value as such, is itself a value. In comparison with Being of any other kind, it gives to the Ideal Being of values that sublimity, that elevation above the relative, that inviolable subsistence beyond Being and Not-being, for which language has no name, and in which the authority of these principles inheres, "in strength and dignity rising above existence," to use the phrase coined by Plato for the Idea of the Good. It is this necessity also which lends to values their very characteristic universality as regards validity—they being valid for every case, even for those which violate them—a universality which holds even in the specialization, the individuality, of content (where only one case comes into consideration) and which perdures unabated, rigorous, inaccessible to every compromise, even in the tragedy of life's conflicts.

The moral sense, while it bows before this incorruptible power, looks up to it as to the object of highest veneration, and rises inwardly to it, while its greatest pride is nothing more than identification with it. This participation is its superiority to the neutral demeanour of impersonal entities. Kant gave the deepest expression to the feeling for the absolute

[1] Cf. Chapter XXIII (c)–(e), Vol. I.

necessity of the Ought in his glorification of duty: respect for
the moral law was regarded by him as the pre-eminent distinction of a rational being. If by such a being we mean one
who discerns values, his expression is exactly fitting. The
rigid one-sidedness of Kant's attitude towards values should
not blind us to the import of this matter. The value which
he here discerned was rightly esteemed.

In this sense the necessity of the Ought-to-Be itself is
rightly held to be a value of the most elementary kind. And
this is confirmed by man's consciousness in his seeking and
looking out for values as yet undiscerned. It is the search for
an ever new and absolute necessity of a higher kind.

And this worth of necessity has its counterpart in the value
of freedom. It is the freedom which these values, even in their
absolute necessity, allow to that being who in his sense of
value participates in them. A person who is acquainted with
their necessity is none the less not constrained by it. This
personal freedom is not the "freedom of necessity" itself, but
is dependent upon it. Were that necessity tied to possibility,
it would be equivalent to ontological necessity, and the person
would thereby be coerced, as by a natural law. Participation in
it would then not be something sublime and a mark of distinction; it would not lift man out of the series of natural
beings. It is precisely the absence of compulsion on the part
of the Ought which is a value; and indeed for a moral being
it is a fundamental value. Acts to which moral value adheres
are only made possible through the absence of power on the
part of the unconditional necessity of the Ought.

This situation is paradoxical enough. Precisely that which
is a kind of deficiency in the mode of existence peculiar to
values, the inability to determine the actual directly, the wide-
reaching inconsistency of reality and of human conduct with
them, is as a moral phenomenon, of infinite value. This powerlessness of values conditions the attitude of the personal
subject in the world, as that factor which mediates their
actualization in real existence. Hence it is only those acts in

which the subject commits himself to the realization of what ought to be, that are the bearers of the higher and moral values. And if this commitment did not exist, there would be nothing in the whole world to which the highest, the moral, values could be attached.

This freedom, therefore, which that necessity peculiar to values allows to the subject, is itself an elementary value. It is —and this is the antinomic feature in it—a value, although it is set over against that necessity which is likewise an elementary value and limits this modally. One may say that here the antinomic relation of these two values, their reciprocal balance, their self-limitation, is itself valuable. For in this relation of suspense between them is rooted the position of the person, together with all the values of which the person thereby becomes the bearer.

(b) The Antinomy of the Real Being and the Non-Being of Values

Parallel to this first antinomy, but not coincident with it, stands a second, equally fundamental. It is of the essence of the Ought to force itself onward into reality. That its contents are in part real does not alter the situation. In ethical actuality values are only in part real; they stand between Being and Non-being. Upon this intermediate position a double relation depends.

It is clear that the reality of a value, whenever and wherever it appears, is itself valuable—and indeed irrespective of how it has come into existence. Likewise it is clear that the non-actuality of a value is a disvalue. As a consequence it follows directly that the actualization of a value is at the same time itself valuable, but that the annihilation of one is contrary to value. These four propositions hold good also for disvalues, with the opposite designations: the reality and the realization of disvalues are contrary to value, the non-actuality and the annihilation of disvalues are valuable.

These propositions hold good not only for complete reality and unreality but also for every advance thereto. This is especially so as regards realization: the tendency to approach reality is valuable. As the act of a person, such a tendency is a carrier of a moral value, a value higher than that which is intended. But as a real process it signifies—according to the teleological form of its advance through the means to the end— the conferring of value upon what was in itself alien or indifferent. The providing of means for the actualization of a value is a giving of value to what is valueless. But the worth of this relationship, controlling the whole sphere of valuational teleology, is the worth of the real existence of values in general.

In antithesis to this stands an equally fundamental value. The non-reality of values also has a value. This becomes perceptible, as soon as we consider that active, intended realization is only possible where a value is non-existent, just as, on the other side, it is the active, intended actualization, in which the higher, the moral, type attains actuality. This means that the reality of the highest values would be altogether impossible, if all valuational situations were real. But since the real existence of the highest values has also the highest value of actuality, it is evident that the unreality of values which might be intended—whether they be situational or in limiting cases moral —is itself for the moral being of the person a basic value.

To resolve this antinomy is impossible. It lies in the very nature of the metaphysical situation, which is given as a relation between, on the one side, the sphere of values and that of existence and, on the other, between the value intended and that of the intention. The paradox of this subtle antithesis is a fundamental feature of the ethical phenomenon. The two contrasted values are of course united in the value of the intended actualization. But the unification is not in principle a synthesis which could meet the antinomy. For viewed from the value of the real existence of values the realization is only a subordinate element, the value of a means. The value of a process, from this point of view, inheres only in the goal, in the resultant; it rises or falls in rank with the grade of the reality aimed at. It is otherwise, when one views the same realization from the value of the unreality of values. Here the actualization as such, the act, the greatness of the commitment is valuable, and indeed without regard to the attainment or non-attainment of the result. The value of the reality of the result as such is not annulled; rather does it remain the basis of the actional value. But this is of another kind, incomparably higher than that; and it varies in its axiological rank by no means proportionately to the actual value which appears in the result. Here another standard sets in, which annuls that dependence. The actualization (although only intended) has the standard of its grade wholly in itself in contrast to the actuality of the intended values. The greatness of the commitment is only one of these standards.

Hence the antinomy is not even here resolved. It returns intensified in the phenomenon of actualization; indeed, it inheres in it and constitutes its axiological ambiguity. This is to be taken in the literal sense. It is a double emphasis upon one and the same thing; it is a selection which in itself is two-sided, and involves a polar contrast. To try to solve it would mean a radical misunderstanding of the problem. We should need to deny the double relation.

(c) FORMULATIONS AND CONJUGATIONS OF THIS ANTINOMY

Under all circumstances the antinomy itself is rightly regarded as genuine. One can most easily bring it home to the sense of value if, abandoning the more exact but difficult modal terminology, one formulates it in the following manner. Actualization is only possible by virtue of the Non-being of that content the Being of which is valuable, and toward the existence of which it is directed. In so far, therefore, as a value proper inheres in the actualization as such, this involves a depreciation of the value being actualized in it. Axiologically the realization of values is self-contradictory. Like every process limited to a goal, it leads to its own nullification. But thereby it deprives the higher value, which adhered to it as such, of reality.

A whole series of values can be subsumed under the two fundamental values of this antinomy. And the antinomy always reappears in them, although of course with very different degrees of sharpness. The wide cleavage between the valuational regions to which they belong, proves the dominating position of the fundamental values. Thus the value of a mere Ought-to-be in something not completed stands in opposition to the value of completion; thus a value peculiar to the living tension towards something unattained—indeed to a certain degree the value in the inability to attain—stands in opposition to the value of success and attainment. For the energy of the tension stands and falls with the unattainability. Attainment and attainability themselves further display a twofold axiological aspect: both have value as well as disvalue. And the same cleavage reappears in the whole of ethically intentional acts. Activity, striving, willing and whatever is like these, are doubly bound, like actualization of which they are the intentional forms. They are valuable for the sake of the goal and at the same time for their own sake. But the realities of both values which attach to them are never in harmony—irrespective of the relation of dependence prevailing between them. The reality of the one excludes that of the other. This exclusion of each other nevertheless does not annul the two-sided character of the value.

But these more special values are no longer properly modal. They belong to a more concrete stratum and must be especially considered in connection with it. There, of course, the discussion will no longer be concerned with their antinomic character. This shows itself distinctly only in the most general elements of value. But it can entirely disappear only in the most concrete valuational fulness.

CHAPTER VIII (XXXIII)

RELATIONAL OPPOSITES

(a) THE ANTINOMY OF THE CARRIER OF VALUE

To every carrier of possible values as such is attached a value. The carrier is the condition of the reality of that value of which it is the carrier. Its quality follows from the value of the reality of values.

But in all ethically fulfilled actuality the carrier is not single nor of one kind but, in agreement with the duality of the valuational classes which are at stake, it is itself cleft in two. The intended value has not the same carrier as the value of the intention. The former adheres to the object; the latter to the subject of the intention. The object and subject of one and the same intention—whether it be a striving or a mere disposition—are both in the same way carriers. This is the root of the opposition between subject and object. Both are carriers, but of different values.

In itself this contrast is far from being an antagonism. But antagonism sets in, as soon as subject and object coincide as carriers.

It occurs in this way. As regards the moral values, the subject assumes the position of substance. As the only carrier of their entire diversity he is a kind of ethical value, not in the sense of the highest, but of the basic value which carries. Yet he is at the same time drawn into the matter of the situational values which can be striven for, because the latter have as content participation of persons in goods. If I do good, it is to "someone"; if evil, that also applies to someone—whether a person or a community, whether it be direct or indirect, makes no difference. This *dativus ethicus* accompanies all human conduct, and is a constituent in the value or disvalue of the conduct. The disposition before every action or volition inevitably concerns someone. Thereby the subject, as a matter of course, is drawn into the value of the intended object (the situation), and is himself an object of the intention.

That it does not contradict the nature of a personal subject to become an object has already been discussed in our criticism of personalism. There it became evident how fundamental for the whole field of ethical reality the objectification of the person is. Otherwise intention could not be directed to persons. Their disposition and striving would be ethically irrelevant. Mere action upon things is not conduct, a disposition towards things or their relations is not disposition in the moral sense. The personal subject as an object is the condition of moral behaviour; and his substantial value as the subject of possible acts (for only as such is he personal) is drawn into the general value of what is objectively to be striven for.

The same thing can be seen from another side. Everything valuable, even the morally valuable, is, in so far as there is a consciousness of it, an object of worth for this consciousness. Now as the highest values are those of the personal subject, these also must appear as objects. And within the limits of what can be striven for, they must also be the objects of the acts of that subject to whose acts they apply. The personal subject is in this sense at the same time an object having worth, and indeed an object of acts pre-eminently moral. Only in the moral value of the currently moral intention itself does this kind of intentionality and objectivity find its boundary. But this boundary allows wide scope. If it did not, all moral work in itself and all such as referred to personal subjects would be illusory.

It is a peculiarity of ethics, that in a double sense the object of intention is an intending subject. Moral values allow of being intended—if at all—only in their natural and particular carrier, the person. When this direction extends widely, as in the ethical formation of ideals and in concrete life under the vision of ideals, then it is immediately evident. But a life under definite ideals is at bottom the essence and the function of every current morality in the total construction of ethical reality.

The antinomic factor in this relation finds expression in the fact that the values of objects and subjects none the less clearly stand in contrast to each other; thus it was in the ancient division into goods and virtues. That the former are realized in the effect, the latter in the disposition, separates them. But in so far as the effect attaches to subjects who are capable of disposition and is meant for them, and on the other hand indeed a decided commitment can be the matter of the effect, the limit is transposed and the two classes of value overlap. It is not only that virtues presuppose goods, but that virtues are themselves the highest goods. This is the meaning of the ancient doctrine that virtue is the "highest good."

(b) THE ANTINOMY OF ACTIVITY AND INERTIA

The opposition between tendency and tenacity, activity and inertia, is closely connected with the second modal antinomy, but from another side. This opposition finds scope within the class of moral values, but it reappears in distorted form among goods-values.

Our categorial analysis showed that the capacity to tend towards something constitutes an essential factor of that entity which alone can grasp and actualize a positive Ought-to-Be. Activity, for its part, therefore converts a subject into a person. The question concerns activity in every form, even in the mere inner direction towards something, as an object beyond oneself, which is to be realized. The value of activity is a value of preoccupation as such with something beyond oneself, of self-transcendence, or to speak categorially, the self-transcendence of the moral substance—even when the aims can exist only in the substance as such—and, indeed, so far as the transcendence is not instigated from without but is an original self-movement, a first starting of something new, a πρῶτον κινοῦν. In a certain sense, of course, every value is in itself a first mover. But again also it is not; from itself it cannot set the real in motion. A second and equally original power must come to its aid. This is the activity of the personal subject. The real tendency can issue from it only.

If one thinks of this activity as a personal form of existence, charged with value and intensified unlimitedly, as Fichte in his youth regarded the moral being of man as issuing wholly in activity, the active entity is completely disintegrated by its own activity. The pouring forth in activity would needs dissolve and destroy the active entity itself. And in fact it was Fichte's opinion that "absolute activity" is without any substratum, and must be lost in the "infinite object" (that which ought to be).

This self-dissolution may be a result of pure activity, but it cannot be the meaning of a person, in so far as he is at the same time a carrier of moral values. As regards the tendency of self-abandonment, it is not simply the natural entity in man with its ontological weight which is set up; for the natural entity is neither a person nor a moral carrier of value. There must also be in the moral nature of the person something which holds the tendency in the scales, a moral being, an obstacle to all tendency, a self-poise of the ethical substance; not a passive substratum which would be only amorphous material, but a counter-tendency peculiar to the substantial character of the person, a tendency towards self-preservation and persistence, a peculiar moral force of inertia. The identity of a person in all his outgoing beyond himself is just as deep a moral requirement as the outgoing itself. We are therefore justified in setting up a value of inertia over against that of activity. It is the value of ethical Being as compared with that of intention. Realized values are indeed not less valuable, because they are not something that positively ought to be. But in every person, at all times, values are real, even without any addition. This ethical Being sets limits to tendency; it furnishes inner resistance to onrushing advance. Its fixity in itself and amidst excitations is its moral self-preservation.

All forward movement rises upon something stable. If this is lacking, the weight of substance is lacking; the movement is not a movement of something, but of nothing; hence it is no movement. The power of inertness is the counterweight of ethical Being against the Ought, its check upon the restlessness of tendency. This inertness is not passivity—that would cripple activity—, it is not ethical inertness (that would be a disvalue), but it is the ontological inertness of ethical substance, the stability of actual valuational content in the stream of activity, the conservative counter-tendency of ethical Being. In this sense it is a value, and indeed the value of potency, not different from that of activity.

The opposition between activity and inertness becomes sharper, if one bears in mind that all activity of a personal subject, at the same time with its outward direction, is also turned back inward upon the person. Striving may spend itself on the object; what is realized in the striving, however, is, besides the object, always something different in the subject, his moral value or disvalue. This reflex effect of acts is anchored in the basic relation of values. The subject cannot escape from it. But if it be true that in all activity the moral content of the subject is itself changed, the persistence of this content is essential. It is in itself a value, regardless of that of the activity.

(c) THE GRADE AND THE RANGE OF THE TYPE

In every structure which is a possible carrier of diverse values a valuational enhancement is conceivable in two different directions: as a one-sided augmentation of a single value (or of a few which are closely related) and as a many-sided adjustment of various values at the same time. Both kinds of enhancement as such are of value. But materially they are opposed to each other, and the further progress of either in one and the same carrier excludes the other.

In the former case we have to do with a rectilineal development towards one value. In the life of peoples and their morality, which is always one-sided, this is generally the case. The strength of this tendency lies in the height of the development of the type which is aimed at in it. One-sided advance naturally comes much nearer to its ideal than a many-sided tendency—with the same access of moral strength. Everything great and decisive in history has needed to rest on the efficient energy of a one-sided enhancement. The unity of the direction in which all energy is led brings about the unfoldment of the ethical substance beyond itself (whether it be that of a person or of a tribal union); it is that which has power to transcend its own existence. But in a pre-eminent sense this is a constructive, creative factor in man, which leads even to the sacrifice of his own substance, to its transformation into something else.

In such a cultivation of one value (or of a narrow group) we may see the fulfilment of the value of activity; and although here it is not a matter of activity as such, yet the value of the height of the type lies materially in the same direction. Transcendence beyond itself and the attainment of the ideal show the same type of value.

In the second case an adjustment takes place in favour of all the values concerned. Here the ethical being of the person develops more towards richness of content and extension. No single value dominates, the height of the type is projected on to the second plane, in favour of its inward diversity and enrichment. It has given way to the value of extension. In place of a transformation of the substance into something else, there is here a development of the substance within itself. Such a growth can take place, only where the valuational enhancement is distributed among all the original tendencies. Here inner breadth of synthesis is aimed at, instead of efficiency of energy. The development of the person (or community) is directed to itself—to its inner destination so far as this is prefigured in the fulness of its possibilities.

This development towards extension also is creative; it is a constructive unification of all accessible contents, even of the most diverse, in the unity of a valuational type. Hence the axiological breadth of the type. Everything of value is here caught up into this unity and saved. Instead of a sacrifice and abrogation of the substance for something else we have abrogation, unlimited as regards tendency, of all else in favour of the substance.

(d) HARMONY AND CONFLICT

The oppositional dimension of harmony and conflict is in another direction. Such harmony—agreement with oneself—in every structure in which it occurs is a value, needs no exposition. A personality, a co-operative group of persons, a community, a development, a human life, may be harmonious. Harmony is always an immediately perceived value, the matter of which is in the static condition of the structure. If it mounts towards completeness, it approaches the value of perfection.

It haunted Aristotle in the "Teleiosis," in which he saw the axiological meaning of eudæmonia. It is evidently akin to the value of breadth of type, although it signifies another element in the same phenomenon. For its content is not the inner breadth but the inner consonance throughout the whole range of diversities.

It is only when viewed from the outside that harmony seems to be a value of poise and stationariness. A structure may very well have movement in itself; it can show an interplay of various powers. What it depends on is only a symmetry of adjustments, a synthetic binding of the inner powers into one another, an absorption of all surplus, a repose of the whole within itself. It is a valuational unity, but the structure of its material is a thoroughly unified manifold. It is only as a whole that this structure is static. The factors in it may be as dynamic as is ever possible. But the unity arises from the fact that the poise of the whole ontologically as well as axiologically dominates the forces within the factors.

But in all ethical actuality, and indeed even within the same structure, this poise is met by an outside force which at the same time lays claim to domination, and is independently marked as a value. In every tendency, in every outward-going, this force is present; it partakes of the type of the value. But at bottom it is something else than an activity. It is the inherent unrest of the opposition, the moving principle of conflict.

What Heraclitus called the cosmic "war" and regarded as the "father and king" of all things, exists also in ethical actuality; the element of restlessness and of "flux" which carries all things, that inexhaustible productivity of new and ever new relations, situations and demands, with their endlessly new conflicts and puzzles. This it is which constitutes the infiniteness of content in ethical Being, its wealth, its eternal freshness and abundance. It is no exaggeration to speak in this sense of conflict as a value. In the domain of knowledge, problems as values, although paler and more restricted, correspond to it. As in knowledge a problem is a basic value, although it is the opposite of insight, so in ethical life conflict is basic, although it means incompleteness, disharmony, indeed a lack of indubitable value.

Conflict is that from which decision, intention, action are born; but the values of intention are the ethical ones. Conflict is that which keeps discernment and the feeling of value alive and opens up new vistas. In discord the sense of value, feeling itself restricted, presses on to escape. Moral life is, in general, life in the midst of conflicts; it is concentration upon them, a constructive solution of them through the commitment of the person; and all ignoring of it is a sin, an irrevocable injury to ethical Being—even to that of one's own personality.

In this way every situation in life is of value. It is the material of all good that is distinctively ethical. For him to whom it is "given" it is the opportunity for creative shaping; indeed, the possibility of all definite conduct. The man is drawn into it and is a member of it; for every situation is built up of ethically intended conduct of persons. And again it is at the same time given to him as the object of possible comprehension, participation, mental attitude and productive activity; to the person as the subject it remains as an object, as that which he is called upon to grapple with. Human life consists in a flux of situations, and these are each presented to the man for a time only and irrevocably. And because life is made up of them they are the valuational foundation of man's existence.

Primarily there exists between harmony and conflict only a contrast, not an antinomy proper. The proof is that concord pertains only to a whole as a collection of elements, but the elements may very well be in antagonism, when they are not held in check.

But that is changed, if we look at the actual conflicts that can be found in a situation. In so far as they require a person to meet an emergency beyond himself, equilibrium and harmony issue from them. This requirement is of value, no less than the harmony which has come about. Thus an antinomy is, of course, produced. And it becomes the more acute when one bears in mind that in ethical reality these two tendencies always confront each other, each trying to get the upper hand. From every harmonious equipoise new conflicts shoot forth; and precisely these conflicts, in that they demand solution, entail new forms of harmony. The perpetual tendency to conflict, beyond any existent harmony, is confronted by the equally perpetual tendency of harmony to embrace, absorb and resolve the conflict. Tendency to co-operation and tendency to disruption, statics and dynamics, continually compete, they constitute an unstable equilibrium of a higher order. It is an equilibrium, which is always just as much an instability, and therefore at the same time a dynamic of a higher order, in the forms of which the life of ethical actuality is unrolled, full of changes and yet bound into a unity.

Whether to this purely ontological synthesis of valuational materials there corresponds an axiological synthesis, cannot be definitely settled. Absolutely certain is only the antithesis of the two values.

(e) Simplicity and Complexity

Within every kind of harmony or conflict there arises the opposition of simplicity and internal multiplicity. This also is a valuational contrast, and indeed between two types of unity. Herein it differs from the previous opposition. There unity in general stood over against discrepancy. But here undifferentiated unity stands in opposition to the differentiated unity which contains the manifold within itself.

That both bear the mark of a distinctive value is easily seen. Simplicity signifies an inner solidity, an innate unity of structure, a primitiveness and a primitive totality. But in personality this is what we call "being straight," it is absolute directness, undividedness, spontaneity, common sense. Its outward sign is quiet collectedness, an absence of vacillation. In content it belongs to the same valuational group as simple-mindedness, innocence and purity. It is, however, not necessarily unmoved by conflicts in the way characteristic of the latter. In a conflict which is felt, there is also such a thing as serenity of conduct; one can be straightforward even to the point of questionable one-sidedness, which may involve serious wrong. Directness of conduct, the making straight for a goal, is none the less, as such, of value. Conflict with another value does not put an end to its own.

But to avoid injuring any value, to survey carefully various aspects, is on the other side no less important. A many-sided interest, however, implies a many-sidedness of personality. And this is the opposite of simplicity. It is ethical complexity itself, or, as one might say, the complexity of the ethos. In distinction from solid, naturally-grown unity there appears another, a secondary, cultivated unity, and indeed this claims to be the higher form. It is the unity of a many-sided development and of the inner unfoldment of the person.

In the direction of this value lies a widening of appreciation for diversity of situation, even for conflict as such, a conscious participation in the manifoldness of life's values, a capacity to commit oneself to the unique and unprecedented, even the astonishing, an intensified flair for undiscovered values in life generally—be it a mere participation and paying of attention, or a taking of the initiative required at the moment, and a constructive effort to master the situation.

There is no need of proof for the fact that the exploitation of values and the transformation of life—and not merely one's own—in the valuational direction can attain quite another greatness than that of simplicity and straightforwardness; nor does the fact need proof that herein is a witness to the unique value of complexity in all moral life. Still this is clearly different from that of "breadth" of type, as well as from that of conflict and harmony; for here the material greatness of participation in values is itself the determining factor, not harmony nor discrepancy, also not contrast to specifically directed striving. It is openness of mind to every form of value, purely as such, irrespective of possible effort and of the worth of harmony. In the axiological sense complexity in itself is a mode of fulfilment, of ripeness, of attainment of height.

QUALITATIVE AND QUANTITATIVE OPPOSITIONS

(a) UNIVERSALITY AND SINGULARITY

THERE is a wide-spread notion that values are generally universal. If by this is meant only that the value of anything must appeal to every person capable of discriminating, the notion is correct and is inapplicable only to persons who are value-blind or have renounced the capacity to discriminate. But it is not merely such subjective validity which is meant, but something objective: the validity of any value for every possible carrier of value.

In this sense universality is by no means a mark of all values. Goods and situational values can be so specialized, that there may be only one instance which comes under consideration. Of this kind are the majority of the spiritual values which inhere in things and relations, for example, the value of the house where one was born, of one's home, of anything made sacred by one's personal experience, of a souvenir, a relic; but the chief example is the value of the specific experience itself, as well as of the situations which constitute the content of the experience.

The same is true in the sphere of personal values, and here the individuation is far more emphatically marked. For the moral being of a person consists of his valuational capital, and what is his personally is not his mere existence. Persons are not transferable and are irrecoverable; what one is to me, no other can be—this is the verdict of every finer personal attachment. In short, there are possessions as individual as are the things of which there is only one of their kind; there are values which have individuality.

The peculiarity—by no means self-evident—is this, that the categorial opposition of universality and singleness, which in this way reappears in the realm of values, has the character of a valuational opposition. In it both sides are charged with value. And, indeed, this contrast is not quantitative, as one might think, but qualitative. The significance inheres not in the extent but in the content, not in the number of cases but in the agreement or the difference.

In this sense the value of universality is "qualitative." The likeness, the common constitution—or, to use the formal expression—the identity of the distinctive mark, is the valuable thing. That the value lies in this can be seen in the idea of justice, which is based wholly upon the value of the equality of all persons before the law. A common claim, and a common duty, the same opportunity and the same burden—this is not merely an opportunistic *modus vivendi*; it corresponds also to a primal demand of the Ought, so that it has meaning, and everybody understands when we say: However different men may be, there are certain basic relations of life, in respect to which men ought to be equal; here every individual advantage has its limit. In these things the same judgment ought to be passed upon all; and the same conscience ought to be in all. The equality of the valuational norm which stands above empirical inequality is, as such, of value. In these matters no one may have a private conscience and no one a private judgment; thereby he would make an exception for his own person, and would violate the equality.

In the categorical imperative Kant has given formal expression to this idea. He has related equality inwardly to the direction and disposition (the maxim) of the intention itself: that mental attitude is good of which I can will that it be the disposition of all. The meaning of "good" is thus, of course, restricted to one single value. But this one value at least thereby receives the most definite expression. It is the value of objective universality binding upon all—and, indeed, binding upon all, not as subjects of possible judgment, but as carriers of possible values, as carriers of moral values.

In the same way individuality, the opposite of this value,

is also "qualitative." The same persons, whose ideal equality before the law is of value, are in actuality unequal, and indeed not only in their nature, but also in their moral being. But, again, this inequality is itself valuable. Indeed, it is easy to see that this value penetrates deeper into the essence of the person than that of equality. The equality that ought to be can only touch the outward station in life; if one wants to apply it to the inner essence of the person, there arises the demand for a universal uniformity of the ethos itself, which plainly contradicts the sense of value. An ethically uniform humanity would in general actualize only one value, or a few narrowly related to one another, and, indeed, these would be not the highest and most fruitful; they would be developed to the neglect of the possible fulness of the realm of values, in a one-sided intensification without concrete unfoldment. The unique formation, the ethical Being *sui generis* of each person as an individuality, peremptorily opposes regular uniformity in the external structures of life. The axiological individuality and uniqueness of the ethos in each person are, as such, of value; in these is rooted all moral diversity. Clearly the value of equality is limited by that of inequality, the common duty and the common claim by that of the special duty and the special claim, such as only the one person can have and only on account of his uniqueness. And however different the deep layers of the human ethos may be, in which the two opposed values claim supremacy, there exists, nevertheless, in all the situations of life a medial line, at which they touch and clash antinomically in their Ought-to-be. Here man is confronted with a conflict and he cannot avoid settling it.

Persons are not the only carriers of valuational individuality. It reappears in units of a higher order, in communities of every kind, where the circumstance that these possess personality of a lower order only, does no injury to the individualization in quality and specific value. Just as little is the value of individuality in such structures brought into question by the fact that analogous structures, with the same position and of the same kind, preserve their value (for instance, in the basic values of international law). Notwithstanding this fact, the value of individuality has its special and inexhaustibly fruitful field in every other ethical entity, however fleeting or constant it may be.

Here we have the special value of the particular situation, the uniqueness and irretrievableness of every situation which opens itself to experience and activity, the diversities of which bring about the wealth of human life. Of course there is a certain uniformity of situation, a conformity to type, and in so far circumstances bear a mark of universality; but here, if anywhere, it is conceivable that every application of a scheme is due to an overlooking of what is properly essential. For analogy and all generalization refer to the surface, they do not force their way into the fulness of ethical actuality. The more differentiated and individualized the sensing of the permanent in a situation, so much the deeper and closer to the essential is the participation in its abundance. All generalization is as such purely schematization, impoverishment, indeed a sin against the fulness of values that is given. And every deeper insight, every appreciation and evaluation, as well as all special transformation of the state of things, is ethical treasure, moral enhancement, axiological unfoldment and fulfilment.

We can see here why all ethical casuistry goes wrong from the beginning. Its defect is not that it allows room for a variety of situations, but that it pretends to do so and yet cannot. For no finite human intelligence can anticipate the individualized fulness of real situations. Casuistry lies in a dead rut, because it thinks to evolve from a principle and to discuss what only the unfalsified fulness of real life, and no other power on earth, is in a position to unroll. It is sunk in schematism, it is an abortion of the letter, which kills.

(b) THE SYNTHESIS IN THE TYPE

Between the two extremes, the universal and the individual, lie the specific degrees in manifold gradation. It would be quite false to assume that the extreme alone is of value, and that the whole continuum of intermediate grades is indifferent. On the contrary, in this polarity, if anywhere, it can be seen that in all positive contrasts the whole valuational dimension between the extremes is throughout positively axiological, that is, that every point in it possesses positive value. From the logical relation of extent and content, which is here the basic categorial structure, this does not by any means follow. It is a law wholly peculiar to the realm of values, which is manifested here, in contrast to the differently ordered law of the relation of value to disvalue.

The value of the specific does not justify casuistry or any other form of bad generalization of what is in itself individual, just as it has nothing to do with relaxed or obscurely discerned generality. On the contrary, there are structures of a specific kind, which according to their own autonomic mode of existence stand between universality and individuality, or, to speak more exactly, which can stand between them at various heights. Of this sort is the typical. It resembles the general in that it shows distinguishing marks common to many individuals, and compared with them has the character of universality. But it resembles the individual in that it has other types near it and, compared with them, manifests the character of an individual. It shares in both, only in different directions. Structurally it is a synthesis. And that is why it axiologically also presents a synthesis. It shares in the value of both extremes. The synthesis reveals a new value of its own, the value of the type.

There are type-values of every kind, by no means merely ethical. There are biological values of race types, as well as those of an æsthetic nature, which accompany these. But some also are moral. To the historian this is a well-known fact; there is the moral type—let us say of the Athenian and the Spartan, the Roman and the German. In the perspective of history these can be easily recognized as real type-values. But a contemporary also knows the same phenomenon within his own world. And even if he can seldom describe with precision wherein the valuational structure of the type consists, his spontaneous sense of value is, nevertheless, sharp enough. It is easier to see what is typical in contemporaries of a foreign nation and to gauge it morally (whether with approval or disapproval) than to see what is individual or universally human. Indeed, an obscure but strong conviction as to one's own type-value accompanies any genuine national conscious- ness. And we meet with the same phenomenon all the way from the large and historically fruitful sense of community down to the narrow and narrowest local and family pride. The excesses of such consciousness, bordering occasionally on the comic, must not blind us to the fundamental ethical fact: the ideal self-existence of all these moral values inherent in types. The axiological variety in the communal forms of ethical reality is essentially conditioned by the extraordinary diversity of stratified type-values, by the way they overlap and cut into one another. In the actual world every individual is a possible carrier at the same time of the most general and the most individual values, and thereby also of the whole scale of intermediate values.

A synthesis of the contrasted extremes occurs therefore in the value of the typical. But the antinomy of universality and individuality is not on that account done away with. The synthesis is not of such a kind that it draws the extremes into itself. It has only the character of an intermediate member, of a link; the extremes remain contrary to each other. In the typical the universal does not become individual, nor the individual universal; and the value of the one does not, as such, approximate to that of the other. They remain outside the synthesis, and the artificial bringing of them into the value of the typical is a compromise.

(c) COMPREHENSIVENESS AND UNIVERSALITY, INDIVIDUALITY AND THE INDIVIDUAL

The contrast between all and the individual is closely related to that between universality and individuality, and yet is quite different and is independent. This is a quantitative opposition, as can be seen in the categorial attitude of comprehensiveness to universality and of the individual to the individualized. And as the quantitative contrast is of especially decisive significance for the placing of concrete values, we must begin with an analysis of this categorial relation.

That universality cannot exist without the totality of all the instances is an analytic proposition. It is just as evident, although not an analytic proposition, that the embracing of instances at least presupposes the universality of a distinguishing mark which characterizes the instances as belonging together. But only in this sense.

Apart from this they mean different things and appear independently of each other. Universality is complete likeness of the cases, but comprehensiveness is the bringing of them together into a larger unity. The former is a qualitative agreement without respect to the concrete connection of the cases; the latter is the quantitative and numerical binding of the cases in their concrete natural relation, without respect to likeness or unlikeness, even in spite of unlikeness. Comprehensiveness is concrete inclusiveness, not comparative but total unity, the higher whole, the integration of the instances; the specific nature and the individuality of the cases are drawn into it. Totality does not need to obliterate unlikeness as such; diversity is compatible with it. The difference shows itself most sharply if we consider that comprehensiveness, as a higher order, does not indicate universality but numerical singularity and qualitative distinctiveness. For it is that form, the essence of which is to have near it nothing of the same kind. As soon as something of the same kind appears, the categorial meaning of comprehensiveness absorbs it. Totality, strictly understood, is that which is in itself the only one, the great singular, which does not allow itself to be generalized.

The same categorial relation reappears in the two-sided counter-members. Individuality certainly always exists only in an individual, presupposing it. This is an analytical proposition. Equally evident is it, even if not an analytical implication of the concept, that an individual must necessarily have at least a minimum of individuality, even if it be only the singleness of its place in space and time. In this thinnest meaning everything real is individual, down to the most attenuated of things or events.

But only in this sense, and only so far as it reaches, do individual and individuality coincide. Beyond this they signify something very different. Individuality is the singularity of the case; the individual on the other hand is the case itself, independently of whether there be other cases similarly or dissimilarly constituted. An individual remains the individual, even if qualitatively it allows itself to be merged into generalities. Its naked categorial existence is indifferent to the uniformity and schematism of the general, as well as to the height of the qualitative individuation. It is not a counterpart of the universal, but of the collective unit; it is the numerically one, the single entity as such. It is that ontologically singular, the essence of which does not exclude the plural (like that of comprehensiveness), but does for ever remain in opposition to the plural as such. This is not contradicted by the fact that it appears always as one along with others, and that all real plurality is necessarily a plurality of individuals. The other individuals are not repetitions of the one, but are likewise original single entities, and are ontologically essential singulars. But their plurality proves most conclusively that being an individual does not mean individuality, that is, the being the only one of its kind. For the being an individual is as such common to them all, it is their fundamental likeness, their universal mark.

Thus arises the paradox, that the whole as such is in the strict sense a singular and something individual, but the individual as such is in the strict sense a something that is general, and as regards all individuation of content is indifferent. It is this which radically distinguishes quantitative correlation from qualitative.

(d) The Contrast of the Collective Unity and the Individual

For ethics this categorial connection of the two correlations (in itself purely ontological) is decisive. In the realm of values the radical separation reappears as a difference in the axiological dimensions of contrast.

There is a specific value in totality, and it is independent of the likeness or diversity of the members. And there is a specific value peculiar to the individual, which is independent of that inherent in its qualitative degree of individuation. That in ethical reality both dimensions often appear so closely related to each other, that at times the individual and individuality appear indissolubly bound together, that we can no longer keep them distinctly apart, must never obscure their essential difference.

The quantitative opposition preserves its axiological colouring through the fact that the unity, of which the singleness, plurality and totality are here under consideration, is the personal entity, the bearer of moral acts and their values. The ethical individual is the person—with all his characteristic functions, as a subject as well as an object of intentional acts, as a value-discerning and value-carrying being. But the ethical totality is the totality of persons—including their reciprocal objectivity to one another and the diversity of all the acts which bind them together or separate them.

According to the ancient conception, which reappears in most of the ethical classicists, the really great moral problems concern the existence of the collective unity (of the legal, social, civic community). The commonalty leads a life on a larger scale than that of individuals; in this way it is the carrier of greater aims and values, in comparison with which those of individuals must take a secondary place. Empirical communities of such a kind are indeed never, strictly speaking, totalities; the idea of humanity stands far removed beyond them. But such limitations are not willed, they do not inhere in the idea of the commonalty; the tendency to expansion is rather a characteristic of every community. In so far we must recognize in every communal ethics, without depreciating it, the fundamental tendency towards comprehensiveness as a value. It is the substance of all ethical values on the grand scale—all the way from simple legal arrangements up to the highest cultural ideals; comprehensiveness is the idea of the universal carrier of these values, and in so far the value of the moral carrier is transferred to it.[1]

The collective being is the bearer of values on the grand scale; whether it is also of a higher order is another question— it depends upon the height of the value that is borne. The collective being is the substance, in which alone distant goals, far-seeing human enterprises, can be pursued. And in so far as the individual can co-operate in these enterprises, when at times he consciously enters into their service (and does not simply allow himself to be used as a means towards them by social organizers), he subordinates himself and his private ends to the enterprises, he recognizes their superiority and con- sciously converts himself into a means; in some cases he sacrifices his personal existence for them. He adjusts his life as a member organically to some grand process which passes beyond him into the future, into the life of the communal being in which he participates only by contributing, not by receiving.

This self-sacrifice—and no one would deny that it is morally of value—is full of meaning only on the supposition that there really exist values, enterprises and goals which cannot be actualized except in the community as such and in it as the bearer of values. Only then may we speak of the exaltation of man through the conferring of value upon the commonalty. Nor can there be any serious doubt concerning the existence of such values. Social organization of every kind and degree is a distinctive value, it is a form, the realization of which, even in the most one-sided distortion, is of worth, because its

[1] Cf. Chapter VIII (a), Vol. II.

annihilation would mean a setting free of private egoism. Whether these values are the highest is quite another question; and still another concerns the limits of realizability. Yet the existence of the values is independent of their height in the ideal scale as well as of the degree to which they can be realized.

But the value of the individual is easy to discern; and again and again it has called forth opposition to the classic morality of the communal being. For the community is never the carrier of full humanity. In the complete categorial sense of the word, it is not a personality. Personality implies a subject, a consciousness, with the fulness of act and content peculiar to it. Only an individual possesses that. If behind the community there were a super-individual subject which as such could be the bearer of the same acts and actional values as the individual subject can be, or if there were a still higher one, the case would of course be different; likewise it would be different if there were such a thing as personality without subjectivity.

But neither of these notions fits the fact. Subject and person stand in a definite categorial relation of dependence; the higher form, the person, is conditioned by the lower, the subject. But it is precisely the phenomenon of the community which forbids our hypostasizing a subject of a higher order; all the personality of a community is a borrowed personality, transferred to it from the individual. A collective person has personality only of a lower order.[1]

This view harmonizes with the fact that precisely the highest values that can be realized in a community are not properly communal, but are those of individuals. The legal and constitutional order, public arrangements of every kind, of course, inhere in the commonalty and not in the single individual; the latter only has a share in them, producing and profiting by them. But even as values such forms are not the highest, for they are not moral values. The communal sentiment, on the

[1] Compare the criticism of Personalism in Chapter XXV (c) and (d), Vol. I.

other hand, is a moral value; so is the civic and political disposition which ripens such fruits. But this disposition is that of individuals, the community as such has no mental attitudes. The renowned civic virtue of the Roman is a value which accrues to the advantage of his republic as a goods-value (for every virtue has in it the reverse side of being a good for someone); but as a moral value, that is, as a value of a higher order, it inheres in individuals. As in a vision, the transformation and the salvation of the community hover before the individual as his ends; he aims at the situational values peculiar to the commonalty. But the morality of his intention is something different from the value of what he intends, as is the case with all moral conduct. On the back of his act, of his effort, appears the value of the higher order— it is actualized by his striving, although not intended. In reality it attaches only to him. While the individual gives himself up to the community, he actualizes in himself the higher values. This is the moral meaning of "sacrifice" for the people and for one's country.

This relation between the values of the individual and the community is in no way reversible, or even displaceable. It is embedded in the rigid law that moral values are based upon situational values. What irritates one is only the circumstance that the situational values—in this case those of the commonalty—are the ones that are striven for. Thus upon a superficial observation it may appear as if they were the higher values, as compared with those of the individual. It is in the sacrifice of the individual for the community that this appearance reaches its highest point, for to yield the higher in favour of the lower would be senseless. One forgets that it is precisely in sacrificing his existence that a person actualizes in himself the supreme value, that therefore in offering up himself he preserves and enhances his Being axiologically and perfects himself morally. The object for which the sacrifice is made must, of course, stand higher than that which is sacrificed. But the moral value of the sacrifice is not that of the thing sacrificed; it is then by no means surrendered, but even actualized in the surrender. It is decidedly higher as compared with the worth of that for which the sacrifice is made; indeed it is the highest of all values.

If one keeps this point in mind and remembers also that what constitutes the standard of actional value is not the height of the thing striven for but the person's greatness of mental attitude, one cannot fail to understand that it is the values of the individual, which in axiological height transcend those of the commonalty. But then it is also clear that, as a carrier of values, the individual himself has higher worth than the community, and that individualistic ethics has a deeply founded right to precedence over a purely social and therefore one-sided ethics.

The claim of communal morality will not on this account be contested; it discloses the highest ends that can be striven for. But the highest values capable of being actualized cannot be those of the community. Purely communal ethics would be an ethics of ends merely, and would run into the danger of becoming an ethics of success.

(e) The Antinomy in the Contrast of Quantity

The valuational opposition between the collective unit and the individual is in itself not antinomic in character. Each side has a certain axiological superiority. The collective unit is a structure on the grand scale, its values are macrocosmic; those of the individual, on the other hand, are moral. But the superiority of the one is not of the same kind as that of the other; they are therefore compatible.

Yet in ethical reality each shows itself to be tyrannical. Each claims to be the sole authority and aims to subordinate the other to itself.

From the standpoint of the collective unit the individual is in itself a meaningless, ephemeral structure; in the life of the collective unit innumerable beings of the same kind come and go. They exist for nothing else than to carry this "higher" life of the whole, to reproduce it and to enhance it. From this point of view any single individual can be ignored. He is merely material for "higher" forms. The collective unit, not the individual, is the substratum of history, only its process and only its goals are historically of significance; and the individual rises to historical greatness only in so far as he sets this process in motion, somehow grasps these goals in vision, advances them, or even hinders them. His significance then is borrowed from that of the collective unit, and is entirely bound by it. Even in the case of great personalities the individual is always there only for the sake of the collective unit.

Indeed, the sole mastery of the collective unit extends still farther. The community tolerates only those individuals who in their conduct conform to its ends; it rejects those that are of no use, stamps them as criminals, puts them out of existence, or renders them harmless by its jurisdiction which is directed to the life of the whole. Its authority meets the individual as a force, as a restraint upon liberty of action, but the individual accommodates himself to this force; he even takes the lead in it, he re-establishes it by voluntary subjection to the "higher" ends of the whole. Thereby he recognizes the inferiority of his own worth to that of the community.

This openly sanctioned attitude—it is in general the natural one among young and vigorous peoples—then finds expression in popular metaphysical theories, according to which the division of mankind into separate persons is a subordinate fact, individuation (the μερισμός) is a mark of imperfection, and there rests upon man the fulfilment of no higher destiny than to merge again into the common substance by devotion to the "whole."

This racial, tribal, social ethics, which reaches back to pre-historic, patriarchal times, is confronted by the growing self-consciousness of the individual with the simple reflection: How can I commit myself to ends which are not my own? They must at least be also my own ends. Only an individual can set up and pursue ends; but he can do that only if he is interested in them and sees in them some value for himself. The community must therefore respect the ends of the individual, it must be so organized that it is unmistakably a means to his ends. He must see himself confirmed in it, otherwise he cannot avoid disavowing it.

History corroborates this view. No community can maintain itself which is not based upon the common interest of the separate persons concerned. But then our thesis is converted into its antithesis: the individual does not exist for the sake of the collective unit, but the collective unit for the individual. The community is nothing but the *modus vivendi* of the individuals; for an organization, a structure of the common life, is needed by the individual for his own private life. Without the private life of the individual and without any value of his own the community were meaningless.

The culminating point of this individualism is that the individual just as unscrupulously credits himself with the worth and claim of the existing community, as the community credits itself with the worth and claim of the individual. And just as the community tolerates only those who serve it, so the individual tolerates only that community which in its organization and trend serves him. He rejects the collective unit which is of no use, opposes it, overthrows it. For him the community is only a means to his own life and his own ends.

In this attitude of mind the individual finds himself objectively strengthened, far beyond the limits of his natural egoism, by the reflection that human greatness is never with the crowd but is always and necessarily an affair of individuals. The conception of great individuals, in the sense of their value to the community, fails to understand the domination of moral values over the community. It is absurd to think that the great exist only for the sake of the small and insignificant, and ought to merge themselves in the struggle for material ends. Their superiority to the crowd is axiological, it can therefore be understood only in the sense of higher standards than the common ones. It is the great individuals who first give light and splendour to the life of the community, who open up a higher order of value which spreads to the rest, singly and collectively. It is they in whom significance is alive, whereby the community attains significance. Their image dominates and survives even in history, after the community has long been extinct. For them therefore, to speak axiologically, the collective unit exists. Not from it is their value borrowed, but from them that of the community is derived.

(f) The Limit of the Antinomy

That in this antinomy the thesis and antithesis are each one-sided is quite plain. Socialism and individualism—each strictly understood in the sense of the above contrast, which corresponds with customary speech only approximately—are typical "isms": the kernel of truth in each is justified, but it cannot be universalized. Both theories commit the error of abstraction, of isolating a value, in a way which in concrete life never occurs. For either value to assume supremacy over the other is usurpation.

In communal ethics the error lies on the surface. The collective unit itself, taken by itself, exists only in abstraction. Apart from individuals it has no being. It exists only in them, for it consists of them. It must therefore grant to the individual his mode of existence and his own worth, it must recognize him and in his independence respect him. It must do this not only because otherwise the individual sets himself above it, but because otherwise it annuls itself. The whole must assert the existence of its constituent parts; but their existence is simply their independence as against the whole. For its own sake, therefore, the community must recognize what, in its structural constitution, it has denied: the axiological self-existence of the individual.

There is no similar dialectic of the "whole" in any ontological totality. The relation of valuational contrasts first introduces it. An individual is not simply a "part." As a building-stone in the whole he is, nevertheless, a higher formation, a person in the full sense—which a collective unit can never be. And in so far as here the relation of means to ends prevails, the means transcends the end. In being a means for the collective unit (a lower order of carrier) the individual is at the same time a carrier of a higher order, and in so far an end in himself. The teleology of the "part" remains independent of the teleology of the "whole," although it is a reversal of the latter. The whole cannot fulfil itself as an end in itself, in so far as it does not at the same moment constitute itself a means to the part.

But the same thing is met with in individualism. Here also a false claim is made. The individual, taken by himself, is only an abstraction. He has no self-existence isolated from the collective unit. A separate isolated person is nowhere found. The separate man exists only in a community, he is entirely bound by it, as by a larger and infinitely stronger structure. He is born into it, draws from it the common goods—by inheritance, innumerable adaptations, education—he gradually falls into the conventional forms of life, which he did not produce, he gains a place in the communal being, in discipline and culture, in the conception of life and the universe, in the "objective mind." Even the man who later isolates himself, the anchorite, Robinson Crusoe, on his island, brings all these possessions with him and for a long time nourishes his life upon them. He rests with all his humanity upon the actualized values of the community. And everything of shape or value which he by himself brings forth, is already latent in those communal values. At the most he lifts himself but a little above them. Even such advance is made only within the limits of what is attainable from the actualized communal values in general. Ordinarily this is little enough. And even when it is much, as with the "great individual," he never loses from under his feet the common basis. Where this is lost, it is to his own detriment.

The individual must needs acknowledge the value peculiar to the collective unit; he cannot otherwise advance a step. It is precisely when he learns to understand himself as a final end, that he must also respect the collective unit as an end in itself, and adapt himself as a means to its macrocosmic teleology. Even the teleology of the individual turns dialectically against itself. It can achieve only by self-conquest.

But thereby in content it coincides with the collective teleology, which shows the same return upon itself. Of course not as regards the end, but certainly as regards the process. There are not, therefore, two different teleologies, which compete with each other; there is only one. Seen from either side, it is the same teleological reciprocity of individual and community. But this means that the two are connected not only ontologically but also axiologically. Within the valuational contrast there is a correlation, in which the union of the members is always stronger than their discrepancy. Herein the antinomical element in the quantitative aspect of the opposition undoubtedly finds its limit.

This is not a solution of the antinomy, rather might one call it an intensification; for the less soluble the oppositions are, the harder do they collide with each other in ethical actuality. Rather to the antinomic relation as such there is an inner limit, inherent in the materials themselves and independent of every radical solution. But perhaps here the axiological unity of the valuational continuum finds expression, for it reaches to the two extremes. And herein is contained a reference to the direction of the concrete tasks of life, before which man is placed by this antinomy.

(g) THE COMPLETELY ANTINOMICAL ELEMENTS IN THE REALM OF VALUES AND OF ONTOLOGICAL REALITY

This unification of values within the quantitative antinomy reaches even to the qualitative opposite, in which as such it does not exist in itself. The collective unit has an interest not only in the individual as its member, but also in the degree of his individualization. The more the single persons differ from one another, the richer in values becomes the whole of the community.

The common life is not a function of uniformity; its structure is a unity of differences. For all the wider enterprises of the social structure the prerequisite is the development of individuals in native gift, understanding and efficiency. For communal tasks the functions of the members must be of many kinds. There can be no schematization of them, it is in their diversity that they fit into the organic unity of the common process and aim. In contrast to this the necessary uniformity constitutes only a sort of basis, a *conditio sine qua non*.

Likewise for his own sake the individual has an interest not only in the collective unit as a concrete entity, but in everything which conditions it. However little his life can be absorbed in the uniformity of the elementary conditions of existence, nevertheless it must consent to these. The height of his qualitative individuation, in which his life culminates, must acknowledge and must by all means preserve the foundation of equal claim and equal duty, even where his life rises high above it. Indeed, it continues to be a unique value, even where it causes conflict. And exactly on this account it means conflict. If the higher value could abolish the lower, if the individual in his elevation above the average could place himself without conflict above the demands of equality, the alternatives between which he has to choose freely would not, as regards his real conduct, continue to exist. But this conflict not only continues, it is the fundamental form of most of the human conflicts, at least it is contained in them as an element.

The individual and the collective unit, just as much as individuality and universality, are fundamentally different directions or regions of value which subsist independently of each other and none the less are materially most closely interwoven in concrete life. Both antinomies run, unresolved, throughout the entire realm of values and on that account are drawn into the axiological structure of all the concrete situations of life.

Everywhere values divide into those of the community and those of the individual, and even in many otherwise harmonious materials they constitute opposed sides. The same specific material—let us say, honesty, steadfastness, energy, obedience, trustworthiness—may have a totally different value according as it inheres in a collective or an individual unit. Indeed, what in the one instance is valuable may very well in the other be indifferent or opposed to value. This double significance of many specific values (and especially the moral ones) should not be obliterated by any artificial cancellation. It is characteristic of the realm of values itself.

That a similar significance of general structural elements adheres to other pairs of opposites, the modal and the relational, so far as they do not have in themselves a tendency to cancellation, needs no proof. But for the philosophical completion of the valuational realm the double contrast of quantity and quality has an instructive significance. In it the general structural character of contrasts is perceptible in a unique way. No other pair of opposites has determined our conscious concepts, even to the setting of its stamp upon their terminology, so authoritatively as this. And in the diversities of positive morals no type of opposites is so consciously and simply developed in history as that of social and individual ethics.

But the task of the moral life, and with it that of philosophical ethics, consists, in spite of this fact, of a synthesis of the two points of view. The resting of each of these two carriers, the individual and the collective unit, upon the other, is by no means, as we have shown, a valuational synthesis. There is here no question of a radical universal solution, seeing that the unity of values is not discernible. But from moment to moment concrete life none the less yearns for permanent solutions. Every new situation confronts a man with a new decision and he can never escape from this necessity. But the task is an endless one, because unceasingly new, on account of the

qualitative infinitude of situational diversities. And this again
is of value for the complete development of the moral life.
For the great extent of the conflict furnishes the strongest
inner stimulus to human productivity, commitment and
acceptance of responsibility. It challenges the utmost spontaneity and the greatest creative energy of man. The ever new
attempts at mastery move forward over the ever unmastered
expanse.

(h) Intermediate Members—the Smaller Community and the Political Party

Just as between qualitative opposites, so between the collective
and the individual unit there appear intermediate members,
variously graded: the smaller association—the group, the con-
gregation, every sort of fellowship with a common interest,
the family, and so on. It unites the characteristics of the
extremes. As a comprehensive union of individuals it is a collective unit and at the same time, being among other societies
of a similar order, it is an individual. Strictly taken, even the
nation and the State, as empirical and limited structures, have
their place here and are not absolute collective units.

Again, the intermediate member displays a value of its own,
which in part has the quality of a synthesis, although of course
without mastering the antinomy. For the individual there is in
the narrower community the value of collectivity. His work in
it and for it goes in that direction. The smallest group has
entirely the inner structure of collectivity, the same kind of
existence and life; indeed, the same way of setting itself in
opposition to the individual. He sees himself in it as an alien
value. But in national life the people throughout play the part
of an individual. Likewise every State is an individual with the
characteristic values of such and is capable of higher combinations with other individuals of the same order. The federation,
the united State, the league of States, even the Idea of a world-
State, which in the history of nations is always alive and is

often striven for—these all lie in the same direction. Every State has an individual life, which moves according to its own laws, laws which cannot be transferred and for any other State would be unnatural. These are not by any means merely the "positive laws" which touch only the surface of the distinctive life. For every community acts as a person and bears responsibility, like one, towards foreign communities as well as towards its own members. Nor can its own moral life be reduced to any positive or ideal law.

Here, of course, it is not to be forgotten, that ultimately in the State consciousness, foresight, action, guilt, fall to individuals. There is no proper communal subject. At best the guilt is that of all (generally, in fact, only of some); but this does not make a person of the community. The representation of the communal consciousness (which is missing) through a single consciousness set into a leading position, is imperfect enough. No empirical person stands on the height of the required communal consciousness. And even if one stood intellectually on this height, he could not do so morally. No individual can so put behind him his individual interests that he can devote himself absolutely to those of the community and be nothing but its representative.

From this point of view we see why it is ethically wise for the subordinate groups in an empirical community to represent independently their own special interest, at the risk of their being in conflict with one another. If a community had an adequate personal consciousness, this would not be necessary; such a consciousness would possess a valuational sense for every justifiable interest. But under the circumstances the independent action of groups in the community is necessary. A political "party" has ethical meaning, because it represents a valuational trend in the communal life itself, which is active in many of its members. The strength of a party is the positive value which guides its interest; its weakness is its inevitable one-sidedness, involved in the championship of only one value. The presumption in making the one value all dominant is in itself a usurpation. But party violence is likewise a sin against this value. Conflict in political life is a necessity, it inheres in the living orderliness of a community. For it is a positive conflict of values and as such is itself of value. But the means by which the contest is carried on may be bad. Typical is the widespread obsession that the conflict is not one of value against value, but of value against disvalue. All disdain and calumniation between parties issue from this obsession. No one will believe that the opposite party also sees values and is striving for them; it is charged with what is humanly impossible and preposterous—the will to do evil for its own sake. There have been times in the historical life of nations, when this immorality of the political intelligence was a disease and made mutual understanding impossible. In such times the life of the community seems undermined; in unrestrained abandon it consumes its own vital energies. But there is a morality of political life, the health and strength of the State depend upon it: the unfalsified, disciplined sensing of the right in an adversary's contention and the inevitable diversity of interests themselves. The meaning of this morality is that as citizens the members of a party must stand above the party conflicts.

(i) HUMANITY AND NATION

A glance at this state of things shows clearly how far the limited empirical community—whether of a higher or lower order— is a properly ethical reality. But it can also be shown in a general way.

Strict collectivity cannot be actualized. It is an Idea. Even the individuality of a person is not commonly actual, it is deeply hidden and is yet to be discovered in its own proper value. The concrete sphere of ethical reality is the empirical community, which has grown up naturally or even been produced historically. In it, not in the collective unit in the strict sense, blossoms the variety of all the values into which the individual grows through birth and development by participation: such values as the biological type, language, customs, mental trends, civilization. There is no one language of humanity nor a single civilization; there are only specific, national languages and civilizations. Compared with these embodiments of the most concrete and abounding values, whatever is universally human is attenuated enough, and ultimately the Idea of humanity as a collective unit is profoundly unreal.

Connected with this is the fact that the values peculiar to a race or people should never be entirely merged into the levelling Idea of humanity. They are and they remain individual and as such show a relation to the general collectivity similar to that of the individual to his national community. Indeed, they stand in contrast to the values of humanity; but the bond and the connection are stronger than the tension of opposing forces. In spite of antagonism the nations require one another, to supplement the deficiencies of each. Even the Idea of humanity can as little do without national individuality as a State could dispense with the personal individuality of its members. Variety and independent differentiation are not less essential for the development of mankind and its ethos than is the perspective of over-arching unity. For not only are disposition, spiritual type, morality, poetry, art and ideal discipline necessarily specific, with a national individuality, inimitable by foreigners, but there is also a national calling, a specific task towards the whole of humanity as such and for its sake, a task which only a definitely organized people with special gifts and with a unique position in the total process of history can fulfil.

Herein lies the purpose of nations, their inner determination, their Idea single and incomparable. Like the Idea of the individual, it exists independently of the degree to which, as its carrier, a people fulfils, actualizes or even comprehends it. Like every axiological ideal, it is never merged into identity with its carrier. A people can also miss its inner determination, its specific values, its world-task. It can give itself up to foreign ideals, it can be diverted from its own course by overpowering influences, it can allow itself to be spiritually violated. History furnishes many a sad example of such an occurrence. But it is a tragic spectacle, when something goes to ruin which was possible only once and only in the life of one people. For nations do not repeat themselves any more than personal types. Conversely, it is something great and sublime in the drama of history, when such an inner destiny fulfils itself. For it is the achieved values of peoples which alone outlive them and which as spiritual heritages continue their work after the nations themselves have fallen into ruin.

Section III

THE VALUES WHICH CONDITION CONTENTS

GENERAL CHARACTER OF THE GROUP

(a) CONCRETENESS AND FULNESS OF CONTENT

IN content the realm of values is an interrelated variety of materials, and perhaps is even in all its dimensions an unbroken continuum. But we are not able to see it as a continuum. We see only single groups, between which whole portions of the intelligible space remain unfilled. The narrowness of our vision does not allow it to be otherwise. The connections, no doubt, are manifested in the recurrence of elementary factors in the more complex materials. But they permit of no inference as to the filling in of the gaps. In every single group which is discernible there is a new and differently formed point of view, with a different clue and a different context. Thus from the outset heterogeneity necessarily strikes the mind.

This is the case with the fundamental values which condition contents. They are a section, just as the contrasts are, and never a complete one. The connecting members are lacking. Many assumptions might perhaps be made in regard to them, but the assumptions are not confirmed in our sensing of values. So we are obliged, throughout the whole methodological difficulty, to allow the fact of discontinuity to stand. From it as such we cannot decide whether we are confronted here with an inherent irrationality of the intermediate members or only with temporary ignorance on our part, as if something were beyond us. We must accept the task of pressing forward into the unknown spaces, a task which is perhaps possible from both sides.

As compared with the former group of values the new one is characterized by a far greater abundance of content; the almost formal emptiness of the valuational contrast, which feeling detects only with difficulty, here entirely disappears.

Here are contents which anyone easily sees to be values. They come into much more intimate contact with our intuition. This is due to the existential form of that structure, in the organization of which they are constitutive factors.

The valuational antitheses were discovered in the categorial analysis of value and of the Ought; hence their abstractness. The values which condition contents are laid bare by an analysis of that structure which, in the sphere of actuality, only a positive Ought-to-be is in a position to grasp, and to transmute into actuality, and which thereby sets up a mediation between the ideal sphere of values and the real sphere of existence.[1] That this structure, with everything which essentially pertains to it, must itself be of value follows from its mediatory function. Its main features, therefore, must necessarily constitute valuational material. And as this structure is exactly the same personal subject (man), who alone can be a carrier of moral values, it is clear that these elements inherent in his nature must be for all moral values the condition determining their contents. The latter inhere in those acts which rest on that constitutional essence and in which, therefore, the conditioning values are already realized. In this sense—and only in this—do the fundamental values in the constitutional essence of the person condition the contents and prove vital for the manifestation of moral values. And likewise they are for the same reason highly concrete and directly accessible to discernment, and not by way of reflection. For in its constitutive ethical elements the nature of a personal subject is something concretely discerned.

(b) THE RELATION OF THE ONE-SIDED SERIES TO THE ANTINOMIES

The peculiarity of this group is that positive oppositions have ceased and have given place to more complex relations. No longer does value stand against value, but throughout only

[1] Cf. Chapter XIX, Vol. I.

against disvalue. The positive opposites are lacking, and even when they do put in an appearance their antinomical characteristic is absent. In place of it there is merely a contradictory relation. This, indeed, is not a new thing, for the positive opposites also have disvalues opposed to them and to their polar system corresponds a similar polar system of disvalues. But here the disvalues have a different axiological importance, because they are not concealed by any positive contrary structure. And for all higher values this feature is dominant.

The axiological dimensions, which appear here, are therefore one-sided series. Between their extremes they embrace a continuum only one half of which is positive; the other half is negative. The line binding value and disvalue is always clearly an ascending one from the negative, over the indifference-point, to the positive.

This unambiguous relation between value and disvalue, from which conflict is absent, is characteristic of all the wider and more concrete values of goods, situations and persons. The strict separation of these latter from one another is not yet carried out on the plane of the basic values. Here general inner situations stand close to acts, with a strain in them that is already clearly moral. In certain cases distinctive marks of both classes of values can be clearly discriminated and yet are inseparably joined. But it may be generally said that in the whole series goods and situations are predominant among the categorially lower materials, but that they diminish towards the higher, while conversely the moral values increase in the same relation and finally attain complete predominance. Herein the transitional position of the group comes clearly into evidence. In regard to valuational height this series shows an ever ascending curve, even if at some points in the intermediate members it is less evident. But under all circumstances it is important to distinguish most carefully this rise of the valuation level itself within the whole group of values from the advancing participation in value of the carrying structure (the personal subject) within each separate dimension of value and disvalue.

On another side the group as a whole has in it the conflict of opposites. The elements of these reappear in it and as such extend into it not otherwise than into the higher strata of values. And where the antagonism between them can be discerned, it is just as insurmountable here as it is there.

But only in a very external sense can one speak, in regard to these values, of their being determined in content by oppositions. They somehow always fall into the general scheme of one or another opposition, they take definite "places" in valuational "space" and within certain limits permit of being subsumed under these. Here we may therefore very well acknowledge a stratification. But it does not constitute the essence of the group. The opposites combine in many ways, but never from such combination can the new material, still less its peculiar value, be discovered. Accordingly, we could not speak of derivation, even if we could survey the whole series of the intermediate members between both groups. In every new value hides a new content which gives it its peculiar quality. To it the axiological essence adheres.

(c) THE SECOND SUPPLEMENTARY GROUP

Along with this group of fundamental values which adheres to the personal subject as such there exists a second series which also conditions the content of moral values, but does so in a different way, namely, by furnishing a material basis. It does not adhere to the personal subject and cannot be discovered by an analysis of the subject.

Ethical actuality is not constructed out of the essential features of man only. Rather are these themselves more widely embedded ontologically in universal structures of existence. And the latter exhibit those valuational qualities which as contents are drawn into the matter of moral values. They are conditions in a more external sense. Their main axiological feature is that of objectivity of value.

This second series differs therefore from the first and more fundamental, referred to under the head: the "antinomy of the carrier of values."[1] As a whole then it is differently articulated. It begins with very general existential structures, in so far as these furnish a basis for personal and actional values; and, rising to more specific materials, it terminates in the unlimited diversity of goods values. It ascends therefore in the opposite direction to that of the first series, to the other lower class of values, which in itself is of course highly enough differentiated. Within the whole ethical space it constitutes that section to which the realm of goods belongs. Here the whole of this region with its variegated specializations does not concern us, but, once more, only the most fundamental, only those which in a pre-eminent way provide a basis, those which are materially decisive for the general axiological problem of human nature in the world and its morally relevant place therein.

But the common element which binds this second series to the first is this, that in the realm of values the two-sidedness of the one is parallel to that of the other. Not only are both series conditioning factors, but they show the same attitude towards the sets of valuational opposites. In them also the contrasts reappear, and likewise only as subordinate elements which deprive the contents of none of their independence. Here also the distinctively positive opposition vanishes and gives place to a simple relation of value and disvalue; here, as in the other series, clearly ascending continuities prevail, one half with negative signs. And in the same way a conflict occasionally breaks out, which then extends to the opposition of actional values, in so far as the acts are directed to objective values.

Finally there is a still more intimate connection in the point from which both series issue. In the lowest types of both there is a close intimacy, without sharp lines of demarca-

[1] Cf. Chapter VIII (a), Vol. II.

tion; it is only with the increasing complexity and height of the contents of both that the series diverge, while, in the one, the character of actional and personal value becomes distinctively evident and, in the other, that of the situational value intended in the act. For the extent of the valuational differences in the ethical life generally, this divergence is of decisive significance.

CHAPTER XI (xxxvi)

VALUATIONAL FOUNDATIONS IN THE SUBJECT

(a) LIFE AS A VALUE

In the first series the most elementary value is that of life. By this is not meant the value of the form and existence of every thing alive, out of all relation to the ethos, but only the much narrower value of life as the ontological basis of the subject, and thereby indirectly also of the moral being and value-carrier, the person. We are acquainted with moral beings only as resting upon a biological basis, only in connection with an organism as a physical carrier. And all higher development of spiritually moral power is conditioned by the development of the life which carries it; it not only stands and falls with the life, but also grows with it.

In this sense vitality, vital strength, the degree of life in man, is a value proper. It is the value of that side of his being by which he is deeply rooted in nature and is himself a natural entity. The footing of the natural being in him is as such of value; it is his secret of Antæus, his hold on existence, without which he would, with all his spirituality, float in the air; it is the source from which all his unconsumed strength is drawn. Here is the earthly weight which holds him down and which he must overcome at every step upward; but here also is the root which sustains spiritual life until it reaches its highest elevation, and with which that life dies when its sustenance has all been consumed.

Over against this value, death stands as a disvalue. It is not only an annihilation of physical life, but with it also of the spiritual and personal. The unique grievousness of this disvalue becomes evident from the seriousness of murder, the moral sin against life. But also every injury to life and every weakness of it bear the same stamp of the elemental anti-value of death: the vital downfall, decay, degeneration. There is serious peril to life in every mental attitude that is hostile to it, in all excessive cultivation and physical weakness, in the suppression of the primal instincts, and consequently in the symptomatic, disintegrating pessimism of those who are sicklied over and unfit for life.

The value of a life that is sound at core peremptorily demands an ethical approval of whatever is natural and instinctive and a reverent preservation and fostering of the inner primal good which has grown naturally. In ancient times man felt this reverence; this ethical attitude found its classic expression in the view that everything natural is innocent and beautiful. The unnatural of every kind, perversity, diseased instincts, are repulsive to it. The individual is built upon the health of the emotional life, the community upon the health of the racial instincts. Even the communal body is rooted in the same biological soil; where the social instinct degenerates, there nation and community are doomed to destruction, with all their higher values.

We may also of course overestimate the value of life. In the ethics of the ancients is found a conception of the soul as a vital organism, and of the "good" as the "healthy," as that which is "wholesome for the soul." Not only with Epicurus and the Stoics is this thought current, the Platonic ethics also is familiar with it, and by no means merely as an analogy. In this way, health in general becomes the "highest good"; and although it is not simply that of the body, nevertheless it is an unjustifiable extension of biological value beyond its limits, a false analogy between soul and body, an ethical naturalism.

But the reverse of this is a more serious error—ethical anti-naturalism, the failure to appreciate and the attempt to oppose the natural. Many ethical theories have committed this mistake. Ordinarily the desires are called in question. In them, it is believed, can be seen something of inferior value, which lures men to evil. In so far as they belong to the "nature" of man, it is thought necessary to explain the natural as evil. Thus arises an attack upon the affections, the tendency to exterminate them entirely, and not only to control them. This is the tendency of asceticism, to kill all craving and pleasure; it is outspoken hostility to the natural and to the value of vitality.

One can see how such tendencies could spring up on the soil of Christian thought, where all value was carried over into the world beyond; here the renunciation of the flesh and of the sinfulness of nature is made a principle. On the other hand, it is astonishing that Stoicism, which sees the meaning of all morally good conduct in "conformity to nature," should take the same path. But the contradiction is only apparent. To the Stoic "nature" means something different: not what ordinary language calls the natural, but a metaphysically ideal conformity to reason. "Desire," however, is held by him to be something in man which is rebellious against the Logos and in this sense is "against nature" ($\tau \grave{o}$ $\pi a \rho \grave{a}$ $\phi \acute{v} \sigma \iota \nu$). Thus it comes about, that in Stoicism two apparently contrary tendencies go hand in hand, ethical naturalism and ethical anti-naturalism. In truth both rest upon the same misunderstanding of value, and nothing but the ambiguity in the concept of nature conceals the source of the error.

Moderate reflection discovered early, that in the natural affections and desires there lies hidden a profoundly significant adaptation to ends, and that their destruction is the destruction of life. However much morality may demand a higher valuational point of view and a control of impulse by it, the preservation of the natural still remains a value proper. Indeed, precisely upon man as a moral being falls the task of conserving life's value and the whole fulness of its phenomena; and so much the more, because he can destroy life, but cannot at will bring it back.

Herein lies the peculiarity of this value: life was not created by man, but it exists, it is real, and it is given to him—it is laid into his hands, as it were, and is entrusted to his care.

He can seize hold on it and with love can lead it to its height. On its foundation he can even evolve something higher than it, he can guide its process to aims of quite another kind. In this tendency natural value passes over into moral value.

(b) CONSCIOUSNESS AS A VALUE

The animal nature in man is confronted by a value in him which is superior to animality. It begins with consciousness. The unconsciousness of the animal is a dull, obscure life, a blind happening. Above this dark background in man rises the "light" of consciousness, the seeing, the knowing life. This is not without qualification to be set on a level with the life of the spirit; the latter possesses a deep stratum of a peculiar kind, different from that of vitality and nevertheless similarly unconscious. Consciousness as a value reaches of course into this depth of the subject. Out of this depth arises the fulness of experience, in so far as it is not conditioned from outside; in it is the world of the emotions, out of it springs the evaluating tendency and attitude of mind, the disposition. Consciousness proper is only a superficial stratum of the soul. Nevertheless, the peculiar emphasis belonging to value is upon consciousness. For only what comes into its light is the spiritual property of man. What remains closed in the depth of the ego he passes by without noticing, however much it may be the kernel of what is most his own. To live without participation in oneself, without being there "for oneself" (to use Hegel's words), is the fate of everything that is unconscious.

By consciousness we must not of course mean simply knowledge by the understanding. There are other forms of experience which reach deeper, to which indeed potentially the whole inner world of the life of the soul stands open. Inward beholding of this kind, qualitatively differentiated feeling, however non-logical it may be, is a consciousness of equal value and is full of content; it is a form of comprehension, although not transmutable into the language of concepts.

But the worth of consciousness rises with the degree of its development, or—what is practically the same thing—with the depth of its penetration, with the extent of its participation. And not only participation in one's own spiritual being. It rises also with the extent and fulness of the outward existence which it mirrors in itself. For exactly the same consciousness in the outward direction is the mirror of the world; and the greater the circle it reflects, so much the more is the function of consciousness fulfilled in the unconscious world. It is that form in the world, to exist "for" which gives a glimmer of meaning to everything real, a meaning which cannot come from the real itself, which is alien to its mode of existence. The actual merely as such, has—in Hegel's phrase—no "being for itself." But to be "for" another is well within its possibility. It depends only upon whether this other for whom it could be, exists in its sphere, that is, in the realm of the actual and exists itself as an actual thing. Now consciousness is this other. In being known, comprehended and experienced, one actuality comes to be "for" another. To the knower the self-existent becomes an "object." Consciousness, as the reflection of what is in itself, as that unique form in which there is a knowing participation in another existent and a representation of it, means the inclusion of something, existing merely in itself, an inclusion within a higher connection of meaning which is built above the ontological connection. In this interpretation, consciousness is actually the miracle of the bestowal of meaning.

It is the foundation of spiritual being. Its value is the basis of the spiritual values. But this rises in the scale, in so far as there is a consciousness not only of existence but of value. The key to this second dimension of participation is the emotional sense of value, and, above that, valuational discernment applied to the diversity of materials. A second realm of the self-existent is here opened to the subject. But his participation in it does not remain a mere discernment, it carries the discerned essences as standards into the world of actuality.

Thereby arises another way of comprehending Being, the comprehension of its worth, participation in its value.

Here is achieved a new and deeper metaphysical definition of man. He is the "measure of things" (according to Protagoras), their standard of value. He is the one who evaluates. We must not misunderstand this in the sense of any kind of valuational subjectivism. Man's "valuing" is not a conferring of values. He does not give them, they are given to him, whether they be ideal or actualized values. But they exist, in the first place, in so far as they present themselves realized in actuality, "for him" as the one who feels and understands them; and, secondly, the whole class of goods-situations is relative to him. Goods are not valuable in themselves, but "for him." And in this sense we must of course speak of a kind of conferring of value: by means of himself, as the point of reference, an appraisement of what in itself is neutral. The appraisement is mediated "through him."

This second, higher kind of participation in the actual is the one which in practice is decisive. In it is consummated the valuational character of consciousness. Not alone the comprehending of things is rooted in it, but man's whole comprehension of life, including his attitude in reaction to everything. All circumstances which confront him, all situations into which he falls, come under his judgments as to value and thereby attain for him sense, meaning, importance. Every consciousness of a situation is at the same time a complex consciousness of values, even if they be not comprehended as such. The axiological dimensions of the actual are superimposed upon the ontological dimensions. By man's penetration into their depth his participation in the valuable things of life increases; and at the same time the mass of values itself increases. For this participation itself is of value, it is one of life's treasures.

Man can no more create consciousness than he can life itself. But he can enhance its energy and heighten its worth not as with life through other values which thrive upon it,

VALUATIONAL FOUNDATIONS IN THE SUBJECT   137

but through the value peculiar to consciousness. Consciousness is to an extreme degree plastic. And here is opened an outlook upon a series of more specific values, like education, training, every kind of mental cultivation; these are enterprises for consciousness in consciousness itself. They require constructive work by it upon itself. But such work carries a value of a different kind, an actional value.

(c) Activity as a Value

Man's moral being, personality, is built upon consciousness, as this is upon life. It is self-evident that personality as such is a distinctive value, and higher than consciousness or life. But as its structure is complex and all its constituent elements have again their own character, its total value is a complex one. It is worth while to analyse it. The following six values are its chief factors: the last is a summary of them.

Beyond mere participation in Being, activity stands forth prominently as the first factor in personality. To it adhere moral values and disvalues in a pre-eminent degree and most unmistakably. In considering contrasts we have already met with activity as a value; inertness stood in contrast as a positive opposite, in the mere sense of persistence. Here the case is different; mere non-activity, passivity, stands over against activity. This is inertness in another sense: not ontological but ethical inertia, standing still, stagnation, indifference to values and ends, in short, negative inertness, as a disvalue.

This gives to activity also a different, a more special, meaning. Not the restlessness of tendency in general is here meant but commitment, the living mobility of the ethos in seizing the initiative and giving one's adherence, even where it does not issue in overt action. It manifests itself even in the evaluating of a situation, in the consciousness of a situation it becomes an inner act. It is the opposite of all purely passive existence, and is the most perceptible feature of the moral constitution.

Activity is not at all a mere means to the higher values

which it aims at. Man himself, as a creative worker and as perhaps the ultimate and highest object, is included among the aims of his creative work. In the widest perspective, the personal subject with his actional powers appears as his own "infinite object," although of course not in his own person.[1] Finally, activity generates itself again; it brings itself forth augmented. In this sense it is a Self-value, without regard to its object. And in this way Fichte identified it with the good; he held inertness to be simply the bad. That is, no doubt, an exaggeration of the value of activity. But it is not so paradoxical as it seems at first glance. For with Fichte not every action is genuine activity. It is not merely natural instinctive tendency; for that is nothing but a surrender to the stream of existence, a passive submission to compulsion, inertia. Only that which aims at what is beyond the existent, only that which pursues an Ought-to-Be, is activity. Then, of course, to be morally "good" inheres in the essence of activity.

Yet ethical activism is an exaggeration. For we cannot invert the sentence and say that there is nothing in the nature of the morally good except activity. Whether the circle of self-reproduction is completed in activity or not—and axiologically at least it is not necessarily so—nevertheless the great store of moral values, such as love, purity, sincerity, faithfulness, personality, remains outside and is by no means exhausted in activity. In such a violent simplification special materials must be completely robbed of their peculiar quality. Yet it remains true that, in general, activity as such is a value in itself, and that even the superior moral values of personality more or less participate in it.

(d) Suffering as a Value

Besides inertness, another opposite—suffering—stands in contrast to activity, and indeed as a value, even if the contrast be only outward and figurative.

[1] Cf. Chapter VIII (a), Vol. II.

There is a special value in suffering. It was unknown to the ancients; and later also it remained alien to rationalistic and eudæmonistic ethics. For from the point of view of hedonism suffering belongs to pain and is an evil. Christianity takes a different attitude towards it, although not on purely ethical grounds. It distinctly recognizes the elevating and liberating effect of suffering and does not regard it as a weakness, but rather as the setting free of a deeply inward and mysterious power.

One need not here think immediately of its purging and transforming powers, the existence of which is undeniable. They are morally differentiated phenomena which do not depend on suffering alone, but simply receive an impetus from it. The value of suffering itself, on the other hand, is more elementary. A glance at the corresponding disvalue may prove instructive on this point. This is the incapacity to suffer, the impossibility of bearing grief and misfortune, collapse under its weight, an inner succumbing, a sinking, the lowering of the human being, a brittleness and inner inelasticity. When a dire misfortune has passed away, it leaves the man who is incapable of suffering broken, morally warped, disfigured, weakened: he can no longer stand up, he has been damaged in his fundamental worth. For him suffering is, in fact, only a disvalue. On the other hand, one who has a capacity for suffering is strengthened in it. His power of endurance, his humanity, his moral Being, grows under it. His suffering is of value, for his reaction is the reverse of that of the fragile and desponding man. It is the positive, assertive reaction of the man under the burden of adverse fate, under the external power against which his own activity cannot prevail.

For even where activity is denied to one and is lamed, where nothing apparently remains but to submit passively, a deeper power of the moral nature in place of ordinary activity is released, a power which at other times is closed, but which now, having been freed, takes up the struggle for moral existence. Suffering is the energy-test of a moral being, the load-test of his elasticity. Not only is there no prostration, but suffering also leads to no mere resistance or endurance or moral self-assertion; there is much rather an actual liberation, an awakening of a deeper moral power—a might of a higher order, as compared with that of activity. For exactly when all activity is destroyed, then strength sets in, the positive ability to suffer.

Naturally everyone has his own limit, as regards the capacity to bear suffering. For each there is an excess which goes beyond his power of endurance and oppresses him. There is therefore for each a limit to the value of suffering; beyond it suffering becomes a disvalue. That is the ugly feature about it, it becomes the opposite of a value; and the point where it changes is not objectively in the amount of suffering, but subjectively in the strength of the man to bear it. Within the limit—and indeed the nearer to it, so much the more—suffering means the awakening of his innermost moral nature, the unlocking of the depths of his being, the liberation of his noblest energies. Whoever has been tested in suffering is tempered steel—for him nothing is too difficult; moral capacity is at the same time stored up in him; he is like a steel spring which returns to its original strength, or, according to Nietzsche's analogy, he is like the strung bow, which waits for the arrow. He is in fact the man who is raised to a higher moral power.

This potency does not spend itself only in active energy. It enters into the still depth of ethical feeling and understanding. Great pain also opens the deep places, in a way the untried person does not dream of. And not only the depths of one's own heart, but of the hearts of others, even the depths of the general life with its inexhaustible richness of opportunity. One's whole attitude towards life is changed. The gaze of the unburdened man falls only upon the sparkling surface; the man matured in suffering sees the same situations and conflicts, the same aspirations and struggles, but he sees below the surface; in another way he shares the life of others, his outlook is broadened and sharpened. Suffering has lent to him the capacity to see values which before were hidden from him. Perhaps it is not too much to say that suffering is the special teacher of the consciousness of values. This statement would be fully confirmed, if it be true that discernment advances with the situations and conflicts that are given and lived through. For a living situation reveals its constituent values only to a person standing in it and gazing into it with penetrating observation.

If with his suffering a man purchases the highest values, the thought of a will to suffer has nothing absurd in it. There is such a will. Whoever assumes great burdens must necessarily have it. It is nothing unusual for a man to want to suffer for the sake of a high goal, of an idea, for the sake of the communal life. But the will to suffer for love's sake, or rather for a person who is loved, is deeper still. This is by no means a merely external or inevitable taking of the risk of suffering, where it is unavoidable. In suffering for a person there is a puzzling and yet unmistakable depth of participation, a communion with him, which for inward depth has no equal. A mother loves her child not the less on account of the suffering which it brings her, but the more; and for nothing in the world would she allow herself to be robbed of this. It is her inmost interest in the child and is independent of all response, of all gratitude or ingratitude. In this way "to suffer for His name's sake" hovered before the first Christians as the highest participation in the person of Jesus.

To the greater potency, elevation and ennobling of personality through suffering there corresponds—as one might have expected—an enhancement of the capacity for happiness. For with suffering the appreciation of happiness deepens. The moral greatness of a tested character is far removed from all anxiety to flee from pain and hardship, from petty fear and worry. The quiet, firm nature of the tried soul does not crave for pleasure and happiness. He does not care for it. And just for that reason—according to the law of happiness—it comes to him.

(e) STRENGTH AS A VALUE

Moral strength is not identical with activity; passivity also can be strong, as well in steadfastness and perseverance as in the endurance of pain. Strength is something which stands behind activity and suffering and both of these grow out of it. Even an active nature can be weak, can allow itself to be diverted and confused, just as a passive nature can be strong and remain inflexible.

The special value of strength is, of course, most evident in will, determination and resolution; for here it can be seen in the execution of plans. A weak will, even when it is well directed and in its tendency constructive, is morally of a lower value, even abject, independently of the value or disvalue of its aim. Agility alone does not signify; perseverance in aim, the overcoming of opposition, even a thriving under it, constitute the value of will as mere will (without respect to its end). But the same holds good of all inner intention which does not come outwardly to manifestation. In just the same way there is also a strength of disposition, of love and of hate, a strength of conviction; just as there is a strength of belief, whatever may be the object of it. The phrase "to remove mountains" may be metaphorical, but it is a closely fitting metaphor. And not only as regards faith.

Strength of will, furthermore, is something different from freedom of will. A strong will can be unfree, wholly determined by something outside itself. But, equally, a free will can be weak. Fichte's ethics, chiefly renowned in regard to freedom and strength, effaced this difference; with him the two values merge into a third, that of activity. Against this view we must bear in mind that freedom concerns the basis of determination and is its origin, while activity is the tendency as such; but strength is the dynamic power. Its value lies, on the one hand, in the force of the determination itself and, as it were, in the weight of the resolution as such; it is in so far a ruling power. But, even in the reverse sense, it has a value of its own, as a serving energy. The moral value of an action does not increase generally with the height of the object intended in it, any more than with its success, but with the degree of the commitment to it; and it attains its highest point when the whole personality without reserve is surrendered to the thing striven for.

This value of strength culminates in that of sacrifice. The peculiar quality of it is here augmented, in that sacrifice does not become morally inferior through the inferiority of the thing for which it is made. He who struggles heroically for a bad object may be to blame that he does so at all, but in itself his bravery would be no different in the service of a good cause. And if anyone should say that it was worthy of a better cause, he would thereby attest its inherent worth.

In the direction of this value lies that of moral consecutiveness, of fidelity, energy, even of work and efficiency, of every kind of service.

(f) FREEDOM OF THE WILL AS A VALUE

A person differs from all other kinds of Being especially in this, that he is not compelled to carry out the determination which he receives from the principles (the values) that hold good for him, but retains the power either to comply with them or to oppose them. This peculiar dignity has always been described as freedom of the will. This is not the same as the freedom which the pure Ought-to-Be of values allows him; the latter is in itself a special value for the personal being, but not one which would subsist in him (as carrier). To this negative free play of values there must correspond another, a positive power of determination in the person himself; without it there would be an indeterminism and at the same time an ineffectuality of values, and there would never be any determination by the will at all.

A will which is not determined by a principle as such, must at least be itself able to determine the principle. For if it cannot do that, all connection between reality and the realm of values is lacking, and the values rest powerless in their ideal Beyond, without laying hold on life. But the essence of the personal subject is that he breaks through the Yonder of values, that in emotion he takes hold of them, can commit himself to them and transform them into reality. This constitutes in him a special power of positive decision. And the positive sense of freedom as the ultimate factor in decision is the counterpart of that merely negative freedom which values grant to him. Consequently the valuational quality of man's real freedom is something different, entirely new, adhering to the personal subject as such, however much it may be conditioned metaphysically in its scope.[1]

Together with the values of consciousness, activity and strength, there also appears the unprecedented value of volitional freedom of the will, personal self-determination in directing the aim of actions morally intentional. This value is quite independent of the much disputed "problem of the freedom of the will"; in that problem the question is whether there is or is not a freedom; here the question is only in regard to its value. This is an ideal form, like all other values; that is, it exists even though there be no carrier of it in reality, and even if there should actually be no real will that was free. Even then the valuable is only unreal, but is none the less valuable. In the strict sense, then, no moral entity would exist. But a moral entity, whether real or not, is of value. Therefore freedom also is valuable.

Freedom is the rising of initiative above the blind happenings of the world. As such this is a value; it lifts man out of the connections of nature in which he is rooted, it allows him to tear himself away, to rise into the "second realm." Lack of freedom is total determination from outside, the serfdom of man under the universal course of events. The profound struggle of human thought to attain a metaphysical proof of freedom of the will is a witness to its worth. However desperate

[1] Cf. Chapter VII (a), Vol. II.

the problem may look, however violently all psychological theories deny it, man cannot and dare not permit himself to be robbed of it. He struggles with all his might to retain his belief in it. He has even a deep consciousness that he is free. He feels that, even if he be not free, he ought to be. For he ought to be a moral being, a person. The will to be unfree, or even to renounce without a struggle the consciousness of freedom, would be a renunciation of his selfhood.

But this same will to freedom exists in a much concreter form, in the midst of the ethical fulness of life. There is the strongest evidence of it where one might least expect it: where responsibility and guilt fall upon the free person, while one who was not free would stand guiltless and untroubled. There is a will to responsibility, even to guilt as regards one's own conduct; there is a repugnance to the presumption of exculpation, as implying a repudiation of guilt. It is not as if one wanted guilt as such—one would be glad not to have it. But once we are laden with it, we cannot allow it to be taken away, without denying our selfhood. A guilty man has a right to carry his guilt. He must refuse deliverance from without. To retain his guilt is valuable for him despite its oppressive load; it signifies for him the retention of his personality, the preservation and recognition of his freedom. With his guilt he would lose a greater moral good: his manhood. In taking upon himself his own deed and his guilt, in asserting his responsibility, in his sincere willingness to carry it, there is a moral pride in the free deed which speaks out; it is the majestic right to manhood, the foundation upon which all moral Being and Non-being rest. To surrender it is moral meanness, betokening incapacity to be free. He who pardons a guilty person, compromises him spiritually. He denies his accountability. The presumption in washing away guilt, in discharging it, the admission of "mitigating circumstances," is at bottom a moral disfranchisement and a degradation of the man. That one who is threatened with severe punishment may very well want to be absolved, implies nothing against this axiological position; it is simply his weakness, his moral abasement, his lack of moral pride, of freedom, responsibility and human dignity. To him unaccountability and disfranchisement are preferable to the consequence of freedom, the merited punishment. But no one will justify this, although he may humanly understand it.

That a conflict of values inheres in the concept of guilt is not to be overlooked. Guilt is and remains a disvalue in man; no one, so long as he is guiltless, could wish for it. But the astonishing thing is that when a man has once burdened himself with it and bears it, it gains the character of a value which contradicts the value of innocence. It is not that the latter would thereby be nullified; it continues to exist, in spite of the value of guilt. Here, in one and the same moral perception, there are denial and affirmation of the value of guilt, a will to be rid of it and an acceptance of it (a will to have it), a will to responsibility and a yearning to be delivered from it. Each is profoundly justifiable.

Behind all this stand the denial and the affirmation of freedom. How far these two can be reconciled with each other, how far they exclude each other, is a different question. It may be that a man cannot bear the degree of freedom which has fallen to him; it is this which places responsibility upon him. And possibly it is his inner destiny, to be obliged finally once more to renounce his freedom—and with it his manhood, because he has not grown to the greatness of the gift. Just as riches and power can become a curse to a man of weak character, so the greatest of inner goods, freedom, can become a curse to a morally small and weak man who has not grown to it. It seems, accordingly, that there is a danger point in the value of freedom, that even freedom is a value to man only up to a certain limit and beyond that becomes a disvalue. Like suffering, freedom presupposes in its carrier an ability to carry it, and in so far as this ability is limited the amount of freedom which the individual carries must also be a limited one. That this amount can increase with the moral growth of the person, need not be disputed. But a limit always exists beyond which freedom would morally oppress him.

The yearning for deliverance from guilt is a sign of inner bankruptcy. Religion builds its scheme of salvation upon this bankruptcy, upon moral insolvency. Salvation, in fact, disfranchises man; it exacts of him the renunciation of his freedom. The result is a sharply pointed antinomy between ethics and religion, that is, between freedom and salvation. This antinomy is far more fundamental and far less capable of solution than that between guilt and innocence. For behind the value of guilt stands that of freedom, and this is in itself no opponent of innocence. Freedom and salvation from guilt, however, cannot be reconciled, at least not as values; for deliverance from guilt involves the renunciation of freedom. It is, however, not for ethics, but for the philosophy of religion, to solve this antinomy—and whether the philosophy of religion can solve it depends upon whether to do so comes within the range of possibility. Ethics knows of no deliverance from guilt. Only religion speaks of it. And upon it alone falls the metaphysical burden of the consequences.

(g) Foresight as a Value

Man's consciousness, merely as such, is not practical. Even activity does not alone make it so. It first becomes so when his capacity to look forward in time, to see the future, to prepare for it beforehand, raises it above the mere reflection of the actual. Mythology has brought this to picturesque expression in the form of Prometheus. His mere name bespeaks "the forward thinker," just as his counterpart, Epimetheus, tells of the backward-looking thinker. The first man is forward-looking. His becoming man is theft from the divinity. And although the myth knows to inform us only of the stealing of fire, it clearly means that something else is stolen, divine prevision ($\pi\rho\acute{o}\nu o\iota\alpha$). Providence is the attribute of godhead.

The ethos of man is his pride, his raising of himself against the divinity, his assumption of its attribute.

Foresight is the intuitive vision in man; in its highest power, it is prophecy. Prevision makes him move forward, conscious of his goal. Man does not live in the present alone. He belongs to the future. And the future belongs to him—within the limit of his prevision. Indeed, to speak exactly, the future is the only thing which practically does belong to him. The past stands eternally still and is not to be changed. Nor is the present to be changed any more than the past, it already has its irrevocable determination in itself. Only that which has not yet entered into the present, that which is coming to us—for this is the meaning of the word "Zukünftig"—can be guided, can be influenced.

All activity, every striving, moves necessarily towards the future. A consciousness to which the future were closed would be condemned to inactivity. It is man's foresight which opens to him his only possible field of action, the future. Here is the key to all his capacity for action. The ability to anticipate breaks through the spell of the present, transfixes the brazen bound of the actual, the temporal flow of which never forestalls the course of time. Thought forestalls, it is timeless, although it is the thought of a real subject who is bound within time. Thought lifts the veil which is spread over the future. And however imperfect prevision may be, only through it are there preparation and execution of something willed.

The opposite of foresight is the thought that holds fast to the present and the finished, that is struck with blindness to what is not actual, the unforeboding push in the stream of events, the dull sinking of oneself in the moment, to which only a backward look and regret remain (μετάνοια and μεταμέλεια instead of πρόνοια and ἐπιμέλεια). Nothing is more indicative of the value of anticipation than man's ceaseless striving to foresee, his struggle and anxiety to know beforehand. From the narrowest outlook of the man absorbed in winning his daily bread to that of the statesman who keeps in mind the distant development of the future, this striving is essentially one and the same. The only difference is in the extent of the perspective. Even in private life we speak of short-sighted and far-sighted behaviour; when we speak of precaution and improvidence, our language implies the same valuational judgment.

This judgment is so much the more urgent, because man's outlook is so essentially limited and even within its limits is so uncertain. It does not deserve the name of knowledge. The future, so long as it is future, does not permit of being made into an object; of all that is real only the present is given as an object. The past must already be viewed at second-hand— by the "traces" which it has left behind. But in the present the future has no equally impressive witness, none comparable to the "traces" of the past. The network of the conditions from which it arises indeed precedes it; and through them it may be anticipated. For the course of events is uniform. But this network is wide and no human eye can survey it. Man grasps only single threads; exactly where it is of practical import—as regards the future—his knowledge is for ever piecemeal. An intuitive understanding might perhaps discern directly what does not yet exist. But, in this sense, man has no intuitive understanding. In theoretical calculation in advance (for instance, in regard to the movements of the stars), where a simple calculable uniformity prevails, he is far-sighted enough; but he is short-sighted and uncertain of himself within the actual sphere which touches him and his life. Here the veil of the future hangs thick before his eyes, and even the richest experience of life gives only a faint glimmer of certainty. But all this does not derogate from the value of foresight. Even the faintest glimmer of light which falls upon what is coming, is of inestimable value. And the Idea of perfect divine providence confirms this value.

Nevertheless, as a value, prevision also has a limit; it has a danger-point in it. In the Cassandra myth this is clearly brought out. Cassandra sees the destiny coming, without being

able to avert it; the prophetic vision poisons her life; for her
the divine gift becomes a curse; she envies the happy ones
who are struck with blindness and can at least spend unem-
bittered the short span that still remains to them. Is the myth
right? Is the gift of prevision a disvalue? If Cassandra could
convince the unforeboding, it would be of supreme value,
it would avert disaster. What then makes it full of disaster?

In the Homeric world fate is overpowering, Moira is un-
avertible. What must happen is predetermined by divine
council, man cannot escape. His foresight is powerless; therefore it is a fatal gift. Blindness to the future is itself decreed.
The seer is condemned to passive vision of what is approaching.
He has indeed the one attribute of divinity, prevision, but
not the other, predetermination. He cannot prevent the thing
he sees; for him to defy fate is also of no use. Such is the
conception of the ancients. Even Laius does not ward off the
curse of the Labdakides, although he believes the oracle and
exposes the son. Heimarmene is stronger, she finds means of
achievement. Philosophically expressed: in a world wholly
determined teleologically, where all that happens is irrevocably
decided beforehand and allows no place for man's predetermination, prevision is in fact an evil. But it is different in a world
that is determined causally. Causal determination permits
itself to be changed, it is not fettered to the final stages of its
process, nor is it imprisoned in the immutable. One single
thread, in the network of the causal interlacement, added
spontaneously by man, is in a position to transform the whole.
In a world determined teleologically the future is as fixed as
the past and the present; in a world determined causally, the
destination is not closed, it stands open, at least in principle,
to the initiative of man. In such a world—and ours is such[1]—
the gift of prevision is a value.

And still a danger-point continues to exist in prevision as a
value. It is the kernel of truth hidden in the myth of Cassandra.
If man knew everything which lies before him, he could not

[1] Cf. Chapter XXI (c), (d), Vol. I.

endure it; with such knowledge life would exceed his moral strength. For to guide and avert everything is far from being within his power. Also in this respect man is intermediate between divinity and beast. By his prevision he lifts himself above the blindly living creature, but even such foresight he could not bear in its fulness. He can live only by having a certain strain in him of irresponsibility and light-heartedness; the full attribute of divinity would overwhelm him. And accordingly the full measure of what is of value in itself becomes for him a disvalue.

Finally, in view of this double-sided risk of danger, we may see an astonishing adaptation to ends in the moral condition of man: he has approximately that measure of prevision only which he can bear, and without that he would not be man. He stands on the dividing line between providence and imprudence. In both directions he can degenerate—into the frivolity of the short-sighted, troubled about nothing, as well as into the crippling pessimism of one who knows and understands too much.

(h) Purposive Efficacy as a Value

That which, beyond freedom and prevision, rounds out the measure of personality, is man's purposive efficacy, his teleology.

After the preceding exposition, little more need be added concerning the value of this fundamental factor in every tendential act. It is the finish and crown of all the partial factors, and it is also the culmination of their valuational qualities. Man is the only being in which we find the power of teleology. And in it lies his qualitative superiority over every real thing that is otherwise constructed; to it is due his position of power in the world.

To all the three stages (or strata) of the finalistic nexus the value of his teleology adheres: it adheres to the capacity to set up ends, to prefigure contents as goals before their actualization in the course of events; to the capacity to find out means for their realization and to use them; and to the not inferior capacity, with the help of these to guide the real process of events toward the goal which was marked out beforehand. This threefold exercise of power in the midst of the broad causal stream of blind events—without interrupting the continuum of the stream and yet as an alien body—this it is which constitutes the unique position of the human being in the world, this it is which enables him to actualize values which without his help would remain unreal. Through this position of power he has—in addition to his inner freedom of will—the outward freedom, that of motion and efficacy in the stream of events. He can enlist the natural forces into his service, with their help he can even steer upon occasion against the current.

The teleology of man is his second attribute of divinity; it is foreordination, predestination. Inwardly his conduct is different from the action of other powers; but outwardly, as a process, it shows the same form of temporal action as everything real, in that it brings to actuality something that was predetermined. Here the natural processes, in so far as man can introduce them into his purposive activity, are linked to values. Man does not create the processes; but he turns them to his own ends. He thereby predestinates their course. To the causal determinants he adds a finalistic determinant. His prevision renders him capable of this. Thus he fulfils his metaphysical rôle of mediator between the realm of values and reality. But at the same time he becomes thereby the bearer of moral values. For it is to acts distinguished by such teleology that the qualities good and bad pertain. And this applies not only to conduct and action proper, but also to every type of inner tendential action, even to the general attitude, disposition and commitment towards life and the surrounding world. For here also in tendency lies the direction towards the telos, and in fact all conduct issues from inner disposition. All intention which is directed to value already contains a factor of predestination. In it are rooted positive decisions, and these are directed by ends.

But, like man's freedom and foresight, his predetermination may be excessive; he cannot bear it in full measure. Foresight at least leaves his responsibility unburdened; predetermination involves him in responsibility. This is the meaning of predetermination: That he who practises it has guilt or credit for everything which it brings about. Unbounded purposive activity means unbounded responsibility, responsibility for everything. Guilt falls upon him who has power. The idea of God as the being who predestinates everything is the idea of an unlimited responsibility, at the same time also the idea of an unlimited capacity for being responsible. The moral strength to endure is here thought of as raised even to the infinite. Man is not such a being. The degree of responsibility which he can bear is narrowly limited; and in real life, when it is exceeded, he collapses under the burden and gives up in despair; then he no longer acknowledges his purposive initiative but looks about for release. The second attribute of divinity he can endure to the full extent still less than the first. The former threatened his happiness, the latter his moral being. In this connection also he is midway between divinity and beast. His peculiar predetermination lifts him high above creatures that are bound to nature; but he can live only with a low degree of predetermination; in this also he needs release from burden. An excess of power falls upon him like a crushing load.

And here also he is anxious to be limited. Indeed, the limits of his predetermination are perhaps still narrower than those of his prevision. Many powers, which in the course of the world he can very well foresee for a considerable distance, escape from his initiative entirely. At best he can control them by submitting to them. Here, however, there does not prevail an equally fitting balance, as in the limitation of his prevision. It may be affirmed that man approximately possesses the degree of predetermination which he can bear. In general his capacity for responsibility (his moral endurance) is smaller than his power to control events. Accordingly in human life it is not a rare phenomenon, that someone may not be able afterwards to carry the guilt with which he loads himself. For this reason there are moral wrecks, who can no longer stand upright; there are the morally stunned, in whom the stupefaction is itself a function of the secret fear of being found out and called to account—a doubtful self-protection against their own conscience and against despair.

Predestination is the most powerful, but also the most dangerous, of the gifts which man has received. For him it is a value only within the limits of his strength of endurance. Beyond that it is a disvalue. But the whole practical life of man is step by step a playing with this dangerous gift; of course it is not an idle play, but necessitated, inevitable. For in it man has no freedom; so long as he breathes, he cannot withdraw from the game. Only how he shall play the game, how he shall use the gift, is within his power. And it happens that the gift, the more he is conscious of the power which is in his hands, leads him astray, lures him to ever higher stakes. But in this frenzy he does not become aware of the limits of his strength, until after he has overstepped them and the game is lost for him.

CHAPTER XII (xxxvii)

GOODS AS VALUES

(a) The Position of the Scale of Goods in the General Ethical Scale

AMONG the ancients the conception was dominant that the ethical values in general come within the scale of goods. Hence the inclusion of "virtue" under goods, as the "highest good." This view allows little scope for the special character of actional values. Nevertheless, it has held its own unweakened in popular morality, and in many theories of modern times (for instance, in Schleiermacher's moral doctrine) it has re-established itself. Directly opposed to it stands the Kantian ethics of duty; and whoever holds with Kant the conviction that only disposition and will can be good or bad, is inclined from the start to exclude the doctrine of goods altogether from ethics.

Both extremes go too far. Goods belong to material and situational values, which as objects to be striven for constitute the basis of actional values. They are not moral, but they are morally relevant. Man's doing as he pleases with them is the sphere of moral goodness and badness. Accordingly they indisputably deserve their place in the ethical scale of values, although it be a subordinate one.

As regards their sphere they are related to the values just discussed, in so far as these also condition moral values and besides manifest a distinct strain of goods-value. Life, consciousness, freedom, foresight are inner goods. In the whole series the character of the "good" in the value of life still occupies the foreground, but it continually becomes less prominent, until in predetermination it has almost entirely vanished in comparison with actional value. In the lowest member of this series, life, the group of goods-values begins immediately; but it then withdraws, giving place to more complex materials always further removed from it, until it falls into the wide region of the variegated hedonistic goods, finishing in a characteristic opposition to them. The two series therefore diverge, materially and axiologically. In valuational height the members of the first are throughout superior to those of the second, and with the divergence this superiority also becomes more pronounced.

In the exposition that follows, only certain chief types from the second series are set forth. A real analysis of the goods scale, together with the inner relations of its grades, is a task by itself, for which there is no room here. If the height of the moral value of striving were proportionate to that of the situation striven for, the concrete ethics of value would need to begin with an exact analysis of the scale of goods. But evidently such a proportion does not exist. The sacrifice of a material possession can be morally more valuable than the wisest ethical advice, if this does not demand any sacrifice on the part of him who gives it. Moral value rises not with the height of the intended object, but with the amount staked.

For this reason the gradations in the values of goods are relatively alien to ethics, however much the values themselves form the foundation.

(b) Existence as a Basic Value

The goods-values proper differ from those of the first series in this, that they do not attach to a subject, although they are values "for" a subject. They attach to an object, to an existent, to the surrounding world. Now it is clear that the general situation, in which a living, conscious, active subject is placed, together with everything that can serve the ends of his life, implies a value. This exists independently of whether or how far it is felt by the subject to be of value. Its content embraces the natural conditions of life, beginning with the earth, with water, air and light, up to the special sources of nourishment and

well-being. A whole system of values is included in the
general concept of the environment. If any one of these elemental goods of nature be temporarily withdrawn, immediately its value, usually unnoticed, rushes overwhelmingly into
consciousness.

But there is a richly organized mass of values at hand, not
only for a man's mere life and its needs, but also for his moral
being, for his activity, freedom and creative enterprise. This
world is so constructed fundamentally, that a free and end-
pursuing agent finds scope in it. One may cite as a chief
feature of this valuational constitution of the world the causal
structure of the order prevailing in it. If the world were just
as completely determined teleologically as it is causally, there
would on that account be no scope in it; the activity and
teleology of a person would be excluded, his freedom would
be an illusion, his power of foresight ominous, unbearable.
But if the same world were entirely undetermined, if it were
neither causally nor finalistically ordered, or even if it were
but partly coherent in its interdependencies, in the sense of
partial indeterminism, prevision would then be impossible.
Freedom and inward strength would indeed be boundless,
but also incapable of outward effectiveness. Purposive efficacy
in man would be as completely cut off at the root, as it would
be in a finalistic world. Every actualization through means to
ends (the third member of the finalistic nexus) presupposes
the causal structure of the world; as a real occurrence it itself
has the form of the causal process. If a definite complex has
not a distinctly definite and necessary effect, there is no specific
means to a specific end. The finalistic nexus in human conduct
has, therefore, as its categorial presupposition the causal
nexus of the world. And hence the latter is a basic and actual
value for the existence of personality. For the moral qualities
attach to the teleology of acts directed to values.

In the valuational scale accordingly this basic value of the
cosmic structure—regardless of its merely secondary and
external goods-character—has a strictly complementary posi-

tion to the inner basic values: activity, strength, freedom, foresight and predetermination. Without its reality these are not really possible. As regards content they have their universal condition in it. Here we see clearly the intimate connection between the two valuational series.

(c) SITUATION AS A VALUE

Within the general situation of man occur the various specific situations. We noted their highly individualized quality when we were speaking of valuational opposites.[1] But their value does not rest simply upon their individualization. Independent of type and singularity of circumstance it consists chiefly in the fact that situations first bring a man face to face with his tasks, challenge him to commit himself and hold him to his decisions. They are his field of action, indeed the material basis of his moral life in general, in so far as the basis is an external one. Their variety constitutes the rich contents of his existence. The multiplicity of interests which cross and recross in the situations is the key to his sense of values. But the new consciousness of value is always absorbed in the novelty of the conflict. No logical combination, however, and no fantasy grasps the depth and abundance of the living situations. Man grows morally with his understanding of the depth of ethical reality and with appreciative participation in it, even when he does not himself stand in the situation nor act creatively in it. Its value differentiates itself for him even down to the most fleeting changes of the moment.

But besides this we may speak of a still higher significance of the same material. There are human connections which take on the character of approximately lasting duration. Personal life is full of them, all the way from economic and utilitarian fellowship up to the deepest spiritual love and friendship. Such relationships have each a distinctive quality, they manifest a kind of life of their own, which is not identical

[1] Cf. Chapter IX (a), Vol. II.

with that of the participating persons; in content it is something different and in moral attributes may rise high above
that of the persons. As a power also it can become stronger
than they, it can so outgrow them that the situation lifts the
persons, upon whom it rests, into a higher moral existence,
raising them above themselves. Who has not met this in real
life, can find it in fiction. A highly significant conflict of a
dramatic nature can be played between persons inherently
insignificant. Its value—not the æsthetic but the ethical—is
objective; it exists as much for those who do not participate
in it as for those who do. But the distinctive life of such situations is thoroughly real and takes its course for a period, like
the life of an individual. It has its hour of birth, its growth,
height, decline and dissolution. All the deeper human relationships show something of this mode of existence. They likewise
show the same valuational type, varying, of course, indefinitely.
Every human situation is a piece of ethical existence. In this
fuller sense the totality of situations constitutes the substance
of moral reality.

(d) POWER AS A VALUE

What is everywhere equally striking in the multiplicity of
situations is one's power to guide them, to mould them to
one's own desire. Here the question does not concern the
determining values in this desire, but the power—outward or
inward—to gratify it. In the sense of being able, of controlling,
power is wholly a distinct value; it is desired for its own sake,
not simply as a means to other values, the realization of which
depends upon it. The will to power—which Nietzsche rightly
placed above the will to life—is an impulse *sui generis* in human
life, although certainly not the only one, as Nietzsche would
have it.

And it is an interesting fact that there exists the same kink
in power, as a typical goods-value, as in freedom, foresight and
predetermination. These also are powers, although inward,
personal, and actional. It is a commonplace bit of worldly

wisdom, that a position of great power confuses one's intelligence, and warps the judgment. Power takes hold of a man like a fit of giddiness, it draws him to its own limits, it shows openly a tendency to destroy him morally; to the inner danger of power which lies in the gift of predetermination is here added the outward one due to failing powers of resistance.[1] Man can bear only a certain measure of outward power; beyond that it becomes for him a disvalue, an infliction. This axiological limiting phenomenon accompanies every degree and kind of growth in power, from the easily aroused activity of the physically strong man to the madness of a despot. Powerlessness still remains a disvalue; but the goods-value of outward power is for man as limited as the actional value of inner power (of freedom and efficacy of will)—a further proof of the kinship of goods-values with actional values.

(e) Happiness as a Value

Happiness, the most popular of the goods-values, which so often passes for the value of values, may in any case be classed along with power, to which it is materially related.

A twofold meaning adheres to happiness; objectively it is favourableness of circumstances, of destiny ($\epsilon \dot{v} \tau v \chi \acute{\iota} a$), but subjectively the enjoyment of favour, appreciative participation in it ($\epsilon \dot{v} \delta a \iota \mu o v \acute{\iota} a$). In the first sense happiness is nothing but a situational value; into its domain fall the agreeable, what is wanted, attainment, success, "happy accident." In the second sense it stands nearer to actional values; it is an inner goods-value, but purely neutral, without initiative directed to a goal, or even without intention, that is, without any moral quality. It includes pleasure, satisfaction, joy, blessedness—and between these an extremely varied scale of spiritual states in the manner of participation in values. The highest stages in the scale are near to moral values; and in this circumstance lies the attraction of eudæmonism as a theory of life. In it

[1] Chapter XI (h), Vol. II.

outer and inner happiness exist relatively in independence of each other. The feeling of happiness is not a function of the goods of fortune but of a special capacity for feeling. And upon this fact is based the meaning of ancient eudæmonism, which detaches the inner disposition of the happy from outward fortune.

In another connection we have already spoken of the very peculiar dialectic of the striving for happiness (as the external good), which stands in the way of its own true goal (happiness as an inward good).[1] But this ambiguity does not derogate from the value of happiness; it attacks only the value of striving for happiness. The value of happiness is itself just as independent of the possibility of its being attained by striving, as are the moral values, although the reason as regards the latter be a different one. In this respect it evidently stands a step nearer to the moral values than do other goods.

On another side it is plainly nearer to the basic values which are attached to a subject; happiness as a value is also not without its dangers. It is a commonplace that anyone who is spoiled by happiness becomes shallow. It is as if the proximity and obtrusiveness of many goods drove the higher values out of the field of vision. A man can bear only a limited measure of happiness without sinking morally; even in happiness there lurks a hidden disvalue. Indeed, in no other value is this limiting phenomenon so paradoxical as in happiness. Perfect happiness is the commonest of all valuational ideals. Even a seriously minded man, one who is by no means bent on gaining hedonistic goods, cannot easily rid himself of this ideal. Nevertheless, it is not free from objection; it does not take the nature of the human constitution into account, for our nature cannot without damage suffer the exclusive cultivation of one value. It morally refuses the extreme of happiness as well as other extremes.

This is related to the fact that happiness as a value stands in clear opposition to suffering as a value (notwithstanding

[1] Chapter X (*f*), Vol. I.

the opposition between suffering and activity), to a value, therefore, which for its part has the same kink in it. Precisely what happiness lacks, suffering furnishes, the deepening and tempering of the man, the sharpening of his perception of value. Surely not all happiness can on this account be called superficial; there is a deep and level happiness. But this latter does not exclude suffering and perhaps does not exist without a strain of it. It stands at the boundary of another order of feeling.

But all theories are entirely wrong, which, because of a more or less hazy consciousness of this boundary, would altogether deny to happiness a value of its own. Philosophical attacks upon eudæmonism have often reached such a blind "rigorism." This is a violation of the sense of values, and indeed of the moral sense. Important moral values are based upon the goods-value of happiness. To see this, one needs only to remember what it means to make a man happy; and likewise what it means to destroy anyone's happiness. Here everyone becomes acutely aware of high moral value and of disvalue. Certainly actional values of this kind are different from that of happiness itself; but they are based upon it. If one deprived it of all value, as fanatics of the ethics of duty wish to do, it would be absurd to see moral goodness and selflessness in the loving attempt to make people happy.

(f) More Special Classes of Goods

The values which have been specified are only the most general types which appear in goods. Under them a variegated diversity of situational and mental goods is brought together. Separate ones share in more than one of the general types. The value of existence is indeed common to them all; but not less so is that of the special situation, and again, in another way that of happiness. Only a shade less general is, perhaps, that of power. But ordinarily one of these stands more in the foreground than the others.

Within the fundamental types one can distinguish more special classes. The lowest and most elementary is that of material goods—with their peculiarly exclusive mode of existence for a particular person: possession and property. The latter, strictly understood, as compared with mere outward possession, implies an inalienable right to possession. Wealth and poverty are here the extremes—wrongly interpreted by rigorism (for example, that of the Stoics) as without value.

The steps in communal life, from the family up to the idea of mankind, constitute a wider class of goods.

Allied to these is the class of structural elements in them all: law, well-being, traffic, language, knowledge, education and all mental goods. To this class belong "free association"; likewise what Schleiermacher called self-revelation, the language of the heart, of the feelings, which does not resort to words but expresses itself in spontaneous symbols of mimicry, or rhythm, indeed of the whole bearing, and which has its truth and untruth, as much as the spoken word.

And, again, there is besides a class of goods which rest upon the morally valuable conduct of one's fellow-men—for a goods-value attaches to all good conduct.[1] Of this kind is the good reputation which a man enjoys, honour which is paid to one, trust which is bestowed upon one, friendship or love which is offered. As to the goods-quality of these values we must not be deceived by the name which language uses for the acts and actional values upon which they rest. The disposition of another has its moral value for itself; but for him to whom it is directed it has the value of a good. He is the recipient of it.

(g) The Limit of the Ethical Problem Concerning the Scale of Goods

The interest of ethics in goods is a limited one. It goes only so far as the dependence between them and the moral values

[1] Cf. Chapter XV (c), Vol. I.

reaches. As this involves no dependence of the grades of the two sides, the order of the rank of the goods is almost a matter of indifference for that of the moral values. Only the kind of dependence is at all of importance. The essential thing is therefore to know when the condition is to be found. What we must know is what should count as a good.

Here it may be said comprehensively that in the sphere of things, in relations and in the personal milieu which fill up the life of a man, there is scarcely anything that would be absolutely indifferent to him. Everything has for him its axiological colouring, be it positive or negative. In the enumerated classes of goods only values proper are touched upon. Much in life does not directly fall under them, but under the means related to them, under the dependent goods which are not on their own account striven for, but for the sake of some other value. The general type of means is the "useful."

In this many-sided permeation of human life with shades of value and disvalue, it can be understood that every step a person takes in the common life with others is a distribution of goods among persons, even where they know nothing about it. But this distribution is exactly that, the moral qualities of which are involved in conduct, in willing and in disposition. For whether the distribution is made merely in tendency, or whether in actuality, is a matter of indifference, both as regards the inclusion of the goods and the moral value of the distribution.

It is therefore in the whole extent of concrete diversity that goods-values are the basis of the moral good and bad in man.

Section IV

FUNDAMENTAL MORAL VALUES

MORAL VALUES IN GENERAL

(a) THE CONNECTION BETWEEN MORAL VALUES AND FREEDOM

THE narrower realm of strictly moral values, upon which we now enter, is, as was shown, that of acts and persons. But this characteristic of the carriers does not suffice to define the class precisely. Activity, strength and endurance are also values of acts and therefore of persons; the same is true of freedom, foresight and purposive activity. There are even æsthetic and perhaps many other actional values of persons. But none of these are moral, however closely connected. In fact anyone who understands their value, knows that good and evil have to do with something else.

Just as little does the way in which they are based on other values, as was explained above, suffice for a definition of the nature of moral values. From it one understands that value of intention is different from intended value. But wherein this difference consists remains uncertain. It is not evident why actions and persons through participation in these values do not simply become goods, as it were inner goods of a higher order. If the whole difference between the two classes—excepting difference in the bearers—were that the one stands higher in the scale than the other, it would necessarily follow that the bearers of moral values would be simply goods of a higher order.

Such, however, is not the fact. Or rather, this higher order of goods also exists; persons are goods for one another and just because of their moral quality; to his fellow-citizen the just man is a good of a higher order, likewise the friend to his friend. But to be a good in this way presupposes the morality of the person. It cannot therefore constitute it. The goods-value depends upon the moral value. For the person has the moral value in himself, in his purely inward, secret disposition, independently of whether he becomes a good to anybody. The goods-value on the contrary is necessarily "for somebody." The mere place in the scale of values, then, does not constitute the difference. Rather does the difference of position in the scale rest on some other difference. And this other difference is not one of degree, but is absolute, one of principle, of quality.

What then is the outstanding feature at this dividing line between values? What is the specific mark of ethical qualities in behaviour, will and disposition?

One grasps it most easily through the contrast involved in the case of the corresponding anti-values. Moral badness is not simply a person's mistake or deficiency, but his fault, his transgression, his culpability. It is charged against him, he is subject to censure, condemnation, disdain, abhorrence. A person is held responsible for his moral anti-value, he is regarded as its author, in whose power it lay to conduct himself differently. He is answerable. This is something which can never be said of situations and things which are opposed to value, of misfortunes of any kind. In these matters there is no question of imputation, responsibility or guilt.

Strictly analogous is the relation to the positive opposites, moral goodness is imputed in the same way as moral badness; it wins acknowledgment, approbation, admiration, reverence. He who meets his responsibility receives credit for doing so. No such treatment is apportioned to things and situations that are valuable.

The outstanding point of difference between the two classes concerns the relation of moral values to freedom. Whatever of value and anti-value is brought about by a being who is free, in virtue of his freedom, that is, in so far as he could have done otherwise, can be imputed to him; its value or disvalue is his own. On this fact alone depend responsibility, accountability, guilt and merit. Only a free being is capable of being good or bad.

Speaking in general, the specific mark of moral values is not their height in the scale nor the fact that they are based upon other values, but their connection with freedom. This is the reason for their general superiority to things and situations in the scale of values.

We cannot confine freedom to cases of actual conscious decisions, resolutions and purposes. Moral conduct does not for the most part manifest these forms of activity at all. We know that freedom is playing its part, not by considering whether the person could have acted or willed otherwise, but solely through our valuational judgment, through our sensing of moral values which proclaims unmistakably the responsibility of the person, even down to the most impalpable shades of his behaviour. That which is decisive in the conduct of a person need by no means rest upon a resolution made consciously at the time; it can emanate from his whole moral make-up, from a comparatively permanent basic attitude. What counts, then, is the total disposition itself. To it accordingly adheres the fault, the responsibility or merit.

(b) The Fundamental Moral Values and the Subordinate Groups

In examining moral values the difficulties we encounter are just the opposite of those which beset us in examining the first groups of values. Whilst there the material was relatively easy to describe but the valuational quality was somewhat unfamiliar to our natural feeling, here our sense of values readily bears witness on the whole to moral qualities (naturally, with exceptions); but the materials become harder to comprehend, the higher they are. That is especially the case as regards goodness; everyone knows dimly what kind of value is meant, everyone knows also quite definitely how to distinguish it from other values, but he does not therefore know what it consists in.

In dealing with moral values the procedure is therefore necessarily different. No categorial analysis here points the way. Instead there is the historico-empirical approach to them —in the details of the positive moral codes, in the diversity of

which is mirrored a considerable part of the manifold moral
values. Certainly this procedure is full of gaps—according to
its nature, like everything which arises out of the empirically
contingent—and ignores, moreover, the more general, more
elemental values (those that are fundamentally moral). But the
more it deals with the concrete and special, the more abundant
is the gain. Completeness, however, is out of the question; one
can only try to win the greatest possible range of vision. The
historical connections will be shown in specific instances.

At the base of all moral values lies a fundamental group, in
which the "good" forms the core. To it belong clearly nobility,
richness of experience and purity, and perhaps others which
cannot be determined a priori. What characterizes these values
is that they are common to many very different kinds of
behaviour and in no way characterize one special kind only.
On these general values turns the basic problem of this whole
class of values.

The next three groups—one can with some historic justification call them the groups of the "virtues"—should not be
taken strictly as groups. Their unity is definitely not rigid or
necessary. Thus the first group includes especially the values of
the ancient moral system, the second that of the Christian
sphere of culture, and the last without a further selective
principle brings together the values which were lacking in the
first two, in so far as they have become accessible to our
modern perception. That a connected picture emerges, despite
the sporadic character of the method and arrangement, must be
due to the nature of the realm of values itself, which together
with its separate parts always reveals something of its connected-
ness. But what can here be felt remains, as regards content,
below the threshold of philosophical formulation.

THE GOOD

(a) GOODNESS AS A FUNDAMENTAL MORAL VALUE

THAT goodness is the fundamental moral value is not disputed. The systems of morality which differ most in content are at one in this, that they are all concerned with moral value in itself and as such. Then "good" and "morally valuable" are one and the same.

That there is something correct in this interpretation of goodness, no one would wish to deny. But it is another question, what exactly is gained by it. It might have seemed to be illuminating, so long as we believed in one single "highest" value on which the others are all dependent. But that belief becomes illusory, as soon as it is seen that the notion of a unifying value is ambiguous, that, for instance, it can refer to the most fundamental, the most elementary, as well as to the axiologically highest or even to the richest in material content. It will at the same time be seen how none of these meanings apply to goodness, and how in it there is a unique relation to other values, which is quite different and structurally more complex. But the singleness of meaning vanishes entirely, when one considers the intelligible fact of the plurality of values and the axiological autonomy of the separate materials. The consequence of this fact is that we see that the "unifying value" itself, even if it should exist in one of the possible directions, still remains unknown, possibly irrational, but anyhow beyond the limit of our view of values. The content of goodness, then, is not given in this conception of its nature.

Nevertheless all recognized moral systems speak of the good as of something known. By it they always mean only one certain, special value, which they hold to be the only one and the highest. And according as they regard pleasure, happiness, collective unity, justice, love and so on, to be the good, the various types of morality are distinguished.[1] Even this diversity itself shows that in reality none of these values is the good. But if, like Plato, one sets over against such limitations of content an "Idea of the Good" and places it above the virtues, even then one does not get a definition of its content. The "Idea" remains empty. The Leibnizian concept of perfection comes perhaps a little nearer to the goal. But even it shows only the barest outline of a possible content.

Finally, this conception of the good as the fundamental value draws it too much into line with special conditioning values, for instance, with activity, freedom and purposive action. The correlation of goodness with these is a blunder, not only because the distinctive character of morality is thereby lost, but also because these conditioning values show a reciprocal dependence; they require and presuppose one another, they are involved in a Platonic interlacing. But goodness is unique, it does not permit of being classified in this way. One might sooner expect its constituent factors to exhibit among themselves a similar relation of interlacing. The good might very well contain a whole system of values.

(b) Indefinability and Partial Irrationality of the Good

One must conclude that the good is not definable—neither directly, *per genus et differentiam*, nor indirectly. Strictly speaking, all values are indefinable; one can at most present their material clearly and unambiguously; the special character of a value as such, the specific quality, one must always leave to the living sense of values to find out. But as the sense responds specifically to each specific content, the quality of the value is thereby inseparably fused with the material. In the case of the good even this indirect definition is denied to us; we do not have access to its material.

Nor do we gain any light from the fact that many of the

[1] Cf. Chapter V (a), Vol. II.

simpler elements of value are united in the good and are included as elements in its contents. The good is clearly not exhausted in them. In fact the character of "moral" value remains quite untouched thereby. The good has evidently a something new in it over and above all combinations of its constituent parts, and it is just on this fact that the question turns. But the new is not accessible as regards content. The usual methods all prove too simple in this case. The nature of the good—however obvious its character may appear to the feeling for values—is highly complex as regards material. Therein lies its partial irrationality.

It is important to make this state of affairs quite clear to oneself. Precisely here, in the centre of ethics, all methods fail, as regards content. This confirms what has already been made clear in another connection: we do not yet know what good is. Neither positive morality nor philosophic ethics knows it. We have first to seek it. Moreover, we have yet to find the path which this investigation should take.

(c) THE AMBIGUITIES CONCERNING GOODNESS

To begin with, the meaning of moral goodness can be outlined negatively by limiting it: that is, it is possible to say what the good is not.

One has here to remember that the ambiguities in regard to the "Good" have been at the root of most appalling historical mistakes. The good is not "good for something," not the useful, not a valuational means. The notion that it could be treated as such is the mistake of Utilitarianism. But just as little is it good "for somebody"; it is not a "good" amongst goods, not even the highest or the sum of all. To have taken it for this is the historical error of all Eudæmonistic theories, even of those which are altruistically coloured. Such is the fundamental error of the Stoic ethics. The good, understood as the "highest good," falsifies the meaning of moral value throughout, apart from setting it in the sphere of goods. A "highest good" is something comparative, but moral value is quite evidently no comparative, but is clearly of the positive degree. It is not the enhancement of something, not even to the superlative degree. Instead, it is precisely the something itself which is no doubt capable of enhancement to an ideal extreme. As such the ἄριστον, of which the ancients spoke, is not the moral good at all. The superlative is just what is superfluous. Not the degree, not the intensity or the completeness constitutes the good as such, but the valuational quality itself, the degree or completion of which is in question.

That moral goodness, apart from all this, may nevertheless be the "highest good" is quite possible—it is in the nature of moral values that they are also, incidentally, goods-values. But that is hardly the concern of ethics. For nothing can be deduced therefrom concerning the essential nature of the good as the fundamental moral value.

(d) Axiological Distance of the Good from the Conditioning Values of Action

The gulf thus formed between the good and all the values which have been mentioned so far corresponds to the fact that moral values are connected with freedom, that the phenomena of imputation, responsibility, guilt and merit, are inseparably bound up with moral values. The good is a unique value in a sense different from that in which the personal values inherent in the subject are unique, although most of these also are actional. It is the first value which appears "on the back of an act"; the first which attaches to a disposition of the mind.

The superiority of its grade is greatly underestimated, when —as often happens—we place it on a level with vitality. Even consciousness, action, suffering, strength, freedom and so on, rise above mere life and its sphere. In order of worth this whole unified, ascending series lies between the value of life and the good, and to each one of the series corresponds a group of values. But between the highest member of the series and the good opens yet another hiatus, which breaks the series by a fundamental heterogeneity: those valuational materials make up the personal being in his character, as depicted, which is still not moral. They must all be realized to some extent in an entity, if it is to be capable at all of goodness and badness. In this capability consists the ethical nature of a person. But thereby the person is still neither good nor bad. After complete realization of these values a person still stands on this side of good and bad; the real crisis still confronts him.

Those values therefore can just as well drive him into immorality. Indeed, only a being who is fully grounded in these values is capable of badness, just as only such a being is capable of goodness. Baldly expressed, even the ability to be bad is a high value, which embraces all the preceding ones— and it is exactly the same value as the ability to be good. But hereby it becomes clear that goodness itself is, over and above that, another and completely different value; but badness is yet another danger, equally unlike the lesser anti-values. Exposure to this danger is the natural reverse side of the ability to be good. It belongs to the fundamental nature of moral Being. It is identical with dependence on freedom.

To this axiological gulf corresponds the old metaphysical conception of the good as a primordial power in human life. The dynamic conception of evil has been still more rigorously carried out. The bad too is represented as a metaphysical primordial power; and both powers struggle for mankind, each tries to drive him into its territory. Religious thought has personified these powers: God and the devil contend for the human soul, damnation and grace stand open to him, and both have vast powers of attraction. No doubt the real ethical problem suffers under this form of representation. The two powers confront the moral consciousness, not outside of it but within it, as its own potentialities. But the powers exist. The question where they exist is identical with the question as to the nature of the good.

(e) The Teleology of the Anti-Values and the Idea of Satan

In face of the impossibility of defining the content of goodness directly, there remains open to ethics but one way of achieving a description, and that is by an analysis of the relation of goodness to other values. This is most likely to succeed if we glance back over the series of the prerequisite actional values.

This series culminates in purposive activity. As regards content, the latter holds the whole series together, embraces the lesser values as factors in itself. It shows personal Being at the height of its development. It is a sum of values. Yet purposive activity lacks the most important essential of complete worth which it can have: the goal itself towards which it is directed is still undetermined; the direction of the tendency is not determined by purposive activity itself and cannot arise out of its nature; it is open to and waits for another kind of determination. Teleology is in itself nothing but the categorial form of the tendency. It is therefore—in principle at least—indifferent to the axiological level of its content. Purposive activity is indifferent to the value or anti-value of its own purpose. That is essential for it, as it is for man. Otherwise man as a teleological being could not have freedom, could not be an entity capable of goodness as well as of badness. But then he would not be a moral being, he would be incapable of responsibility and accountability. Capacity to be bad belongs necessarily to the capacity for goodness. An animal cannot be bad.

The same holds true of the other factors which are involved in purposive activity, of action, strength, freedom and foresight. It is to be seen most clearly in the case of freedom. There is no freedom to be good, which would not be at the same time a freedom to be bad. In short, it inheres in the nature of all those acts, which are themselves valuable, that they can be directed equally towards something of value or something contrary to it. The intended values or anti-values are on that account far from constituting the moral worth or worthlessness of these factors. Yet the worth or worthlessness stands in a relation of dependence upon the intended values. Goodness and badness form then a second layer of axiological qualities on the very same actions which presuppose the value of action, freedom, strength, and so on, as already actualized. The latter value is independent of the direction and purpose of the acts; goodness and badness, on the contrary, emerge only with the specific determination of direction. The moral value of the intention depends on the value and disvalue of what is intended.

There arises then the question: is there such a thing as a teleology of badness? Is not man so created that he must always desire something positive, and can never for its own sake desire anything negative, anything contrary to value? This must certainly be admitted. No one does wrong for the sake of the wrong; something positively valuable always hovers before him. This view has not been seriously challenged since Socrates. He who plots injury to another, does not desire the other's harm, but his own advantage; and no one would deny that this is a value. But that does not tell us much. He who destroys another's happiness for his own gain is as much to blame as one would be who willed the unhappiness for its own sake. Not all valuable things are of equal value. And the standard of moral goodness indicates exactly the boundary between worthy and unworthy intentions. But that reveals another side to goodness, with which we shall have to deal. For the moment what matters is only that there should be a pursuit of evil ends at all, irrespective of whether they be absolute or relative, whether they be directed towards anti-values, as such, or only towards the lower values, thus violating far higher ones. But that human teleology can very well be turned towards what is less worthy, even towards what is contrary to value—even if not for its own sake—is beyond question.

Apart, however, from this question concerning mankind, it

must be said that an absolute teleology of anti-values is not in itself an absurdity. If man is not capable of it, that is not because of the nature of teleology but solely because of the nature of man. In this connection, however, the latter is not under discussion but only the nature of teleology. Now this certainly is not confined to values as ends. Its categorial nature is exhausted in the capacity to take unreal circumstances as ends and to actualize them. In this is involved no relation at all to the value or anti-value of these circumstances. This in no way diminishes the value of purposive activity as such. Still it remains true that, had man in his feeling for values no other link with them but this, he would be perfectly capable of an absolute teleology of the bad.

Were this not so, the ancient idea of Satan would be absurd. That is clearly not the case, or it could not have been imagined and have held its place in religious thought. But however thinkable, metaphysically, the personification as such may be, axiologically as regards content it is unthinkable. The idea of Satan is that of a being who pursues anti-values for their own sake. He does the very thing which a man cannot do, he does the bad for the sake of the bad; his nature is axiologically destructive, annihilating. He is the pursuit of evil personified. Should he—as subtle interpreters have often maintained—be himself the dupe and, without willing it, create the good, that would only prove his weakness over against the strength of God, but it would not imply a lack of harmony within his nature. His will would still have the categorial form of the teleology of evil, just the same.

Now the lesson to be learned from the idea of Satan is this: anti-values as such are not bad, but the attitude towards them. This, however, is always at the same time an attitude towards positive values. What constitutes the existence of evil in the world is not that disvalues ideally exist, or even that the anti-values actually emerge in the world, but that some actualizing power in the world is directed towards these things. Such a power can only take the form of purposive activity; indeed it takes this form necessarily even where it exists only in a tendency or disposition. It does so, irrespective of whether the actualizing power, as with Satan, pursues what is "as such" contrary to value, or in a blinded way, as with man, under an illusion of its worth.

Hence it follows that evil is neither the ideal Being of dis-values nor the real existence of what is contrary to value, but only the pursuit of anti-values as ends in the real world.

(f) GOODNESS: THE PURSUIT OF VALUES AS ENDS

And hence it follows further that goodness is neither the ideal Being or concept of values, nor simply their actual existence, but only the pursuit of them as ends in the real world.

Pursuit of values as ends is in itself valuable, and indeed in a sense different from and higher than the mere power of pur-posive action in general. The attitude of a purposive Being to values is the only thing which as such is good or bad. Neither in the intended situation, then, nor in the categorial form of the intention—however valuable this may be—lies the substance of goodness and badness, but in the relation of the latter to the former. And this is why it is impossible to give a satisfactory definition of the content of the good. It would involve, as its presupposition, the whole material diversity of values as well as the categorial diversity of actions.

Now we can see how the conceptual definition would need to shape itself, if thought could embrace this two-fold diversity. The worth of an end is not given with that of purposive activity, it must be added as a new factor. The directional determination of an intention is identical with the content of the purpose. Therefore the value or anti-value of this content is necessarily a new axiological factor, which is superior to purposive activity as such. The more the latter is intensified, that is, the stronger and more compelling the purposive action, the greater the weight of the new factor, the inflowing determination of concrete purpose. For the greater also is the strength to actualize the content of the purpose. If the content is of value, the moral value of the act rises with the increasing value of the purposiveness; but if the goal is not of value, the moral value of the act sinks, as purposiveness rises in value. But that means that the greater the actional potency (valuable in itself), so much the greater is not only its goodness but also its badness. This also can be seen projected on a large scale in the idea of Satan: were Satan impotent, of less teleological drive, he would not be the dreaded lord of this world; just the greatness and strength of his pursuit of his ends convert him into absolute evil. But this strength in itself is anything but evil. It is the same as it would be if in the service of the good. In all striving towards positive values the increase in the basic activity means then an increase in goodness, but in all striving towards negative values an increase in evil.

Here now, if anywhere, we must be able to grasp how utterly different goodness is from all previous values. Purposive action, the highest point of all activity, indicates at the same time the greatest scope for morality and immorality. This is the reverse side of freedom. There is no compulsion to goodness. Possibility of goodness is also, to the same degree, possibility of badness. The greatest power is also the greatest danger. It belongs to the nature of man to stand in this danger. The danger is itself the foundation of his ethos. Through it he is a moral being. To him is given this power, the teleology of tendency, of striving, of committing himself—not absolutely, it is true, but in principle. The gift cuts both ways. It can become a curse to him, as it can a blessing. This is the cryptic meaning of the danger-point in those actional values, which constitute the power of moral being. Man bears his danger in himself, in the creative force which he is. To be suspended thus, with both vistas continually before one, to be menaced from the depths within, and to be a menace to others, through one's own highest and noblest capacity, this is what it is to be a moral creature, to be a man. Dangers outside themselves are also common to other creatures. But it is only man who has his danger in himself, and indeed

at the very heart of his finest inner gift. He must be on guard
against himself, must struggle against himself. The life of a
moral being is a journey along the edge of an abyss. Every
retreat from the abyss is an abandonment of moral being, an
approach to a second abyss. A narrow ridge between the two is
the path for the morally good. He must not sink into evil, but
must retain the capacity for evil. For without it there exists no
capacity for goodness. And on this everything depends.

Goodness is the first value in which such deep inner difficulties are involved. Therein are most strikingly revealed the
uniqueness and the novelty of the whole class of values which
now emerge, and of which goodness is the basis. One describes
it as a kind of dialectic of moral values, that here the modal
antinomies reappear; and not in such a way that the thesis of
one value is the antithesis of another, but always in such a
way that both depend on one and the same value. Thus it is
true of goodness that its necessity (its absolute Ought-to-Be) is
of value equally with the freedom which it permits to mankind,
with the opportunity it allows for badness. In just the same way
there is value in its reality (where it is actualized in an act) as
well as in its non-actualization, for this latter is the opportunity
for badness. This inner antithesis of the valuational factors
is essential to goodness, and equally—although in very different
degrees—to all moral values. It is the inevitable reverse side of
that connection with freedom, which is the hall-mark of the
whole class.

The new element in goodness, if one accepts it as the conversion of values into ends, is then not so simple as it might
appear at first sight. It is that wherein the indifference of
purposive action to the value of its content ceases and gives
place to fixed direction and definite value. Yet that indifference
to value must not be completely surrendered. Else being good
would at once supersede the capacity for goodness, thus blocking
its own path. For with indifference the capacity for badness
would vanish.

It is then quite right, although ambiguous, to describe goodness
and moral values in general as actional values. Activity, strength,
freedom and purposive effort are also actional values. Goodness
is such in another sense. It is not attached to acts (and those
the same acts) as such, but only in so far as they have a definite
quality. And that quality lies in the intended value. Goodness
and, with it, all moral values are values of the intention of the
act, not values of the act itself. But the quality of the intention,
which is the point at issue, depends on its own content, on the
intended value.

Nevertheless goodness does not inhere in the intended values.
These are and remain situational values, and cannot through
any power on earth, not even through being intended, be turned
into anything else. Goodness does not spread from the intention
to the thing intended; but vice versâ, the value of the thing
aimed at only conditions (is the basis of) the goodness. The
thing aimed at is not on this account itself morally good.

The intentional value of a purposive act depends on the
character of its intention. In the expression, "the pursuit of
values as ends," it is not the value of the intention but only
the intended values which are referred to. But exactly on this
account the expression defines, as regards content, value of the
intention. The intention is the material of goodness as it is
of the intentional value of the act. The material of the intended
value, on the other hand, is comparatively irrelevant. Granted
that happiness is in no way the "highest good," yet to destroy
someone's happiness is bad, while to foster and advance it is
morally good. It is only the intentional fostering of it, not the
happiness of the other, which is "good."

Two aspects of this relationship of dependence now become
clear.

In the first place, one sees that there are not two but three
different classes of value involved, which here come together,

merge organically into one another, and form a distinct stratum of values: (1) the intended situational values, (2) the values of the intending acts, as such, and (3) the qualitative value of the intention. The first two condition and are pre-supposed in the last, but they condition it in very different degree. Only the situational value is materially basic, it alone gives to the intention its direction and determines its quality. The value of the act as such has nothing to do with the content and direction of the intention, and therefore does not affect its quality. Its material is only the potency of the act as such, but this is a potency for good and evil equally. Upon the intended situational value alone, then, depends the alternative between goodness and badness. What depends upon the value of the act itself is the height in the scale of goodness or the degree of badness. This does not mean that the alternative between goodness and badness and their respective intensities is conditioned solely by these two factors. To the former must be added the diversity of situational values, and to the latter the differentiation in the special moral values.

Secondly, the greatness of the difference which separates the intended value from the value of the intention is here for the first time made evident. The ambiguities of the term "goodness" have repeatedly succeeded in obscuring this difference. If we say that someone does good, we imply thereby both that (1) what he does is good and that (2) he is good in doing what he does. Language objectifies the goodness of the person, and at the same time renders subjective the goodness of the thing done. It reduces the two classes of value to one level. Moral good is indeed founded upon the situational value, and this relationship finds expression in our formula, the conversion of values into ends. But the value of the moral good is not that of the intended situation nor comparable to it; indeed it does not even stand in any demonstrable relationship to the intended situation in the scale of values. In fact between it and the situational values on which it rests must be inserted the actional potency itself. Only with this does the degree of the moral worth rise and fall—but also correspondingly the obliquity of the moral worthlessness. This is something which the formula "the teleology of values" does not adequately express, but which must nevertheless be understood by it.

(h) THE DEPENDENCE OF GOODNESS UPON THE SCALE OF VALUES IN RESPECT OF MATERIAL

The meaning of goodness, at which we have arrived, now branches out farther. Were there only one value, then in saying that goodness is the pursuit of it we should have said all that was necessary. But since we have to do with a diversity of values which may be aimed at, goodness is also a thing of manifold branches.

In the first place, within each series of values the direction towards disvalue is "evil," while that towards value is "good." But this difference would not at all apply to man, who is not a Satanic being and cannot aim at negative value as such, were it not that the diversity of values and participation in them introduce conflict. The acceptance of one value may involve the rejection of another; the former may be right, the latter wrong. This phenomenon is more striking, where there is a question of material goods. It is in the nature of these to be of value only to those who can enjoy the use of them, others being excluded from a share. Every situation which brings such an acquisition at the same time necessarily involves a corresponding exclusion. If then the possession is a good and the deprivation an evil, the act which aims at possession (whether for oneself or another), and which in so far might be altogether good, may very well at the same time be bad, in so far as it involves the intended exclusion of another. The conflict of interests in society would alone suffice, therefore, to hold open the path of evil to man, and to insure to him the freedom and capacity for both good and evil, although he be a creature who is ever aiming at positive values only.

But this is only a minor matter. The significance of goodness becomes infinitely more serious and varied, if one takes into account the diversity of the values themselves. This diversity, as has been shown, has several dimensions. The groups are differentiated according to universality and particularity, simplicity and complexity, according to strength and weakness of determination, according to the carrier of the value, whether it be an individuality or a collective unit, and so on—not to mention dependence as regards content or the resting of one value upon another. Goodness is indifferent to all these various gradations. On the other hand, it is intimately connected with the difference of rank amongst values.

All the concrete situations of life are such that several values are involved in them at the same time. But the intention of the person who stands in the situation cannot as a rule be directed towards all at once. It is essential to choose one (or a few) and to pass over the others. Now within such a constellation of values, goodness is always the turning towards the higher value, evil a turning towards the lower. Goodness does not require of us the denial of the lower value (for instance, our own advantage or happiness)—that would be a misinterpretation of our feeling for values and would lead to resentment—but it does require the surrender of the lower in favour of a higher (for instance, another's right or welfare). Goodness, as the value of the intention in an act, consists materially in preferring the higher, while evil consists in preferring the lower. It is quite consistent with the nature of goodness to discern and appreciate the lower. The honest man knows the value of another's property, and as such he respects it. And only on this presupposition is his respect for it real honesty. Only then is it a real preference for a higher value.

This case is typical of all ethical situations. There exists absolutely no situation in which value simply stands over against disvalue; there is always value against value. And interest in the lower is not only ethically justifiable—perhaps because it is natural—but it is also morally essential in the choice of the higher. The greater the renunciation involved in choosing the higher and the greater the triumph over "natural" desire or interest, the more completely does the character of moral goodness reveal itself in the choice.

Preference for the axiologically higher to the lower—despite personal interest, and even in face of much stronger interest in the lower—is the second general and positive aspect of goodness. It accompanies the pursuit of values as ends or rather is contained in the pursuit and passes beyond it. If we wanted to express both aspects at once, we could say: Goodness is the conversion of the higher value into an end.

It would be a complete misunderstanding to interpret this analysis as if it were intellectual. Anyone who can conceive of preference only as a logically explicit form of judgment is naturally not in a position to avoid the misunderstanding. The good man does not spend time in weighing and choosing; his feeling for values guides him surely, even in axiologically complicated predicaments. The conflicting values need not appear as such to him; he does not resort primarily to deliberation. None the less his decision for the one value and against the other has the weight of a deliberate preference on principle. How this is possible, is the innermost secret of the feeling for values. But the fact that such decisions exist—perfectly spontaneous and unreflective—shows that the appraisement of values consists not only in a recognition of the content and the nature of its value, but also in a recognition of its status and comparative worth.

Goodness consists then in selecting values, according to their relative height, from among the diversity which is always met with in any given circumstance; a selection therefore which cannot be made *semel vitæ* or purely theoretically, once and for all, but must be made anew each time from the very foundation, out of an ever-living sense of value; there can be no diagram to assist us in this, no help from precepts or rules of life; it is selection not by way of contemplative deliberation, but through the intuitive element in our impulse towards the higher: an element which is always already generated in our actions (dispositions, desires and behaviour) or, on the other hand, is sometimes lacking. The selection of values according to their real worth is inherent in the pursuit itself of values as ends and guides it as regards content. Strictly speaking, it is implied in the very nature of valuational teleology. For the higher value is simply the more valuable, that which is worth more, compared with which the lower is insipid. In pursuing values we must necessarily aim at that which is most purely valuable.

On superficial consideration one might see in this a contradiction of the earlier statement that the worth of the intention is independent of the worth of the intended value on which it rests. This statement of course still holds good. The moral value of love bestowed does not rise or sink with the situational value aimed at in a labour of love. But it turns instantly into moral disvalue, if in a given situation a less valuable service is rendered, instead of one which is fully recognized to be perfectly possible and greater. Such a choice is really a pursuit of the lower value, whether the lower value is bound up with one's own advantage or comfort or any other pressing consideration. The absolute worth of the thing aimed at does not determine the value of the intention, for we cannot at will transfer ourselves into a more agreeable situation in search of greater values; we are always strictly confined to the values which are offered in a given situation. On the other hand, the relative worth of the intended value, from among the situational values actually offered, is vitally important in determining the moral worth of a particular line of conduct arising out of a particular situation. Thus in pursuing the higher value we in no way deny the indifference of moral value to the status of the intended value on which it rests.

But despite the apparent simplicity of the formula, the demand which is implied in the pursuit of the higher is very complex. The whole scale of values is presupposed in it. This scale is the objective order of preference which alone can guide our subjective choice in a concrete situation. And this is the decisive reason why it is impossible to give an unambiguous account of the content of goodness. For that content embraces the whole table of values, including the principle on which they are arranged, but neither the table nor the principle is ever given in its entirety. And for this very reason the content of goodness varies from case to case and must remain undetermined in our conception of it. One can never lay one's finger on it and say with absolute universality: this or this is goodness. It is always this and yet it is also not. But that which is universal and applicable to all cases, that which can really be demonstrated as to the nature of goodness, is not a certain content, but simply the relation of the actional value of the intention to the axiologically graded contents in general.

Here the problem of the gradational order for the first time becomes real. Misplaced philosophical eagerness does not invent it. It is the most real of all problems; man takes no step in life—at least not as a moral being—without becoming cognizant of it. We have already in another connection seen reason to believe that such an ideal and unalterable scale exists. But it does not follow that the scale has been presented in its clarity and totality to our human sense of values. Man can always have but a segment before his eyes; and, since he lacks the perspective of the whole, he may be subject to errors even within the segment. It is to be expected, then, that every gradation of values being discerned and dimly felt, has an element of subjectivity in it and should always be counted as only an approximation to the objective scale itself. The multiplicity of moral codes, and the variety of things which have been considered to be the "highest value," are historical evidence of this fact.

(i) THE GRADATION IN OUR SENSE OF HEIGHT AND THE "ORDER OF THE HEART"

But thus much can be said for certain: the rudiments of an absolute scale of values are contained in all moral feeling for values. It is clear even to a very primitive moral sense, that

honourableness takes precedence of outward advantage, that
doing one's duty goes before pleasure. The same holds good as
a whole of the more obvious gradations in the scale, for instance,
in the general preference for moral worth before goods-values.
In any case, so far as a feeling for the values themselves reaches,
a sense of their relative importance usually accompanies it. The
closer the values are in grade, the less clearly can we discern the
order of their precedence. Thus the inner situation approaches
a conflict of values, which actually exists objectively only where
values of equal rank stand over against each other.

Despite all the deficiency in our awareness of the gradational
order, there are evidences at hand of a sense of valuational
height. In fact, there is an astonishing infallibility, a strength
of conviction in the sense of relative grade, which is enough
to justify the old belief in a "moral organ" (Hemsterhuis), an
"order of the heart" or even a "logic of the heart" (Pascal,
Scheler). It is a unique kind of order, with its own laws, which
cannot be proved intellectually, but which equally scorns every
intellectual argument brought against it. This is well enough
known in the phenomenon of conscience, as in the unerring
imputation of guilt, in the sense of responsibility and in the
consciousness of guilt, but no less in the infallibility of the
prohibitive shrinking from a deed beforehand.

Certainly this sense of grade varies, both in scope and discrimination, exactly as does the sense of each value. There is
also such a thing as blindness to the rank of a value, just as there
is blindness to material things, and there is perhaps even a
perverted or a quite dead valuational sense. But this is no
objection to the certainty and real apriority of the sense of rank,
where and in so far as it is present. Exactly the same is true of
all genuine apriority; its universal validity is independent of
how many people have the insight; and even if only one, or no
one, actually has it, the fact remains that whoever is capable of
it, necessarily has it just as it is in itself and not otherwise.

"Goodness," as the controlling moral "order of the heart"
hidden in man, is not simply the objective order of values, but

is the decisive rôle which this order—so far as it is revealed in the sense of values—plays in the disposition, will and behaviour. The ideal gradation of values is in this respect only the pre-supposition, the metaphysical condition of the possibility of moral goodness. But the "order of the heart," as a real sense of the comparative worth of values and as a power giving direction to the pursuit of them—or, if one prefers, as the hidden system of the laws of preference in the acts themselves —is the narrower and specific basis of moral goodness in man, as well as of the value in the intention of his acts.

(k) Universality in the Ought-to-Be of Goodness

Goodness is distinguished from all actional values which are not intentional, in that a person does not find it in himself, but must first create it out of nothing. This does not mean that he is radically bad; no doctrine of original sin can be based upon it. Man, as the product of conditions, is neither good nor bad, however much disposition, upbringing and milieu may smooth or make difficult the way to moral goodness. He can only become one or the other, in so far as he enters the conflicts of life and makes decisions in their midst. Moral goodness is realized in him only as the value of rightly directed behaviour. In this sense everyone builds entirely his own moral being— for good or bad. The orientation of our whole personal life according to the scale of values is the objective ideal of goodness.

Thus it is that goodness forms a kind of fundamental moral claim, which is made upon everybody. The Ought-to-Be in man is strictly universal. Heroism and moral greatness cannot be demanded for everybody; but it is demanded that, within the limits of their ethos, all men shall be good. Goodness leaves unlimited scope for special moral values, for values which are by no means materially completed in mere goodness. It is only a minimum as regards definite content, but on that account a maximum as regards the extent of its claim. All special moral values (virtues) are good. But over and above that, each one of them is also a something more.

This universality of the claim of goodness characterizes it as essentially a universal value. It is by no means on that account a collective value. The communal and the individual good form rather specializations of value within it, which emerge adequately differentiated in connection with the more special moral value. In content the meaning of goodness over-arches that conflict between the collective unit and the individual. Both have equal weight as regards goodness. But it is different with the universality and individuality of the claim itself. Goodness is a strictly universal claim; that lies in the nature of the basic moral value. Nor is this contradicted by the fact that the content of goodness varies not only from person to person but also from situation to situation. Indeed, as a principle, its content remains indefinite. Together with the supreme universality of its claim, it is capable of the highest and most unlimited individuation. But the individuation belongs no longer to its own material, but to that of the special moral values.

THE NOBLE

(a) THE RELATION OF NOBLE-MINDEDNESS TO GOODNESS, AND OF ITS OPPOSITE TO BADNESS

CAN any fundamental moral value be placed axiologically side by side with goodness, or even in contrast to it? In any case it cannot be of equal generality, else it would have to be included under goodness. But there is no question as to something equally general. Nobility coincides neither in content nor extent with goodness; it is neither an intensification nor a specialization of it, but something specifically new. The word of course expresses its character but feebly; it is only a makeshift, in as much as language does not reflect the delicate shades of valuational distinction.

The opposite of the noble is the common. This latter is far from being identical with badness. It is not reprehensible at all in the same way; it is merely the inferior and as such perhaps contemptible; it is the attitude of mind which turns to the inferior but not to what is in itself bad. Of course in its extreme degree it is also extreme badness, it is meanness. But a mind is noble which is directed towards the high, the ideal, and is detached from everything trivial and secondary (even where one's own interests are concerned). Nobility of character is what language designates as magnanimity, generosity, large-heartedness, high-mindedness, because there is no word for it except such one-sided figurative expressions. Goodness can also be commonplace. There is such a thing as hackneyed virtue, ignoble contentment, narrow-minded virtue and righteousness. Certainly one would be perverting the meaning of goodness, if one tried to characterize it as such a habit of mind. But it cannot be denied that it gives scope for such failings and that the worthlessness of hackneyed virtue is by no means badness.

Conversely, within certain limits, that which is bad can also

be noble. Wrath, hatred, revenge are definitely bad in themselves; disdain and ambition come at least very close to badness.
But who would deny that there is a noble wrath, hatred and
ambition, a noble disdain, indeed even a noble revenge? This is
as certain as the very common fact that there is ignoble revenge,
petty wrath, low hatred and ambition. Here clearly we have a
second and different way of valuing the same act over and above
the first and basic one. It furnishes unmistakable evidence of a
unique valuational antithesis between noble and common, independent of and beyond that between good and bad.

Nobility is not everyone's concern as goodness is. It is
"uncommon"; it is always and necessarily common to few.
As a claim it is not directed to all, at least not immediately
and not in the same way, but only to those who are already in
some way morally outstanding; it separates its chosen ones,
raises them up—not according to human estimation but
according to their own ethical being, their own moral greatness
or strength. For its demand is itself uncommon; more properly
speaking, it is the demand which the uncommon makes. Of
itself it casts off the narrow and petty. Goodness is a strictly
universal value; on that account it can well be common.
Nobility is pre-eminent as a value which distinguishes between
man and man, and indeed even in the ethos itself, in the fundamental disposition. Its opposite is the usual, the ordinary, the
well-worn track, in so far as upon it goodness as well as badness
can be found. By its very nature the noble is not everybody's
concern. It divides men—not indeed according to birth and
social status, but according to their innermost disposition,
according to the ethical claim itself. It divides even the good
into the noble and the not noble. It consists in nothing but
an aristocracy of disposition.

(b) The Relation of Nobility to Vitality as a Value

A radical misunderstanding must here be avoided. The axiological dimension of the noble and the common—in sharp

contrast to that of goodness and badness—belongs by no means to the class of moral values alone. Rather does it characterize the whole realm of values, even the non-ethical. It is best known in the domain of the biological values; but it extends also down into the inorganic realm and upwards into that of mind. One speaks rightly of precious metals and stones, of noble æsthetic line, form or figure. Everywhere the pure cultivation of a certain quality is noble, but impurity, impoverishment of type, the paralysing effect of compromise is ignoble. This is most clear in the sphere of the living organism.

Here the noble is the culmination of the type, the thoroughbred, the genuine. Also in man there is a biological value of nobility; in him also purity of racial type is a special quality, as well of the body as of the mind. As the former does not coincide at all with vitality in general, so the latter is not identical with the moral type. Now it is here that one might see oneself tempted to strike nobility out of the series of ethical values altogether. Scheler, for instance, took this step in his doctrine of the "valuational modalities." With him not only did nobility count exclusively as a vitalistic value, but actually as the fundamental value of the biological sphere. The result is a double confusion.

In the first place this sphere is itself thereby unduly restricted. There are biological values which can in no way be classified as noble. To these belongs well-being—properly a whole region of values—which Scheler explicitly counts amongst the noble. This alone would suffice to wreck his scheme; every undistorted sense of value would far sooner count it as amongst common things; this is a sure sign that the sphere of vital qualities does not resolve itself into the contrast between the noble and common but is of more than one dimension. For there is no doubt that well-being is a genuine life-value.

In the second place, under this biological view other classes of nobleness do not receive adequate recognition, especially the spiritual kinds; quite clearly the æsthetic and ethical. Also in these there are unquestionably a noble and a common, in addition to other qualities which characterize them, such as beauty and ugliness, goodness and badness.

Here only the ethical realm concerns us. How nobility of character, magnanimity, high-mindedness, could resolve themselves into biological qualities of breed is at least not apparent. But if one means to reserve the word "noble" for biological values—which is linguistically arbitrary, since the word is clearly not only capable of moral application but is actually coined out of it—then one must look about for another word, which denotes the analogous tone of value in the moral sphere. The word as such is naturally of no account. But that there is an analogous series of values in the region of morality cannot be brought in question. With this reservation, we may allow the word "noble"—which is certainly rather ambiguous—to be retained, on the understanding that only the morally noble is meant.

(c) The Pursuit of the Uncommon as an End

Nobility shares with goodness the trend towards value, also the dependence upon the gradational order of values—in every way it presupposes goodness. But it brings with it a special attitude of its own in the selecting of values. What is common to all, as a moral claim, counts with it as secondary; it looks out for something else which ought to be, something divergent which in content surpasses the good common to all. It is therefore not the pursuit of values in general, but only of certain ones; nor is it always the pursuit of higher values (within the given situation), therefore not merely the devotion to the discerned and felt scale of values. Instead, it selects afresh from among the given values and does so according to a new and special standard of preference: it aims only at values which are not common at all—which are uncommon not only as regards achievement, but even as regards claim; it aims at uncommon values, of which the very claim does not hold good for all, and which tend to raise a man above the level of common goodness (whatever the height of its actualization).

This tendency does not necessarily gainsay that which is directed towards valuational height. The realm of values has other dimensions besides that of height; it has also a width spreading at right angles to height, in which various and co-ordinated values stand side by side on the same level. In the realm of values every grade is a whole plane; and the manifold, which is grasped by feeling at any time, is always only a section within that plane. As regards every accepted morality, the search for what has not yet been grasped by it, is a thoroughly justified tendency. And selection according to height gives unlimited scope for selection of a different order. But, ultimately, even in the upward direction of height there is something higher than what is grasped by the prevailing view; and to this also the searching glance of nobility is directed. Progress, therefore, in selecting values, even within the range of goodness, is itself a function of the noble. For nobility of character is the pursuit of the uncommon.

The exceptional inheres in the essence of the noble. Of course every recognized body of values has a tendency to draw the ethos of the many after it; therefore, to become universal, even as a moral claim, that is, common. But as soon as it has become general, it is no longer noble but simply common goodness. Then some new body of values becomes the noble. The content of nobility changes, although its direction towards the uncommon remains the same. In the historic process of the displacement of values, the essence of nobility is the perpetual anticipation, the searching and testing, the moving forward which transforms the ethos of an epoch. Its content at any given moment must therefore be the moral claim of the uncommon. Without the noble the process must needs stagnate and —since to stand still is an impossibility—become retrogressive.

On the grand scale, nobility is the onward striving life of the historical ethos; in the individual, it is the spirit of the pioneer.

(d) SELECTION OF VALUES AND SELECTION OF INDIVIDUALS (ARISTOLOGY)

The noble must then be the exclusive; it chooses the special—and in this sense the "aristocratic"—as much in contrast to the mass of people as to the multitude of values which are in vogue at the time. In both these directions it implies selection. It is choice of individuals according to values and at the same time choice of values according to preference—a preferred direction in the realm of values. The two kinds of selection are closely related to each other. Selection of individuals if not according to value is pointless and valueless; it is presumption, vain pre-eminence; but selection of values without selection of individuals means ineffectuality in real life. Genuine superiority involves the heaviest obligation. But even it is utterly impotent if it does not derive efficiency from the co-operation of the few who are of the same mind. At the same time true superiority always exhibits forcefulness. Where that is lacking, it becomes an idle game.

In this connection, too, nobility must be axiologically equated with goodness plus something new. Its trend is not individualistic. Simply because it goes beyond the common standards, it does not aim at the individual as such, but only at the exceptional, the type or the group of those who are aiming at the same value. And even this is not a finality in the noble. It is only its way of actualizing itself, its starting point in ethical reality.

It sets itself against the tendency to flock like sheep and against all mass-production. Differences of level in the individual ethos are essential to nobility. They offer it support. It does not abolish the good any more than the common possession of the good; but from amongst good people it picks out those who from its new point of view are "the best," just as it ranges what is in its sense the "best" (ἄριστον) above what is simply good (ἀγαθόν). The noble thus restores the discrimination which the good discards. In this it is justified, for detachment from ordinary goodness gives pre-eminence to the noble. Herein at the same time nobility becomes dependent upon goodness, it becomes relative to goodness as the basic value. But in all selection of individuals the discriminative point of view of the "ariston" never is the same as that of an "aristocracy"—as usually understood. For it is not interested in rulership (the κρατεῖν of the ἄριστοι), but only in selection and moral Being itself. One might therefore speak of "aristology" in this connection and that only in reference to the guiding values themselves.

In this sense ethical leadership and control follow of their own accord. The higher type of moral claims, and therewith of man himself, stands over against commonplace goodness. Thus the tendency of the noble is first to create the axiologically superior type, the ideal of man. All idealistic education is forward-looking. But it is only capable of efficiency in life, if at the same time it gains a real following—at least in a group of individuals. Without this the ethos of the wider group dies out. It sinks to a lower level, for stagnation is decline.

As regards its content, the higher development of the human type always depends upon the actual tendency (not perhaps the conscious aims) of the noble. It necessarily clashes with the interest of those who are accounted "good," and is always to some extent aloof from the community at large and stands in open opposition to the universality of their standards. An improvement in the standard is made possible by concentration of energy upon a narrower sphere. Hence the necessary remoteness of the selecting group from the general public.

(e) Ethical Ascendency and the Morality of the Group

In nobility man possesses the power of freeing his own development, the unfoldment of his type, from mere accident, from blind necessity, and, by foresight, of prescribing the ends to be pursued; at the same time he possesses the still higher power of working efficiently towards these apprehended goals.

These assertions sound audacious, if one takes them in a
literal and intellectual sense—as though men needed only to
have certain views concerning values, in order, with them as
ideals, to guide the real historic process. This is of course not
true. No sophisticated "superman" can lead mankind to higher
levels, not to mention the extremely limited power, particularly
in such matters, of human foresight and predetermination.
The power of the ethos in man does not take on the form of
deliberate reflection and choice. Still the consciousness which
seeks and turns towards values is the guiding factor even here.
Not a conceiving or understanding, but a clairvoyant discernment, a conscious emotional rapport with the transcendent
powers of the genuine self-subsisting ideal, is the moving
principle. The ascending trend, which has its root here, is
nevertheless on this account a genuinely foreseeing and morally
creative advance in contrast to all naturalistic evolution, which
moves merely towards the biological value of the fittest to
survive. In the natural life-process man goes on quite blindly
according to natural laws; in his adaptation to ends he only seems
to be purposive in his activity. Here, on the other hand, is
purposive activity foreseeingly directed, guided, drawn towards
perceived values; here is a thin and perhaps weak, but not
on that account less significant, thread of historical teleology
within the colossal web of blind necessity—necessity with its
determinant strands, indifferent to ends (and not alone those
of the causal nexus). It is not at all necessary to attribute an
extraordinarily revolutionizing power to this weak element of
genuine predetermination in the spiritual life of an age. Its
power and its moral worth are to be seen not so much in its
results as in its ethically real existence and in the high axiological
quality of such determination as issues from it.

In this we can see, more plainly than in anything previously
said, how nobility of character differs from the sphere of
biological values. The creative powers in it are themselves
fundamentally different, even if they work themselves out in the
same dimension of reality, in the temporal line of the develop-

ment of a type. In fact, these powers clearly fall within the one common reality, forming, as it were, a superstructure upon the powers of the biological process, whereby the tendencies of a higher development, directed towards values, find characteristic scope above the tendencies of the lower development prompted by nature, a scope which the higher determination always finds above the lower.

The moral ascent of man never proceeds historically from the wide-spread multitude and does not actualize itself directly through them, but always at first through a narrow group of pioneers. This pioneering is the path-finding rôle of the noble in the life and creation of the commonwealth. The many are strongly conservative, they hold hard and fast to what they have grasped. The noble does not immediately trail this ballast with him in his advance; he quietly leaves it behind him and hastens forward untrammelled as the champion of the human ethos. Thus arises the isolation of the group, even its antagonism to the community. The isolation is not intentional, it is inevitable.

But in it the moral purpose of the group is as little fulfilled as is the meaning of nobility. In isolation there is no fulfilment; eventually whatever is really achieved contributes anew to the good of the community. The group transforms the multitude into its own likeness, draws it to itself. Drawing after is different from trailing with. Different forces are at work here. In embryo, every spiritual movement is weak, it needs a chance to find itself and must have freedom of movement. But once it is strengthened and matured, it moves the heaviest mass. Herein lies the law of nobility and at the same time its right to segregation and selection.

In the history of the ethos nobility takes the place of the revolutionary tendency. Not out of dissatisfaction is its revolution born, but out of the fulness and progressive readiness for change in the outlook upon values. In nobility lies the tendency to an ever-renewed grasping of values. But this tendency is perpetual, just because the group of the noble is continually drawing the many after it. For that is why all values which are vividly conceived show a tendency to become common. But as soon as a mass of values has become common, it has forthwith ceased to be the substance of the noble. And the noble passes over it to some new contents. The noble is always laying hold upon the untried and uncommon.

(f) The Moral Characteristics of the Noble

In harmony with this incessant reaching forward, which is the fundamental attitude of the noble, is a whole group of further characteristics, which, strictly taken, constitute yet another variety of values and avouch the rich content of this basic value.

The noble man hates all compromise as to values, even those that are wise and beneficent. His salvation lies in another direction, in the exclusive fostering of the value which he thinks should be preferred—even at the expense of all others. It is the same with nobility of a lower order (for example, with biological nobility in regard to race); but it is really true only of moral nobility. All admixture of alien tendencies with regard to values is common, is a deformity, a diminution of personality and of its free action, as it is in the life of the community. To the noble all half-measures are despicable. Singleness and absolute integrity are his taste, even at the risk of one-sidedness, ruthlessness and violation of values. Where his own purpose demands it, he does not shrink from responsibility and blame. The weight of both fall only on his own person, and to him that is of no importance.

Native to the noble is a wide outlook, the grand style in the inner life and work, even under outwardly narrow circumstances. With him response to everything great and for its own sake goes without saying. His aim always rises above all individuals—and not only above himself. In the same way it passes beyond any given community. The noble man is the sworn enemy of all that is narrow and petty. He lives above the commonplace and morally insignificant. He is raised above misjudgments and pretensions. He does not strike back, where he cannot respect his opponent. He wants even his enemy to be of his own kind. But he knows how to honour an opponent of equal calibre and sees himself honoured in him. His bearing and his intensified sensitiveness arise from an inner immunity to everything that is mean.

The free, unbounded devotion to what is great accords with a capacity for genuine enthusiasm, for real absorption in an enterprise, not only an ability to make sacrifices but even a delight in doing so. The joy of devotion is the knightly virtue of the morally strong. And on that again rests the strong man's power over others, the ability to carry them with him, to make them capable of nobility. It is the power of his ethos itself, the kindling example of the pioneer.

The magnanimity of the noble penetrates everything, even what is in itself most trifling. It selects not only ends, but even ways and means. The noble man spurns low means, which do not seem to him justified by the end, but which drag it down and dishonour it. Here again he can make no compromise, he remains true to himself in the selection of means. This is at the same time the drawback in his ethos, his inner handicap, his weakness. He is defenceless against baser forces, which shrink from nothing. Against the peculiar strength of the common he has no armour; he can battle only with his peers, and contend only in great things, not in small. To the common pretensions he is unresponsive; but his very aversion or his noble indignation is a no less effective weapon. He succumbs, where the base fall upon him by stealth. He has more in common with a noble enemy than with an ignoble friend.

Where this ethos arrives at self-consciousness, it becomes noble pride. The noble man must rely on himself; his conception of honour is severe, elevated and wholly inconceivable by commonplace men. Yet he is not absorbed in self-respect and self-esteem, his attention is not turned upon himself. To the noble another's unwavering commitment to what is honourable and worthy is as easy to understand as his own. With him good

taste in personal intercourse is not conventionality but his own
sensitive respect for the nobleness in everyone. He keeps his
distance, is not pushing, but modest in pride. Obtrusiveness
and boastfulness seem to him equally common. Even in sympathy and love he is sensitive in approach, from regard for
the other's individuality. His respect for others is thus a pure,
happy and even joyful recognition. In this way he is capable
of unenvious reverence for the morally superior, of admiration
without jealousy.

He admires only what is above him. From what is below him
he looks away—not intentionally nor out of disdain, but because
his purview is occupied with other things. The noble man lives
in what he can admire. If he wished to drag it down and tread
upon it as the envious do, he would need to drag himself
down.

(g) Discrimination and Co-ordination

There is a whole galaxy of values in the moral disposition
of a noble nature. These all appear "on the back" of his purpose
and by no means are the same as the values he pursues. The
latter vary with the historical changes of the ethos; inevitably
the objects aimed at by the noble are never for long the same,
because they tend to become common. But the finer moral
shades of the intention itself remain the same. They belong to the
forward-looking attitude as such and are independent of their
momentary content.

If one is inclined to protest against our proposition that this
complex of moral values is not to be included under goodness,
since they are in a pre-eminent sense morally good, no objection
can be offered. In a certain sense all moral values remain within
the circumference of the good. This can undoubtedly be asserted
of the noble. But one must not therefore ignore the fact that
here a more special value, more definite in content and at the
same time narrower in its range, emerges. And this requires
special delineation. It is also no mere accident that the content

of nobility is definable in quite other terms than that of goodness. The same of course holds true even of all the other more special moral values. If one tried to ignore this, one would be denying the rich variety of moral values in general.

In the case of all other moral values this is more evident than with the noble. For it is too near to goodness. The new feature, which distinguishes it, looks too much like the original. But the difficulty does not release one from the philosophic task of making the distinction and granting its validity so far as it holds good. To ignore dividing lines is without exception the commonest fault in our treatment of values. Only by means of the sharpest differentiation can one succeed in making ideal contents discernible. The emphasis must be on the distinctions, in order to grasp the diversity. The feeling for values is not lacking in power to reconcile and co-ordinate

RICHNESS OF EXPERIENCE

(a) RELATIONSHIP TO GOODNESS AND NOBILITY. THE WITH-
DRAWAL OF TELEOLOGY

BESIDES goodness itself and nobility, we may count among
moral values richness of experience and purity, which are both
admittedly more specialized and show greater definiteness of
content; but yet they fall short of being virtues in the proper
sense and—like goodness and nobility—are presupposed in the
virtues.

An interesting feature of both is the distinct reappearance in
them of positive valuational contrasts. This of itself shows,
what is otherwise confirmed, that together they constitute a
narrower group of values. But a similar set of opposites links
richness of experience with nobility. To this double antithesis
is due the axiological position of richness of experience between nobility and purity. The relation to goodness, on the
other hand, is essentially the same in all three.

The strength of nobility lies in its concentration upon preferred values. Its weakness is its one-sidedness. The pursuit
of the uncommon cannot include the pursuit of all values. But
this inclusion of all—within the limits of human possibility—
is at the same time a task and also a distinctive value. And there
is a tendency in the human ethos, which makes for this inclusiveness, for all-round breadth and diversity. In its concreteness
it is related to breadth of type, to harmony, to conflict and
complexity, while nobility is allied to elevation of type, to unity
and simplicity.

This tendency, as a basic moral disposition, has fulness of experience as its value. The task, which it imposes, is the unification of diversities and of the antagonisms observable at any given
time. From this point of view, not unity of effort is the highest

concern, but many-sidedness and diversity of interest, all-round participation in values as an ideal, the ethical exploitation of life which understands and embraces everything, and with this also axiological richness of content and development of personality, ethical greatness in the sense of spacious capacity for everything that is in itself valuable, positive breadth of valuational judgment. Its opposite is the disvalue of moral and emotional narrowness, inability to participate in values and appreciate them, the blinding simplification of life, the condemnation and misjudgment of the actual realm of values, inner impoverishment and shrinkage of the ethos.

In so far as every moral attitude—at least in tendency—has to do with the pursuit of values, fulness of life, in comparison with goodness and nobility, has to do not with the pursuit of the higher or the uncommon, but of all values, in so far as they are known. But that is an impossibility. Striving must be towards one goal or it dissipates itself. Hence it happens that in the ethos of inclusiveness pursuit as a factor falls into the background. Its place is taken by an inward attitude of many-sided openness, of participation and appreciation. Of course one may speak here also of a purely inward teleology of commitment, of interest, of participation even. And in fact this would necessarily be inseparable from many-sidedness. But the actuality of this tendency wanes with increasing breadth of content.

In the same sense one may say that here also the importance of the order of rank fades. Even the lower values come into their own in the ethos of inclusiveness. The valuational fulness of the real, like that of the ideal realm, extends in every direction. Here the domination by the order of rank and by the higher values finds its counterpoise.

(b) THE SYNTHESIS OF VALUES IN THE ETHOS OF MANY-SIDEDNESS

Inclusiveness is a general axiological synthesis of human life. The high degree of the interweaving of factors constitutes the new element in it. Of course the extent of the diversities must not destroy the unity. But the unity itself is synthetic, something constructed, an organic combination. With the extent of the contents the unit must expand. The objective fulness itself—and every experience adds something—imposes upon the person an ever-new task of synthesis.

In this objective sense we may express the principle of the fulness of life as the greatest unity of the greatest diversity. In other fields also this principle holds good, for example, in the æsthetic realm. But in our field it is a principle of the ethical attitude of the individual and of the concrete organization of life. The rudiments of values are everywhere; each one makes a demand on the individual and at the same time imposes obligations upon his understanding, his power of initiative and executive ability. Every experience is full of values; but not everyone is in a position to appreciate what he is privileged to experience. One's ethos must have fed upon the fruit which has fallen into one's lap. Ordinarily men refuse life's fulness, they ignore the riches in themselves and the world. Yet to the moral nature belongs the synthetic unity of the ethos itself as a fundamental condition of its existence.

Man is never morally completed. With his moral growth he constructs himself; even without intending it, he makes himself the object of actualization. He achieves his own synthesis in his preoccupation with the manifold values of life, by increase of understanding and participation. In evaluating the world—and the more objective the process is, so much the better—he succeeds in transforming his own unique, irrevocable life into a general harmony, a real symphony of values.

What applies to the individual person, applies *mutatis mutandis* to all ethical Being. The relationships among men permit of the same valuational synthesis. Every situation manifests germs of values, each one of which can be appraised after its own kind; neglected it can become stunted. Even in this connection man is, in part, responsible creator of existence, into whose hand all riches are given; he is, in part, fashioner of the ethical reality in which he lives. And it is the same with the synthesis of ethical ideals. Even here, in his prospective vision, the abundant diversity is of value. The ideals of morally narrow and poverty-stricken men are themselves narrow and poverty-stricken ideals. And finally it is not otherwise in the building up of the community; here also reappear the diversity and the demand for a valuational synthesis. The only difference is that here the synthesis is made above and beyond the ethos of the individual. Here man sees himself to be a building-stone in a larger structure.

(c) BREADTH OF MIND AND ITS RELATION TO BADNESS

The ethos of many-sidedness presupposes mental breadth, space for everything. This is of especial significance in respect to moral conflict. Conflict widens as well as deepens a man. Precisely in it and while standing in the midst of it a man becomes conscious of life's richness of content. From this point of view conflict is seen to be pre-eminently positive and valuable. To shrink from conflict, to avoid it, is moral shortsightedness. There must be room even for tragic conflict, from which there is no escape without guilt. Especially in it the ethos is widened. Whoever is incapable of conflict is incapable of tragedy. He is morally blighted who in life's earnest conflict is cursed with the sense of the comic; he bears the stamp of the tragi-comedian.

From this it becomes clear that in one point fulness of life is the exact opposite of nobleness: it is not exclusive, and not only does not bar out lower values but also within certain limits not even what is directly opposed to value. From the point of view of inclusiveness there adheres in fact a value to every content of the moral life, even to strife, suffering, misfortune, fruitless striving, cares and yearnings, to yielding as well as to overcoming, indeed to failure, deficiency, wrong-doing and the burden of guilt. Here there is no question as to the value of suffering or of freedom (which are also deeply involved); but rather is there still another pure concrete value in all this— we might call it width of experience or richness of the moral

life. For the morally narrow man everything ultimately becomes
worthless, even what is in itself of value. For the open-hearted
man, on the contrary, everything is valuable, even what in itself
is contrary thereto. There is certainly no other way to ethical
maturity and expansion than through the conflicts of life itself,
through "moral experience"—even experience of wrong-doing,
and this perhaps most of all. Here is the absolute limit of the
principle that virtue can be taught. No one can hand over to
another his moral experience with its inner meaning which he
has lived through and suffered. All the lessons which can be
drawn from it and told to another are empty, unless one has
had the experience itself; and the lessons sound like moralizing.
The living and intertwined situations, with their mass of
ethical conflicts, are the only thing which really discipline
morally, open, train and widen the valuational vision and thus
disclose the fulness of life. In this way it is of value to have
gone through, to have been overcome, and to have failed.

Although so familiar a fact, this is certainly a paradox and
is not without its danger-point. But it is true. Here is certainly
manifested a deeper valuational conflict with the good; it is a
genuine, indisputable antinomy. The pursuit of a higher value
has its limit in the intrinsic value of the lower. Not as if the
pursuit of ends were here directed to the lower as such; in the
ethos of inclusiveness the pursuit of ends has entered upon the
second stage. And precisely where there is no striving but yet a
gaining by participation, the differently organized relationship
to values in general reveals to a certain degree an intrinsic
worth in what teleologically is the contrary of value. And this
relationship is not to be understood as if the evil needed first
to justify itself for the sake of variety of experience; rather does
it become justified through the value of inclusiveness, at least
in so far as in contents it is a part of life's fulness and is not
simply negative and disruptive. It is not as though the bad
became good. It is a quite differently dimensioned quality,
which is here superimposed upon goodness and badness. Just
this is the new feature here, and we learn from fulness of life

that, precisely in the higher moral sphere, there exists a point of view from which everything that is ethically actual has ultimately a side that is of value. Ethics needs no metaphysical theodicy. In itself—in fully diversified unity as a value—ethics has an anthropodicy, the axiological justification of man in his imperfection.

The passion of this value is that of an all-sided optimism. Only we must be on our guard against interpreting this optimism eudæmonistically. On principle it is beyond happiness and unhappiness.

Ethical actuality is richer than all human phantasy, than dream and fiction. To live apathetically from moment to moment amid the abundance, is nothing short of sin. The narrowness of a man's participating sense of value makes him poor. It is because of his prejudice, his blindness, that he does not see the abundance, in the midst of which he stands. The ethos of openness to all values is the tendency to do inward justice to life, to win from it its greatness. Its passion springs from reverence for the unbounded abundance of the things that are of worth, it is knowledge filled with gratitude; and, where knowledge fails, it is the presentiment that the values of existence are inexhaustible. Whoever lives in this attitude, by him every restriction of experience is recognized as superficiality, dullness, barrenness, a waste of life and, when it degenerates into a pose, as an unworthy renunciation, a petty pessimism, a moral ingratitude.

PURITY

(a) CONTRAST TO GOODNESS AND MANY-SIDEDNESS

As a value, purity is more akin to goodness than many-sidedness is. One has often been inclined, especially when morality has been dominated by religious sentiments, to see in purity the whole meaning of moral goodness. But that is going too far. Unquestionably purity is also "good," just as its opposite, sin, pollution, defilement ($\mu\acute{\iota}\alpha\sigma\mu\alpha$), is bad. But it is not only much more restricted, it is also qualitatively different. The meaning of goodness is entirely positive, that of purity—as the word itself implies—is negative as regards the intended content; it means untainted by evil. Here the pursuit of values, even of the higher ones, is confronted by the non-pursuit of disvalues, especially of those that are lower and elemental. He is pure whom no desire leads astray, no temptation allures. His ethos consists of an inner tendency turned away from disvalues altogether and as such.

But the contrast of purity to many-sidedness is much more striking than its contrast to goodness, with which it is in harmony. Between it and many-sidedness there exists a distinct antinomy. The ethos of the latter opens itself to everything and esteems of positive worth even what is contrary to value. But purity bars out everything which is in conflict with any value. It is isolation as regards evil, untaintedness and immunity. A lack of moral experience is here of value. Experience, in proportion as it is rich in content, must have already come into contact with everything; and something of everything must have adhered to the person. The man of experience has passed through conflicts; his eyes have been opened—yet at the price of innocence. From the point of view of purity, however, guilt is the greatest of evils, innocence the highest good. For there is no question of innocence as conquest over guilt, but only as the original state before any guilt, the state of not having been tempted, the virtue of the child, which has no merit in it and yet is a moral quality of the highest worth.

Ignorance, simplicity, childishness, have here a positive worth. They constitute *sancta simplicitas*. The morally complex character is uncertain; it is caught in the struggle for life, it does not easily walk in the straight path. To purity belongs the moral phenomenon of ingenuousness, steadiness and immediate perception of the right way—a sort of moral instinct whereby one turns away from evil without any proper knowledge of good and evil. This phenomenon is often met with among the morally unripe, or among those who are just at the threshold of maturity, in so far as they are unspoilt and unperverted. It reveals a fulness of fine, even the finest, shades of value, which the understanding cannot grasp but can only have an intimation of. It would mar them to bring them under fixed concepts. Our capacity to appraise values here shows itself to be infinitely more discriminating than the rude logic of thought. The simplicity, straightforwardness, guilelessness of the pure possess, for the man standing in the midst of his diversified experiences and burdened by them, something convincing, irresistible and redemptive. Although he is aware of the spiritual poverty of the pure, still in the midst of his riches he longs for it.

(b) CHRISTIANITY AND ANTIQUITY. PURITY AS A BASIC VALUE

Purity of heart is the primal Christian virtue. With it mental riches pass as an evil. Blessed are they who are poor in spirit. Blessedness is the ethos of the child. Of such is the kingdom of heaven; to be such is the yearning of the sinner.

Surely such an ethics of conversion is radically one-sided— without raising the question whether for any man a return to innocence be possible. Yet the basic value is correctly estimated. With this estimate Christian ethics opened up new roads, with this more than with its commandment in regard to loving one's neighbour. Not only did ancient ethics not know the value of purity in this sense, but by the greatest representatives of philosophy it was consciously set aside. Aristotle denied to the child capacity for happiness; yet in happiness he saw moral fulfilment, the τελείωσις of goodness, a synthesis of the virtues. Insight lies in this: only he who is set in the midst of moral conflict can show virtue or its opposite. Now if virtue consists in ἐνέργεια alone, this is indisputable. But if there be an ethos in an attitude of mind which is anterior to all conflict and in contrast to all energy, then the peculiar value of such an attitude is overlooked in the ancient ethics.[1]

Like goodness and nobleness, purity also is the basis of a series of well-known moral values. In the same direction lie sincerity, frankness, openness. These are natural to one who is morally unspoiled in sensitiveness. One who is pure has nothing to conceal; to him concealment, secretiveness, is alien. He willingly lets others know; the shame of the guilty is lacking in him. He needs no covering, no mask; his nudity is not nakedness.

The same is true of his directness in conduct. He takes hold of an enterprise without reflection, he makes straight for the matter in hand. He lacks both the occasion and the worldly wisdom for subterfuge. He does not need to mislead others. But it is not his fault that to the man of the world he is in his ultimate nature unaccountable and incomprehensible and is in fact misleading; it is due to the worldly man's incapacity to be straightforward and clear-sighted. Whoever attributes ingenuousness to no one, must, when he really meets with it, inevitably mistake it for something else; his own calculating and intricate nature prevents him from understanding simplicity. But the pure can understand the pure, without any difficulty.

[1] Cf. Aristotle, *Eth. Nic.*, 1100a, p. 1 ff.

(c) Purity as a Moral Power

To the pure-minded man distrust is as alien as is every crooked
way. He believes in the good in man, he trusts in the right and
in the good cause, he is optimistic in a childlike way. He holds
fast this faith against all appearances and especially where he
does not understand motives and tendencies. He cannot comprehend the gnawing ethical pessimism which imputes evil to
everyone. He does not avert his glance from known evil—for
the valuational judgment of the pure mind is clear; but, as his
own conscience is easy and free, is without compromise and
without self-torture, and as his own capacity for happiness and
his right to it rest on this, he attributes the same to others. And,
despite all its naïveté, his trustfulness is a power, the greatness
of which he is unaware of, in proportion as he really possesses it.

As the impure mind has an evil influence and infects with
evil, so the pure mind has an influence for good. In this respect
pure-mindedness, despite its originally negative character,
shows itself to be an eminently positive and creative energy in
life. Nothing perhaps works so powerfully, so convincingly, for
good, and so transforms others in their innermost character,
as the mere presence of a pure-minded person who pursues
the right undisturbed, just as he sees and understands it in his
simplicity. Precisely in his obliviousness to evil, in his failure to
understand it and to react to it, he becomes a symbol and
attracts the fallen and the morally prostrate. In this—and by no
means in the very doubtful superiority of the mature man—lies
the charm of association with a child, the assuaging and
liberating effect of childhood upon the experienced and worldly-
wise man—the education of the grown-up person through the
child.

This power is the secret of purity, its veritable mystery.
Innocence does not resist evil, simply because it does not see
it, or, seeing, does not understand and believe. Outwardly it is
defenceless. And yet it is clad in a coat of mail and is equipped
as no other type of ethos is. Its failure to defend itself is not a

weakness. It is the guilty man who is powerless against it. He never feels his weakness more acutely than when he encounters the glance of the pure-minded who does not see the evil in him and, even in seeing, cannot believe it. In that the pure-minded man reacts to him, as if he himself were pure, the guilty sees himself denied in his innermost being, sees himself judged, cast out—as no conscious judgment could censure and condemn.

By its nature evil shuns the light. It shrinks from the glance of the pure, hides from it, keeps away from it. It cannot tolerate the transparency of the innocent. The ethos of the pure draws a charmed circle about itself, which extends into the busy human world beyond; and whoever with only a faint spark of moral perception enters into the circle, falls under its spell. The existence of the pure in heart is the power of goodness, moving about unconsciously but palpably; it is the power of goodness become flesh; in it the otherwise merely ideal power of the realm of values possesses reality, although it is not of this world and although it is felt by those who experience it in themselves to be not of this world. This is no metaphor, nor is it a poetical exaggeration. It may be true that many are not acquainted with this phenomenon. That proves nothing against it, it still remains a real phenomenon. Whoever is acquainted with it is held by it from within. On a great scale it may of course be rare enough; but in a small way it is met at every step by anyone who has not become quite insensitive to it. The great example is pictured over-poweringly by the Gospels in the figure of Jesus—and indeed not in its divinity, but precisely in its humanity. At the sight of Jesus, by his mere word, shrewd calculation and subtlety are silenced. Here certainly the spiritual superiority of the person supplements the Idea itself; but behind it is still something else which gives support to it, the moral pre-eminence of purity of heart. And not solitary in the grey past does the one great example stand as a legend; ever again arise great representatives of this ethos, filled with its spirit. In a modern setting one finds it in many of Dostoiewski's characters,[1] most convincingly in

[1] Alexei Karamasow is also a beautiful example of this.

his book *The Idiot*. Palpable as an atmosphere is the precinct of purity; no one can withdraw himself from it; but the power which it exercises does not lie in the word or deed of the one who is pure but entirely in his mere moral existence. He who is pure does not actualize; his ethos is not a pursuit of ends. He is only himself a monition, a wandering conscience for the impure mind; this he is, without on his part judging or condemning. For when baser passions, hate, envy, injured dignity, resentment, encounter purity, it is always as if there came from out its inmost nature those words before which all condemnation is silenced: He who is without sin, let him cast the first stone.

Perfect purity borders on holiness. Although holiness is not an ethical value and is not adapted to human measurement, it has always been revered as such in the great types of purity. Aloofness, "existence for itself," comes into the foreground here. Hence the gleam of other-worldliness in this ideal.

(d) The Forms in which Purity Appears

The ethos of purity extends throughout all the grades of human conduct as well as over all kinds of acts. And everywhere it has its own special impress. As purity of deed, it is the perfectly straightforward way of acting, the absence of all cunning and of all concealment of one's true aim behind plausible aims. As purity of word, it is the frankness which admits of no double meaning, ambiguity, veiling or offensiveness. Deeper still is purity of thought, the simple presentation of fact, unpremeditated objectivity, absence of masked motives and ulterior purposes.

But at the centre of all this stands purity of disposition— single-mindedness in love and hate, in admiration and contempt, in good-will and anger. In this sense that attitude which is not transparent is impure, is involved and complicated with cross-currents in the treatment of other persons—such as envious admiration, jealous or suspicious love, suppressed or impotent rage and, above all, the dark corrupting dregs of resentment. To purity in this sense belongs the recoil from all secret, unavowed cravings which lurk in the background of one's own nature, as well as revulsion against suppressed complexes, such as false shame in love or admiration, which is moral cowardice in disguise. The pure-minded man confesses freely his own real feelings, not only to himself but also, when occasion arises, to others. He does not stop to reflect how his attitude may be regarded by others or what sort of a light it may throw upon himself. He does not assume a pose foreign to his own true state of mind. This on the contrary forces its way through and fills his whole nature. His inward attitude harmonizes with his outward, his unconscious with his conscious.

In the same way we may speak of purity of will; it is whole-hearted and unbounded surrender to the end in view. As regards the pure-minded man, we all feel certain that his real nature is expressed in his pursuits. Whoever has a sense for such things, may always rely upon it. Hence the pure-minded man is the one who is perfectly trustworthy, even without having the special intention of justifying the trust bestowed.

The same characteristic reappears on the lower level of impulsive and instinctive life. The pure man is not the one who has no desires, but the one in whom they preserve their unperverted nature and beauty. To him both suppression and misuse are equally impure. Sensitiveness, chastity, modesty, constitute purity in the sphere of the senses. To the innocent man they are as natural as the sensuous impulse itself; with their loss his natural purity is corrupted.

(e) PURITY IRRECOVERABLE WHEN LOST

A peculiarity of purity and of all the more specialized shades of value which are related to it, is that it can neither be striven for nor actualized. One may yearn for it, may waste away in desire of it; but one can neither make it the goal and content of one's pursuit, nor actualize it in one's own nature quite apart from any direct aim. The latter is the usual way in which all moral values become actual, but the former is at least in general possible.[1]

The reason for this is not to be found in the nature of striving and of actualization, but in the nature of purity itself. It is a constitutional peculiarity of its material. This is fundamentally negative, an absence, an aloofness from something, an insulation, a state of being untouched, which once being violated cannot be restored. Only something positive can be actualized. But in purity the only positive element is the valuational quality, not the material. Furthermore, the accompanying phenomena are also positive; for example, the influence for good. But the essence proper, the attitude of the intention towards the dis-values, continues to be negative. Hence purity stands alone among the moral values; it is radically different from every one which may be otherwise related to it: it is either fulfilled in person or it is for ever unattainable. Hence of it may further be said: one may indeed lose it when one has it, but not gain it if one has it not. It is a primal state of the ethos before conflict has set in, before real "life" has begun, before experience and guilt. It falls into the lap of the young; but, once it has been forfeited, the mature man longs in vain to have it back. He can still rescue only what has not been forfeited. The purity that is lost is irretrievable—just as guilt is unescapable, just as the deed that is done cannot be undone.

Purity is no merit in one who has it; it was not acquired, it was given. But so much the more is the loss of it a moral fault. Although it is not possible to acquire it, yet to preserve it is altogether possible. Also purity as a value is thus related to freedom, not otherwise than are all the other moral values. Indeed there lies something like a positive task in the Ought-to-Be of purity. And in this way it can very well be aimed at. The impulse towards its preservation is the strictly moral element in the ethos of the pure. In it consists the inner watch and ward against evil. At this point we begin to see that the ethos of purity is not limited to an ideal primal state of child-

[1] Cf. Chapter II (d), (e), Vol. II.

likeness before all conflict and responsibility, that man can much rather retain something of it far into the depths of his life. He does not lose innocence with one fell stroke. It is precisely the beginning of guilt which permits him to feel what kind of a value is at stake. And the deeper he sinks and the more he loses of his purity, so much the stronger can the positive ethos of preserving it become in him. For so much the better can he measure the value of the purity which he has forfeited and also the purity that is still enjoyed.

If there existed only absolute purity and absolute impurity, it might be said that the value of purity bars out its own existence-for-itself, that is, the consciousness of itself. Whoever would have the maturity and experience to appreciate it, must already have lost it; but whoever still possessed it, would be unable to appreciate it. For the extremes this holds good. But the extremes are not given in the moral life and are not actual. The human ethos moves through the long scale of intermediate stages. And there the law of relativity holds good: the deeper the consciousness of guilt, the higher the estimate set upon purity. This means: the less a man possesses of a value, the more he may have a feeling for its worth.[1]

(f) THE INNER DIALECTIC OF PURITY AND MANY-SIDEDNESS

We have already spoken of the antinomic relation of purity and many-sidedness. They exclude each other. But the peculiarity which distinguishes this relation from other pairs of opposites is this: the ethos of many-sidedness requires the value of purity, and the ethos of purity requires the value of many-sidedness. Each is incomplete without the other. One

[1] More than this "may" must not be asserted. We cannot say that the sense of the value of purity "necessarily" increases in proportion to the impurity. Here other, value-obscuring factors set in, which work in the opposite direction. With impurity, moral obtuseness also increases. It naturally first obscures that value which it assails. In this case it is the value of purity. Hence after a certain grade of impurity the relation is reversed.

might even say that after a certain degree there arises in each kind of ethos the diametrically opposite tendency, that is, they exchange intentions.

This fact is well known. In the person who is replete with experience, there is a yearning to return to the purity which he has lost, the yearning of the morally mature, indeed of the person who has grown up, for the original state of child-like innocence, simplicity and guilelessness. Similarly the one who has remained pure yearns for the fulness of experience which he has missed, just as the child longs for the rich humanity of his elders—a yearning which makes straight for the darkly foreboded earnestness of conflicts, of responsibility, even of tragedy. The difference between these two yearnings is apparent: that of the pure moves toward its own fulfilment, although the fulfilment will not be what was anticipated; while the yearning of the other for purity remains necessarily unfulfilled, it is inevitably an eternal yearning. And both kinds are rooted in the essence of their respective values, each is the inner destiny of its own ethos. But the process of change which is irreversible moves only in the one direction, from purity to fulness of experience. The child does not escape the seriousness and manifoldness of life, but the matured mind longs for ever in vain for the lost innocence. The child's yearning passes over into striving and actualization; that of the other cannot. The value of purity can neither be striven for nor actualized.

In this antinomy one may speak of a positive connection between the opposites, a dialectic in the values themselves. The synthesis of the two in a single character remains of course for ever imperfect; the reciprocal exclusion of the two permits of nothing else. But the real stages in the transformation of character may very well be approximately described as a synthesis. And the more strongly the ethos of purity stands fast as a bulwark, while experience becomes many-sided, so much the more is the synthetic unification of the two values achieved in the one character. But the limit to the synthesis is due to the essence of the values themselves, it can never be

annulled. And perhaps in nothing do moral types differ so
fundamentally as in the preponderance of the one or the other
ethos.

(g) PURITY AND FREEDOM, BELIEF AND CHARACTER

It is natural that the human spirit should not be satisfied with
this dialectic, which is decisively unfavourable to purity, that
it should look about for help from another quarter and for
another kind of enrichment of life. The higher a man's estimate
of the value of purity, so much the more does he struggle
against his irretrievable loss, and so much the stronger becomes
his "metaphysical need" of restoration to innocence. For ages
past religious thought has met this need, just at the point where
the value of purity as such is drawn into the centre of moral
consciousness. The ancient concept of "purification" ($\kappa \acute{a} \theta \alpha \rho \sigma \iota s$)
as the superstitious "wiping away of guilt" is here joined with
the thought of forgiveness and salvation through the suffering
and sacrifice of the divinity intervening for man. Purity returns
as a gift of grace. The condition which man must fulfil is
simply belief. The mystery of the new birth resolves the antinomy of the values.

The fact that the mystery itself conjures up indeed another
and more serious antinomy—that between purity and freedom
—would inevitably have dawned some time or other to its full
extent upon the religious consciousness. In considering freedom
as a value we have already met with this conflict in its more
general form. It unavoidably develops into a comprehensive
antinomy between ethics and religion. But it is not for ethics
to resolve the antinomy; ethics says nothing of a work of salvation. The burden of clearing up the difficulty falls solely to
the lot of religious thought. For ethics, on the other hand,
which takes its stand on this side of metaphysical needs, the
law of purity retains its power, the law which inheres in the
essence of the matter: that purity, once lost, can never be
restored.

Were purity the one moral value, or even only the central one, that would mean for ethics a radical pessimism. But purity is neither the one nor the other. It is only one of the two members in a perfectly poised opposition of values. And above this contrast a basic value is to be sought solely in the positive pursuit of the higher as conditioning the lower, solely in the pursuit of the "good." But this basic value leaves open to actualization and the steadfast will the whole manifoldness of the special moral values, even up to the highest.

To dispute over the impossible is folly. Actual life, however, is full to the brim of that which can be striven for and attained.

Section V

SPECIAL MORAL VALUES

(FIRST GROUP)

CHAPTER XVIII (XLIII)

THE VIRTUES IN GENERAL

WHAT was true of the basic moral values, is true also of the more special ones, the virtues. They are the values of human conduct itself; and as conduct extends over very different kinds of situation, they necessarily show a rich variety, differentiated according to their material.

What is common to them all is the valuational mark of virtue as such, as the good connected with certain relations. Among them the proposition holds necessarily, that moral values are based upon situational values, that is, that they attach to the intention which is directed to valuable situations, and that their specific character as compared with the latter is neverthe-less independent of the connection. As regards method, this point is of importance here; for the virtues are distinguished in content according to the situational value. Ever since Aristotle, who approached the single virtues everywhere with the question concerning the περὶ τί ("with what the conduct is connected"), the attempt has been made to distinguish them in this circuitous way. For every virtue has a different situational value in view. This is the traditional method of procedure.

Of course there is a certain danger here, namely, that in considering the situation one might lose sight of the virtue. When one is new to this kind of analysis, one continually forgets that the conditioned value is at best but indirectly indicated by the value which conditions it but is in no way determined in valuational quality by the latter. In fact, even the conditioning relation itself does not permit of being brought into a definite scheme; it varies with the variety of content itself. And the specific characteristic can be here disclosed, as everywhere else, only by the living sense of values, or by its way of expressing itself, the response and the predicate. The conditioning relation can offer here only an access, an approach of the valuational sense itself to its object, the moral value.

To give a complete diagram of the virtues would mean to exhaust the realm of moral values. That is a task which cannot be carried out. There is no question of doing so. We can only pick out what the consciousness of the age has elaborated and has to a certain extent made palpable. But we must entirely leave out of consideration what has been understood by the "doctrine of virtue"; to such a doctrine belongs not only a description of the virtues, but even instruction as to their actualization. Instruction of this kind has at all times missed its aim and inevitably, for no one becomes good through instruction. Such instruction everyone of morally fine discrimination has always dismissed, not only as arrogance but as a trifling with what is highest and most serious, as that which has degraded even the words "moral" and "virtue" into something tiresome and half ridiculous. Ethics has no occasion to "moralize." Everyone can provide himself with a "doctrine of virtue." But the moral values themselves permit of being simply pointed out within the limits of the current valuational vision, without reference to their practical tendencies.

An historical survey shows that several specific groups of virtues can be distinguished, but that between them the intermediate members are evidently still lacking. We must seize upon the values, where and how we can, at the risk of losing their unity in their variety and of making mistakes as to their gradational order. Thus in the following presentation three groups are to be discriminated. For the first two a basic value can be assigned (justice and brotherly love), about which the others cluster. The first corresponds nearest to the ethos of antiquity, the second to that of Christianity. But both are undoubtedly much richer in content than would appear from a limited numerical survey. Here there is no question as to completeness, but as to the quality of the manifold values, as to the contrasting character of the groups, the valuational relations produced, the conflicts between values, and so on. Besides all this the gradational order remains as an important desideratum. But this is difficult to trace, at least in the present state of research.

The following analyses do not go beyond the task outlined above. The seriousness and positive nature of the moral problems concerning value permit of nothing else. Every overstepping of this boundary—and the older doctrines of virtue have always overstepped it—must degenerate into the ambiguity of "moralizing." For us the only question is concerning the valuational quality of the single virtue itself, so far as it can be seen and defined. The greater the variety which can here be surveyed, the closer shall we approach to the general character of the realm of values.

CHAPTER XIX (XLIV)

JUSTICE

(a) LAW, EQUALITY AND PERSONAL JUSTICE

THE Platonic system of virtues culminated in justice (δικαιοσύνη). It was to be a sort of crown to self-control, courage and wisdom. This was in harmony with Plato's fundamental interest in the value of the community. In itself this arrangement does not inhere in the essence of the four virtues. But justice retains the central position in the group. We accordingly give it the first place here.

The primary significance of justice is its tendency to counteract the crude egoism of the individual. As regards the good things of life the egoist's standpoint is: everything for me, whether anything remains over for others or not. Against this, justice maintains: not everything for me, but the same for myself and others. All grievous sinning against one's fellow-man, whether against body, life, property, social status, reputation or honour, finds in this fundamental attitude a complete check. The essential feature in it is from the outset the idea of equality: equal rights, equal duty with others, whether the individual or the whole of the community, on the principle that this is the basic condition of all communal life.

As regards its contents this principle may mean various things. To the ancients it meant primarily only this: equal with equals; which involved the reverse side: unequal with unequals. The principle does not then extend its authority beyond the current inequality of the given individuals. Against this position there was a widening of the claim, under the influence of Christianity, until it meant: equal rights for all. That signifies: however unlike men may be in character, disposition or social position, there exists a court of appeal, before which they are all equal. This idea of equality is a strictly idealistic demand; it does not deny the differences, nor does it extend to all the relations of life, but only to quite definite ones, to certain fundamental interests and primal rights of mankind in general. All positive law seeks to formulate these elementary rights in their various ramifications. A violation of them is injustice, and according to their intent men "ought" to be equal. But the justification of this demand for equality implies that even the man who violates it in fact makes a claim upon it for his own person, and therefore goes counter to his own interest in violating it. Who steals another's property, claims that it is now his property—which is only possible where in general property is held to be inviolable. The criminal by his deed denies the legal basis upon which he himself rests in the temporary advantage accruing from his deed. In practice he excludes himself from the very law which he puts into requisition.

Justice is not objective right, nor even ideal right. At best the latter is the object of the just man's intention. But ordinary language adds to the confusion. In the wider sense, a law, an arrangement, an established order of things can be "just," in so far as it tallies with the idea of the right. But in this sense the word "just" does not mean a moral value of a person. Here the carrier of the value is not a person at all; the value, although human conduct may first have made it actual, is that of an object; it is a situational value, a good for someone. In this sense all positive and all ideal right is valuable. But in another sense the man is "just" who does right or aims to do it, and sees and treats his fellowmen in the light of the equality that is required, whether in disposition or in conduct. In this case "justice" is the value of a person, it is a moral value.

(b) Doing Wrong and Suffering Wrong

This point comes to clear expression in Plato's attack in the *Gorgias* and the *Republic* upon the sophistical conception of justice. The Sophists, Callicles and Thrasymachus appear as champions of a kind of morality of power, according to which the "just" is that which is useful for the stronger person but is disadvantageous for the weaker. One might describe this as the natural, the pre-moral view. One can also separate it from the morality of power and universalize it. Established law has merely the significance of means, man's legal sense has merely that of consequences, for instance, protection against outside aggression. The greatest injury is to suffer wrong. "Good" means to maintain one's rights, "bad" to surrender them. Here only the situational value of justice is meant. This is quite right, but it is not the moral meaning of justice.

Over against it Plato advances the thesis: to suffer wrong is better than to do wrong. At a flash the moral value is revealed. To enjoy justice is a great good, but nothing more. To do justice, on the other hand, is a value of a totally different kind. It is not a good, but a moral dignity of the person instead. Nothing brings this more fully to expression than the Platonic dictum: The man who suffers wrong, may still be 729 times as happy as he who does wrong. This sounds like a joke. But the meaning is clear: the value of being just is simply not commensurable with that of experiencing another's justice— it is on a wholly different plane. No suffering of an injustice justifies a man in violating justice.

Thus we can understand how Plato could assign to justice the highest place in the scale of moral values. If virtue consists in right conduct toward one's fellow-man, it is reasonable to allow justice to pass as the sum of virtue. Still the three other Platonic virtues have more the quality of a merely inner disposition, at least as compared with justice.

(c) JUSTICE AS THE LOWEST AND MOST ELEMENTARY MORAL VALUE

Plato did not overestimate justice. The discovery of the moral value proper to it, in the ethics of Socrates and Plato, could not be placed too high in their newly awakened consciousness of value. Still, what was quite right in the Platonic ethics is not tenable for a widened survey. If one adds the variety of moral values which since then have been disclosed—and that on the basis of the original discovery—one must reverse the proposition. Among the virtues proper, justice is to be classed not as the highest, but rather as the lowest.

This is seen in the fact that in justice the Ought-to-Be puts forth not the maximum of moral demand, but quite evidently the minimum. Its claim upon a man's conduct is purely negative: not to do injustice, to commit no transgression, not to encroach upon another's liberty, not to injure another nor anything that belongs to him. It is this which is unmistakably expressed in the Commandments of the second table of the Decalogue; they are prohibitions: Thou shalt not murder, steal, commit adultery, bear false witness nor covet what is not thine. If that is the whole meaning of morality, its tendency is merely conservative, not constructive. The one concern is the protection of the lower, the elementary goods: life, property, family, and so on. If that is the whole of justice, then it is only a means to those goods-values.

Of course that by no means exhausts the essence of justice. In the first place, behind those goods-values is hidden something of positive moral value, the sphere of personal freedom. Justice merges into respect for this. But beyond it there rises something still greater. Law with its objective order and equality, as the just man strives for it, is indeed a court of protection, but by no means merely of the lower goods-values, but also and pre-eminently of the higher and the highest values, which are not directly affected by its arrangements. The higher spiritual, the communal and cultural values one and all can flourish only where body, life, property, personal freedom of action, and the like, are secured. There only is scope found for the higher purposes. Justice, then, makes room in the sphere of actuality for the higher values. The more diversified moral life cannot begin, till the simple conditions are supplied. Justice is the moral tendency to supply these conditions. It is the prerequisite of all further realizations of value. At the same time it is the pioneer among the virtues. Justice is the minimum of morality that paves the way for all the higher forms.

(d) LEGALITY AND MORALITY

Consonant with its being a minimum is the fact that the objective content of justice, law, permits of being pressed into fixed formulæ, of being codified, and even within certain limits where it is not voluntarily fulfilled by individuals, of being enforced by a public power watching over its fulfilment.

Such fixation and such enforcement go counter to the meaning of morality, the essence of which consists precisely in the freedom of fulfilment from instance to instance and in the spontaneous finding of the right. A commandment authoritative and leaving nothing undetermined is not a moral commandment at all. The disposition does not permit its aims to be prescribed from without, not to mention forced into actualization. But it is just this which legality would do; the legal claim does not appeal to the disposition but looks exclusively to the action. Legality is not morality; legal force leads only to the former, not to the latter. But the lower goods are of so elemental an importance—simply because they constitute the basis of all higher valuational reality—that they need such a stronger weapon of defence. For them the good will, so easily deficient, is not an adequate security.

This does not preclude the possibility that the minimal and predominantly negative stratum of requirements can be purposed and achieved without force, that is, from a genuinely moral disposition, for their own sake. Such purpose and such fulfilment are naturally the moral ideal, which is involved in all legal claims. In this instance, morality in content coincides with legality. And only in this case is man's moral attitude "just" in the narrower, moral sense of the word. All voluntary subjection, all genuine obedience to the existing order and the laws, all real virtue of the citizen as such—from simple

unerring honesty and truthfulness up to unhesitating sacrifice—
all this rests upon such an attitude of mind.

This is the ethically decisive factor in justice. Its moral
distinction lies not at all in the direction of the objective
situation, public or private, towards which the intention issues,
but in its value as a disposition of the person. Here also, as
everywhere else, the moral value of the intention is not the
same as the intended value, however important this may be.
Justice as a value of the disposition is indeed based upon the
situational value of the legal order; but this dependence does
not constitute the value peculiar to the disposition. The will
to justice is a value, and as such, independently of the inci-
dental value of what it demands, protects or secures. The will
to justice is right, even when the intention is objectively
wrong, when the situational value of the law has been misunderstood—exactly as it is right independently of the consequence. The rightly disposed man respects the property of
another, but not because as a material piece of goods it is
worth so much; also he respects it not in proportion to its
relative height in the scale of goods, but because it is the
property of another and as such sets an absolute limit to his
possessive intention. Between persons and their rightful
spheres there exists a dividing line. It is the sphere as such
which is respected.

But even here the objective and inherent value of the sphere
does not yet constitute the moral value of the self-limiting
intention; a new value appears, that of the intention itself. The
free commitment to the right, the inner conquest of contrary
impulses of desire and fear, of ambition and will to power, are as
regards value incomparably higher than all situational values,
which can ensue upon such a commitment. It is this which
lifts justice immeasurably above the mere utility of means and
constitutes the awe-inspiring element in a simple life of homely
justice. In the objective law this moral value remains latent.
The juridical point of view cannot recognize this distinction
between legality and morality. The distinction does not lie in

the action—in the action the two are indistinguishable; but the inner disposition is withdrawn from any human judge.

(e) LAW AND SOLIDARITY

There is a still deeper connection between justice as a virtue and justice as an objective order in the community. Justice as a situational value adheres not alone to the individual as a carrier, but also to the collective unit. It is a value which is actualized in the community. The regulation which it establishes is for the community as such. The objective forms in political, civil, penal law, and the like, are moral creations of individual peoples, in which each people actualizes in its own being the idea of law, as it understands the idea. These creations express the moral attitude of a people exactly as his judgments express the disposition of an individual man. And so far there is something more in legal institutions than mere situational values.

This view is limited by the fact that a community as such never attains to full personality, that moral initiative even in the creation of law always rests ultimately in the mind of the individual, however much the individual may be bound by the voluntary co-operation of others. Co-operation itself is, once more, just such a primal act of individual initiative. Finally it comes to this, that the individual holds a twofold position in regard to the law current in the community. On the one side, he is the one affected by the legal arrangements, the one who owes submission to them, and at the same time enjoys their protection; on the other side, he is there also as a law-giver, who, either directly or indirectly, participates creatively in the continual process of legal development in the community. He also has his share in the responsibility for the existing law. This joint responsibility is the inevitable reverse side of his subjection; otherwise this latter would contradict his personal freedom, the preservation of which is inherent in the very meaning of law. The consciousness of such joint responsibility is the second moral factor of importance in the individual as

a member of the community. It is the foundation of his legal
and civil solidarity with the mass of others similarly placed.

This solidarity is the deepest formative factor in the historical
life of peoples. It is also the primal element in the ethical being
of the citizen of a State; and wherever it is strong and outweighs
the special claims of the individual, the community flourishes
upon it. Its decline spells downfall. The history of the Roman
Republic with its classical blossoming of the communal life is
an instructive instance of the rise and fall of solidarity. This
solidarity, which consists in the unhesitating devotion of the
individual person to the whole, is a genuine virtue. For it is a
dispositional value in separate persons, even if the greatness of
its influence is first manifested in its communal effects.

For our modern sentiment this value is not fused with that of
justice. But for the ancient Greek it blended throughout with
δικαιοσύνη, it constituted its essential element, as it was tacitly
assumed. The ancient ethics never brought it, as such, fully
into consciousness.

In idea there is more contained in solidarity than the joint
responsibility for the whole. Joint responsibility for the individual is also contained therein, indeed for the individual even
when he goes astray and violates the common right. To punish
the criminal, to render him innocuous, to kill or banish him,
is an embarrassing duty for the one who, jointly responsible,
has to fulfil it, that is, ultimately for every citizen. The various
attempts at penal theory, which for all their differences are
equally unsatisfactory, fail at this point, because they start
exclusively from the position of the collective unit and from
responsibility for it, while they leave out of account responsibility for the criminal, a responsibility which has in itself
exactly the same import. But if we consider that in the criminal
a citizen has been lost to the community, who as such is at the
same time an appointed law-giver, the situation is changed,
and the question as to responsibility for the criminal becomes
very serious. It behoves that he be won back to the community, that he be rehabilitated legally and civilly; and

atonement through punishment is seen to be the means to
this end.

As to the question of guilt it is important to arrive at the
final ground for it, its super-individual, social ground. This
question coincides with that concerning joint responsibility.
For if the criminal acts from need, he is of course not excused,
but the guilt then falls not upon him alone; it touches those also
who tolerate the public condition which engenders or prolongs
the need. The idea of joint responsibility leads to the question
as to "whether the criminal has not lost his orientation in the
collective unit because the State as compared with him is only
a majority" (that is, only a party, only a group). If his sphere of
liberty was too narrowly confined by the view of the empirical
"majority," "the moral problem arises for the State as to a
widening of the limits, therefore as to an adaptation in the most
genuine sense to the criminal, who in truth had orientated
himself in the collective unit, but not in the defective representation of the collective unit."[1]

If we bear in mind that the State together with its legal
institutions is a structure continually undergoing an inner
revolution and never attaining finality, so that there are always
individual cases in which something inadequate is visible in it
and in which a new formation should be striven for—if we bear
this in mind, the revision of the existing law appears as an
inevitable consequence of the universal legislative trusteeship, a
revision issuing from the solidarity of all with all (including
even the criminal), from that solidarity which rests on the idea
of justice. In fact all have a share in the guilt of each individual.
And all are called to bring about that transformation of things
which is required by the sense of justice.

This solidarity is a disposition of the individual; but nevertheless it is a disposition which he can have only in connection
with the collective unit. And in so far it is at the same time a

[1] The sentences cited are taken from M. Salomon, *Die Idee der
Strafe*, in *Philosophische Abhandlungen* (H. Cohen, Berlin, 1912),
p. 241.

value of the community, just as justice in general is. But, besides
all this, solidarity is also a claim made in the same way upon
all, it is something wherein men ought to be equal and ought
to feel themselves equal. Solidarity is therefore a strictly
universal value. Indeed, it is the strictest and most absolute
value conceivable in its universality, because the uniformity of
the dominant moral claim inheres in its very essence. If one
takes it in the complete fulness of the moral tasks which it
imposes, this uniformity loses immediately every trace of
schematism; it does not in the least exclude the diversities of
claim, their vividness and their perpetual novelty from case
to case. On the contrary, in it alone does the rigidity of the
objective meaning of law and justice become relaxed. Through
solidarity man outgrows himself, by devotion to his perpetual
task as the architect of the community and the creator of law.

CHAPTER XX (xlv)

WISDOM

(a) The Ethical Meaning of Σοφία and Sapientia

PLATO regarded σοφία as the virtue of a part of the soul, although of its highest part; with Aristotle it is already supreme as the dianoetic virtue; but from the Stoics onward the whole contents of ethics is treated under the "ideal of the wise man." In this historical process σοφία becomes more and more a concept embracing every virtue.

It is not to be wondered at that in this way its special meaning was lost sight of, and that finally there remained only a form pale in colour, which could at times become a mirror of virtue, at times a repellent phantom of morally good men. Yet despite every absurdity which arose in this process of profanation, there is hidden in σοφία a high and genuinely ethical ideal, a moral quality of a unique kind. One can easily conceive of it as the exact opposite of justice, the contents of which refers to the community. Wisdom has no such reference. In tendency it is wider.

It has only a peripheral contact with the intellectual values of insight, truth and knowledge. These appear in it as instrumental values, but they are remote from its essence. For this reason alone Aristotle's conception of it as dianoetic was a mistake. Through it one was drawn hazardously near to contemplative self-indulgence and unpractical remoteness from the world. In the practical significance of wisdom there is a complete rapport with the world, a sensing of everything which contains value.

Yet it does not consist in mere valuational lucidity or a priori ethical intuition, just as little as in the mere foresight of the practical consciousness (prudentia), which, taken by itself, is only worldly shrewdness and has no value as a disposition at all. Likewise it is an error to see its meaning in a synthesis of these factors, in an orientation of life, as it were, to the many sides of value. Even that would still be too near to intellectual insight. As a virtue, it can be only a fundamental and really moral commitment, a primal direction of acts. None of those factors, in so far as they pertain to their own kind of value, can be properly attributed to the person; they are a matter of individual endowment or of involuntary perception. Only to a very limited degree does the responsibility for their failure fall upon the man himself.

In wisdom the disposition is a special kind of commitment of the man to life in general, whether his own or that of others. We come a step nearer to it when we start from the literal meaning of the term with which the Latins translated the word σοφία: *sapientia*. Through it resounds distinctly the *sapere* (to taste). *Sapientia* is moral taste, and indeed fine, differentiated, discriminating, cultivated taste, the refinement of moral capacity, in so far as this capacity, directed towards fulness of life, signifies appreciation of everything and an affirming, evaluating, attitude towards whatever is of value. This is fundamentally different from knowledge, insight, foresight or circumspection. It is the penetration of the valuational sense into life, into all discrimination, into every reaction and action; even down to the spontaneous valuational responses which accompany every experience; it is the fulfilment of one's whole ethical Being with its points of view, the fixed and basic attitude of the practical consciousness towards values. In a strictly anti-intellectualistic sense one might indeed call it ethical spirituality, the attitude of the ethos as the ultimate spiritual factor in humanity, dominating the whole life.

(b) The Socratic Ideal of Life

Socratic self-knowledge is the first fruit of this attitude. Only upon it do the more positive valuational factors rise. Although it is negative, self-knowledge has nothing in common with fear, remorse, despair, despondency. On the contrary, a certain dispassionateness in looking upon oneself is peculiar to it. It signifies knowledge exactly at that point where it is most difficult, where all our natural tendencies check objectivity of knowledge—knowledge of one's own ethical Non-being, failure and short-coming. The ethical import of this knowledge can be measured by the value of that which it brings with it, the right appreciation of the moral life which is demanded, the appreciation of what a man ought to be.

Here the Socratic proposition that there is knowledge inherent in virtue is justified, but of course without the exaggeration which identifies virtue with knowledge. On the contrary, genuine self-knowledge sets the limit even to this error of intellectualism, and it does so not only in theory but in the moral perception of the individual. Here knowledge itself counteracts all over-valuation of mere knowledge. It does so, as it is a knowledge of the fact that no insight into the good is sufficient to make a man good, that insight must be reinforced by volition, determination, active energy and self-mastery.

The attitude of the wise man is the commitment which is directed from out the modesty of his self-knowledge to the ethical values. It is therefore not the direction towards values in general, as goodness is, nor indeed towards the higher value; wisdom does not coincide with goodness, although it lies in the same general direction. To it belongs pre-eminently the preservation in one's own person of moral "taste" in its objectivity, and indeed not by paying attention to it, but in every transient intention. This it is before all else, which constitutes the distinguished feature of lucidity and calm, of inward superiority and spiritual mastery, the feature which makes itself unmistakably felt in the ancient ethos of σοφία, even in its onesidedness. To the wise man the domination of values in their ideality (the domination, in Platonic phrase, of moral Ideas) is something natural. Motives and ends of other kinds fall into the background. In this sense Plato was right when he joined this virtue to the beholding of Ideas, and indeed in such a way that a man, returning from the vision of ideas, sees in their light everything which appears to him in life. The wise man carries into all the relations of life the standards of value which he possesses in his spiritual "taste," he saturates his outlook upon life with them. This domination of values does not come to him by way of reflection, or through knowledge of commandments, but is an immediate, intuitive, emotionally toned domination, which from the centre of moral perception penetrates all unobserved and impulsive excitations, and is therefore already alive in them.

In the figure of Socrates, which for centuries has fixed our ideal of the wise man, there is still a second factor, which has been of service in the evolution of our conception. The man who took the words "Know thyself" as the motto of his life, describes himself as the bearer of an inner voice, which warns him prophetically when he is on the point of doing wrong. He calls it divine, his "daimon." There has been much dispute as to the nature of this daimon. But so much is certain: it is a kind of ethical divination, a foreboding presentiment of the wider perspective, in so far as this is not included in the given situation. For the wise man the intuitive grasping of the situation is in part determined by this wider perspective, by that of the Idea. The understanding of the significance of a situation depends upon the perspective in which it is seen. The larger the perspective, the deeper the insight into the situation. Ethical divination is the bestowal of meaning. For at bottom it is the living sense of value—but obscure, foreboding, not yet clear as to content. With a thousand tentacles the wise man reaches out beyond himself and his own limited understanding; he does not live in what he already knows of himself, but always a span beyond. This is the strict meaning of *sapientia*.

(c) Ethical Optimism and the Capacity for Happiness

It goes without saying that fulness of the prophetic sense augments the power to evaluate situations, whether it be as

active construction or as mere participation. And this reacts
upon the attitude of the wise man and upon his general estimation of life. His total mental outlook is an intelligent optimism.
Of course not one that is eudæmonistic, but one that is
genuinely ethical, a sense of the presence of inexhaustible
riches. The wise man is he who is open-minded towards every
value and is recipient, always learning more, never ceasing to
investigate. Everything administers to his moral growth and
heightens the potential value of his own life, although at this
he is not aiming; and at the same time, in so far as he influences
others, they also receive an access of spiritual power.

The attitude of the wise man towards the life and personality
of others is by no means exhausted in right action. It is an
interest of a distinct kind, a desire to understand another
from within, a surrender to the values peculiar to him. The
wise man has the rare virtue of wishing to understand before
he understands, of giving credit, even where he fails to understand. When we consider how the lack of the wish to understand prevents our doing so, and on the other hand how great
is the spiritual need of all those who their life long yearn in
vain to be understood by one single soul, it becomes easy for
us to appreciate how one truly wise man among the unwise
may bring salvation, freedom and happiness. He is the born
friend, the spiritual helper. And not less is he the moral leader,
the educator. The guidance of another's life does not consist
in burdening him with requirements, but in directing him to
the personal values in himself which he has not understood.
Even in this there is ethical divination which extends the vision
beyond the limits of what is actually seen.

However little the optimism of the wise man is eudæmonistic
in theory, it nevertheless brings him near to real happiness.
The proposition of the ancients, that the wise man is the happy
man, does not point out the ethical kernel of wisdom, but it
is true all the same. It calls attention to the natural effect of
σοφία. Calmness and clearness of vision, a loving recognition
of the individuality and intrinsic merit of others, are the

extreme opposite of the hunt for happiness, and therefore of any sort of eudæmonism proper. But it is of the essence of happiness that it always comes to him who does not pursue it.[1] He combines with a heart for ideals the modesty to which extravagant expectations are as alien as is indifference to genuine values, or envy or resentment. He does not take another's happiness as his standard, but his own claim to happiness; this, however, in the case of one who lives under strict self-criticism, is always greatly exceeded by the abundance of the happiness which real life offers. Cynic philosophy with its extreme depreciation of demands upon life is an exaggeration of this principle, as is also the Stoic doctrine of self-sufficiency ($\alpha\dot{v}\tau\acute{\alpha}\rho\kappa\epsilon\iota\alpha$). Yet in the tendency to be independent of external goods is seen a genuine characteristic of the wise man. And, if stripped of its exaggeration, the Epicurean ideal is no less right; it commends the acceptance of the happiness near at hand. The wise man does not spend his life in grasping, but in appreciating with fine feeling the various values of life and participating in them continually and wisely. He lives in the fulness of life; whatever he understands and knows how to appreciate, belongs to him. When viewed from within, the comprehending perception, the living appreciation and the expansion of the mind with the richness of reality, are increments in spiritual wealth.

In this synthesis of the Stoic and Epicurean ideal is found the true concept of the wise man. A sense of reality, guided by a sense of its values, is the secret of the wise man. With him, to overlook the fulness of values is just as much a sin against life as to make Utopian claims which are incapable of being gratified. Pure joy in everything which is worthy of joy has its criterion in the unenvious delight one takes in the happiness of others, which is denied to oneself, and in the admiring recognition one gives to superiority in others. It culminates ultimately in a deep sentiment of gratitude, in a great and profound sense of reverential wonder at the richness of life.

[1] Cf. Chapter X (*f.*), Vol. I.

To the wise man the real world is infinitely richer than that of fiction or imagination. He lives in the consciousness of his own littleness and narrowness, of his backwardness and his inability to exhaust the resources of life. He sees himself as one who is too rich, who is overwhelmed, and whose power to receive is not equal to the gifts bestowed. His cup is already overflowing, his capacity is exceeded by his possessions. And in that he in this way exercises unintentionally an influence as an example, he is a true educator of men in inner spiritual freedom and in the one true happiness.

CHAPTER XXI (XLVI)

COURAGE

(a) PERSONAL COMMITMENT AND MORAL ADVENTURE

WISDOM is a value which spurs man on to the choice of ends; bravery, to the execution of them. The former lies in the valuational direction of the fulness of life; the latter, in that of strength and freedom, activity and the ability to suffer. The wisest outlook is morally impotent unless active energy, which is ready to cope with obstacles, reinforces it, especially when one's own life, welfare and happiness must be risked.

The most conspicuous form in which this value manifests itself is outward bravery, the ability to stake one's life, the spontaneous facing of extreme danger, the standing at one's post, or manliness (ἀνδρεία, *virtus*), as the ancients called it. In the early war-waging period of a nation's life this is held to be synonymous with all virtue.

But it is more general still. It inheres in all decisive effort, in all steadfast perseverance, in all quietly persistent tenacity; that is, wherever there is an element of adventure in a situation, which requires personal commitment and demands sacrifice. Perhaps there is something of it in all genuine effort, at least so far as adventure enters into it. In this more general sense ἀνδρεία means courage.

Indicative of its separateness as a value is the fact that it is independent of the value of the objects for which the commitment is made. A brave act can be worthy of a better cause, as was Cataline's. We may therefore morally condemn the object and still morally admire the high spirit which is devoted to it. This independence of its object has no connection with that caricature of bravery, impetuous foolhardiness, the gambling with danger (which can become mere delight in excitement). On the one hand, there is genuine bravery; and, although the object be a bad one, yet, subjectively, faith in it is the presupposition of the commitment. On the other hand, foolhardiness has only an outward resemblance to it. In it the principal thing is lacking, the felt seriousness of the commitment and the seriousness, although only presumed, of the object in view. Nothing but the deliberate entering into the danger of a project, a staking one's life upon it—which is reasonable only if the value of the project is more precious than one's own life—is genuine fortitude in the sense of this distinctively moral value.

Even in its most primitive stage it has the characteristic of self-conquest. But it can rise until it is a capacity to deny oneself and to take delight in sacrifice. Here the paradox is due to the fact that the increase in fortitude and active energy keeps pace with the increase in the resistance offered. It is a special mark of genuine bravery that it is not diminished with the greatness of the opposition, of the venture and the danger, but grows and is at the same time strengthened by it. It is as if ever new moral powers were liberated, as the burden becomes heavier.

Ethically this psychologically puzzling phenomenon is very easy to understand. At bottom fortitude is an act of freedom. But freedom is never a fact existing beforehand; it is always awakened in the given conflict, and indeed in proportion to its greatness. In this particular no one can know himself before life puts him to the test. Many a man honestly believes himself in the highest degree brave, and yet fails under the first stress of circumstance. Many a one is timid, so long as no great emergency arises, but at the critical moment proves himself to be strong and steadfast. What, then, comes to light is a sort of individual sterling quality that was hidden. It is this which constitutes the virtue of bravery.

(b) MORAL VALUE AND THE DELIGHT IN RESPONSIBILITY

Hazardous enterprise is always the acceptance not only of actual consequences but of moral responsibility. This may be of many kinds, according to what it is that the person stakes. It need not be life and limb, it may be another's welfare, happiness or destiny. In this case is added to the free determination of one's own fate that of others. Here fortitude takes on the significance—ethically more profound—of the will-to-assume-responsibility, the courage to be under obligation. Wherever a man's circumstances place him in a position of leadership, the courage to act is a function of the capacity to assume responsibility and to delight in it. To determine another's life—and this is demanded by the circumstance of the ordinary man from day to day—is for everyone who is not lacking in conscience, incomparably the greater adventure, the severer test of courage. For here guilt is the danger which he exposes himself to. Nevertheless, one who rejoices in responsibility, who runs the risk of guilt, is morally the greater, while one who fights shy of responsibility is less worthy—he is cowardly. It depends upon moral courage; with that the issue rests.

In fact, all courage to act is at the same time fortitude in suffering, in the bearing of consequences, of disaster and guilt. In the case of illustrious examples this is well known, as in the tragedy of heroism and moral greatness. It is less evident in the conflicts of ordinary life. Still the principle is the same here as there. Every actual conflict demands the courage of deciding. The moral coward is always prone to remain inactive, to let things go, not reflecting that he thereby—and indeed especially thereby—incurs guilt. He preserves only the appearance of not having been a participant; in truth, what it was in his power to change remains a charge upon him. Self-deception hides from him his moral self-indulgence and his incapacity to take the initiative and to assume responsibility.

Moral life is a venture and requires courage at every turn. Along with the courageous deed must be classed the courageous word, conviction and opinion, bravery in truth, confession and thought; and not less, courage towards oneself and one's real feelings, one's own personality, the courage of great emotions, of love, of fateful passion (the special field of false shame, fear of public opinion, a cowardly hiding of oneself). Indeed there is such a thing as the courage to live, to undergo experiences, to see things through and know their quality, not less than the courage to be happy. Thus it comes about that merely participant wisdom refers us step by step to the complementary virtue of courage.

SELF-CONTROL

(a) σωφροσύνη AND ἐγκράτεια

WHAT the ancients called σωφροσύνη has been set in a false light by being ordinarily translated as circumspection. It does not refer to deliberation, but to spiritual proportion and symmetry, to the restraint of destructive excess and to the moral strength of self-control. This is best expressed by the Stoic conception of ἐγκράτεια, which means: having oneself in hand; being master of oneself.

Antiquity brought it into close connection with σοφία and ἀνδρεία. Both of these reappear as elements in it, the one as guiding, the other as giving strength. But, as compared with both, it is an entirely new and distinctive value. For it is not concerned with guidance or strength as such, but with the subordination of one's own inner life to them. Nor is the point which is here in question personal devotion to a cause, but the rejection of inward excess for one's own sake, self-limitation as an independent value, the combating of exuberance, of inner turmoil, in the interest of inward harmony.

Self-control is by no means to be understood as purely negative, as a rejection and suppression, as if the natural were nothing but evil. It is the inner construction and transformation of everything natural in man, of all the obscure powers which he finds present there, which, rising up out of the unconscious depths, confront consciousness as something real. Instincts, impulses, emotions, passions are in themselves by no means neutral in value, though they are primarily and strictly neutral. In content and power they constitute a mighty material, constructive and destructive, an inner world, which, like the outer world, waits to be exploited.

Only too long has the Stoic notion of the badness and per-

niciousness of the feelings prevailed in ethics. Its consequence
was the demand for the extermination or deadening of emotions. This ascetic ideal was encouraged by the Christian view
that human nature is radically sinful. If desires are nothing
but disturbances or weaknesses in man, the result was inevitable
that morality should adopt the unnatural ideal of asceticism.
We have already considered[1] the serious misunderstanding at
the root of asceticism, concerning not only human nature in
general but also concerning an autonomous value, that of life
itself, the manifest form of which it absolutely denies. But the
fact that asceticism likewise loses altogether the ethical meaning of σωφροσύνη requires a chapter by itself.

In the first place, it is psychologically false. The affections
and everything which in kind belongs to them are the root of
our emotional life, of our spiritual strength; they are the substance of the inner content of life, the basis of its fulness. With
its eradication the spiritual life itself would be eradicated.
Hence the ethical penury of asceticism.

But in the second place it is false ethically. Every genuine
Ought is positive. It demands not destruction but construction, the creation of the higher out of the lower. Out of
"nothing" no value can be actualized. The world of desires is
the material for the building of the inner life; of course in
itself it is not unshaped, but it is of a lower kind of structure.
If this be destroyed, all formation becomes impossible.

The only tenable meaning of the situational value presupposed in σωφροσύνη is exactly the opposite of extermination;
it is reconstruction, the unfoldment of the affective life itself,
its completion, its organic transformation, its advancement
into harmony, the fostering and protection of its bloom. For
this safeguarding no more emanates from the affective life
itself than does its harmony. The psycho-physical character of
the affective impulses is tyrannical; every one of them tends
to crowd out the others and to extend itself at their cost. This
conservative strength of the emotional energies is an inner

[1] Cf. Chapter XI (b), Vol. II.

danger, man is menaced by them from within. We might say that their equipoise is for ever unstable. Its stabilization must come from some other quarter.

The negative side of self-control is directed exclusively against excess, lack of balance, the state of being divided against oneself. Its positive aspect is ἐγκράτεια in the strict sense, as the possession of power over affective impulses, the virtue of inward right proportion, of positive transformation of the emotional life and its appraisement from points of view that unify and guide. It is a kind of inward setting of one's house in order, a lawfulness and rightfulness in one's spiritual *modus vivendi*—similar to δικαιοσύνη in the outer life. With the ancients, in so far as they did not lose their bearings through asceticism, σωφροσύνη culminated in the inward reconciling beauty of the man whose character was completed and had become steadfast, in καλοκἀγαθία. Nothing is so radically contrary to this ideal as the Stoic blunting and coarsening of the emotions, simply for the sake of serenity and of the ability to endure everything. Far more akin to it is the Epicurean refinement, the enrichment, the rounding out of the emotional life, ultimately the enhancement of the capacity for enjoyment in the sense of ethical "good taste" (of sapientia), although the eudæmonism involved in it lacks the objectivity and unique character of self-control, as a moral quality of the disposition.

(b) Obedience, Discipline, the Education of Character

A peculiarity of this virtue is that in a high degree it can be acquired and developed, and can even be induced in others. This is due to its essential character; it consists in becoming master inwardly over that part of man's nature which in itself is without a master. It is perhaps the lowest value among the virtues (it was already so appraised by Plato); it is the least claim which a man must impose upon himself; yet upon it, as a basis, do the higher moral tasks rest. According to Aristotle it attains only the level of the "not bad." That may be an exaggeration; we need only to regard it in comparison with the high ethos of bravery and wisdom—which can become heroism or moral greatness—in order to feel the difference in valuational height.

Nevertheless the attainment of it is by no means on that account easy and native to everyone who, according to his personal constitution, satisfies the requirements of many a higher value. But, then, in the moral being of such men there is a void, which makes their ethos incomplete. In all these respects self-control is akin to justice.

Because it is morally basic and because it can be trained, very definite educational tasks adhere to the valuational direction of self-control. That self-conquest can be acquired in little things, that obedience and discipline can be learned, that the form of the inner life can be striven for and gained, that one can accustom oneself to the domination of chosen ends over vacillating inclination, in short, to inner discipline, which finally becomes self-correction, spontaneous self-command and guidance—that all this can be done has been well known to educators from ancient times. Accordingly many have often fallen into the error of mistaking "discipline" for the whole of morality. That is as untrue as the notion that all virtue is justice or bravery.

But a more serious danger to education lies in a purely external drill: for example, that of mere obedience. Equipped with submission of the will alone, however valuable that may be, a man is not ready for active life; he must also be capable of independent self-direction. But this is far less teachable, simply because it is more positively and more highly organized in content and transcends considerably the limit of mere self-control. In the edifice of character, discipline is only the ground-floor. The whole training of the lower powers in man is only a prerequisite, to provide scope for the higher moral qualities.

CHAPTER XXIII (XLVIII)

THE ARISTOTELIAN VIRTUES

(a) THE THEORY OF THE GOLDEN MEAN

THE table of the virtues, as antiquity constructed it, is not exhausted in the four Platonic virtues. For example, Aristotle and the older Stoic school contributed much which has proved to be of abiding worth. To this day the *Nicomachean Ethics* is a veritable treasure-house for the explorer of values. Without any pretence to completeness, we may study it here, because of the wealth of its contents. Since the words by which these values may be described are highly inadequate—ordinary speech does not distinguish as finely as does our sense of values, and even Aristotle found words inadequate and saw himself constrained to coin clumsy new ones—we cannot at this point avoid taking a glance at the whole method of determining the content of values as Aristotle elaborated it. But this presupposes his very peculiarly planned theory of the virtues in general. And since a series of traditional misunderstandings attaches to it, it is necessary at the start to restore the meaning of this theory itself.

It is well known that Aristotle defines virtue as a mean (μεσότης) between two extremes (ἄκρα), which are both evils (κακίαι). Of the evils one is always too much, the other too little (ὑπερβολή and ἔλλειψις). An analysis of the contents of the values is the only way to test this theory. σωφροσύνη (moderation) provides the best example; according to Aristotle, it is a mean between licentiousness and apathy or emotional dullness (ἀκολασία and ἀναισθησία). Likewise bravery is the mean between cowardice and foolhardiness (δειλία and θρασύτης), justice between doing wrong and suffering wrong (ἀδικεῖν and ἀδικεῖσθαι), ἐλευθεριότης (that is, liberality with one's money and possessions) between penuriousness and squandering (ἀνελευθερία and ἀσωτία); πραότης, which is

akin to σωφροσύνη—it seems to mean equable temper almost
more than gentleness—between violent temper and incapacity
to feel righteous indignation (ὀργιλότης and ἀοργησία).

From these examples it is already evident that there is a
different mean in each one—now more now less than the exact
middle point. Nor does Aristotle keep throughout to this
conception; he drops it in regard to φιλία and the "dianoetic
virtues." Whether the principle can be universalized is therefore from the beginning a futile question. But it is carried out
as a guiding hypothesis in the case of the "ethical virtues."
Each one of these is referred (περὶ τί) to something else, to a
specific content, as to a material, in relation to which there
exists a whole scale of human habits (ἕξεις). Thus σωφροσύνη
refers to pleasure and pain, bravery to danger and fright,
liberality to money as a value. And each time the specific virtue
is a habit in the series of possible habits, and indeed an intermediate one.

This theory has always been subjected to the mockery of
critics. It appears only too ridiculous that the seriousness of
virtue should resolve itself into the triviality of a "golden
mean," that is, into a mediocrity. Even the reflection that with
the Greeks "measure" and "beauty" were wellnigh identical,
helps us very little here. It is still more absurd that a further
enhancement of a moral good should lead back to a vice, even
if to another one than that above which it arose as an opposite.
Rather is it evident that a virtue can be augmented in itself,
without ever losing its distinctive value, that is, that its quality
is absolute and is an axiological extreme (ἄκρον). Self-control,
bravery, justice, taken as values, have no upper limit at all.
It is impossible to transcend them.

This cannot be the sense of the doctrine of the mean. However much one may see in it of the popular motto "nothing in
excess," the absoluteness of the virtues, after Plato's doctrine
of Ideas had philosophically discovered it, could not have
escaped the mind of Aristotle. What, then, is the positive
meaning of his theory?

One need not go far to find it. Aristotle himself expresses it most baldly in a passage of the second book of the *Nicomachean Ethics*, the philosophical importance of which has not been sufficiently appreciated by its interpreters: "Therefore from the point of view of Being and of Reason which expressly defines essence ontologically, virtue is a mean; but from the point of view of the best and of the good generally, it is an extreme."[1] Here it is clearly stated that virtue is always at the same time both a mean and an extreme, but in different connections. In every virtue two points of view stand over against each other, one ontological (suggested by οὐσία and τί ἦν εἶναι) which refers to the existential form of the conduct—we might say, the material of the value—and one axiological, which concerns the valuational quality itself (κατὰ τὸ ἄριστον καὶ τὸ εὖ). In the sense of the latter, virtue is an extreme; in the sense of the former, a mean. This affirms unequivocally that as an ethical value it is something absolute, beyond which there can be no "too-much" (ὑπερβολή). It is a mean only according to existential reality.

If we analyse the situation more precisely, we find that two dimensions of heterogeneous opposites cut into each other, or stand at right angles to each other: one, that of excess and deficiency, is the ontological dimension; and the other, that of the good and the bad, is the axiological. Ontologically, in every species of habit, which refers to a definite content, the continuum of possible habits would be rectilinear, between the extremes of excess and deficiency. But the adding thereto of the axiological dimension bends the straight line into a parabola; for both the ontological extremes are in meaning vices

[1] The passage in the text, *Eth. Nic.*, II. 6. 1107a, 5–8: διὸ κατὰ μὲν τὴν οὐσίαν καὶ τὸν λόγον τὸν τὸ τί ἦν εἶναι λέγοντα μεσότης ἐστὶν ἡ ἀρετή, κατὰ δὲ τὸ ἄριστον καὶ τὸ εὖ ἀκρότης.
The suggestiveness of the contrast suffers in every translation, because the heaping of the ontological terms οὐσία and τί ἦν εἶναι can in no way be reproduced. In the interpretation of this passage, as in many details of this chapter, I follow the expositions of the work by M. v. Kohoutek on *Die Differenzierung des ἀνθρώπινον ἀγαθόν*, I. Kap. 6 (compare the remark on p. 58, Vol. II).

(the lower extremes), while the intermediate elements approximate to the good (the higher extreme) and in a culminating point attain the status of ἀρετή. This therefore is ontologically at a point midway, but axiologically it is at the highest point. From it the curve falls away again towards another vice. Thus there exists, if we bear in mind the two oppositional dimensions, no rectilinear transition from vice to vice, but only a parabolic path over ἀρετή.[1]

Hence it is to be understood that according to Aristotle there is no passing beyond ἀρετή in a further enhancement of the valuational quality of right conduct. For the extension of the curve cannot rise above its culminating point, but can only fall. The mean is not a valuational intermediate. But, as a highest point, it is a behaviour which is not qualitatively (ontologically) an extreme. Hence the ontologically intermediate position is justified.

Of course in this it remains unexplained, why there is exactly the one point in the curve, the one kind of behaviour among the infinitely many gradations, which has the one value. Here evidently a higher point of view enters tacitly in, which for the first time connects unequivocally the two dimensions in every single case. That Aristotle discerns this in the higher formation can be inferred with considerable certainty from the concrete relation to his metaphysics. But this is a problem by itself, which as such is not brought out by him.

[1] M. v. Kohoutek (p. 55) provides for this point the accompanying diagram (Fig. 1). The horizontal line represents the ontological, the vertical line the axiological dimension. The essence of ἀρετή, as Aristotle understands it, inheres in its double position as μεσότης in the first and as ἀκρότης in the latter.

GOODNESS

DEFICIENCY   BADNESS   EXCESS

FIG. 1.

The whole theory—however much it may require to be supplemented[1]—must have been right in its main point, that in general virtue is a structure based upon two dimensions which cut into each other. For virtue, as human behaviour (according to its matter), is something real, and falls within the variety of real forms of existence; but, as moral value, it is an ideal formation, the autonomy of which is preserved in the actualization. To this extent it actually passes, precisely as regards its ethical essence, into another dimension. But this means that all human behaviour, besides its incorporation into the specific determinations of existence, falls also under the ethical dimension of the opposites: "Value—anti-value" (ἀγαθόν-κακόν).

(b) σωφροσύνη IN THE LIGHT OF THE μεσότης

It is not so much the theory itself as the point of view hidden in it which proves to be empirically fruitful in showing forth moral values. In fact Aristotle has discovered values by it and made them clearly evident, but no one before or after has done anything similar. The fact that their quality as dispositional values does not receive full recognition in Aristotle's work does not detract from the service he has rendered.

From this procedure less benefit accrued to the Platonic virtues, which apart from it are well known. For instance, concerning the essence of bravery, it is of little help to know that it lies between timidity and rashness; it is only too evident that it lies much nearer to the latter (the excess) than to the former, and that its distinctive opposite is cowardice. Still weaker is the intermediate position of justice; to it as a dispositional value only doing wrong (ἀδικεῖν) is a moral opposite, not suffering wrong (ἀδικεῖσθαι). This latter is not a badness, but only an evil.

The sense of the mean comes out more strictly in the case

---

[1] For a systematic appraisement of the μεσότης theory, cf. Chapter XXXVI (d) and (e), Vol. II.

of moderation. Here the essence of the matter is precisely a keeping within limits. In contrast to the Cynic and Stoic morality of blunting and deadening, it was a great merit on the part of Aristotle to have recognized ἀναισθησία (that is, lack of the feeling for pleasure and for the values of possession), as an inferiority (κακία) of moral worth. Thus a limit is set to every form of asceticism. Here also the virtue does not properly lie in the ontological middle point, but nearer to ἀναισθησία. Licentiousness is the badness which is really to be fought against. For—so argues Aristotle—to turn away from pleasure, to strive against emotion, is contrary to human nature.

(c) LIBERALITY IN GIVING, MILDNESS, MAGNIFICENCE

From the cases cited above we see that it is exactly the less known virtues, to which the doctrine of the mean, as an empirical principle for the determination of values, applies more closely. They are at the same time the values which are more special and less central. Liberality in regard to money (ἐλευθεριότης) is in fact finely characterized through the double contrast to penuriousness and extravagance—although Aristotle sees in the latter the lesser fault.

But with regard to mildness of temper a special merit lies in the view that not only easy excitability to anger but also complete incapacity to feel wrath is a moral defect. The presupposition of this view is that anger in itself is something valuable, therefore, indirectly, that in general there is moral value in emotion, and that here also, as generally in the realm of the emotions, the crisis of good and evil is to be found in right guidance—one might say: in the direction of the emotion towards the object which is proportionate to it. It is evident that here a far deeper appreciation of emotion is expressed than we find elsewhere among the ancients.

For the completion of the table of values it is of especial interest that Aristotle supplements liberality, which refers to the lowest material possessions, by a virtue which is higher, but which refers to the same fundamental value, the virtue of μεγαλοπρέπεια. One might translate this admirable word, which was current among the Greeks, most closely by the word magnificence. The meaning may be more exactly given by saying that it is behaviour which befits great circumstance. It is not a virtue for every man. It only concerns him to whom much has been given. The thought is that from him much also will be required. In so far as one who has great possessions is exposed to special moral aberrations, such a higher claim upon him is justified. Here, then, the ontological opposition appears on another plane: the two extremes are shabbiness and vulgar display. The former is that ridiculous care for the farthings which is unsuited to the man's circumstances, but which would be commendable in one of little means (the literal significance of the word μικροπρέπεια). In connection with ἀπειροκαλία the love of vulgar display is equivalent to purse-pride, the swindler's desire to outdo others. The common factor in both these vices is the radical failure to recognize the ethically subordinate value of riches and of outward possessions. But even here there is clearly a tacit recognition of the lower goods-value, which the Stoics lost.

(d) Ambition and Magnanimity

It is a trite commonplace that ambition is axiologically a variable concept, in which both a value and a disvalue are contained. Language does not specially indicate either the virtue or the vice involved in it. The same is true of the Greek word φιλοτιμία except that the vice perhaps is somewhat more strongly suggested. Hence the moral value in ambition is without a name (ἀνώνυμος). Over against it appear as vices excessive ambition and complete lack of it or, so to speak, place-hunting and an inability to strive (inertness of will). φιλοτιμία is a genuine mean, a strict virtue of right proportion. Of all the special values of the *Nicomachean Ethics* it appears as the one least independent; it coincides completely with moderation. Even here the underlying emotional factor as such is of value.

As with liberality in giving, Aristotle raises over ambition a higher value, μεγαλοψυχία. The relation of the two is obscured in the *Nicomachean Ethics* by the form of presentation and the context, but it is nevertheless unmistakable. This remarkable new value, for which the later schools had little appreciation, is with Aristotle a kind of crown, a moral ideal. The name, which literally means greatness of soul, tells us very little. In this virtue is hidden a whole system of specific values. But its fundamental distinction is this, that with it as with ambition the point at issue is a relation to honour as a goods-value (περὶ τιμάς). But like magnificence it is not every man's concern, but an exceptional value. It has to do with great privileges, or, as one might say, with the highest values (τιμὴ μεγάλη) and not at all with the more serviceable, the useful, ones. The μεγαλόψυχος is the high-minded man, his ethos is in the valuational direction of the noble. He demands for himself what is great and justifies his requirement, in that he is really worthy and capable of it. His pre-eminent characteristic is the high self-esteem which he justifies or, more correctly said perhaps, the achieved justification, the moral pride, which rests upon genuine greatness and worth. Self-depreciation in one who stands morally high, the belittling of oneself, the humility of self-disparagement (μικροψυχία) is according to Aristotle of as little value as over-estimation of self and arrogance (χαυνότης). These two extremes are not properly vices: they bring about no harm. But still they are morally of less value. Greatness of soul, which stands as the mean between them, is a virtue of a higher order. The mean here is self-appreciation itself, moral self-consciousness (ἀξιοῦν ἑαυτόν). Descriptive of it is the definition of the μεγαλόψυχος[1] as the μεγάλων ἑαυτὸν ἀξιῶν ἄξιος ὤν, that is, the man who thinks he is worthy of great things, in so far as he really is so. All disparity between one's self-estimate and one's real moral being is unworthy; not only

[1] *Eth. Nic.*, 1123*b*. 2.

the false pride which one's personal being does not justify, but equally that lack of pride which leads to moral deterioration. The former is vain, the latter worthless. The μεγαλόψυχος is he who on great issues is justifiably appreciative of himself; he is in little matters simply σώφρων (the sane man) who knows his own moral limitations. For moral self-consciousness is to be named pride only in connection with great worth; in connection with slight worth it is just as naturally humility. Only real greatness of moral being is entitled to be proud.

Genuine moral pride does not constitute the whole essence of μεγαλοψυχία, but it is nevertheless the central factor and also the interesting element in it. For that there is at all a moral value in pride is not self-evident. Nor is it essential for our consideration to decide whether there exists such a value; it is sufficient, if we make clear that antiquity recognized it, and that its philosophical representative Aristotle knew how to define it very exactly and even saw in it a kind of moral completeness, a world of excellences. It is also important to note that he had as little respect for idle gazing at oneself in the looking-glass as for the boasted moral pride of the Stoics, in their ideal of self-sufficiency. That there is always danger that this value may be counterfeited should not tempt us to deny its existence. But it would be quite a mistake to suppose that genuine pride would exclude genuine humility. The man who is justified in being proud will always, if he sees himself clearly, have something before which he humbles himself, although it be only the ideal which he aims to satisfy. But the humble man, if he does not wish to become worthless, must always have something in himself which he prizes. This combination may be morally difficult; for the contrast between these values and the ethical attitudes corresponding to them is clearly evident. Yet it does not assume the form of a valuational antinomy proper.

(e) Giving Each his Due

νέμεσις, the detailed analysis of which we owe to Aristotle, is a virtue related in content to justice. We might describe its content as morally justifiable participation in what befalls others, in their happiness and sufferings. Like justice, it is directed towards others, but not in reference to their possessions and their modes of conduct, but exclusively in reference to their emotional susceptibility. Aristotle starts from the view that there are here two kinds of badness: the one is displeasure at seeing a fellow-man happy, envy; the other is pleasure at seeing him unhappy, delight in another's misfortune (φθόνος and ἐπιχαιρεκακία). As the mean between these he sets up νέμεσις. It does not entirely escape his notice that these two extremes are not strictly opposites. He is clearly aware that a more complex relationship is here involved. For what interests the man who wishes to give everyone his due is not another's happiness and suffering as such, but the relation of both of these to the man's deserts. It pains him who would give every man his due, when anyone suffers undeservedly (ἀναξίως), and likewise when anyone is undeservedly happy, as when the triumphant rogue enjoys the fruits of his deeds.

Accordingly it might be thought that the one extreme of badness must consist of delight in seeing undeserved happiness or suffering; and therefore that the other extreme would be displeasure at the sight of deserved happiness or suffering. Both are involved in the nature of the matter, but with Aristotle they do not come fully to recognition. Yet, however it may be with the mean and its deficiency, the matter itself is conceived correctly in its central feature: namely, there is such a thing as a right attitude towards another's enjoyment and suffering, and this does not consist, so to speak, of sharing in the enjoyment and suffering—such participation may in itself have value but of a different type—but of a kind of inward justice which enters sympathetically into another's life, in proportion to his worthiness and desert. Morally such inward justice penetrates deeper than outward justice.

(f) The Sense of Shame

In the *Nicomachean Ethics* αἰδώς, the sense of shame, is
treated as a kind of step-child. Aristotle does not wish to
recognize it fully as a virtue; for a morally good man ought
to be good in every respect, so that he has nothing to be
ashamed of—how, then, can being ashamed of oneself count
as a virtue? Nevertheless it is to be commended (ἐπαινεῖται).
Men actually do very much which they ought to be ashamed
of; but in that case it is better for them to feel ashamed than
not to. The sense of shame also restrains them from many
things; a man feels that he would need to be ashamed if he
should do a certain thing; accordingly he is ashamed to do it.
Thus indirectly αἰδώς is a value. It is at the same time a substitute for the sense of right, when this is lacking. We shrink
from the condemnation of others, from a bad reputation (φόβος
ἀδοξίας). This is a kind of surrogate, when the voice of conscience does not speak directly.

This value has many shades, when one considers its position as a mean. According to Aristotle the man who is ashamed
stands midway between the timid and the shameless. This
mood, again, is strictly a mean, since shamelessness is worse
than excessive shyness. The sense of shame falls short of
virtue, because it is not properly a habit of conduct but is
more a passive state. In the young, Aristotle is willing to concede that this passivity is a positive value, inasmuch as the life
of the immature is more a life of passive acceptance than of
conscious worth. From his position, Aristotle could not of
course recognize that a sense of value—although immature and
indirect—was concealed behind the sense of shame.

In a certain respect the sense of shame is closely related to
meekness, the sense of honour and the sense of what others
deserve. In common with these qualities it has the peculiarity
of being an emotional value. Equally with the moral sense of
shame, sympathetic justice, noble ambition, righteous indignation (when blended with gentleness) are passive states. Indeed,

we could include greatness of soul in this group, in so far as in genuine pride there is an element of moral emotion. Aristotle has expressly recognized such an element only in the sense of shame. But, in spite of their difference, the whole group is significant, because in the sphere of the emotions generally there exist positive moral values, and indeed a variety of them. In recognizing this fact Aristotle was far in advance of the Stoics and of most of the later philosophers.[1]

[1] Further examples of Aristotelian virtues in Chapter XXIX (c), Vol. II.

Section VI

SPECIAL MORAL VALUES
(SECOND GROUP)

CHAPTER XXIV (xlix)

BROTHERLY LOVE

(a) Interest in the Welfare of Others

WITH the transformation which the ancient ethos underwent through Christianity there emerged into consciousness a new class of moral values. Whether this was from every point of view a higher class may remain an open question—the facts quite clearly speak for themselves—but in so far as its fundamental value, brotherly love, surpasses justice, the fundamental value of the ancient world, it is undoubtedly on a higher plane.

To disentangle this change of outlook from its religious basis is not easy, but in itself is altogether possible. Especially can this be done without distortion in the case of its main feature, brotherly love. It is harder in the case of ideal purity, which relaxed the concentration of the older ethos upon plenitude and variety of experience. It becomes impossible only where Christianity permeated the ancient outlook, obscuring it. The idea of wisdom, for instance, was submerged under the new, all-controlling relationship of man to God; in the same way σωφροσύνη was submerged under the religious conception of sin and grace, and the ethos of courage and pride under steadfastness of faith and humility of the sinner. Here opens an antinomy between the values of this world and those of the Beyond—of ethics proper and religion, an antinomy which as such is no longer an ethical problem.[1] But we must not therefore misconstrue the fact that here, although in a transcendent connection, new values do come upon the scene, which have to do exclusively with the relation of man to man.

Love of one's neighbour (ἀγάπη), as the Evangelists meant it, is not love in general—neither the Platonic ἔρως which turns

[1] Cf. Chapter XI (f), Vol. II.

to the Idea, nor Aristotle's "love of a friend" (φιλία); also it is not the Stoic ἀγάπησις, which in its universalistic tendency does indeed come nearer to brotherly love but plays only a secondary rôle. Love of one's neighbour is primarily directed towards whoever is nearest, towards the other person, and it is a positive affirmative tendency, the transference of interest from the I to the Thou. The word "love" is therefore misleading in so far as it stresses the emotional side too much, while the essence of the matter lies in one's disposition, one's intention, finally—and not least—in one's conduct. It all depends on an inner propinquity to another; but it manifests itself in consideration for him as a person, in intercession for him as if for oneself.

The modern word, altruism, which admittedly is much misused, gives exact expression to this fundamental tendency in its opposition to all egoism—and by no means to its more blatant forms only. In altruism the centre of one's whole sphere of interests is transferred from oneself to the other person. It is the abrogation of the self-centred tendency and a transference of interest to the being of another for his own sake. Where this new commitment is reciprocal among several persons, at once there appears a spontaneous devotion of all to each, in contrast to the indifference or even antagonism of mere proximity to one another. For each the sphere of values of the others falls into line with his own. This is the fundamental structure of the mental attitude on which the moral value of brotherly love depends.

(b) Positive Contents and Creative Spontaneity

The nature of brotherly love is familiar enough. But for all that it is not easy to outline exactly. For this purpose a comparison with justice is especially illuminating. Justice also consists in an attitude towards one's fellows (πρὸς ἕτερον). But it is only concerned with recognized claims, the rights of the other, not with whatever affects him, and not with his own personal being. Brotherly love is concerned with the person himself and for his own sake—irrespective of his rights, deserts or worthiness. The same contrast holds good in relation to νέμεσις, which also accepts or rejects the joy or suffering of others according to their deserts. Brotherly love affirms and welcomes the entire well-being of others, deploring and contending against their hardships of every kind.

This tendency, however, goes only one step of the way. The valuational point of view, the moral claim, is itself a different one. Justice puts all men on a level, expanding ultimately into uniform collectivism. Neighbourly love only places one's own ego on a level with that of others, concerning itself merely with those who are nearest at hand, those accidentally present, with the narrow circle of those who are within reach. Indirectly, of course, it applies to the whole community as much as justice does; but it begins at the other end, not with conduct that is outwardly right, but with the central point of one's disposition, which determines all positive treatment of others.

This is due to a still more radical difference. Justice in its ultimate purpose is indeed constructive, but in its basis it is negative; its primary demands are prohibitions and restrictions. Love of one's neighbour is positive from beginning to end. Its command forthwith declares what one ought to do. Certainly it thereby says also what one ought not to do. But its negation is secondary. Therefore in its total tendency it includes justice—except the objective regulations of the community—and surpasses it in richness of content. Aristotle saw this clearly in the nature of φιλία: if all men were friends, there would be no need of law—a statement of which the converse cannot be affirmed; for even if all were just, they would still have need of love.[1] Even more cogently do the Gospels define the relation of the new morality of love to the old morality of justice: "I have not come to destroy

---

[1] *Eth. Nic.*, 1155a. 26; compare also 1159b. 25: justice and love are περὶ τὰ αὐτὰ καὶ ἐν τοῖς αὐτοῖς.

but to fulfil"; or "Herein lies the whole Law and the Prophets."

Of course brotherly love is not in every respect an adequate substitute for justice. In the community as a whole there is need for the firm structure, the formal system, of law. Social structure on the grand scale cannot remain a matter of feeling. Justice retains its unique value. Within a small circle, on the other hand, love of one's neighbour has a much greater influence. In content it is richer; it meets every single case. For it there is no legal formula. Yet it finds a new law each time. It would be pointless to prescribe for it anything definite, since from any given situation it constructively discovers what is needed; and, as it is continually making new laws, its content is always different. This inner spontaneity raises it above the uniformity of a fixed standard.

(c) ANTINOMICAL RELATION TO JUSTICE

Unlike justice, love of one's neighbour has its root deep in the spirit. In so far as both have to do with the binding of person to person, justice unites merely surface with surface (hence its origin in social frictions and the negative character of its commands); but brotherly love directly links the inward life of one person to that of another. This is why it cannot tie itself down to laws and standards, indeed cannot set up any laws or make any general rules. It extends over the whole life of man and into all his spheres of interest and all situations. For such love there is nothing too small or too trivial; even the least weighty matter has significance for it, in so far as it expresses the mental attitude of the one who loves. In this way it hallows what seems of no account, filling it with meaning and import. Accordingly, in every new emergency it is a living orientation, an ingenious discovery of the commandment inherent in the situation itself. Its vitality is due to the fact that it is rooted in the concrete fulness of everyday life.

This concrete fulness is not accessible to justice, because

justice ignores the inner world of the individual person. Justice is not allowed to see it. A judge, who respects the person, is unjust. The ancients depicted Themis with eyes bandaged, and holding in her hands a pair of scales and a sword. Justice is blind, weighing objectively, judging rigidly. Love for one's neighbour sees, is responsive and judges not. It understands everything, having brooded over all the details of the situation. It is not a sitting in judgment upon the deed, but an entering of the spirit into the spirit of the doer.

From this point of view early Christianity saw in brotherly love the unifying principle of all virtue; it was "the greatest," even when compared with "faith and hope." Whatever good a man might do was only accounted morally good by the Christian, provided it was an outcome of love. For him all other values derived their worth only from this one. The basal implication here is that dispositions are the only moral values. What could only be seen dimly when justice was the dominant value, now becomes clear: that the question is not concerning the action itself but the motive. From the point of view of love, the value of the intention is plainly distinguished from the intended value.

Brotherly love is certainly not on this account the unifying principle of all virtue. That was an exaggeration. Its very contrast to justice can teach much on this point. Justice may be unloving, brotherly love quite unjust. Desire for justice, even when combined with hate, enmity, disdain, still remains a desire for justice, and as such is of value, while love even in cases of obvious injustice still remains love and is valuable in its own way. This lies in the nature of both values; their difference is basic. The various attempts also to bring them both under one law should be looked upon as having miscarried. Kant's categorical imperative aspired to be such an attempt. In fact, however, through its legal form alone, it remained suspiciously close to justice. It could not draw into itself the spontaneousness and creativeness of love. The reflection as to whether the particular maxim could become a law for all, weakened its vitality. From this it followed naturally that Kant rejected love as a motive, together with all other "inclinations" and—quite in accord with the Stoic doctrine concerning the affections—described it as pathological.

Love and justice make fundamentally different demands. They take only the first step together—this is what occasions error—and then their ways diverge, each with its own justification; and in the richness of their concrete consequences they stand in antinomic opposition—just because and in so far as they relate to the same situation. Thus it happens that in any single situation, if it be of this kind, they may confront each other in open conflict. Here we have a case of antinomy among the virtues themselves. It is the more significant, in that it exists between the basic values of two distinct groups. But the strange thing in this case is that the two values are obviously not of the same axiological grade. Brotherly love is morally the higher.

(d) RESENTMENT, FALSE LOVE AND PITY

A neighbour in the context: Love thy neighbour, is primarily the needy person, the one who is in want. Hence has arisen the impression that love is merely an aspect of pity. This misunderstanding, out of which Schopenhauer constructed a theory, led further to Nietzsche's criticism of brotherly love. If love is devoted essentially to the weak and oppressed, the notion is not far-fetched that in itself love is not really a value, but has been falsely set up as such by the oppressed themselves in resentment. Their resentment is of this nature: the things they really long for but cannot attain, such as power, strength, wealth, prosperity, they declare to be of no value but to be the very opposite. By this falsification of values, in so far as they succeed in believing it, they escape the pangs of envy. It is clear also that the oppressed would inevitably be disposed to see value in a benefactor's brotherly love, even if it were not in itself of any moral worth. That this psychological process might suffice to form a hidden basis for a morality of pity at least cannot be denied. Nor can it be disputed that the morality of brotherly love, like every one-sided moral code, has led to a depreciation of values of a different kind. Even so, the argument is faulty: for it ignores the main issue.

The essence of neighbour-love is not pity at all nor suffering, but a feeling, a striving, which approves another person as such. One suffers sympathetically only with what is poor, weak and sickly in a human being. But love does not spend itself upon this at all, but upon something else. By its nature it turns toward what is of value, never toward the opposite. "What is loved in a person who is sick and poor is not his sickness and poverty, but something behind these; and from this alone comes help."[1] Brotherly love is the living sense of another's worth; and in so far as this is endangered—whether from without or from within—it comes to the rescue. It is fundamentally positive, spending itself upon a man's total humanity, upon that in him which is capable and worthy of life. This alone love accounts valuable. Only as an effect of this attitude does devotion to one who is in want and misery follow; and it does so, because want and misery stifle the man's free humanity. As a basic tendency love is not at all a reaction to the person's momentary condition, but is a spontaneous, original interest in him as a person, including all that concerns him, like the interest one has in oneself and all that concerns oneself.

This tendency, which appeals directly to our sense of values as of eminent worth, cannot in any way be explained by resent-

---

[1] For this and for the more exact analysis, as well as for the refutation of Nietzsche's theory concerning Christian love of one's neighbour, see Max Scheler, *Ueber Ressentiment und moralisches Werturteil* (Leipsig, 1912), p. 29. The explanation of the altruism of brotherly love, which is given there, must not be accepted without reservation. In fact, only a special form of altruism, one that does not exhaust the concept, is considered there. But what is said is true of that special form.

ment. On the contrary, the resentment theory expressly denies
it. But to deny it is quite impossible, if one at all grasps the
phenomenon of brotherly love. What is true in the theory
is the fact that there exists a kind of attitude which is sufficiently
like neighbour-love to be mistaken for it, without being like
it in substance. There is, indeed, such a thing as resentful
renunciation of strength and the fulness of life, which in its
unnatural distortion turns toward sickness and weakness as
such, as though these were in themselves something valuable.
But to anyone who is acquainted with real love, whether in his
own experience or by observation of others, it is self-evident
that such an attitude is never genuine pity, much less genuine
love, and indeed that genuine pity, like sympathy with joy, is
always born of love, while the converse is never true.

Confusion on this point, however, as we come across it
again and again, even in the form of self-deception, is very
natural. For the capacity to love is as unequally distributed
as the inclination to feel resentment. Spurious love, like a
weed, springs up everywhere, side by side with real love.
Outwardly they are indistinguishable. The deceptive mimicry
of the spurious extends even to the highest and finest flowers
of the ethos. Only an unperverted sense of values, which, as
it were, listening, can detect the emotional tone itself, is able
to distinguish the one from the other.

(e) EMOTIONAL TRANSCENDENCE OF THE SPHERE OF SELF

Genuine brotherly love is altogether wonderful, a phenomenon,
the mere recognition of which requires a certain amount of
faith. It is a curious invasion of one ego into the experience,
the emotional life and even the moral being of another ego, an
ethical communication between the two worlds, otherwise
eternally separated, of the Self and the Not-self. It is not
knowledge which brings this about. To knowledge each consciousness is closed in upon itself. What a consciousness
"experiences" of the outer world must be given to it, either

by aprioristic discernment or through perception. Now the senses give only physical reality. They cannot disclose another person to view. Is there perhaps an a priori insight, which penetrates so far? At all events there is no cognitive insight of this kind. But there is indeed an emotional apriorism of love which pierces through the dividing wall. How it comes about, how it is possible, we cannot say. But it is an accomplished fact in the aprioristic focusing of one's mind upon another person, together with the whole sphere of his inner life. Emotion, disposition, ultimately will and deed, with their intercession in favour of the other person, perform this miracle of positively transmitting the ethos from man to man. It is different from the passing from subject to object in the cognitive act. Love as a trend forces its way whither knowledge cannot reach, into the sphere of another's inner experience, his feelings, struggles and failures, his happiness and sufferings. Indirectly, of course, it has the character of knowledge. In it there is a recognition of that, in someone else, which otherwise each person knows only in himself, a kind of emotional anamnesis (which, like that of Plato, does not refer back to one's own experience), a feeling-after and with, a living-through by participation.

In this eminently transcending act is accomplished the extension of one's sphere of feeling and experience to another person. The limits which otherwise are rigidly individual are here projected in an outward direction and at the same time externalized; they now include a world quite different in richness and variety of content, the world of a plurality of persons. This does not mean a fusion of persons; in the act of participation the other does not become oneself, although as regards content what is experienced becomes one's own experience. Another's interests become one's own concern, affecting one with the same directness. This is why in him who loves the impulse to help another, to take part, to intervene, is primal, and not at all due to reflection—as little so as it would be in regard to one's own concerns. Deliberation and judgment ordinarily play just as small a part in stimulating the desire to intervene on another's behalf, as they would in prompting one to look to one's own interests. Conversely, all understanding of another's ethos, in fact any real knowledge of human nature which deserves the name, rests upon the emotional act of transcending one's own ego. And this understanding is fundamentally different from that of psychology, which builds on experience and infers from analogy. It is intuitive, it even begins at a point which psychology never reaches—another person's experience and feeling.

(f) The Apriorism and Metaphysic of Brotherly Love

The apriorism of brotherly love does not of course extend to the material, external details of another's experience, or to its provocations, but, on the assumption that these are empirically given, to the emotional character of the experience. Only from the outward situation in which he is placed, through outward signs in his behaviour, can I know that he suffers, grieves, and so on. But what suffering means, and indeed any specific suffering (this particular distress), or how some special suffering works, this I can only "feel a priori." Hence all loving comprehension, which can create a sense of oneness with another person, is intuitive in character. The loving glance is full of insight, of divination. From the slightest sign—from a half-word, a pained smile—it sees in a flash the most complex inner conditions. Even before any stimulus or occasion, it rests on one's own sensitive aprioristic attitude towards the other person. Whenever in this way another's inner life is intuitively disclosed to us, it is always as if we had long known. What is puzzling in this is at any rate common to all aprioristic insight, including the theoretical. Even the infallibility of genuine sympathy is strictly analogous to the certainty of the theoretically aprioristic; like the latter it is by no means granted to everyone, and it is not to be acquired by any generalization from experience.

If one wants to specify this kind of apriority more exactly, it is more akin to the knowledge of things than to the discernment of values. The latter is only the grasping of an ideal form (although ideally self-existent); but aprioristic knowledge of things is a grasping of something actual. In it the gulf that is crossed is greater. So it is in the participation of one who loves. Here also the object grasped is ontologically real in the fullest sense. Its subjectivity does not contradict this in any way. It is real mental life, the psychic and ethical reality of another person.

The fact that moral feeling discovers in its object another personal subject, together with all his ethical prerogatives, a subject who discerns values, pursues them and is himself a carrier of them, in short, that it discovers its own ethical mode of existence in a fellow human being, has from ancient times lured metaphysics into speculative interpretations designed to explain the mystery of sympathy. There is an attempt of this kind in the Stoic συμπάθεια, the universal cosmic emotion of one who in the unity of the λόγος senses all things. More deeply anchored still is the Neo-Platonic co-operation of each and all in emotional intimacy, wherein all individuation (μερισμός) is a later breaking up of the primal One (ἕν), as Godhead. But the thought that all entities are ultimately one Being, and that only man's blindness causes him to see himself and others as separate beings, is as old as philosophy; it goes back to the Vedantic teaching. According to this view, individual life is only an appearance, not a reality, for all life is one. By the path of sympathetic presentiment man breaks through the appearance and returns to identity with primal Being.

This ancient and respected view of the universe, which has become widely known through Schopenhauer's metaphysic of "pity," rests upon a simple proposition of identity and suffers from the characteristic defects of such a proposition. It overshoots the mark. It destroys the phenomenon, the mystery, the act of self-transcendence. For this act belongs to the phenomenon and must not be denied. On what the bridge over the intervening gulf rests is the eternally enigmatic, the metaphysical, factor in the problem of brotherly love. If in its place one simply posits the identity of all finite entities, one misunderstands its nature, just as much as one misunderstands the nature of knowledge of things, if one simply identifies "thought and Being." Here once more the essential thing is to stand by the phenomenon.

(g) THE AUTONOMY OF THE MORAL VALUE IN BROTHERLY LOVE

Independently of any interpretation and of any metaphysic the moral value of brotherly love, as such, subsists. One cannot maintain that this value was brought, in its full purity, that is, in its complete autonomy, into current acceptance by Christianity. In it there stood behind brotherly love the love of God, which no longer has the ethical impress. In his neighbour the Christian loves the Christian God. "Whatsoever ye do unto one of the least of these, my brethren, ye do unto me." This savours of the traditional metaphysic. Still more doubtful does the morality of love become, when it is linked to the notion of "laying up treasure in heaven." Here a transcendent, other-worldly eudæmonism discloses itself. Neither of these aspects of Christianity is compatible with the ethical nature of brotherly love. Even in Christianity one must first free this virtue from traditional errors.

Precisely in brotherly love can the self-subsistence of moral, that is, purely dispositional, values be more clearly seen than anywhere else. Not that it is not based on goods and situational values; these are all that it intends and achieves. Its striving is directed throughout to the procuring of goods for one's fellowman. That he should have and enjoy them is the object in view. The value of the disposition is conditioned by the fact that the things aimed at are of value. But this condition only provides a basis. Not only is the value of the loving intention different and of an order altogether higher, but it is also quite independent of the actual grade of the goods in the scale of values. The greater amount of help rendered is not attached to the greater moral value. On the contrary, the amount and genuineness of the love ennobles the help it bestows; something of the value of the disposition goes over into the lifeless thing and appears in it as a finer lustre. This is what the Gospels so eloquently proclaim in the story of the widow's mite. The moral value does not increase with the greatness of the gift, but with the greatness of the love, with the depth of the intention which is directed toward the other person. The distance between it and egoism, the degree of self-abnegation and self-transcendence, constitute the measure of brotherly love. For therein alone lies the proof of its reality, of the living participation in the value-carrying personality of another.

The self-subsistence of its value becomes still clearer, if one takes into account that brotherly love is a kind of solidarity, and a kind different from justice, corresponding to the different sort of union between person and person. It does not bear the whole social structure on its back; it resists any fixed form. Yet it by no means spends itself wholly in the strong sentiments which bind us to those who are near and dear to us. In contrast to the solidarity of justice, it is truly universal, not being confined by any boundaries of nation or State. For although only one who is near is the object of sympathy, yet potentially every human being is a neighbour—and this is no mere possibility, for there are many ways of coming into contact. But, above all, through brotherly love the fact of being jointly responsible grows into universal participation in the fate, the sufferings and actions of the rest of the world. On account of the relatively small share of each, this may have only a subjective significance. But when a wider section of the multitude encircles the world with the same love, and actively concentrates upon doing what is enjoined upon them by sympathy and the fact of a common destiny, this solidarity rises to such a power that it can determine the fate of whole classes of society.

The common responsibility is then something in the highest degree real and positive. And perhaps of all the active forces of social life it is the deepest and purest. In this respect it is stronger and more fundamental than the solidarity of justice. As it springs from union of a deeper kind, it radiates over a wider area.

TRUTHFULNESS AND UPRIGHTNESS

(a) Truth and Truthfulness

TRUTH and truthfulness are not the same. Both are of value, but only the latter is a moral value. Truth is the objective agreement of thought, or conviction, with the existing situation. The agreement is not in the least dependent upon the free will of man. Hence it has no moral value.[1]

Truthfulness, on the other hand, is agreement of one's word with one's thought, or conviction. It is in the power of man to establish this agreement; he bears the responsibility of doing so. Truthfulness is a moral value. One's word, the object of which is to be a witness to one's real opinion, conviction and attitude, ought to achieve this end solely. For as this is its object, everyone assumes involuntarily that one's word is truthful—unless there exists some special ground for distrust. The thing said is taken as really meant. Nothing is presupposed, but that the sense peculiar to the words will be fulfilled. Herein consists the natural and good trust of anyone who is not morally corrupted, the faith he puts in the words he hears. The lie is the misuse of this good trust. It is not simply a violation of the sense of the words, but at the same

---

[1] This sounds paradoxical, but only because one is not accustomed to distinguish truth from truthfulness. The merging of the two concepts has worked confusion even in the theory of knowledge. In fact the two are altogether indifferent to each other. The truthful man may very well say what is untrue, of course *bona fide*, in that he is in error. And a liar may very well speak the truth, of course against his will, in that he mistakes the truth for untruth. For the essence of the lie is not to present as true what is untrue, but what one holds to be untrue. Thus it comes about that an untrue word may be truthful and a true word may be a lie. It is the same relation as that which exists in all action (and speech is action) between the inward disposition and its effects. The best Will may bring about evil; the worst, good.

time a deception of another person, based upon his trustfulness.

Inasmuch as words are not the only form of expressing one's actual attitude of mind, there is together with truthfulness of word also truthfulness of act, of allowing oneself to appear to be such or such, indeed of conduct in general. One can tell a lie by means of a deed, by one's bearing, one's pose. Straight-forwardness, or uprightness, is related to pretence not other-wise than truthfulness to a lie. Still, mere silence can be a lie. One who pretends and conceals is a liar in the wider sense of the word.

A lie injures the deceived person in his life; it leads him astray. Sincere expression is a good for the other person, since he can depend upon it; and under these circumstances it is a high and inestimable good. One might accordingly think that the dispositional value of truthfulness is only a special instance of neighbourly love. A lie is, in fact, loveless. This connection may exist; and a trace of it must always be at hand. But it is not the distinguishing mark of truthfulness as such. There is something here besides. The unloving man, for instance, is merely less worthy from the moral point of view, but he is not reprehensible, not despicable. But the untruthful man is indeed so. He heaps upon himself an odium of an entirely different kind. He is "branded" as a liar, as one in whom we can have no confidence, as an untrustworthy person. Trust-worthiness is a quite distinctive moral value; it inheres as a constituent element in what gives a man "integrity." The liar is precisely the man who cannot be regarded as an "in-teger," his worth as a witness is damaged.

In truthfulness and uprightness there is an element of purity. A lie is a kind of stain—which one cannot say of a failure to love; it is a degradation of one's own personality, something to be ashamed of. In it there is always a certain breach of trust. And there is also in it an element of cowardice. For in truthfulness there inheres "the courage of truth." All this distinguishes it from neighbourly love. A truthful man may in some other respects be immoral; likewise one who loves may be untruthful. For there are lies which do not at all injure the person who is deceived; indeed, there are some which one commits out of genuine love. And conversely there is a truthfulness which is highly unloving.

But, despite everything, the essential connection between truth and truthfulness is by no means broken. Objective truth is still the value which is intended and striven for by the truthful person. It is the goods-value upon which truthfulness is based. The situation which the truth-speaker aims to bring about is that the other person shall experience the truth. Upon this reference to objective truth—in which the general connection between the intended value and the value of the intention re-appears—depends the high situational value of truthfulness in private as well as in public life. There is also a public truthfulness, just as there is a fraudulent and falsified public opinion. Freedom of speech, of conviction, of instruction, of confession, is a fundamental moral requirement of a healthy communal life. In the ethos of nations the struggle for such freedom is a special chapter on truthfulness; likewise the official lie, the deliberate misleading of the masses to attain particular ends, even down to the practice of official calumniation and instigation to hatred, constitute another special chapter. Truthfulness as a community-value is a permanent ideal of the moral life, which in history for ever meets with new obstacles.

(*b*) VALUATIONAL CONFLICTS BETWEEN TRUTHFULNESS AND THE SO-CALLED "NECESSARY LIE"

Truthfulness as a value, with its specific moral claim, admits of no exceptions at all. What is called the necessary lie is always an anti-value—at least from the point of view of truthfulness as a value. No end can justify deliberate deception as a means —certainly not in the sense of causing it to cease to be a moral wrong.

Still we are confronted here with a very serious moral problem, which is by no means solved by the simple rejection of each and every lie. There are situations which place before a man the unescapable alternative either of sinning against truthfulness or against some other equally high, or even some higher, value. A physician violates his professional duty, if he tells a patient who is dangerously ill the critical state of his health; the imprisoned soldier who, when questioned by the enemy, allows the truth about his country's tactics to be extorted from him, is guilty of high treason; a friend, who does not try to conceal information given to him in strictest personal confidence, is guilty of breach of confidence. In all such cases the mere virtue of silence is not adequate. Where suspicions are aroused, mere silence may be extremely eloquent. If the physician, the prisoner, the possessor of confidential information will do their duty of warding off a calamity that threatens, they must resort to a lie. But if they do so, they make themselves guilty on the side of truthfulness.

It is a portentous error to believe that such questions may be solved theoretically. Every attempt of the kind leads either to a one-sided and inflexible rigorism concerning one value at the expense of the rest, or to a fruitless casuistry devoid of all significance—not to mention the danger of opportunism. Both rigorism and casuistry are offences against the intention of genuine moral feeling. The examples cited are so chosen that truthfulness always seems to be inferior to the other value which is placed in opposition to it. It is the morally mature and seriously minded person who is here inclined to decide in favour of the other value and to take upon himself the responsibility for the lie. But such situations do not permit of being universalized. They are extreme cases in which the conflict of conscience is heavy enough and in which a different solution is required according to the peculiar ethos of the man. For it is inherent in the essence of such moral conflicts that in them value stands against value and that it is not possible to escape from them without being guilty. Here it is not the values as such in their pure ideality which are in conflict; between the claim of truthfulness as such and the duty of the soldier or friend there exists no antinomy at all. The conflict arises from the structure of the situation. This makes it impossible to satisfy both at the same time. But if from this one should think to make out a universal justification of the necessary lie, one would err, as much as if one were to attempt a universal justification for violating one's duty to one's country or the duty of keeping one's promise.

Nevertheless a man who is in such a situation cannot avoid making a decision. Every attempt to remain neutral only makes the difficulty worse, in that he thereby violates both values; the attempt not to commit oneself is at bottom moral cowardice, a lack of the sense of responsibility and of the willingness to assume it; and often enough it is also due to moral immaturity, if not to the fear of others. What a man ought to do, when he is confronted with a serious conflict that is fraught with responsibility, is this: to decide according to his best conscience; that is, according to his own living sense of the relative height of the respective values, and to take upon himself the consequences, external as well as inward, ultimately the guilt involved in the violation of the one value. He ought to carry the guilt and in so doing become stronger, so that he can carry it with pride.

Real moral life is not such that one can stand guiltless in it. And that each person must step by step in life settle conflicts, insoluble theoretically, by his own free sense of values and his own creative energy, should be regarded as a feature of the highest spiritual significance in complete humanity and genuine freedom. Yet one must not make of this a comfortable theory, as the vulgar mind makes of the permissible lie, imagining that one brings upon oneself no guilt in offending against clearly discerned values. It is only unavoidable guilt which can preserve a man from moral decay.

CHAPTER XXVI (LI)

TRUSTWORTHINESS AND FIDELITY

(a) THE ABILITY TO MAKE PROMISES

IN valuational quality, reliability is closely allied to truthfulness. Both refer to the trustworthiness of the person. But in their more specific content they are wellnigh opposite to each other. The reliable man vouches for his word by his deed; the truthful man vouches for a fact (as he understands it) by his word. In both cases it is a guarantee of agreement by the person; only in the one case it is the guarantee of one's word regarding an actually existing situation; in the other it is the guarantee of a situation, still unactualized and outstanding, by one's permanent word. The situational value therefore in truthfulness rests upon the certainty of the witness; in the case of reliability it rests upon the certainty of a future deed, in its actualization, or generally in its future existence. Accordingly the moral worth of these two certainties is not the same.

It inheres in the essence of a promise, that with it a claim arises on the one side; on the other, an obligation.[1] Every stipulation, every compact, every treaty—even that which is ideally at the basis of positive law—rests upon this connection. A treaty is a two-sided promise. This connection as such is independent of whether there is an intention of keeping the promise. A promise, on the contrary, has worth only if the intention is there.

If the intention is only a momentary one, which vanished in the hour when it was discharged, its worth is slight. If the will remains unchanged, it is great. The reliable man is the one whose promise is of value, whose will is fixed by his word

[1] Adolph Reinach, *Die apriorischen Grundlagen des bürgerlichen Rechtes, Jahrbuch für Philos. und Phänom. Forschung,* I. 2, 1912, p. 718 ff.

(he will abide by it) until it is discharged, however much his mind may have changed afterwards. He holds himself bound by his promise. And it is exactly his being bound, upon which the man relies, who has the claim upon him.

It does not need to be proved, that by far the greatest part of all existing co-operation and order in public as in private social life rests upon treaty—whether it was overtly entered into, or arose according to custom, or was tacitly recognized. But then it is evident that only the reliable man is capable of keeping to such co-operation and order, that is, of living in the community. Reliability is the capacity of a man so to promise that the other man can be sure that the promise will be discharged, a capacity for treaty, compact, valid assent, to undertake or desist. It is therefore the moral strength of the person to speak for himself, to determine beforehand his future conduct, to guarantee in his own person future conduct not yet actual but yet under his control, therefore to guarantee for himself beyond the present moment.

(b) THE IDENTITY AND SUBSTANCE OF THE MORAL PERSON

This is not one of the natural endowments of man. The natural man follows impulsively the momentary excitations. He cannot know what he will afterwards decide to do, for he does not know what determines him. He cannot promise. The self-predestination, which is involved in the binding promise, is a specifically ethical power in man, which, as an identical and abiding element, stands over against the coming and going of the determinational factor, whether inward or external. The morally mature man has this power; he can determine beforehand what he is going to will and to do. His present will has power over his future will, and can be a substitute for it; or, more correctly, he knows that it is not merely his momentary Will but one that will preserve itself in the future Will—however this may be otherwise directed. All depends upon the element of self-conservation. In the fixed resolution there is something which remains the same, the continuity of which overleaps the temporal process, something which not only determines but is aware also of this determining power, and from it derives certainty.

But behind this volitional identity there is ultimately the identity of the person himself. One who promises identifies himself as he is now with what he will be later. He can do this, in so far as he is certain that he, as he will be then, will be identical with himself as he is now. The breaking of a promise would be a renunciation of himself, its fulfilment a holding fast to himself, a remaining true to himself. On this personal identity depends a man's moral continuity in contrast to all natural and empirical instability; on it, therefore, depends at the same time the ethical substance of the person.

It is the essential basic superiority of the moral over the natural constitution of man, that he possesses such identity, such substantiality. A man is rightly estimated among men to be moral, in proportion to the value of his pledged word. So far as he is worthy of trust, capable of treaty, so far can one reckon upon him as the same person. Whoever has once realized this has moral pride in being trustworthy. To him the unreliable man is despicable, is morally defective.

(c) The Ethos of Fidelity

Thus it comes about that in the moral life the ethos of reliability has won a decisive and dominating position. But in its universalization it bears the lofty name of fidelity.

Fidelity is not confined to the keeping of promises and agreements. Its field is wider. There is an obligation which holds although no word has been given; only very few of the fixed human relations upon which the individual relies in life rest upon definitely made bargains. Everyone tacitly recognizes a host of claims of other persons upon him, so far at least as he also makes them upon others.

But fidelity extends beyond this to the disposition itself.

A change of mental attitude is itself infidelity. For instance, it is fundamentally true that every avowed disposition—good-will that has been shown, love that has been manifested—carries with it the expectation of its own continuance, as well objectively in its meaning and nature as subjectively in the emotion of him to whom it is expressed. Sympathy, friendship, love, if it is only a transient mood, bears the impress of spurious-ness, and is not worthy of the name. False, inconstant disposition deceives the person who accepts it, exactly in the same way as does a lightly given, quickly forgotten promise. Even the outer symbols and signs of love have something binding in them, something holy, postulating inviolability. It is sense-less to give to anyone friendship or love, in order to take it back on the next occasion. All love which has been felt and expressed has already in truth the character of a promise; in essence it is of full promise and thus awakens a justifiable hope. Therefore fidelity is the test of a genuine disposition. The unfaithful person esteems lightly a promise given in outward deed. But the faithful man is he who preserves the moral identity of himself as a person in the constancy of his attitude towards others.

This preservation extends to all human relations as a moral requirement, from the most external and physical to the inner-most and least palpable. The ethos of fidelity is that of the preservation of every disposition universally. Upon its worth depends the holiness of the ancient German fidelity of man to man, celebrated in song, as also the holiness of personal and intimate loyalty; outward apostacy and treachery offend against this value, like a hidden breach of faith. Fidelity extends to everything to which the human will can commit itself. One may be faithful or unfaithful to a goal, to a cause. Un-faithfulness even to a cause is morally of low worth, but con-stancy in disposition is a sign of full and permanent moral worth; and like bravery it is independent of the value of the object in view. To the person, however, who puts his trust in an avowed disposition, unfaithfulness is a moral crime.

Here it always has something of the character of a breach of confidence.

The ethos of fidelity is fundamentally personal stability. It stands in antinomic contrast to the ethos of excitability and variability, which inheres in so many other values (for example, in fulness of life). There reverberates through it a dominant motive from the sphere of the most general contrasts of values: inertia as the perseverance of ethical substance.[1] The substance is the person. Its active excitability, so valuable in itself, always brings with it the danger of its losing itself. Against this stands as a check the strict moral requirement of persistence. All valuational factors of habit, which lie in this direction, belong to the ethos of fidelity: every tenacious clinging to ends of pursuit, to precepts, to life-tasks, to persons—be it in love or friendship, reverence or contempt—every loyalty to nation, home, State, to communal interests of every kind. All fidelity, because as continuity of disposition it is at the same time a conservation of personality, is ultimately fidelity to oneself, all unfaithfulness is unfaithfulness to self.

[1] Cf. Chapter VIII (b), Vol. II.

TRUST AND FAITH

(a) ADVENTURE, COURAGE AND THE SPIRITUAL POWER OF TRUST

JUSTICE and brotherly love, as well as whatever is related to them in the way of conduct, have a meaning for everyone to whom they are manifested. They need here no special praise in order to receive recognition; no virtue is required on the part of him who stands in the enjoyment of them. But it is otherwise with truthfulness and reliability. Their value as such is indeed just as independent of any definite recognition on the part of others. But the goods-value attached to them—and both are accounted among the highest possessions for one's fellow-men—is dependent upon a certain attitude in which one meets it. This attitude is faith, or trust. It is a new and distinct moral value, fundamentally different from that of truthfulness and reliability and still related to both these, which are presupposed in the other person; and it is rational only in this relation; it is a complementary value. Fidelity is rational only for him who really trusts himself to it, truthfulness only for him who believes the word he utters. Once more, trust, unless another's truthfulness and reliability justify it, floats in the air, is imprudent, frivolous, pernicious.

Credulity, too ready trustfulness, is a serious fault. One may indeed excuse it, for a knowledge of human nature is not every man's business. But habitual distrust, the opposite fault, is morally far more flagrant, a rooted scepticism in regard to moral character. The distrustful man sins against the one who is trustworthy; in him is lacking the feeling for the goodness of an upright disposition, when it is presented to him. By his doubt he belittles the truthful and faithful man. The excuse for him, of course, lies again in the restrictedness of human insight. All trust, all faith, is an adventure; it always requires something of moral courage and spiritual strength. It is always accompanied by a certain commitment of the person. And where the trust is far-reaching, where the faith is impregnable, there the commitment is unlimited, and with it the moral value of the trust rises proportionately.

Real trust is always a claim imposed upon the other person —namely, to justify the trust—but at the same time and along with this it is a precious gift, an honour conferred upon the person, which can be raised to marked distinction. One entrusts one's own interests to another and appreciates his trustworthiness. This gift is comparable to that of love and, as a value, can even transcend it. But the principal difference is not in the degree of the value, but in the character of the gift itself. The one who loves does not surrender himself; he stakes nothing, he gives only from himself; his own personality remains untouched. The trustful person, on the contrary, puts himself into the hands of him whom he trusts; he stakes himself. In this way his gift is morally the higher, and presupposes a greater moral strength. This is reflected in the fact that one can and ought to love everybody in the sense of neighbour-love, but cannot and ought not to trust everybody. Trust and faith have something discriminating in them. From the point of view of love, no one is entirely unworthy; its gift is never squandered, not even when it is rewarded with ingratitude. He who loves is thereby never endangered. But he who trusts exposes himself to danger. If his gift is trampled underfoot, he himself is trodden upon. Hence the unequalled depth of moral indignation which a deliberate breach of faith calls forth even in those who are not betrayed by it.

(b) BLIND FAITH

The ability to trust is spiritual strength, a moral energy of a unique kind. Its foundation is not experience, not previous testing. For it is only by showing trust that a man can be tested; and doing so presupposes that spiritual energy. Faith exists prior to experience. It alone is the foundation of genuine trust. What justifies such faith is only a sensing of moral value in the person. This sensing may be erroneous. Faith is for ever an adventure. It is always at bottom "blind faith."

This blindness is just what is essential to it. A "seeing" faith, which has good grounds or objective certainty, is not at all genuine faith; there is no risk in it to one's own personality: for example, when one is certain of the discharge of a pledge, because it is to the interest of the other person to discharge it. "Not to see and yet to believe," that is the heart of the matter. Even religious faith is subject to the same sensing of values. A faith which requires "signs and wonders" is not real faith. Indeed, one might add that he who sees and knows can no longer take on trust, that is, can no longer believe autonomously and properly—simply because he knows. Knowledge steals a march on faith, rendering it superfluous. Hence genuine blind faith—for example, simply holding fast to the mere word of a man, where all evidence of the facts is overwhelmingly against him—is a unique phenomenon, bordering on the marvellous. Blind faith, blind trust, is the supreme endurance-test of moral strength, the true criterion of genuineness in all the deeper dispositional relations of man with man. How many a person believes himself to be capable of "friendship" in the high sense of the word, and yet loses faith upon the first occasion, where the apparent "facts" are unfavourable to the friend. Afterwards he would need to confess that his friendship was morally of little worth—even when his loss of trust proved correct. For fidelity is often at a loss, when it sees itself to be mistaken.

(c) SOLIDARITY AND THE EDUCATIVE POWER OF FAITH

That faith "removes mountains," that it is eminently a creative power in life, this fact, long known in the domain of religion, has never attained its rightful recognition in ethics. All human relationships, from external material "credit" up to the highest forms of delegated power in public life and of personal trust in private life, are based upon faith. All the strength derived from co-operation consists in men's reliance upon one another; this holds good in the highest degree, where a common faith enters in and binds men in devotion to high purposes. It is pre-eminently a communal value; it is the most positive unifying energy, which welds together a variety of individual persons, with their separate interests, into a collective unit; it is more elemental than justice or neighbour-love—the former being deliberate and a matter of judgment, the latter too unequal and far too private an affair of the emotions. There is a type of solidarity different from that of love and the sense of justice, a standing together "like one man" in the unity of a conviction and in the consciousness of standing together, that is, in sure and reciprocal trust. Solidarity of faith is more fundamental than any other kind, it is the basis of all commonalty. Community, whether national or intimately private, is always community of faith. The distrustful man is not adapted to it; he excludes himself. Distrust breaks all bonds. Lack of faith in a cause, like lack of faith in a man, means separation. Faith is capacity for co-operation. Upon it rests the tremendous extension of the individual's sphere of power by his uniting with many; it is like solid earth under his feet at every step in life. The distinctively moral value of life begins in the sphere of those who trust one another. In that sphere as the substantial element their best qualities and capacities first unfold. In it alone is found outward freedom, on the basis of which the education of a race towards inner freedom and the capacity to assume responsibility and to delight in it, becomes for the first time possible. When a community as a whole lacks faith, the individual seeks it in a small circle, whether in the family or among those of like mind (among natural friends, according to the ancient conception), or in a personally chosen friend.

The proof that faith is a creative power is that it actually generates in another person that which is believed to exist in him. The moral energy issuing from one who believes is in a high degree an educative force. It is capable of making the man who is trusted, reliable and deserving of faith and trust. Of course this holds good only within definite limits, and pre-supposes certain moral conditions (certain endowments) in the other person. But it remains true that in general trusting a man makes him good, distrusting him makes him bad. He to whom nothing good is ever attributed, never learns to be good or to justify the placing of confidence in him. A man who has undeservedly acquired the reputation of being a liar easily becomes one; he lacks the moral incentive of satisfying faith placed in him. He is driven towards that which is attributed to him.

Conversely, in the unreliable man there exists a sensing of the value which he has not but is believed to possess; and this feeling can be aroused and educated into a moral pride to deserve the trust put in him. So long as a man retains a spark of moral feeling, the impulse lives in him, not to fall short of what is expected of him. This is a well-known method of moral discipline; but that there is in faith a general power of awakening the moral life, has been less widely recognized; yet it deserves to become a common possession. Finally, there is somthing good in everyone. And it grows with the exercise of it and through encouragement. It languishes through lack of appreciation. Faith can transform a man, towards good or evil, according to what he believes. This is its secret, its power to remove mountains. Distrust is impotence. Trust imposes an obligation. The ethos of fidelity increases with faith. It is carried by the consciousness of what is attributed to it. This inner dependence is not reversible. Of the narrower valua-tional group of "truthfulness, fidelity, faith," faith is the basis which supports everything else, however much the contrary may appear to be true to external and traditional observation.

(d) Faith as a Factor in Friendship

Trust as a value becomes complete only when it is reciprocal. The reciprocity produces among men a unity of a higher kind: a certainty, a stable and fixed security. When such a relation is justified by uprightness on either side, by reliability and fidelity, we see on a small scale the ideal ethical form of life.

This is the foundation of friendship. A still further factor, personal love, is essential—friendship is indeed a highly complex value; but trust, including its complementary values, is its basis. In relation to these values love is autonomous; it can subsist without faith, it rests on a foundation of its own, however much a tendency to good faith may be native to it. Friendship is different. A friend is pre-eminently one whose faith in us is unwavering; nothing can shatter it, not even our lack of love for him. Friendship is more objectively based than love; of course this dispositional foundation by itself is without the higher qualities of love, without its depth of feeling, without the richness of content, the glowing devotion. Friendship comes to fruition in love, but does not arise out of it.

(e) Optimism and Hope

In an individual the ethos of faith may develop into an all-dominating view of life. It is the view of the morally strong man, the strength of whose faith is not to be overborne by disappointments. As there is an inclination to love and justice, so a man may have a predisposition which inclines him to trust. It consists of a kind of general faith in the goodness of man. It is not incompatible with a prudent reserve on the part of a person of experience. It manifests itself in a capacity to detect what is good and genuine in another's disposition amidst less worthy tendencies and to seize upon the good, even to draw it out and develop it by the influence of one's trust.

In such an ethos there is a peculiar form of optimism—

fundamentally different from that of wisdom, and yet, like that of wisdom, not eudæmonistic but purely ethical. It is akin to the simplicity of a child, to purity, which is supported by a similar faith in the good, and has the same power for good over human hearts.[1] In this optimism is preserved an element of genuine innocence in the midst of mature life; indeed, in the strengthening of this disposition there takes place something like a substitute for the return to the ethos of purity, which in the nature of things cannot return. And with it comes a capacity for happiness, which is astonishingly like that revealed in the spirit of a child.

Yet the parallel to purity must not be carried too far. For faith is attained by striving—at least it may be; it is a fruit of moral ripeness, a power developed to a certain height. Certainly it is not found in the "pure fool," who has no suspicion of evil, but rather in him who sees evil but who is not deterred by it from holding fast to the good in man.

Beyond this there is still a higher ethos of faith—in the vision of the great moral ideals of life, which the individual person does not actualize, and in the vision of the great upward strivings of humanity. Distant goals and vast enterprises require a different kind of faith, a faith which temporal un-attainability does not stifle. It inheres in the essence of all such outlooks upon life—and these are those which lend its highest meaning to our existence—that the non-actuality of the goal does not prejudice the reality of the undertaking. Herein the potent moral element of "not seeing and yet believing" attains its culminating point. For it is the high ideals, which man never sees actualized. To this lofty spirit of faith corresponds Hope—a valuational sense of a distinct kind. It is not properly a moral value, like faith; it is not a new "virtue," but only an accompanying emotional factor, the form of happiness which accords with faith and which anticipates its contents.

[1] Cf. Chapter XVII (c), Vol. II.

CHAPTER XXVIII (LIII)

MODESTY, HUMILITY, ALOOFNESS

(a) THE ETHOS OF THE UPWARD GAZE

TOGETHER with all their divergences the values of the second group, which we have thus far considered, have this in common, that they are the values of human neighbourliness. Their ethos is directed to the inner world of another person. But this tendency may go too far. It finds its limit in the rightful claim of the person himself, to remain unmolested in his intimate sphere. Trust, neighbour-love, and especially the sympathy which flows from it, may become aggressive. As a counterpoise they require aloofness. Indeed even truthfulness, uprightness and fidelity (the latter in the form of attachment) must be kept within bounds. It is the same with the values of the first group. Wisdom, justice, valour and especially pride may presume too much; they have a secret tendency towards vanity and haughtiness. They need a similar limit set to them, only in another direction, in the direction of modesty and humility. These are the limiting values of moral self-consciousness and, as such, are genuine and unique. They constitute a narrower group by themselves.

Modesty is according to Socrates the primal virtue of the knowledge of one's own moral nothingness. It appears as the basis even of the proud ethos of "irony." What it is in an inward direction—self-knowledge, self-criticism, judgment of one's own value (and thus the true beginning of wisdom),[1] this it is also in the outward direction, in relation to others: it is reticence in the presence of another's moral worth, due to the consciousness of one's own unworthiness.

The modest man is not at all the one who belittles himself, even there where his total habit of mind tends towards general

[1] Cf. Chapter XX (b), Vol. II.

humility. He is rather the one who aims high in his moral standards, whose points of comparison lie decidedly above him. He thus from the start raises himself above the arrogant and haughty man. The haughty person makes it easy for himself, because he aims low. For purposes of comparison, morally, a worse man is always easy to find, especially if one is helped by having an unsympathetic eye.

As there is an art of being happy and contented by keeping before one's mind those who are less fortunate in worldly goods, so there is a finer art, peculiar to modesty, of keeping before one's mind those who stand on a higher moral level. But as the ethos of modesty is an enduring one, which pervades the whole disposition, it not only attends to those who are morally superior, but extends to the conduct of everyone. In the presence of men morally inferior to him, the modest man is not more exalted than usual; for he does not measure himself by them. Where one is thoroughly conscious of this relationship, it brings about, in an eminent degree, a morally discriminating habit of mind. The modest man is the despair of one who is arrogant, in that he ignores everything which makes the arrogant man feel important. The gaze of the haughty man is directed downward, that of the modest man upward. And on this account the former sees only what is below him, the latter only what is above him. In life there is always something to which a man can look up. The upward gaze is not a result, but a cause. It does not arise out of comparison, but itself selects the points of comparison. In the ethos of the upward gaze all reverence and awe have their basis, as everyone who is morally unspoiled proves by his reverence and awe for real worth and merit, for antiquity or for persons in positions of higher responsibility.

(b) HUMILITY AND PRIDE

What modesty is in relation to others, humility is as an inner form of the character itself. It is the consciousness of falling infinitely short of the mark, in which all comparison with others is ignored. It measures one's own moral being by perfection, as this is understood, by divinity, as the moral ideal or as some sublime exemplar. Unattainability gives the sense of remoteness, which at the same time both oppresses and exalts; the oppression is the sense of one's own nothingness; the exaltation, the sense of being in direct relation with what is transcendently great.

Man does not feel humility in the presence of man—that would be false humility, self-degradation, servility. False humility is a moral aberration, exactly as arrogance is; it lacks all feeling for the infinite distance between oneself and the ethical Ideal. All humility towards what is external is at bottom a false ethos; some moral defect is always concealed in it, a perplexity, a pettiness of spirit, an anxiety, or indeed some spurious passion, such as false shame, or fear of others. Equally adrift is all arrogance, self-righteousness, Pharisaism, when it is organic and not merely a pose. The haughty man has no conception of the loftiness and the inexorability of the moral claim under which he actually stands. To anyone who has a living sense of values, arrogance is something absurd and truly degraded. Genuine humility, on the other hand, is in contradiction neither to the dignity of man nor to justifiable pride. Indeed, correctly understood, it is compatible with genuine pride, which is far removed from vain self-admiration. The ultimate reason for true moral pride is that one measures oneself by a standard which is absolute and unattainably high.

The seemingly antinomic relation between humility and pride is therefore easily broken down. At least in principle. It is not a genuine valuational antinomy. On the contrary, genuine pride and genuine humility evidently belong necessarily together, re-enforce each other and can exist only in synthesis. In this of course it is not said that the synthesis is established of itself, where the attitude of the man inclines to the one or the other side. Rather does there subsist in the human inclination a certain opposition, and this is to blame for the appearance of the antinomy. Humility is just as dangerous a virtue as pride. Both lie close to the boundary of fantastic aberrations. Pride without humility is always on the brink of arrogance and vanity; humility without pride, on the brink of self-degradation, worthlessness and hypocrisy. Each by itself is unstable, is without balance. Only when together, in synthesis, do they become stable, each gaining support from the other.

Their grappling hold of each other, their inward union, constitutes a moral value for which there is no suitable word in language, but the content of which is recognizable from the circumstance that here the two elements, otherwise so easily manifesting themselves outwardly and so disposed to falsification and posing, are wholly bound together inwardly and hold close to the standard of absolute ideals.

(c) KEEPING ONE'S DISTANCE

On another side modesty is connected with reserve, the feeling and the keeping of one's distance in relation to another person. All human proximity requires a limit, as a protection against aggressiveness which takes advantage of proximity itself.

Keeping one's distance is a kind of moral shame, different of course from that of the Aristotelian αἰδώς. The latter is a feeling arising from the exposure of oneself. The ethos of reserve, on the contrary, is shame felt out of respect for another because of his nearness and his exposure, or even only at the thought of his defencelessness; it is the preservation of the intimate privacy of another. There is an intimate sphere for each person, which does not endure the clear, cold, and too intrusive observation of others, even of those who love. All near approach is fundamentally an intrusion. A person stands defenceless against intrusion; and indeed so much the more so, the purer and more transparent he is. Much curiosity and sensationalism may go hand in hand with a loving interest in one's neighbour, for even one who loves is subject to human weaknesses. Sympathy, moreover, is easily shameless, easily vexatious. The proud and the noble want no sympathy. They accordingly are themselves chary of sympathy, not from lack of affection, but from a sense of shame, out of respect for others. Every man in his unique divergence from others, where this is exposed to view, has an alluring effect by the attraction of secrecy. But his human dignity suffers under uncalled-for inspection. Shyness about the good which one does is a characteristic of the truly good deed. Even towards a friend a friend cannot dispense with the sense of reticence. The tacit relationship of trust also, by its very nature, needs retirement. In this case the limit to willing exposure simply lies deeper within one's inner being. But it is never altogether absent. One who is entirely without reticence cannot be a friend. He would be unbearable in his lack of shame.

The truly loving glance is one which covers up and veils. It does not dare to observe even when it might. This holds true still more in the case of the proud man. He is precisely the one who is especially reticent—and not from regard for himself but for the other person. Only he who has a sense of his own worth can respect another's. With him a failure to keep one's distance is a violation of good taste. We might describe the ethos of the man who keeps his distance as that of social distinction. In him we see, clearly outlined and finely felt, the synthesis of pride and modesty, analogous to that of pride and humility. Social distinction in one's attitude towards others is the same as the fusion of pride and humility in one's attitude towards the absolute standard of the moral ideal.

A man of social distinction creates about him a permanent sphere of reserve, which not only wards off aggressive persons, but protects others from too great exposure. He sets up the claim for himself as for them, and in so doing manifests a kind of justice within the most intimate relationships of feeling. He preserves reverence for personality, even where it does not know how to protect itself. He thus provides an area of intimate intercourse, wherein, even when the danger of exposure is nearest, its approach is checked. Only under the protection of such security, as a finely discriminating and inward arrangement of emotional justice, can the flower of human neighbourliness best thrive. For it does not bar out sympathy, love, trust— these are absolute and their value knows no boundary—but only their substitutes, only the imitations and distorting caricatures of the genuine ethos.

THE VALUES OF SOCIAL INTERCOURSE

(a) THE MORAL CHARACTER OF CONVENTIONALITIES

THE ethos of reticence introduces us immediately into a further group of values, which can no longer pass as dispositional in the strict sense, but still are values of conduct. They are more on the surface of human nature, where it exists in the outward contact of individuals, in the friction, as it were, of social intercourse. The depths of consciousness, the sphere where intentions originate, are not touched by them. But every intention, moving outward, receives the stamp of their impress; independently of its deeper value, in passing to the surface it falls under the standard of other values, which affect only its form of expression.

Such forms are by no means without significance in life. A person's "bad form" may be intolerable and make the life of others unendurable. However accidental and conventional the existing forms of social intercourse may be, however absurd they may appear to anyone introduced among them from another circle of society, they are still profoundly necessary to life, and anyone who violates them sins against his fellow-men exactly as much as a person who is unjust or heartless. Indeed by doing so, he is unjust and heartless; he is a transgressor in little things and shows all the signs of such a one; he refuses to others what he claims from them for himself; and like a real criminal, he is subject to condemnation and punishment, to boycott and ostracism.

True neighbourliness applies itself very seriously to the preservation of social forms, even to a delicate and minute conformity to them; it shows deference and it wishes to be inoffensive to others. In these matters one feels a serious responsibility. And a quite definite attitude of mind corresponds to it, when once it is grasped; and thus the formal values of social intercourse prove to be indirectly genuine dispositional values.

Like justice and love, the remaining values of the inner ethos reappear in social forms, diminished and yet unmistakable. This is most clearly seen in offence against social custom. In this sphere a person who lacks self-control is petulant, the unwise man is inconsiderate, blasé or disappointed with the world; cowardice reappears as irresoluteness and vacillation; lack of pride and dignity, as familiarity or boisterousness; untruthfulness, as deliberate pose or affectation; immodesty and lack of reticence, as insolence of manner and petty obtrusiveness; arrogance, as self-assertion and superciliousness.

But in this sphere reliability and trust play a special rôle. In view of generally existing forms it is of the essence of social life, that each individual depends upon every other for the maintenance of forms. Trust of this most external kind is a condition of social intercourse; one who violates the form cannot be relied upon. Finally, in this sphere, the distrustful person, who is suspicious of everyone's deportment, becomes himself uncertain in behaviour and spreads about him a sense of insecurity. He never knows how he stands with others; and they do not know how they stand with him. The whole circle of outward association rests ultimately upon a relationship of trust transferred to the plane of everyday life. All propriety in social encounter with others calls imperatively for a like propriety in them. All human relationships, even if external and apparently of no account, rest upon the power of good faith. In the domain of social forms the man who is heartless and unjust is merely inconsiderate and intolerable; the suspicious man disintegrates, dissolves and even destroys all the bonds of social converse.

(b) EXISTING CUSTOMS

The content of this sphere is an extraordinarily variegated, but an essential, constituent of human civilization, changeable like it and capable of unlimited improvement. Whatever is "custom" in the narrower sense of the word, from external usages to the imponderables of a cultivated style of living, is an illustration. Existing custom is of course historically accidental, perishable, a conventionality, and it is never possible to know a priori why it is just so and not otherwise. There is no axiological reason for its special form. But it is never on that account neutral in value. For it is always a formation of actual values: for instance, of moral values such as considerateness, tact, simplicity, friendly welcome, politeness, quiet demeanour, a sense of propriety and fitness, fine judgment as to when to advance and when to retire—projected into the sphere of outward associations.

These latter qualities and much that is related to them are genuine and permanent values, which recur in every conventional structure, however differently selected and graded the details may be. They do not themselves constitute the existing custom; but custom is the specific form into which they seem to be cast. For without some special form these values cannot become actual.

Here the historical diversity is so great, that it is in fact easy to overlook the moral unity of all customs. This may be unambiguously outlined as follows: The separate existing custom as such is never of absolute value; yet it is relatively so; for it is altogether an absolute value that, in general, customs of some special kind should prevail. Without established customs mankind sinks into formlessness and savagery. Indeed, without them development of the inner ethos is hindered, because it is as dependent upon fixed forms, however superficial, as upon forms of law. The moral value of custom is accordingly a very peculiar one. As its material it has not the special contents but only what is essential in them, their real power of self-maintenance in the special environment. Indirectly there is moral value in the social forms which in themselves are morally indifferent.

We by no means deny that the moral cultivation of these

superficial forms may have a high quality, indeed a peculiar
depth of its own. One need not have in mind simply the more
æsthetic kinds of moral refinement, urbanity (τὸ ἀστεῖον) and
the social graces. In the varied structure of this sphere is
included a considerable amount of heart-culture, fine feeling and
humanity generally. The work devoted to it can never be a
matter of indifference to a morally mature personality, and it
will never come to an end; it therefore holds an important place
in the education of the young.

(c) Aristotle's Virtues of Social Intercourse

The view that there are special values in outward converse is
not a new one. In its table of the virtues the *Nicomachean
Ethics* enumerates three such, but in characteristic fashion two
of these are said to have no name. But where language fails,
paraphrase comes to the rescue. These virtues are described,
according to Aristotle's custom, as μεσότητες, and as such
referred to converse in word and act.[1]

The first has reference to conflict of opinions, to the practical
clash of conviction with conviction. The two extremes inhere
in the attitude of the ἄρεσκος and that of the δύσκολος. The
former is the man who is excessively anxious to please, who
talks blindly and never ventures to defend any conviction; the
latter is unapproachable, difficult, insisting on his own opinion
and refusing further discussion. The implied virtue therefore is
evidently a synthesis of willingness to welcome opinions and an
actual holding by what is known to be right, or a defence of
one's own conviction and a recognition of the other person's
view.

A second virtue of this kind refers to one's being true to
what one really is. Aristotle describes it as a being true in one's
outward demeanour (ἀληθεύειν). As it has only a loose connection with truthfulness, its name is misleading. What is
meant is here again to be inferred from what is said concerning

[1] *Eth. Nic.*, Chapters XII–XIV, p. 1126b ff.

the intermediate position. The virtue is a mean between ἀλαζονεία and εἰρωνεία. The former is boasting, the latter self-depreciation. Both are untrue, disingenuous, assumed. Between them is the presenting of oneself simply as one is, without self-display and without concealment, in short, without posing. One might name it the virtue of straightforwardness. Outwardly, in reporting oneself, it is what inwardly μεγαλοψυχία is in self-estimation.[1]

A degree still nearer to the surface is the third Aristotelian virtue of social deportment. It is on that account of special interest. Its realm is light conversation, the social tone; its subject matter is pleasantry and seriousness. There is a virtue of pleasantry, a genuine ethical attitude of mind, not as it were, the art of being witty (this as such is ethically indifferent), but the rightly balanced, tactful relation to jesting, which is dignified and yet is appreciative of humour. The Aristotelian descriptions ἐπιδεξιότης and εὐτραπελία express but imperfectly the nature of the matter. In German it is very difficult to describe. The *Sinn für Humor* misses the necessary note. This becomes evident if we glance at the extremes which are specified by Aristotle; ἀγροικία and βωμολοχία. The former is a deficient sense of the comic, the latter is frivolity, which converts everything into a subject of jest. The ethos of the mean between these extremes becomes still clearer, if we relate it to the way one takes the utterances of another person. The ἀγροῖκος is the man who cannot see a joke, the βωμολόχος is the one who refuses to take anything seriously.

Genuine moral values inhere in these three virtues. By taking them as models, it would not be too difficult to discover further values in the same sphere. But the examples given are sufficient. None of them is of great ethical import, although they may rise to a considerable height. The entire domain of social intercourse is a border region of the ethical table of values. On the whole its significance lies only in its connection with the relative autonomy of the fundamental values.

[1] Cf. Chapter XXIII (*d*), Vol. II.

Section VII

SPECIAL MORAL VALUES
(THIRD GROUP)

LOVE OF THE REMOTE

(a) THE LIMITING VALUES IN THE ETHICAL SURVEY

As the virtues in the first two groups were but loosely connected, so those of the third do not properly constitute a group at all. Rather may we conceive of each of the four following values as itself a narrower group. Compared with those previously considered, each lies in a special valuational region, points to a perspective reaching into the infinite and passes into the sphere of the axiologically irrational. In direction they are diverging limits, not indeed of the realm of values (for we could not know that), but of human vision.

With some of them it is not easy to outline their content in words, or even to name them exactly. This is true of the first two. There is no historical ethos which corresponds precisely to them. On this account they have never had a name, like so much else that our feeling for values knows very well and discriminates. And as even analogies are inadequate, the attempt to define them objectively is a bold venture.

Still the attempt must be made. We must seize upon the central themes, where and in as far as we can find them. Here Nietzsche has been the pioneer in more than one direction. The exaggerations of his aphorisms, which often spring from his craving for paradox, must not divert us from what he positively saw. The sensationalism of two decades ago, which fell greedily upon these exaggerations and cast suspicion upon the seriousness of the problem, must be entirely ignored. So far as it was right, what was prophetically seen under the pressure of passion must now be calmly surveyed.

(b) EFFORT AS AN ELEMENT IN THE FOLLOWING VIRTUES

All ethically active life is prospective, it is a living in the future and for the future. This inheres in the nature of activity. Only the future belongs to striving. The will has no power over what has already transpired, once it exists.[1] The great gift of foresight and pre-determination (teleology), which is peculiar to man, imposes a profound obligation. It loads him with responsibility for the future, in so far as the future is in his power. How far it is so, cannot of course be estimated beforehand. But no absolute limits can here be set. Man's power of intervening in the cosmic process and determining its course extends just so far as he knows how to expand his capacity by his own energies. The fact that his will goes beyond his capacity is here irrelevant.

This absence of known limits stands in bold contradiction to the fact that man ordinarily is inclined to restrict himself to what lies nearest to him, to what is most evident and close in front of him. His thought does not reach beyond the next day. The pressure of the moment constrains him. What is near absorbs his activity, thrusts itself between him and all wider perspectives and causes them to fall into oblivion.

To this is added the natural tendency to inertia. It is most comfortable to exercise the minimum of activity along beaten tracks. It is much, if a man rises to a perspective which surveys his own life. In so far as such a survey concerns his outward career, every normal man attains it at least in certain moments. This is little, especially as such a "practical" outlook seldom reaches beyond material and eudæmonistic ends. Of course there are noted exceptions, men with high ideals of life. But they usually suffer from the opposite mistake, their idealism is unpractical, visionary, exhausting itself in perpetual yearning and inevitable disappointments. In these cases there is no proper foresight, none gained by serious experience and made critical by it. Ethically this dreamy idealism is just as worthless as dull absorption in the passing moment. In both, the thing that is most important is lacking, complete earnestness of effort.

To combine a life, viewed in the light of ideals, with a cool eye for the actual and the possible, requires an ethos con-

[1] Cf. Chapter XI (g), Vol. II.

siderably above the average. Such a synthesis gives to the bearer of it a certain dignity, which grows with the greatness of the ends he pursues and with the practical effect. In such a life is fulfilled something of man's destiny, which is to become a participant in the creation of the world. But just here it is seen that the perspective of any one individual's life is too small for the actualization of human ideals. One individual can advance a few steps upon such a path. And also in the work which he accomplishes he can go far; he can draw a group of men into the circle of his own idea, and under favourable circumstances he may evoke a total transformation of historical importance. But what will that signify, if his life-work dies with him, or soon after? It is just such work that requires permanence, continuation, a living energy of its own. It inheres in the nature of all effort that looks to an objective value, to go on beyond the life and enterprise of the individual, into a future which he no longer can enjoy. It is not only the fate but is also the pride of a creative mind and is inseparable from his task, that his work survives him, and therefore passes from him to others, in whose life he has no part.

But it is also in the nature of man, that he wishes to see the fruits of his struggle. He also wants to have something for himself; there is something in him which resists the passing of his work out of his hands. Whether it be a strain of egoism which is concealed here, or some more deeply justified need of participation, the fact is that almost all human effort is held fast in this tendency. To free oneself from it requires a self-conquest and self-renunciation of a radical kind. But it is just such conquests upon which the issue turns. With it is ushered in the new moral value, which we are now to consider.

It is important to keep clearly in mind that it is by no means merely the natural propensity in man, or the "anti-moral impulse," which brings with it the desire to participate in the consummation of creative effort. Many a lofty character betrays this tendency. It is most conspicuous in brotherly love. Why does this kind of love attach itself especially to the one who is closest, and not equally to him who is remote, to the man of future times? It is because our neighbour is present to us, we know him, his life, his need, and we see in him every effect of our love. It is easy to love him, he is just at hand, he offers himself. What is overcome is only egoism of the vulgar type which demands all for self; the egoism of emotional participation, the higher egoism, that of sympathetic delight in another's welfare, still remains.

(c) THE PLATONIC ἔρως

It is an abiding service rendered by the Platonic philosophy, to have seen clearly the unique value of that kind of striving, which leaves behind it not only all personal ends but even those of one's own social environment and of one's contemporaries. The question is not whether we regard the ἔρως of the *Symposium* as a figure of speech or strictly as the concept of a value. The subject-matter itself is alone important, and that is unmistakable. ἔρως is participation in immortality. Animal nature, in that it reproduces itself, survives in what it brings forth. Its care for its young, its capacity to die for them, the fixed attachment to the future life of the species, is symbolical. It is an immortality in the mortal. But besides physical procreation, man knows another kind, spiritual procreation, whereby he passes into the imperishable. His work survives him, he participates in the eternal through immortal virtue. He too can live and die for his offspring.

The Platonic ἔρως—when we strip it of everything else and attend only to its ethical substance—is deeper absorption in the Idea, great passion for it, personal commitment to it. This passion brings it about that a man is transported beyond himself and beyond his environment. It is a man's losing of himself in his work, his inward life in what is not yet, in what is "still on the way from Non-being to Being"; it is the abandonment of the present for what is future, uncertain; the sacrifice of his life for another life, for one more valuable, but one that is not his own.

There is a potency *sui generis* in man, which here emerges, a germinal capacity with a distant aim, a generative energy of the ethos. Plato called it a pregnancy and a bringing to the birth (κύησις, γέννησις). The driving force is the Idea. The creative worker is carried with it. It is the generating power of values in man, for instance, of his ideals which are laden with values. Through them he outgrows himself. He transcends himself. But the direction and the extent of the transcendence are not the same as in the case of brotherly love and of everything akin to it. It lies in another dimension of life; it does not tend to fellowship with individuals nor even to union with the community, but is prospective towards some future time which is still asleep in the non-existent. The trend of its intention has exchanged the breadth of simultaneity for the depth of succession. Herein the transcendence advances not only in degree but in quality: it goes beyond the boundary of the actual and present and plunges into the unreal, which can be discerned only in the Idea, in order to actualize it.

This kind of purpose is only an extension of the direction which in tendency exists in all striving, in all devotion to a cause, however near and insignificant. Even in self-fulfilment the basis is self-conquest. Likewise all communal progress rests upon the self-subjection of the individual. From its beginning the perpetual revolution of the collective life is composed of the differentiations in the intentions of individuals. But as a communal process it is purposeless and aimless, so long as man as such does not give it a special aim and gain power over it, to lead it.

(d) The Human Outlook and Historical Solidarity

Here is a field of human foresight and activity which, although itself unlimited in extent and richness of tasks, is subjectively limited by the narrow bounds of human foresight and self-conquest. It is of no use to man to excuse himself on the score of his small equipment of capabilities; the responsibility for the course which public life takes falls ultimately upon him alone. At least he alone has the gift of foresight and predetermination.

In political life moral transgression is not due to the narrowness of this gift, but to the failure to use it in a spirit of glad responsibility. The type of the statesman, as we know him in our day, and as history repeatedly shows him, does not act from a sense of responsibility for the wider future of nation and State, but from the need and opportunity of the moment. He is not a conscious carrier of the great and far-reaching responsibility which actually rests upon him. He works for immediate ends, as if beyond them there were no wider and more important perspectives.

To-day we generally know only the short-sighted politics of the moment. The survey of centuries, to which we have become accustomed in historical retrospect, we omit to make prospectively; yet it is most urgently needed in regard to the future. The past gives us examples of truly far-seeing politicians. But they stand there apart; the present age has little understanding of them, perhaps as little as any former age. To-day we know only party politics and party rule. We form groups to meet transient emergencies. So long as no one is superior to their petty conflicts, only immediate issues are visible in public life. The truly political spirit is lacking, the spirit of self-subjection and great historical responsibility. To us it may sound Utopian, if we are asked to consider the children of generations which will be of another mind and another circumstance. Nevertheless it is true that those generations will be our heirs and will reap the fruits of our actions, and that we bear the responsibility for what we load them with. It is the moral business of all to reform political life. There is no escape from this claim.

Political life, however, is only one example. Our responsibility is wider. It reaches to all the departments of life. Everywhere the same law of spiritual inheritance holds good, the same historical continuity. Everywhere, besides being linked to the community of our own time, we stand in another connection. In every cultural relationship each one sees himself in the setting of another community, that of the following generation, which teaches him that he himself is but a link in a chain. The responsibility which arises therefrom signifies a solidarity of a newer and greater kind than that of justice, brotherly love and faith. Like these it is a bond, a fellowship, a pledge, a joint responsibility of person for person. And still it is altogether different. In it the man of to-day feels himself one with the man of the far-away future, though the latter will have forgotten him and cannot be of help to him. The temporal direction of cause and effect is not reversible. The influence of man on man, solidarity itself, is only one-sided. Only he who lived previously can be of service to him who lives afterwards. The successor bears no retrospective obligation. Instead, there falls to him a new obligation towards the generations coming after him. Solidarity is directed forward only; its form is progress, not co-existence. Still it is a bond which is great not only in extent but great in the quality of its task.

That it is a bond of a more fragile kind, that it is taken so much less earnestly by the living than is the solidarity of justice or love, this is not due to its own nature. It is due to the moral immaturity of the living, to their not having wakened to their greatest task. It is their lack of thorough self-conquest, which transcends the sphere of the Now and the Near.

(e) LOVE OF THE NEAREST AND LOVE OF THE REMOTEST

There is an ethos which brings about this new transcendence with the emotional strength of the Platonic $\xi\rho\omega s$. It is an ethos of love, but of another love than that for one's neighbour, a love for the man who is to be, as he is conceivable in Idea by the living. It is a love which knows no return of love, which radiates only, gives only, devotes, overcomes, sacrifices, which lives in the high yearning that cannot be fulfilled for the one who loves, but which knows that there is always a future and that indifference to it is a sin. Such love is "Fernstenliebe" (Love of the Remotest).

This is the name Nietzsche gave to the newly discerned virtue, to contrast it with "Nächstenliebe" (Love of the Nearest). His denial of the latter may be disregarded here; it overshot the mark and only damaged his own contention.[1] That the discoverer of the new value could go to extremes is understandable. The conflict of the two values is undeniable. But to see the antinomy is one thing; positively to approve it is another. To resolve the antinomy in favour of one side is always a temptation. But it leads inevitably to a misunderstanding of the other value.

The antinomy shows itself in this, that love of the remotest at first really requires an overcoming of one's commitment to the nearest. It is the same overcoming which generally inheres in the nature of a future intention. Everything which is dear and entrusted to man attaches to the immediate environment. Here an attachment of love to the remote is demanded. Hence not only natural inclination, but also genuine moral habit, must be overcome. A valuable commitment, not acquired without moral struggle, is to retire into the background and give way to another ethos. It is the conquering of a product of previous self-conquest. Love of the nearest (altruism) went counter to self-love (egoism); it was a tremendous extension of the sphere of life, efficiency, evaluation, participation. Now even this widened sphere is seen to be too narrow, to be a drag on the intention of love. Love of the nearest does not go beyond one's contemporary. Its effect does not endure, it dies with its object; it is not adapted to the continuation of its object, but to his present existence. Love of the remotest seeks a different measure of efficiency, an efficacy which will last. It is Plato's "immortal virtue." Of course it can attach itself only to the nearest, for all effectiveness has the form of teleology and must seek its first means in what is at hand. But its aims do not centre in the nearest. It sees in that only a means to something

[1] Cf. Chapter XXIV (d), Vol. II.

greater, which cannot be actualized in the nearest. It derives the end from a valuational view which does not concern itself with the individual person, which in itself is also indifferent both to the near and the far, and points into the distance, only because it finds no ground in the near.

In love of the nearest the energy of striving, as it has no choice, reconciles itself with whoever is accidentally at hand. Whether he be the worthiest, it does not ask. For it there are none unworthy; it does not judge. With love of the remotest the reverse is true. The energy of striving shall serve not the nearest but the best, whom it will bring to further fruition. Herein a selection of persons from the point of view of values is introduced, a selection which on its side does not refer to the given person at all, but to the type of man.

In love of the nearest there is a characteristic which must make a morally thoughtful man pause, a weakness in its constitution. It responds to the need of the nearest, it prefers the helpless, the sick, the injured (even if not, as was shown, for the sake of their weakness). From the point of view of the weak this is pre-eminently right. But for the wider perspective such service is entirely wasted. At best it raises the fallen to the level of the average. And from the point of view of general progress this is of no use. For the advancement of the community those who are above the average are the persons who are worth encouraging. And they are the individuals whom neighbour-love sends empty away. Indirectly they are even oppressed, they are burdened with the weakness of the weak. Their level is lowered. Logically neighbour-love leads to a levelling of mankind, it is a cause of stagnation and of retrogression—since there is never an arrest of change. Levelling makes selection impossible, it leads to an inversion of development, past recovery.

This is what love of the remotest, as the ethos of progress, must disavow. It must unearth again the principle of selection which love of the nearest has buried. It must reinstate the worthiest, the ethically strong and aspiring, and favour him at the cost of the man who is sinking. This is straightforward and reasonable. It has nothing to do with the lofty passion for ideals for which it opens the way, any more than with Nietzsche's well-known exaggerations and his passionate disparagement of brotherly love. "What is inclined to fall, we should throw down": whether this is true, whether it follows from the alleged weakness of neighbour-love, is very questionable. The fact of their antinomy does not release us from the task of blending the two values. In itself love of the nearest is right and must not be discarded. If precedence should be given to a higher value, the lower at most should be restricted in its domination. The complete abandonment of brotherly love would also vitiate the life of the remotest, vitiate it more perhaps than it would vitiate the life of the nearest.

Here the conflict is deep-rooted. To treat the nearest merely as a means is a dangerous principle. Kant's categorical imperative rightly demanded the opposite: everyone's personality is to be regarded, never merely as a means, but always at the same time as an end in itself. Of course this was directed against the egoism of the individual. But if the personality of the one nearest at hand is threatened by a high ideal just as much as by crude egoism, should not the Kantian demand be directed with equal right against the ideal? At least on principle no one would question the right of so directing it. But how the conflict is to be overcome is not thereby settled. In itself a synthesis is very well possible. Love of the remotest, as such, does not require that the nearest should be treated "merely" as a means. It allows him scope as an end in himself. It only insists that he should "also" be regarded as a means to a farther end. But, so far, this gives us only an empty space for a possible synthesis, by no means the synthesis itself. The phrase "but also as an end" shows an entirely different practical aspect. And if we consider that the problem concerns a claim of the remotest and a responsibility for him together with the claim of the nearest, we see that the conflict leads to a reciprocal restriction of both values, that is, that in every synthesis the conflict must on principle be retained.

It penetrates into the inner disposition. Neighbour-love is sympathetic, soft, long-suffering; its yoke is easy. The way of the creative spirit is hard. It is as hard towards oneself as towards another. It does not set much store by either, both are means. To be a means is what is hard for any man; all that is sensitive in him protests. Here the apriorism of sympathy must be silenced. Another apriorism, which is also fraught with value, rises up against it, a prophetic sense of the ethical potentiality in man, his latent capacity, the future value which transcends his own person and his own environment.

(f) JUSTICE AND THE LOVE OF THE REMOTEST

The relation to justice is similar. With it also there is conflict. Of course justice does not entirely shut out the distant perspective, as love of the nearest does; it requires a wide vision. But love of the far distant is not on that account just, it cannot be so. It must disregard the single individual and even the community, for it aims neither at the individual nor the existing community, but at the type. What preserves this, is right. But here another right prevails.

In the eyes of justice men are equal; and, in so far as they are not equal, they ought to be. Love of the remotest sees the opposite: men are not equal, and not only in nature and character, but also ethically they are not of equal worth in their human potentiality. It is precisely in this inequality that a peculiar strength inheres in the human race, its ability to evolve. Only where among the many there exist individuals who excel, who in some quality or other are the "best," is upward evolution possible, for it issues from these "best" as from humble beginnings. Where there exists a love which fosters what is best in the few who are best, progress is the result. In this respect justice is only a foundation, a preliminary. It is directed only against the selfishness of the lower ethos. Absolute justice would result in as absolute a levelling as would brotherly love; and thereby an inversion of development would ensue.

Love of the remotest goes a step farther: not only are men ethically unequal, but they also ought to be. The more unequal they are, so much the more movement there will be in the process of development, and so much the higher will be the ends aimed at. This is the absolute antithesis of justice: it recognizes inequality as a principle, as a value, not of course as an end in itself, but as indirectly of pre-eminent worth, as a means to ends which are superior to those of justice.

At the same time it would be a mistake if we wished to trace back this antinomy to that between the universal and the particular.[1] Only the one element, universality, agrees with it, the other does not. The opposite here is not the singularity of the individual, but the type, and indeed not the actual but the non-existing "ideal" type. And only so far as the ethical potency of the ideal type appears in the special species of the individual, is any emphasis laid here upon the individual. But this is enough to bring about a transvaluation of equality; or, to speak more exactly, not a transvaluation of the value—for values remain what they are—but a trans-orientation of our feeling in regard to the relative grade of the value. Equality is now no longer dominant; it recedes in the presence of other values for the sake of which inequality is demanded.

Nietzsche saw correctly that from this point of view social ideas must yield to higher ethical ideas, although his polemic shoots far beyond the mark. The demand that our feelings for values be revolutionized is right; and this is hard enough, more difficult than the rigour of justice. A self-conquest of a peculiar kind is required; elsewhere only one's weakness is to be overcome, but here a virtue also. The man must now overcome the very end for which he had conquered his egoism, but not in order to return to selfishness, but to move forward to a new ethos. This is the most difficult sort of self-conquest, to unlearn one's estimate of the values which have penetrated deep into one's emotions and to subordinate them to newly discerned values.

[1] Cf. Chapter IX (a), Vol. II.

(g) The Formation of One's Ethical Ideal

In all this the moving principle is the ethical ideal, the Idea of man as he ought to be. This too is a Platonic doctrine, the ἔρως looks to the Idea and is a passion for it.

But just here there is a danger. Nothing is so much suspected as human ideals. The man of experience in life is accustomed to have only an indulgent smile for "ideals." This is certainly not without ground. Perhaps everyone has his ideals—at least once in his life. But our idealistic visions are seldom forward-looking, practically feasible or ethically significant. Likewise there are many low ideals, of a strongly materialistic and eudæmonistic nature. There is also such a thing as an exalted but impracticable and chimerical ideal. The latter is as worthless ethically as the former; and a life, directed towards it, is wasted. Of this kind are the childish ideals, one or the other of which most men take with them through life. As play, they are innocent enough and beautiful; they are also harmless, even when the mature mind is delighted by them, provided it be only in fancy. But they are pernicious when they take hold of a man's life and determine its course. They should be put away with childish things.

In the life of everyone who is ethically alert there is a critical period when ideals which are lovingly entertained lead him astray. While one is still immature, one is abashed before the real world and disappointed; it appears not worth living in, deprived of its values and its divine attributes. The disappointment is nothing but a fall to the solid earth from the heaven of impracticable ideals. It can become a danger to anyone who is morally weak. But if the childish ideal is not dispersed, if the man continues under the spell of the dream, if he means even by violence to put it into practice, sacrificing himself and others to the phantom, he remains morally a child his life long, unteachable, a world-reformer; and to his grief he is under the curse of being comically tragic.

Not everyone attains to morally positive ideals, which are

capable of transforming real life. In every moral struggle there is a contest for ideals. But more is required. Not all positive ideals are forward-looking. Much rather is the disenchantment only in reference to one's own life, at best to one's own immediate world. Ultimately the earnest seeker finds the aim in life which is *his*. With it he shuts out the wider perspective. Love for the remotest is not everyone's concern. Its claim is wider. The question is how to transfer high faith and strong hope from the sphere of youthful dreams into one's later life, without remaining subject to its unclarified contents. There is genuine and invaluable moral strength inherent in the ethos of immature ideals. It must be retained in later life.

This is what makes the formation of one's ethical ideal such a serious problem. The discarding of the impracticable and barren ideal must accompany the creation of ideals which are adapted to the future and are capable of reproducing themselves, and must contain at least a tendency towards the creation of them. For the process is a living one and develops with the deepening of valuational discernment.

The procreative power of an ideal, however, depends upon two factors: a genuine discernment of values on the one hand, and, on the other, conditions of actualization. What altogether contradicts the latter cannot be actualized in life. But what is not valuable is not worth actualizing. The former belongs to an ethically fabulous world, the latter to a realm that is morally irrelevant. The content of a fruitful ideal necessarily lies beyond the momentarily actual. And because it reaches beyond the limits of an individual life, it naturally reduces the individual to a link in the chain of life, which connects the past with the future. Man sees himself caught up into a larger providence, which looks beyond him and yet is his own.

Such an ideal, as a value, manifests itself in life as a really creative power. It is the form in which values become driving energies in personal life and in history. It attracts the faith of the strong to itself, like a magnet. And with this power of faith it transforms man and his human world. For in content it is objective, it is never the possession of one man, even if he be the only one who discerns it. It draws others after it, binds together all who are able to grasp it. At first it separates the few, the seeing and believing, the noble and self-sacrificing, and forms them into a group. And this closed group moves forward in the process.[1]

As can be easily seen, the nature of love for the remotest is akin to nobility of character. It is preferential in its discrimination. Like the noble in general it selects not only persons but values—the former from the point of view of values, the latter from the point of view of the excellence of the values as regards their rank or other aspects. The formation of an ideal is a valuational selection, a process whereby the inertia of consciousness is overcome. This self-conquest Neitzsche rightly felt to be the most difficult; man clings to nothing more tenaciously than to the values which he has appropriated as his own, for which he has striven and suffered. The whole weight of the community as well as the individual resists such self-conquest. Thus the conflict of values expands into the vaster clash between the two solidarities of the moment and of history. The formation of the ideal is a passing beyond recognized values, an anticipation of others, a revolution in consciousness. It avenges itself upon the person in whom it takes place, upon the hero, prophet or thinker. He destroys the solidarity of his own times and is regarded as an offender.

(h) The Content of Prospective Ideals

The ideals which we are considering are human ideals. But they are by no means merely ethical. They embrace all sides of humanity. Nietzsche regarded their content as consisting predominantly of vitalistic and æsthetic qualities: strength, fulness of life, beauty and whatever is related to these. These qualities are profoundly important and must not be omitted; but they

[1] Cf. Chapter XV (d) and (e), Vol. II.

are one-sided and, on that account, when projected into the Idea, are misleading. The Idea of man requires the rounding out of his whole nature, physical as well as spiritual, of all capacities and all the splendid possessions which are within his power. The great yearning of the creative spirit is for a humanity which is altogether more nearly perfect, more abounding in life and richer than mankind is at present. Out of the abundance which his prophetic sense discerns, the creative spirit gives to the ideal a vastness which it does not find in itself nor in its environment and which it is not able to actualize. And it is unable, because to actualize it is not the work of one man but of generations.

This yearning is itself inherent in primitive man. It is found in the early myths. But there it lacks the ethical impress. Its ideal is passive, eudæmonistic, an enjoyment, not a creation, of values. Besides this, it looks back to the beginning of time; the process of human history is more and more away from it. "Paradise," the "golden age," are retrospective ideals, the ideals of a lost happiness. The mood which corresponds to them is that of a downward course, the vain mourning for a vanished splendour. In the primitive vision of himself man is powerless, he can only consume himself in idle longing for the irrevocable. The one alternative is to wait for divine assistance.

The breaking away of ethical thought from mythology is the passing of man out of the stage of childhood with its day-dreaming ideal, a reversal of his perspective, the discovery of his own power and of the significance of the ideal as a guide. The process is now understood as one of advancement, as a development to something higher. Man began in a rudimentary state, but potentially he can attain the highest. The ideal is prospective. The future is disclosed: everything must and can be achieved by effort. This is the point of view of the Platonic ἔρως. Man stands midway (ἐν μέσῳ) between wanting (ἔνδεια) and the Idea which is discerned; his task is to strive towards it (ἐπιθυμία). His gaze is directed forward; what is about to be is his. He lives in hope, in ardent desire.

Of course the history of the human mind, as we survey it to-day, only partially justifies this reversal of perspective. Together with various kinds of progress it shows much retrogression. But here historical experience cannot be decisive. The creative element in man is necessarily in opposition to it. And if it should be true that the human race is declining, it is only the more true that mankind must bestir itself about its destiny, and must do what is in its power to transform its downward movement into an upward course. The chief question is not how much or how little is in his power, but how fully or how little he grasps the task which looms before him. For historical experience cannot dispute the possibility as such.

Now here the formation of the prospective ideal receives concrete significance. With it the weight of responsibility falls upon man. No longer is it a question of imaginary happiness, but of the objective constituents in hardly discernible but imperative "ideas"; it is a question of strenuous claims. Not at one glance can the ideal of man be grasped. Only what discloses itself to the vision of values tends to converge in it. And the valuational view itself advances. The formation of the ideal emerges in a second process, which in content anticipates the real process of development. Even the discerned ideal as such remains incomplete at every step. It is not achieved by the mere bringing together of separate values; and even Nietzsche only brings such together. This produces no concrete unity. The ideal must be seen from the point of view of the manifold values in their fulness, and as a unity. That the human vision is always restricted is due only to an empirical limitation.

When in any age ethical perception is strong and vivid, not only is no original insight lacking but also no concrete embodiment and plastic expression of the ideal. Doctrine and personal example accomplish nothing here. There is need of another kind of language. It is chiefly the creative artist, the poet, who contributes suggestive speech to the prospective ethos. Homer created for the Greeks not only their gods but their men, the Greeks themselves. The Hellene of the flowering time measured himself by his heroic figures. Among the Romans the poet was called the seer (vates). And everywhere the poets are the greatest of the creative minds, they set before men the ideals visualized in palpable form. This does not mean that the content of the ideals has been transferred to the realm of æsthetics. Nor does it mean that the distinctively æsthetic values, so entirely different in structure, have had violence done to them. Much rather do these values always develop most vigorously where more positive valuational material requires expression and shape. How the artist fashions them remains his secret. It is his super-æsthetic significance in the historical process of humanization, that he does give expression to the more positive values. All artistic transformation is born of aspiration. This aristocracy of birth connects the æsthetic vision with the seriousness of ethical struggle. In the groping of the spirit from age to age the universal moving power is the discerned and envisaged ideal. For within the limits of actual possibility the astonishing fact is this, that in the long run man always becomes what he wills to become.

(i) LOVE OF THE REMOTEST, ITS MORAL CHARACTER

In love of the remotest the content of ideals only plays the rôle of a situational value which gives a basis. In this kind of love the content of ideals is the object of intention and at best is actualized. But the distinctive moral value of the love is not to be found in the content. The moral value exists, here also, exclusively in the disposition of the person who loves. It is purely a value inherent in the intention. It is based upon the content of ideals, but raises itself above them. Yet the height of its value as such stands in no discernible relation to the height of the intended value. The intention of the ideal is in itself valuable, without reference to its content and the valuational grade of the content; the intention of the ideal is valuable purely as a disposition, as an act of love, in so far as only a discerned value is intended. On the other hand, the rank of the moral value in it rises in proportion to its strength, to the commitment of the person and to his self-conquest. In this respect it is not different from love of the nearest; in that also the value of the disposition is not commensurate with the greatness of the work intended. The value of the work is irrelevant to it. It remains what it is, even in case of outward error and failure. In this respect the two kinds of love are exactly alike in fundamental structure. The relation to the basis of each is the same: the value of the moral act is autonomous in spite of its material dependence. The fact that in love of the remotest moral values are found also in the content of what is intended, causes no change. Those values belong to the intended complex and on this account should be assigned to the situational value. In the discipline of a person there is also the same phenomenon in the case of love of the nearest. Here as there another value, that of the love itself, appears on the back of the intention.[1]

In a twofold connection this situation is fraught with consequences. The construction of the human ideal is problematical. It is always a venture, the issue of which the adventurer does not experience. In this venture love of the remotest is for ever problematical in its real effect. If one wished to estimate its value by its effect, one would be forced to be in despair about it. Nevertheless history itself teaches that human progress is open to question. Certainly we must not here infer from analogy; but it is still doubtful whether man can have influence upon the distant future, whether venture and sacrifice are not

---

[1] Here the inner relationship of the two kinds of love becomes clearly apparent. It is natural to see in both a fundamental value, although only a moral one. This shows the same valuational factors. There is a cleavage between these in regard to the intended values. Only between these is there any conflict. One can observe between them a concrete superstructure, such as the *Nicomachean Ethics* presents between ἐλευθεριότης and μεγαλοπρέπεια, or between φιλοτιμία and μεγαλοψυχία (cf. Chapter XXIII (c) and (d), Vol. II). Love of the nearest is on a small scale what love of the remotest is on a large scale. The former is an everyday virtue, the latter an exceptional one. The relation between the good and the noble is similar.

sins against contemporary man—presumptuous gambling in
"futures." In this respect love of the remotest is worse than
any other virtue, but especially so in its damage to brotherly
love, which is always sure of its immediate objects and which,
even when it does not achieve them, is sure that they are
reasonable.

Yet who would take it upon himself on this account to
abandon the ἔρως which reaches out towards the future! That
would be a moral scepticism, a flaccid pessimism, a renunciation of the higher meaning and value of life. In spite of everything, responsibility for the future is of a provident nature
and is capable of actively determining beforehand. No scepticism
can free us from that responsibility.

This difficulty inherent in love of the remotest is easily
solved, provided its moral value is independent of its success
or failure, of whether it attains or misses its objective goal,
indeed provided it is also independent of the valuational
height of what it aims at. However much man may err and
fail in his intended object, the moral quality of his intention
can nevertheless be right and possess the higher value. Indeed,
it is a distinctive moral quality, in which love of the remotest on
this account excels brotherly love and every other virtue:
greatness of moral spirit, intensity of spiritual energy, which
is required in the taking upon oneself of what is inherently
uncertain. The venture is great. Only a deep and mighty faith,
permeating a person's whole being, is equal to it. It is a faith
of a unique kind, different from trust between man and man;
a faith which reaches out to the whole of things and can do no
other than stake all it has. It is faith on the grand scale, faith
in a higher order, which determines the cosmic meaning of
man. When it becomes active and carries out its schemes, its
work is of historic import. In a pre-eminent sense the expression "Remove mountains" may apply to it. And this energy is
harmonious with a similar feeling—hope, when it is raised to
its highest power, the basic feeling of ethical idealism, which
bears all things and gladly suffers for an Idea, never despairing:

hope, the peculiar assurance which takes hold on one who risks all on a single issue.

There is yet another consequence. The situation which love of the remotest strives for is incomparably greater than that which neighbour-love aims to achieve; as for height of value the well-being of one's neighbour cannot be weighed in the great scales in which the ideal value of humanity, as always understood, must be weighed. If the whole value of the two lay in the values aimed at, their axiological relation would prove so utterly unfavourable to neighbour-love that one could never speak of a conflict between them. Love of the nearest would need to withdraw from comparison with love of the remotest. Perhaps it was thus that Nietzsche conceived the relationship; so it was easy for him to reject love of one's neighbour. But the presupposition is simply false. The whole value is not that of the object intended. On the contrary, all the moral value lies in the intention. But in the two kinds of love the value of the intention itself is practically the same. In principle the values of both stand on the same plane. Thus the balance between the two is restored, and at the same time also the antinomy existing between them. It is impossible to impugn the one in favour of the other. Although the goals of the two are incommensurable, the dispositions stand in height of value close to each other.

CHAPTER XXXI (LVI)

RADIANT VIRTUE

(a) SPIRITUAL GOODS AND THE PERSONAL CHARACTER ACCORDANT WITH THEM

IF anyone approaches the realm of values from the point of view of love of the remotest, which is one of its high summits, whatever is near and present must appear to him small. He will be dazed by the Ideal. Yet so long as ἔρως in its grandeur stands there as a solitary peak, it is an absurdity. We need only to ask: Ought the lives of those who will be living in the far-distant future also to culminate in love for the remotest? And likewise the lives of those in the still more distant future, and so on *ad infinitum*? If that were so, sacrifice and self-surrender would become the ultimate goal of all goals, and the axiological process would throughout remain empty of content.

Futuristic ideals cannot be the ultimate, even if we disregard their uncertainty. In them must be contained absolute values of immediate significance; otherwise the future mirrored in the ideal is valueless. We cannot always seek for the meaning of moral tasks, even though they be everlasting, in further tasks. Somewhere or other in this process a value of fulfilment must lie hidden which can be seized upon forthwith. But such a value is by its nature a present one. This does not mean that at every given moment it could be actualized, but that it is applicable at all times and retains its inherent and absolute validity. All humanity at every moment must carry a part of this value in itself. Otherwise the ideal construction is incredible.

This is what gives self-sufficiency to the whole series of the following virtues. But they do not exhaust the realm of what is attainable at any time. In the three following types of value we find fulfilment of another sort. And each one of them is in its own way an axiological summit. The first, although it often enough finds fulfilment in individual persons, is without a name of its own. Nietzsche was the first to attempt its definition. He names it *Schenkende Tugend*—Radiant Virtue.

The law of giving and taking which prevails in the realm of spiritual goods is different from that which reigns in the domain of material goods. As a single individual, no one can be an exclusive possessor of spiritual goods; they belong to everyone who can seize upon them. Possession of them always contains something of mere sharing and controlling. One may indeed keep them back by force from others, one may treat them contrary to their nature, as if they were a personal possession. Such conduct is spiritual miserliness. But a man may also, in so far as he is himself participant in them, have special regard to their nature and to the idealistic claim of his fellow-men, in that he offers them, makes them accessible and, where no access exists, opens up an avenue to them. That is the moral attitude of one who dispenses spiritual goods. It is clearly a form of love, for the giver is concerned not with the gift, but with the receiver of it. As compared with love for one's neighbour and for the remotest, it is a different kind of love, having a new valuational accent.

Inherent in the essence of spiritual imparting, as distinguished from material giving, is the peculiarity that he who bestows does not give away, does not become the poorer, but himself stands by as a recipient of gifts. Imparting to others is the only attitude of mind which accords with the nature of spiritual goods, for they can never be really surrendered. Radiance is the life of spiritual fulness; its life is not the fulness itself—the presence and value of which are here presupposed—but personal living in accord therewith, a vast overflowing, the ability to share, to make rich, to scatter broadcast; and in addition to this a delight in so doing and in enhancing the spiritual insight of those who accept.

(b) IMPARTING AND RECEIVING. VIRTUE WITHOUT SACRIFICE

In contrast to neighbour-love the distinctive value of radiant virtue becomes evident. In the one as in the other we may in the wider sense speak of imparting. But here the process is different. In the former there is a dispensing because of the other's need and from our knowledge of the need; in the latter the bestowing is from the pressure of the fulness of life within. Neighbour-love bestows upon the weak, the needy, the unfortunate as such; radiant virtue imparts to everyone who knows how to take, who stands on a level with the gift, who is capable of appreciating its value. Everyone is in a position to receive the gifts of neighbour-love. It is otherwise with those of radiant virtue. In regard to them men are divided into the appreciative, those with minds that are opened and those with shut minds, the deaf. The parable of the sower, who scatters seed both on barren and on fruitful ground, is a true picture of him who imparts spiritual goods.

A bestower is allotted to the moral height of a recipient. He goes forth in yearning for him who will receive his gift. Such in all times is the spiritually great man, the poet, the artist, the thinker, and everyone who partakes of the abounding fulness of life. With this abundance he cannot keep to himself, because it inheres in the nature of the fulness of life to radiate. His misfortune is his solitude on the height, when there is no one within his sphere who is of his mind. Herein he is like light which finds no world to illuminate. The tragedy of his greatness is the smallness of the small; he misses the fellowship of a mind that receives. His greatest fortune is someone who can take his gift. All his love turns to such a one. In the acceptance the outpouring finds its meaning.

Neighbour-love ordinarily dispenses lower gifts; its task is the well-being, the happiness, of another. It is fully justified, since the other's distress is most painfully felt. Misery accordingly summons brotherly love to its aid. But radiant virtue must first awaken a need for its gift, and must therefore plead for itself. It dispenses gifts which stand in no universal relation to other values, which are not serviceable for other ends, having worth only in their own content, in their own structures, which as means are worthless but as ends in themselves are autonomous; they are imponderables which hover above the weighty and positive values of life. Of this kind is everything æsthetically of value, such as the artist bestows; but not less of this kind is mere admission to participation in the fulness of the real, the opening of eyes to the hidden riches everywhere; also, all making of others sensitive to the imponderables, all disclosure of meanings even within the sphere of common everyday life.

But the difference in the moral attitude itself is still greater. The kind of gift which neighbour-love bestows concerns only the conditioning values. It sacrifices, divesting itself of what it gives; its greatness depends upon the greatness of its commitment and self-denial. The imparter of spiritual values makes no sacrifice, for he does not give anything away; his ethos is not to be measured by his commitment. Nevertheless his is a genuine virtue, a genuine love, but merely a fundamentally different one. The imparter simply overflows—out of the fulness of his life. Thereby he obeys the basic law of spiritual Being, putting himself at its service as a faithful steward. He yields in his personality to this high law. For this he lives. And in so doing he lives pre-eminently for those who receive his gifts.

(c) "A Useless Virtue"

To define the ethical value of this attitude concretely is more difficult than to make it felt. The imparter of spiritual values is akin to the noble-minded man, the proud, the loving, the great-hearted; he combines values in a peculiar way, and something new is the result. He is lavish of himself; like the sun, he shines on the just and the unjust. His tendency is to dispense to all— and yet to none. Not only because the recipients are selected through the nature of the gift, but also because the one who accepts strikes against a barrier which he cannot surmount. The imparter stands on the further side of reciprocal love; no one may lovingly own him. He never imparts to the individual from love of the individual, but to all who are there to receive for the sake of the receiving and of the outpouring. The law of his gift requires this; a law which can be hard even for the giver himself. For only as a giver does he stand on the further side of reciprocal love; he cannot do so as a man. And he must remain human. A love that is beyond human measure is the law to which he is subject, as unlike love of the nearest as it is unlike love of the remotest or even personal love.

But that kind of greatness of spiritual energy which distinguishes creative genius is not properly characteristic of the radiant type. The imparter need by no means be a heroic spirit. There are besides in life remarkable men to whom hearts are attracted as by some secret spell; or perhaps another metaphor fits more closely: in their presence all hearts are opened. No one goes away from them except laden with gifts, yet no one can say what he has received. One only feels that in such men the meaning of life is somehow perceptibly fulfilled, the meaning which one elsewhere seeks in vain. And one feels that in mere communion with them something of this meaning is carried over into one's own personality. A stream of light, a splendour, a spiritual grace floods one's life. But one does not comprehend it, one only feels the mystery of it. Comprehension is confined to the sphere of discerned values and of what is serviceable for them. Radiant virtue, however, is of service in no direction. No other values lie behind it. It is only for its own sake, "a useless virtue."

Its moral value for him who imparts has no equivalent in the value of the gift. And again this gift has no other value except what is inherent in itself. Hence radiant virtue can never be common to all. And yet the moral wealth of every virtue is somehow related to it, as if it gave to each a meaning. As Nietzsche expresses it in his comparison with gold: "But tell me, how did gold come to have the highest value? For this reason, that it is uncommon and of no use and bright and mellow in lustre. It is always radiant."[1]

These are the precise characteristics of the virtue which imparts spiritual values. In no respect is it of service, it has no further purpose beyond itself, such as justice has, or brotherly love, wisdom, courage, self-control, or indeed even love for the far distant, all of which possess something of value "for" someone. It has no end in view, it is the absolutely final member among the values, a bloom, which, even without fruit, purely in itself, is its own excuse for being. And even where it is enclosed in the circle of generation, seed, growth and fresh ripeness, nevertheless it is not of value for this circular course; but this course is for its sake. Here is the valuational boundary of creation and elaboration and at the same time of the Ought. The highest value of life is inevitably a spending of life. And even where this virtue is creative, it does not consist in creating. It is itself the final creation, the ultimate meaning, an ethical Being in and for itself—a kingly virtue.

What happens from need remains under pressure of necessity. "To do nothing more than is needed" is a phrase which refers only to serviceable values, to the useful. But only that which exceeds above want, only the useless, the superfluous, the overflowing never ceases to possess the highest value.

Radiant virtue is not the ethos of the fulness of life, but the meaning which the fulness of life acquires through its overflow; it is an issuing forth without anxiety as to whither it goes. It is a pure out-streaming, but with no diminution of itself; it endows the human heart with riches. The fulness of life is justified by its peculiar way of passing beyond the man's own personality. It is a transcendence of a unique kind, different from that of sympathetic participation in the life of one's fellow-men; it is the objective transcendence of the contents, a pure transference of spiritual goods with their imponderable elements, and in addition thereto, a calm blissful consciousness of the out-going, which is given by the priestly consecration

[1] *Thus Spake Zarathustra.*

of him who administers the mystery; it is a partaking of the
eternal in time, a palpable manifestation of the Timeless within
the current of human life, above its compulsion and beyond
its aims. Hence it comes about that to the imparter of spiritual
goods it is not the just, the truthful, the loving or the faithful
man who is worthiest, but he who receives with an open heart,
the unspoilt spirit which is still capable of unlearning everything.
That is why the man of radiant virtue loves those who are
ethically imperfect, unripe, unspent and still flexible, with the
love peculiar to one who has mellowed, is blessed and is filled
with gratitude. He is the eternal ἐραστής of youth.[1]

(d) THE GIVING OF MEANING TO LIFE, ANTHROPODICY

Uselessness is not fruitlessness, not meaningless waste. It is
compatible with the greatest fruitfulness, but only of a kind
that is not willed, not aimed at. Just as happiness follows virtue
as its inevitable result but is disturbed if striven for, so fruitfulness, unaimed at, follows inevitably from the conduct of the
dispenser of spiritual values; but, if striven for, it violates the
meaning of the gift.

The man of radiant virtue is also of course creative, and
possibly to an eminent degree; but his ethos is fundamentally
different from that of a creative genius. Unplanned prodigality
is the true form in which spiritual values are propagated. The
superabundance, which arises naturally from their character,
makes prodigality the adequate form of reproduction. It is like
wind-scattered pollen, which with its tremendous over-produc-
tion most easily attains its result, without the least selectiveness.
Accordingly uselessness is not worthlessness, but the absence
of an end in view; it is not only not "adaptation to an end
without an end," but also not "purposive activity without a

---

[1] The figure of Socrates is here seen from a new point of view—the
man whom the ancients honoured as their greatest dispenser of
spiritual goods. Compare the passage in Plato concerning the divine
images within the statue of Silenus (*Symposium*, 215 B).

purpose." Rather do end and means return upon each other; the means in the final end. All teleology here finds its limit.

It is a great thing that life, together with its moral Being and Not-being, derives its meaning from such values and through them becomes worth living. Radiant virtue is not the only value of this kind (the two which follow are of the same order). But it is the one in which this characteristic can be seen in the very structure of its content. In the useless as such man justifies his existence as well as his claim upon life, his strivings and failures—for they are never final. He finds herein his anthropodicy.

It does not matter that radiant virtue is uncommon and is a moral power found in the few only. The vindication of man need not devolve upon all men. It may devolve upon the few, upon single individuals. Indeed it might devolve upon one only. Values are not diminished through the narrowness of the area in which they are actualized. A single individual can be the giver of meaning for a whole world, in so far as it participates in him. A life in which only one such exists becomes full of significance for everybody. This does not at all imply individualism. The import here does not depend upon the individual value of the one. Nothing rests with him merely as "this person here." It is only the vindication of all and the giving of meaning for all, which wins through in him. The virtue of the exceptional man inheres precisely in the fact that he is uncommon, yet again in a higher sense is all-common. As it is an overflowing of the fulness of life upon all who are reaching in any way towards its value, so too it is, morally, a shining-forth upon all who have any degree of sensibility for the meaning and its vindication. Thus finally, its unplanned work is a solidarity of a unique and novel kind, a solidarity not of aims or of guilt or of responsibility, but of participation and fulfilment.

Here even love of the remotest finds a special vindication. Its yearning and its hope have before them a portion of fulfilment. What one can otherwise behold only in vision as an ideal, can be seen here in flesh and blood. Radiant virtue is a power of the ethos, it instils the Ideal into the race; and where this occurs, it is as though the ideal man were already a reality. Certainly there is here only a fragment, but for all that a real one. Here the real anticipates the Ideal, a living proof that the Ideal is possible in the world of actuality.

CHAPTER XXXII (LVII)

PERSONALITY

(a) RELATION TO INDIVIDUALITY

In a certain sense every man is by nature a personality, that is, he has a certain human attribute which does not reappear outside of himself. This is more than mere personality in general. The latter is common to all, but every one has personality distinctive of himself. It is individual. Nevertheless it is not identical with individuality. A communal being, an institution, a situation, a thing also, is individual. Only an individual person is a personality.

We must distinguish this fact of personality from its valuational character, although they are never separate. Like all values, this also is independent of actuality; it has an ideal self-existence. Personality as a value, therefore, cannot coincide with the actual personality. It must always be something which stands over against the actual, which does not accompany the changes of its empirical being, but to which the latter is specifically related as to something that ought to be, just as every human and actual disposition is related to universal moral values.

Personality as a value differs radically from all those previously considered, in that it cannot be decisively fixed for all persons; it is not a universal value. Its claim as an Ought is applicable only to one special person: only that one ought to be "so." This cannot be said of individuality in general, as a value.[1] The latter is common to all. That in contents it is different in everyone, does not affect its universal character. The very singularity is itself universal. It is otherwise with personality. By this is meant what distinguishes the individuality of one from that of another. There is no "personality

[1] Cf. Chapter IX (a), Vol. II.

in general." Or more correctly perhaps: one may very well conceive of such a thing, without inner contradiction; but here something else is meant. In contrast to personality in general as the common factor, that which distinguishes personalities, that which distinguishes them qualitatively in idea, is meant. Strictly, then, one may speak here only in the plural, or point to this or that personality. In this sense we are to consider it as a value.

In reality then we have to deal not with a single value but with an unlimited variety, with a whole new stratum, with an entire perspective into which the table of values issues. Ethics naturally is not in a position to follow this diversity as such. Its task is simply to elaborate what is common to the whole stratum in contrast to the universal values. It is inherent in the nature of the case that ethics cannot do justice to the varieties of personality. Its task embraces only the universal, and this is not the essence of the personal, as the sense of value conceives it in the concrete case.

(b) The Real Being and the Ideal Ethos of Personality (Its Intelligible Character)

We must not describe personality as the person's ethical "Being for himself." Personality is pre-eminently what it is "for others." On the other hand, it is for oneself only in so far as the self-discernment of the special person reaches; and this does not reach far. Were the Being of one's personality bound to one's moral self-consciousness, there would be little personality in the world. In truth there is much more of it than human consciousness conceives. Only, as a rule, it does not exist where rummaging and vain self-consciousness seek it. Its values are the most concrete of all the ingredients which everywhere in life make up the variegated abundance of values. Only with difficulty does consciousness trace this fulness; and it always flags far behind.

The matter of personality is different in every man. It is

built up from a mass of components. These are general values. But the kind of composition is always different. And, as such combinations everywhere and always produce new characteristics, so this is specially the case here. For this reason one may describe personalities as "individual values": each individual has his own for itself.

This does not mean that the specific complex is actualized in the real personality. It only expresses the axiological Ideal and is its ideal ethos. The empirical man falls short of his Ideal to the exact extent to which he falls short of the claim of the general moral values which the Ought makes. His actual moral being never coincides with its ideal. In this respect personality is like the universal values; it has a strictly ideal self-existence, which holds its own independently of the degree of its actualization. It is a norm, like the other values, only not a universal one. It may be achieved or missed in all conceivable degrees by the actual person. The achievement, even approximately, need by no means be conditioned by a consciousness of the values. Much rather is there, independently of all valuational discernment, in every person at every moment a specific disparity between the ideal personality, as a value, and the real. This disparity varies greatly, it is in continual movement. But the variation is always only on the side of the actual personality. Its ideal value stands fast, like all ideal Being. The movement also need not in any way be an approximation. There is also a withdrawal of oneself from the Ideal, an advancing failure of one's own ethos. Wherever a man lapses into imitation of another's personal ethos—and this happens with the strongest personalities—he is on a road that leads away from self-fulfilment. Likewise there is a host of lower powers in him, whose unrestraint can cause him to miss his own higher ethos. Finally also the tyrannical domination of some one universal value can repress the personality. In this case the man perhaps fulfils in a high degree certain common claims, but he misses the inner claim of his own essential being. One might rightly call the ideal ethos of personality its inner culmination; it is the

special form of moral Being, to which under the most favourable circumstances a man may raise himself. In the nature,
however, of such a form there is, at least in principle, the possibility of failure.

It inheres in the nature of all values, that their actualization
as such is of value. Likewise the realization of the ideal ethos
of a personality is a moral value. This manifests itself in a very
palpable genuineness of a man's nature, in a special fidelity to
himself, indeed in a general fixity and sterling worth. That in
contents it is different in each personality is not at all to its
prejudice. The moral being of a personality as such is a kind
of anchorage of his whole nature to its ideal, an inner foundation, a penetration of the ideal into the empirical character.
The Kantian phrase, "intelligible character"—if one discards
the Kantian metaphysics of reason with its universalism and
falls back upon the strict meaning of the phrase—might be
used as the exact equivalent of "personality as a value." For
the realm of values is a realm of "intelligible" essences, while
"character" in contrast to everything merely typical is an
expression for individual originality.[1] The moral value of a
personality could then be described quite unequivocally as the
fulfilment of the intelligible character in the empirical person.
If one reflects that even the neglect of an outward talent is a
sin, and by no means against oneself only, but as much against
others, the same principle, applied to the inner factors of moral
determination, gives one a stern sense of what a real actualization of values means. And in this sense one may speak of personality as a virtue.

But it is an entirely different question, whether there is a
conscious striving towards the value of one's own personality.
Such a striving would presuppose a valuational consciousness
complete in contents, such as can scarcely exist explicitly in

[1] One may perhaps best understand it from the popular application
of the older theories of the "thought of God" in a man. If one allows
the theological drapery to fall away, what remains is the intelligible
character.

regard to an individual and highly complex value. Indeed it is open to doubt whether, even if it were possible, it could fulfil its ethical meaning, whether the very reflection upon oneself, and upon the ideal Self, would not prevent its actualization. But all the components of personality are directed outwards, toward other persons, toward situational values. This preoccupation with what is beyond oneself is the basic form of the moral attitude of mind, and it is contradicted by preoccupation with oneself, such as would occur in a conscious striving for the values of personality.

But in this respect personality, as a value, by no means stands alone. The same difficulty is common to all moral values, although of course in different degrees. The moral value is never identical with the value aimed at. This does not absolutely exclude the pursuit of moral values, but limits it to the extent that the moral value which is striven for is not the same as that of the striving. Ordinarily the actualization of moral values ensues without an effort directed toward them; and this so much the more, the more specific and individualized the value is. Within certain limits moral values that are easily comprehended permit of being actualized by effort; thus at least there is a striving to be just, truthful or faithful. Whether in the same sense one can become loving by trying to be so, is very questionable. But it is impossible to attain the value of personality by effort; the reason, however, is not the same as in the case of purity. This cannot be actualized, but it well may be yearned for. Personality, on the contrary, is perfectly attainable—for instance, in the pursuit of other values, in so far as one's personal ethos is fulfilled in that kind of pursuit—but it cannot be made the object of pursuit without one's missing its essence. For by its very nature it inheres in a purpose directed to something else. Indeed it is a question whether the mere yearning for it does not induce the same falsification of it. In principle at least it is the same inversion of the general basic direction of moral intention.[1]

[1] Cf. Chapter II (c), (d), (e), Vol. II.

But this is not saying that a man is not responsible for the fulfilment of his personal ethos, that to miss it is not a sin and does not involve him in guilt. To incur responsibility, it is not at all necessary that a moral value be capable of being attained by direct effort. It is sufficient, if the conditioning values can be striven for. While every man individually in his own way and according to his own moral feeling pursues values in general, he is thereby actualizing his individual ethos. If he neglects this general determination, he is thereby neglecting his own self-determination. For this consists essentially in the special way of achieving the general determination. The responsibility for fulfilling one's own ethos is coincident with the responsibility for whatever one is free and able to do. But naturally this does not mean that the constituent values of one's ethos coincide with those of the objects pursued. In his deed a man bears guilt for the failure of his own moral being; and the fulfilment of it is, in the true sense of the word, his virtue.

(c) SUBJECTIVE UNIVERSALITY AND OBJECTIVE INDIVIDUALITY

The significance of individuality in relation to personality has not yet been clearly presented. Only so much is clear: these values are highly complex, but their constituent elements are universal values. By itself there is nothing astonishing in the fact that the area of validity becomes narrowed in proportion to the degree of concrete complexity. Thus there are virtues which apply only to a group of individuals, while to others, not included therein, they would involve a falsification of the ethos. The group has its own special virtue. The area of validity may be so small as to include only one individual. Then we have personality as the value; and in this way there is a "virtue" peculiar to everyone, besides that which is common to all, but the moral claim of the former in no wise displaces that of the latter.

Now values are ideal essences, and their cognizability is purely aprioristic. Universality necessarily belongs both to essences and their cognizability. How is this compatible with the individuality of personal values? Are these not genuine essences? Then they would also not be genuine values. Values cannot be individual in the sense in which their carrier may be; hence the values of personality also cannot be individual in the sense in which the personalities themselves are. In fact, then, they also as values are universal, and indeed in two respects.

In the first place they are "subjectively universal," that is, they are valid for every subject who grasps values, not of course in the sense that every subject must be able to grasp them; his sense of value may be limited, it may very well be so constituted that it does not discriminate certain values of personality. But they are valid for everyone in the other sense, which alone holds good in regard to all aprioristic knowledge: every subject, in so far as he at all discerns the value, must necessarily conceive it as it is in itself, including its specific valuational quality, and not as anything else. Even mathematical propositions are subjectively universal only in this sense; not everyone can understand every principle, but whoever understands a principle at all, necessarily sees it just as it is in itself, and not otherwise.

This meaning of subjective universality has no bearing upon objective individuality. For this fact æsthetic values furnish the clearest evidence. Taken in their full concreteness they are always only values of one single object (for instance, of a work of art), but as such they are nevertheless valid for everyone who grasps the object in its æsthetic meaning. One can of course pass it by unnoticed, but by doing so one cannot change its value. In the same way one can overlook moral personality; indeed there are always only a few who really perceive its value. But this is nevertheless universally valid for anyone who perceives it at all. It is of no consequence that someone, perceiving the nature of the personality, should find in it another distinct value than that which is there. Rather does he then not even perceive its nature.

(d) Objective Universality and Individuality in the Personal Value

In the second place, objective universality is also found here. It inheres in the nature of the essence.

In its structures the ideal sphere attains the highest concreteness and complexity, but does not attain strict individuality. The latter is singleness, hence it is something more than the extreme degree of concrete complexity. An ideal structure can be so specific that some single real instance corresponds to it, at least approximately. Then one may say that in the real world it is represented individually, singly. But the ideal structure as such is not on that account individual. Its nature would not be at all contradicted, if a second real entity or several corresponded to it. That this is not the case, is not due to it, but to the actual world. All singularity, as seen from the point of view of the ideal, is accidental, merely a fact, an affair of actual existence.

But this fact is sufficient to indicate the only kind of individuality which pertains to personality as a value. Strictly taken, the latter is not an individual value, but only the value of an individual, that is, of a single actual person. Here, as everywhere, then, individuality does not pertain to the valuational quality of the ideal as such, but to its connection with the actual. The real essential singleness of the carrier of a value constitutes the individuality of personality.

Here the question concerns a peculiar tie between the ideal and the actual, between a specific value and an empirical person; it concerns a bond which exists between the two, notwithstanding the perpetual disparity between them. However little the actual person tallies with his own ideal self, yet he is bound to it; his moral Being or Non-Being consists in the degree of his approximation to it. It is his own individual virtue, else it is no one's virtue, because in any other person it would not be virtue. But this means that personalities are indeed in a certain sense individual despite their universality, but are so only indirectly. In themselves they are not individual, but only "in actuality individual," that is, only in their actualization, or in their bondage to actuality. Hence, logically, they are not individual—that would be an impossibility—but only through the alogical, the actual carrier, therefore, as it were, *per nefas logicum*.

It is important to keep this basic relationship in mind. According to their genus personalities are not in absolute opposition to universal values. They are the extreme case of the concretion and individualization of valuational matter. The chain of separateness, all the way from the first and almost empty universalities to the unique value of this or that particular person, does not break off. Diversity and gradation of typical values bind the two extremes. Thus also we are to interpret the fact that the ideal character of Being perdures unabated, that it is the same in personality as in the "good" generally. Not only "is" personality different in every single individual, but it also "ought" to be different. And precisely through the difference a man in his Ought-to-be becomes unique, irreplaceable. The specific direction of his nature actually exists only once, and only in him. In him it co-exists with the universal direction of human nature. In him the individual ethos entrenches itself upon the universal ethos. The moral Ought-to-Be in man is not spent in that of the general moral values. It is not fulfilled until it reaches a culminating point in the special moral value of "this" particular person. Thus arises an opposition of values, indeed an antinomy between personal value that is universal and the value of personality. For the same person ought at the same time in the same disposition to respond to both.

(*e*) THE LAW OF PREFERENCE IN THE INDIVIDUAL ETHOS; ITS RELATION TO THE ORDER OF RANK

As in all stratification of essential features, so with personality as a value; it is not complexity alone which constitutes the distinctive character of the new structure. Something new is added, by which the reappearing and more general factors are for the first time brought together into unity; but the new element was by no means contained in the old ones. The idiosyncrasy of the complex constitutes the new factor. To trace it in detail is not possible for human thought. But what in general characterizes it can be discovered.

Our analysis of the good has shown that in all morally positive conduct there is found a trend not only towards values, but towards what is always the higher value. In the noble character it was seen that the content of this trend changes according to the momentary area of the valuational feeling, and that there is a self-direction in man towards new and not yet explicitly discerned values; but at the basis of both these characteristics there is reference to a fixed and self-existent order of rank among the values.[1] If now the systematic order of the values were merely a linear order of gradation in height, and if into the bargain this as a whole were set before every valuational consciousness, then the law of the good would allow no scope either to the preferential ethos of the noble or to the individual ethos of personality. But neither of these is actually the case. There neither is a consciousness adequate to the "system" of values, nor is the "system" a one-dimensional gradation of height. Values constitute a manifold of many dimensions.[2] Various, materially different values stand side by side on the same level; and often enough between them there exists an opposition, as regards contents, which may become direct antagonism. We have seen examples of this. But it is clear that the antinomies are more numerous than the examples can show, since the number and the variations of the values are far greater than those cited. Upon nearer observation almost every more specialized value opened to view an entire group of values. But it is by no means only the antinomies proper which here come under consideration. Many values,

[1] Cf. Chapters XIV (h) and XV (c), Vol. II.
[2] Cf. Chapter III (d), Vol. II.

which do not at all contradict each other, nevertheless cannot at the same time be actualized, on account of the structure of the given situation. Then the conflict is secondary, being conditioned only by the empirical situation. But it is not on that account less actual or less important ethically.

Now here it is left to the person himself to make a decision from case to case. And this is the point at which the conduct of the particular individual becomes differentiated axiologically, and indeed not simply in regard to preference for the higher or lower value, that is, not merely from the general point of view of good and bad, but according to a far greater variety of possibilities in axiological distinction. Under some circumstances, in one and the same complex situation, innumerable kinds of conduct and of resolution are possible, according to which of the values touched upon is taken as fixing the standard. Every human ethos brings with it preferential trends in specific valuational directions; every ethos thereby neglects other values which also are at stake. And still in its way each one is right—and not only subjectively; for at any given time no one can do justice to all the values concerned.

The individual ethos consists of such preferential trends, which are relatively indifferent to valuational height, because they move within the co-ordinated manifoldness of values, in other words, lie in a line perpendicular to the order of rank. The ethos naturally cannot spend itself in a single line of preference. It reaches out to all human objects and to every conceivable grade of the manifold values. The more richly and highly the personality is individualized, so much the more does it permeate the realm of values with its many-sided system of preferences. Such an arrangement of preferences therefore does not signify a rearrangement of the order of rank, at least it need not. For the order of rank remains absolute, in itself. A rearrangement of it could only spell failure. There may of course be such failure, and it may occasionally attack the individual system of preference. But it cannot on that account be asserted that the individual ethos is nothing but a failure to reflect the universal order of rank. Personality would then not be a value but a disvalue. Often enough on this ground ethics, basing itself only upon general commandments, misjudges the valuational quality of the individual ethos. If morality consists of nothing else than the carrying out of one or a few general laws, then personal individuality, which attempts anything beyond, is utterly immoral.

The case is different, if there exists a real realm of values, in the overwhelming variety of which the order of height in the scale is only one of many dimensions. Here there is room for an order of preference with its variety according to one's liking, together with the order of rank in the scale of values. Thus we can also understand that an individual ethos has its own Ought-to-Be. In all concrete situations there is need of definiteness of preference; only in this way will their valuational resources be exploited. The mere order of rank cannot do this. Its law is too abstract and too devoid of contents; it leaves all the other dimensions of the realm of values undetermined. It is related to the finer differentiations as justice is to love. The type-values of whole groups of persons, of peoples and epochs constitute here an indispensable and positive addition to the picture; for they also consist of such preferential trends, although relatively universal ones. But just for this reason they do not exhaust the variety in what is morally of value. Only the strictly individual values of personality form a kind of culmination in this direction. In them the human ethos exhausts its positive possibilities, latent in the structure of the realm of values. In the sense of such extremes in the unique axiological trends of the ethos—and of course only in this sense—the values of personality are the highest morally and, taken as a whole, make up an entire stratum of the realm of values, which rests everywhere upon the stratum of the universal virtues.

In these values, which are super-imposed upon the "virtues," the single individual as such is axiologically autonomous, spontaneous, creative. In these values he is, what in the "virtues" he is not, the law-giver of moral Being, in the strict sense of the word law-giver. He is this, of course, not self-consciously, but only on that account the more so in his ideal moral existence itself. He is this moreover only "for" himself. But he ought to be it only for himself. In general, law-giving appertains exclusively to all the moral values. But only the pure values of personality are a self-legislation.

(f) THE RANK OF PERSONALITY IN THE SCALE OF MORAL VALUES

However little the material structure of the values of personality has to do with the axiological height of its constituent parts, yet the grade of its distinctive character varies greatly in the scale of values. A man's individual ethos may be highly or little endowed, significant or insignificant. Perhaps one might say that in the majority of men it differs but slightly from the type. Such men have "little personality."

On the other hand, what one calls "great personality" is by no means always a highly individualized ethos. What one ordinarily so describes, for example, in history, is much rather the especially marked and energetic representative of a general ethos, or even merely the historically productive, efficient, stimulating man, the hero, the intercessor, the pioneer in a common cause.

It is not in this sense that we are here discussing personality, but exclusively in the sense of individuation of the ethos itself and of its impress in the actual man. In it historical greatness is by no means involved. The brave man, the wise, the just, the loving, the faithful or the trustful, can also possess moral greatness. The strict sense of personality, on the other hand, applies solely to the uniqueness and differentiation of that valuational complex which constitutes in a man's ethos the preferential trend of his inner disposition. Only through such a trend, or perhaps a number of such trends—in so far as they are somehow bound organically together into a unity of an ethos—does a man really rise above the Ought-to-Be that applies to everyone. Personality, in the strict sense, is not to be found among famous persons—the moral significance of the hero is precisely his super-individual quality—but away from the noisy stress of great ends and services. The greatness of personality is much more a purely inner greatness; it has scope in the most narrow sphere of life, for it is nothing else than uniqueness of commitment to values and, indirectly, uniqueness of the valuational perspectives with which a man permeates his sphere in life. Whoever is really a marked personality, carries his standards beyond all question in himself; in following them he is loyal to himself. He shows very definite and unmistakable sympathies and antipathies, for which he can give no other account than that which is to be found in their existence and their felt necessity. He sees the world, in a light of his own, as no one else sees it, in the light of his preferred values; and lives in accord with them. He is a world for himself, in the true sense of the word.

This is the reason that genuine personality possesses such attraction for others. Participation in it is a second life in a second world. Who sees the personal element in a man and lovingly comprehends it—and only to the appreciative glance is it visible—lives amidst abounding values of another order from those of one who is blind to personality. His world is infinitely richer, fuller and higher, diversified in values and vast.

(g) TWO KINDS OF GRADATION IN PERSONALITY

Personality increases and decreases in two respects.

First, the amount of individuation varies greatly. In its lower stages it is lost in the typical. Only in the higher stages does personality proper appear. But even, then, towards the boundary where the typical, where even all similarity, ceases, there are still many gradations which are distinguishable to the fine sense of values, although no longer to understanding proper. They consist in differentiations of preference for one value over another.

In the second place, there are gradations in the approximation of the actual person to his ideal ethos. Here also there is a long series of stages. But its relation to the other kind of gradation is one of indifference. The two kinds vary independently of each other. There exists a highly individual ethos with little actualization of it, and again a high degree of actualization with not much individuation. Personalities of the former kind are disrupted, inward failures and unsteady; but in spite of that they possess for any discriminating observer the extraordinary attraction of originality and distinction which glimmer through all the self-contradictions. Conversely, personalities of the other kind manifest their inward unity, definiteness of outline, organic harmony, but they do not rise— or only a little—above the typical and they are morally uninteresting.

There is something else, moreover, which binds the degree of axiological approximation to that of individuation. If the ideal ethos of a person is merely typical or little beyond, his individuality does not increase with the greater fulfilment of his ethos; for individuation attaches to man as a natural entity independently of the ethos. The natural difference between individuals may decrease along with an increasing adaptation to a uniform ethos. It is otherwise when the ethos is really distinctive; then increasing individuation is accompanied by increasing self-fulfilment. And here for the first time appears personality proper, as a moral value. Hence there are not only two conditions, which must be fulfilled in this connection; but the genuinely ethical phenomenon of personality does not exist until there is a certain amount of fulfilment and until there is reciprocal penetration of the two conditions.

(*h*) ANTINOMIC RELATION TO GENERAL VALUES AND THE CONVERSION OF THE CATEGORICAL IMPERATIVE

It is a mistake to construct a general individualism out of the ethical recognition of personality. But there can be no doubt that a one-sided presentation of the matter naturally leads to such a mistake. For the values of personality stand in undeniably antinomic relation to universal values, especially to justice, in so far as it demands equality, but also to brotherly love which at least ignores differences of worthiness. Whoever is under the spell of the universal values is always prone to misjudge the worth of personality; and anyone who appreciates it is inclined to depreciate them.

We have already encountered this antinomy among the valuational oppositions; there it became clear that in principle it cannot be solved, and that it introduces a lively conflict into all human relationships.[1] But it must be remembered that in life personality has an especially difficult position. In the equalitarian ethos of justice all stand against the one. They demand the same from everybody. And certainly in general this is right, for personality ought to claim nothing for itself in the sphere of outward life and of goods, in so far as it is subject to the law of justice. Its realm belongs to another world, where no legal relationship should enter. But naturally there is a wide border region in which the two spheres overlap, and it is just here that life is most strenuous; here the relative wrong of justice is as glaring as the defencelessness and outlawry of personality. For all legal protection extends only to the "person" as such, as an individual, not as individuality, therefore not to personality. This is outside the pale of law, as law is impersonal.

In order to see this, we need not especially stress the conflict; indeed there is no occasion for casuistical reflection. Law is not wrong in regarding the individual person as a means; for so to regard him is not its true intention. But by the strength of its solidarity it oppresses personality; this, where it supports injustice, stands alone against all. In life, the lower moral value shows itself to be the stronger; the higher is subject to it.

This relation can be discussed in connection with Kant's

[1] Cf. Chapter IX (e)–(g), Vol. II.

categorical imperative, as the general formula of equalitarian ethics. The formula says that one ought so to act as to be able to will that everyone should act so. In so far as this affirms that the moral test for every act is whether its maxim could at the same time be a universal law, there is evidently something here which in principle man as a personality cannot will. Rather must he at the same time will that over and above all universal applicability there should be in his conduct something of his own, which no other in his position ought to do or need do. If he neglects this, he is a mere numeral in the crowd and could be replaced by anyone else; his personal existence is futile and meaningless.

In personality there is the tendency always to have something personal in its volition and action, such that no one else can will it, or even imitate it—the tendency in every deed, together with all the general claims, to be something "more" than one of many, to have a value of one's own in life, and thereby to prove one's individual moral right to existence. Of course this tendency can never assume the form of a deliberate principle deliberately determining the will. It can inhere only in the feeling for values—as is the case with other moral values also— in so far as the concrete value of personality has already the form of an inward individual law of preference.

But in the abstract we can very well formulate it as a law and set it over against the categorical imperative, as its converse, which also is indeed only an abstract formula for a general moral disposition. The law would then run: So act, that the maxim of thy will could never become the principle of a universal legislation without a remainder. One might also express it in this way: Never act merely according to a system of universal values but always at the same time in accordance with the individual values of thine own personal nature. Or: Always act not only in accord with thy universal conscience (the sense of moral value in general) but also at the same time follow thy private conscience (thine individual sense of values).

The paradoxical nature of the formulations is not intentional. It inheres in the essence of the matter. If we remember exactly what a private conscience is—a feeling of preference or rejection which is not indicated in the general scale of values—we cannot challenge the rightness of such a categorical counterclaim, especially as it leaves untouched the universal values which the Kantian imperative advocates. The conflict therefore, when we go to the root of it, is seen to be not so glaring as it appears on the surface. Of course the antinomy is not removed. But we can see how it is at least in principle possible for anyone from case to case to solve it practically by his act.

Indeed, we can go a step farther in this direction. It can be shown that the converse of the categorical imperative does not at all clash with it, when it is strictly taken, or—expressed dialectically—that it already contains in itself its own opposite, that is, that it is antinomic in its very nature. The imperative, for example, does not declare that all men ought to will the "same"; also it does not say that I ought universally and absolutely to will as all others ought to will. It cannot at all imply that; for then it would also require that all others ought to come into the same situation. The maxim, for example, is altogether relative to the situation; to act according to the same rule in another situation would indeed be morally wrong. But to will that the momentary situation in its uniqueness should return, would be meaningless. Rather does the imperative presuppose a certain type of situation. Likewise it is intelligible only so far as the assumption may be made that others come into the same predicament. This assumption is justified within the limits of that similarity which as a fact exists in situations, however individualized they may be. But it overlooks the fact that the structure of situations is not exhausted in any such similarities, that in reality they are strictly individual, indeed— to be exact—that two perfectly similar situations no more exist than do two persons who are altogether alike, or even two things. Situations are real; and every real thing, understood in its entire concreteness, is single, once for all, and never

recurs. One must remember that even a situation outwardly
altogether the same—in case there should be such—would be
inwardly, that is, ethically, a different situation, provided only
that it existed between persons differently constituted, between
persons whose specific mode of intention was involved in the
situation. We forget this only too easily, because we are
accustomed to keep all deliberate moral reflections within the
boundary of perspicuity, that is, of a certain classification.
But how narrow are the bounds of deliberate reflection! It is
reflection and its classifications which deny the value of personality. Here is the limit of all grouping into classes, as well
for persons as for situations in life.

At this point the meaning, correctly understood, of the
categorical imperative[1] itself gives preference to the limit. Its
real demand is: I ought so to will, as under literally the same
circumstances everyone else ought to will. But "literally the
same circumstances" includes the peculiar nature of my individual ethos. The imperative, accordingly, when the complete
structure of the case is borne in mind, not only excludes the
moral justification of a will exactly the same in others, but it
positively demands also the unique factor in my own will,
without prejudice to the classification which brings my will
and that of others under a rude uniformity of the Ought. The
Ought allows unlimited scope for an individually articulated
will. But that the categorical imperative actually demands individuation for the will—the uniqueness of "my" maxim—is
inherent in its essence, in so far as its demand is a universal
one and includes everything that can be universally demanded
of everyone. For that everyone should will individually and
act in the spirit of his own personal ethos, and that consequently every maxim of a definite person in a definite situation
should have a distinctive character which is in accord with

[1] It is self-evident that this "correctly understood" does not refer to
the historical correctness of understanding as to Kant's meaning. The
interpretation here given in no wise pretends to be an historical
interpretation.

this definiteness—this is an eminently universal moral requirement. In short, the individuality of personal behaviour, as an ethical claim of the Ought, is just as general as the universality of the Ought itself within the limits of the class of possible situations. Hence the categorical imperative has within itself its own opposite. It involves its own converse. Its limitation lies not outside of it, but in it.

Therefore we might say: the converse of the categorical imperative does not lie outside of the proper meaning of its formula. One does not need first to suspend it, in order to establish the peculiar right of the personal will. Rather does the imperative itself establish it. The demand, so to will as not everyone ought or may, is not in contradiction to the universal demand, so to will as everyone ought to will. The two demands do not clash, because they move on different levels. It is this which makes the right of personality compatible with that of the universal virtues, and vouchsafes scope for it as a moral value of a peculiar order along with them.

This is of decisive significance for the understanding of personality as a separate moral value. Not everyone is able to see such scope in his life. Hence arises the blindness of that rigorism which always believes that the universal requirements are endangered, where personality sets up its claims. Whoever has breadth of vision, feels that to everyone should be granted a right of a higher order: "this" man may do what no other may, and ought to do it, because he is what he is. Whoever does not at least occasionally feel this in the presence of some living personality, and is not aware that precisely in this way the strictest demand of the universal Ought is also best vindicated, has neither insight nor spirit for the moral Being of personality. His sense of values does not extend so far. But he is the very one who is least able to cope with that individualism which is just as one-sided, is always ready to spring and is in fact ethically dangerous. Only he can keep individualism within bounds who understands and appreciates its limited rights.

(i) GENUINE AND SPURIOUS PERSONALITY

The Ought-to-Be in the values of personality is only apparently different from that of the remaining virtues. Every man ought to "be" in accord with his own individual ethos, he ought to fulfil it in his Being. Of course he ought not to do this at the cost of the universal values, but so much the more within the bounds which these allow him. The area, however, is wide, as wide as the distance between the contents of the universal and the individual claims. To be a personality without fulfilling the commandment of justice, truthfulness, fidelity or brotherly love, produces an inner displacement, a chaotic and false morality without any ethical foundation; such a personality operates in vain, it is a moral swindle.

The universal values constitute the basis of all morality and as such take unconditional precedence. Only upon them, as the foundation, can the more highly differentiated form of personal values be raised.

But in principle this changes nothing as to the character of the Ought-to-Be, which adheres to the values of personality. On this point a man may easily err, in that he, as is right, gives scope before all else to the universal requirements. But the Ought-to-Be which is valid only for one appears less absolutely binding. We confuse only too easily objective extent of validity with the existential character (the modality) of the validity itself, with the Ought-to-Be as such. This blunder is very natural—and pardonable—but it is none the less an error on that account.

It is another matter with the Ought-to-Do. We cannot say that a man ought to "strive for" the fulfilment of his individual ethos. But the same holds good within certain limits of all moral values. The phenomena, in which a certain striving for the universal virtues is manifested—such as conversion, repentance, the desire for one's own improvement, self-discipline, the imitation of an exemplar—are not ethically primary phenomena. In all these cases there is a prior disposition of a special kind. Personality, however, as a value is never by its very nature actualized in reflection upon itself, but in reflection upon other values. It accordingly assumes a special attitude only in so far as it constitutes the limiting case in this respect. As regards attainment by striving, the Ought-to-Do forbids it. But this is not a difference of principle but only one of degree. Ought-to-Do is not the basic form of the Ought of moral values; for a person it is the direct form of the Ought only in regard to situational values. But it is these which in personally formed effort are the intended values; and upon them appears to be based also the individual intentional value (together with the universal) in the special quality of the intention.

Herewith is connected the fact that, in the carrier of personality as a value, all awakening to consciousness of it entails the danger of failing in it, or even of falsifying its nature. It inheres in the essence of the individual ethos to take part in all conduct of the person as a special determinant, but not to be an object of explicit self-consciousness. Much rather is it inclined to make the individual ethos of someone else the object of attention. Another person is throughout made the object of inspection. The power of inspection can penetrate deep into one's own being. Indeed it may be that, under the dangerous pressure to be a personality himself, while a man has before his mind the personality of another, he mistakes his own. Whoever stands under the spell of a powerful personality, only too easily lapses in this way. But precisely this shows how austerely individual the values of personality are, how utterly they exist only for the one as "his" ethos, but for everyone else they mean a falsification of his own nature, indeed a moral disintegration. The values of personality can very well be in content opposed to one another; what for A is a valuable preferential trend, is possibly for B an anti-value, in so far as in his ethos the preferential trend is different. Thus are produced innumerable conflicts, as soon as the one, by universalizing his own idiosyncrasy (for him quite warranted), overpowers the other. Life abounds in instances of such conflicts.[1]

The proof of the individual Ought-to-Be and of the genuineness of personality as a moral value is that any imitation of another's personality is ridiculous. When the law of his own inner value is lacking in a man, he seizes upon another man's law, where and as he understands it. By so doing he achieves the opposite of what he seeks. The law can issue only from one's own moral being. Only then is it a necessity, even in the way it manifests itself. In moral striving, to follow an exemplar is something altogether different from copying an individual. The disciple chooses his model among historic persons from valuational points of view which he himself already has— how else should he distinguish the worthy from the unworthy model?—and for the sake of the values which the model embodies. Naturally this is wise only when the values are universal, valid for everyone, or at least for many, that is, are typical. There can be discipleship in brotherly love, justice, truthfulness and the like, but not in personality. Such imitation is essentially linked to general values. If applied to personality, it becomes mere copying and brings about only a counterfeit of personality. One who merely copies is not only not a personality, but is positively a destroyer and falsifier of his own true personal essence; not a man, but a human ape.

So it is with all deliberate effort to be a personality, even when its content is not appropriated from another personality. Within certain limits we can construct for ourselves an ethos which we do not possess. But the result is only a pose. This is shown by its hollowness and brittleness; it is merely outward behaviour. Whoever takes the trouble to probe it, finds an entirely different ethos behind it, and indeed, as might be expected, one that is undeveloped, impoverished, chaotic and stunted through adulteration. A genuine personality is cast in one mould, is solid, a moral entity which, as it were, has

[1] Dramatic art has a special predilection for cases of this kind. One may recall Tasso and Antonio, Rosmer and Rebecca.

grown naturally. It can never be found where there has been deliberate effort to become a personality. It is not a thing willed; over against the will it is autonomous; it has its law in itself and follows its law without deliberating.

(k) THE VALUES OF PERSONALITY, DISCERNIBLE AND APRIORISTIC

Wherever there are real personalities, their values can be felt. Through such feeling they are no less capable of being known than the universal values, notwithstanding that a full sensing of any particular value of personality generally arises merely as a particular experience.

But the question as to whether they can be known is essentially changed, if one is referring to a clear understanding of their inherent structure. Practically, values of personality cannot be understood explicitly, being essentially irrational. Their complexity is a barrier to one's penetration. Only typical factors in them can be distinctly discerned. And these forms not only do not contain the values without a remainder, but are intrinsically contrasted with them. The values of personality are indeed within the limits of possible discrimination through the feeling for values, but they are beyond the limits set to our discernment of valuational structure.

This circumstance, however, sets no limit at all to the significance of the values of personality for practical life. As regards the specific value of a living personality, our sensing of it can assume an extraordinarily concrete and differentiated form. Of course, by the mere sensing of values no value of the kind in question can be anticipated, unless the personality is empirically at hand or at least unless a picture is concretely delineated (as may be done in fiction). The actual presence in some form or other, although only incomplete, must always be presupposed. And in this point our sensing of the values of personality is essentially different from our sensing of other kinds of value. It would seem accordingly as if this sensing were not aprioristic, but empirical and bound down to the presentation of the actual case. This impression becomes still stronger when we bear in mind that anyone sensing a value is in the presence of a variety of single values which is practically infinite in quantity and quality, and, again, that every one of these in itself is of an impenetrable complexity. How should a man's sense of value discover them a priori? In fact he always waits, until the actual personality is presented before him; and even then he senses the distinctive value in it only in relatively rare cases.

The question, therefore, is: Have we not here reached the limit of valuational apriority, and does not the sensing of values extend beyond it? In fact, does not valuational empiricism set in at this point, in contrast to the complete apriority of the universal values? This would be a conceivable inference. Values are essences, and essences can be discerned only a priori (it is all one whether by feeling, thinking or in some other way). Then, either the values of personality would not be genuine essences, or else what is presented by experience of the actual person is not a valuational quality.

It is not difficult to show that the latter view is correct. What is mediated empirically is by no means the value itself. What is in fact grasped empirically, and only empirically, is nothing but the fact that there exists an individual ethos of "this" peculiar structure—we cannot a priori conceive or construct personality. But that this ethos, discerned in the actual person, is something morally of value we never know from its empirical presentation, but only by an aprioristic sensing. This is evident, when we consider that by no means everything in an empirical personality is morally of value. The value in it must first be discovered. And only an aprioristic norm, which the sense of values brings with it, can furnish the criterion.

But if we look more closely, we find that in this matter the case is not fundamentally different in regard to the knowledge of all the other values. The sensing of the universal values is not purely an inward contemplation, but proceeds by way of observing an actual moral life. The valuational vision does not unfold itself through reflection and rummaging, but under the stress of an actual situation, through conflict, by taking sides, by approval and disapproval. And here also in the first instance the materials of values and disvalues are always known in the given case; but that one material is of value and another contrary thereto, only a norm that is applied a priori can decide. The sensing is in reaction to the empirical case, it is a valuational response. But the response itself is aprioristic.

This interpenetration of empirical presentation and aprioristic insight is especially important in the case of personality, only because here the general, constant and familiar norms do not fit and must be applied from case to case. This newly gained norm sets up a new valuational feeling, the prophetic dawning of a value not yet discerned and unanticipated. Here the aprioristic feeling widens step by step with the expansion of ethical experience. In that, new human idiosyncracies are continually being presented.

Finally one becomes convinced of the strict apriority of the feeling directed towards personality, if one takes into consideration that an individual ethos is never completely actualized in any real individual, that there is always a disparity, always only an approximation. The value of a personality therefore is never actually given adequately—as little as are the general values; for this reason then it cannot be simply derived from experience. It is never empirically given. Nevertheless there exists a feeling for the pure ideal ethos of a man, an intuitive, often a lightning-like illumination of his personality, and precisely in so far as it is not fully actualized in him. What takes place here is very marvellous. The intuitive glance forces its way, as it were, through the actual personality, it breaks through the boundaries of the empirical man and beholds something different, which in the man himself is only intimated. To the intuitive glance the personality is transparent. But what shines through it is its ideal essence, its true ethos, the value which is its inner destiny, its intelligible character.

No empirical knowledge is adapted to such perception. What

is beheld stands in contrast to what the eyes see. If seen at all, the values of personality are seen purely a priori. But we must not forget that aprioristic discernment—here as throughout the realm of values—never stands detached from empirical presentation of the actual and can succeed only when in connection with it. The actuality experienced is here as elsewhere the occasion which incites the mind to the beholding of Ideas.

CHAPTER XXXIII (LVIII)

PERSONAL LOVE

(a) PERSONAL BEING, THE FULFILMENT OF ITS MEANING

EVERYONE who does not lead a shadow-like existence amidst generalities and principles is well aware that besides universal love of one's neighbour and of the far distant, and besides the love which dispenses spiritual gifts, there is another, closer and richer, an intimate love directed exclusively to one individual person. The other types are impersonal, do not participate in the innermost nature of anyone nor seek after it in its entirety and fulness. But personal love aims at personality as such and for its own sake. In tendency it is all-embracing, a human intimacy far greater than that between neighbours.

It is the virtue of one personality towards another; it is the devotion of him who loves to the personality of the loved one. Indeed all love aims at values, all ἔρως in one way or other looks to the Ideal. Such reference to the Ideal is characteristic of personal love. Brotherly love attends to the universally human value of a person; on that account it overlooks nothing. Love of the far distant fixes its gaze upon the discerned ideal of man; radiant virtue, upon participation in spiritual good. In none of these cases does the individual entity receive the recognition that is its due, as an object of love. It too has a claim, it is in need of appraisement by a special sympathetic sensing of its specific value. For whatever in itself is of worth finds its fulfilment only by becoming a value "for someone."

Personality also craves such fulfilment. Otherwise its very existence, its blossoming, is overlooked in the exhaustive search for values. But in mere existence-for-itself it cannot become actualized. For self-consciousness is contrary to its nature, which is not valuational consciousness but moral Being wholly and solely. It necessarily seeks someone "for" whom it could Be. Only another personality can satisfy this yearning and be the counter-pole in the fulfilment of its meaning. And the mystery of love is that it satisfies this deepest and least understood craving. One who loves gives this unique gift to the person he loves. He gives a new dimension to the Being of the loved one, enabling him to be "for himself," what otherwise he is only "in himself." Personal love is the value complementary to personality, a communication to it of its own meaning. It provides what a personality cannot acquire for itself, a mirror which it cannot itself hold before itself. To picture one's own personality is to distort it. But here is a mirror which gives back a perfect reflection. In the nature of things consciousness of one's personality must be another's consciousness. For it is a consciousness of the value of the personality. Such is personal love.

Since empirical personality never strictly corresponds to its own ideal value, but love looks exclusively to the latter, it inheres in the essence of personal love, to pierce through the empirical person to his ideal value. This is at least its tendency. Thus we can understand how it may attach itself to one who is morally undeveloped and imperfect, indeed to one whose ideal ethos is deficient. Its commitment merges into the ideal of personality; it lets this stand for the empirical individual, accepting him as equivalent to his highest possibilities, as raised to a power above his actual being. It loves in him what inheres in his essential tendency, the axiological idiosyncrasy of his Ideal, yet not as an Ideal, but as a trend towards actuality, just as if it were already actualized in him. In this way, looking back from the Ideal upon its imperfect carrier, it loves the empirical individual in his characteristic peculiarity. For it the man, as he is, in the trend of his ethical preference, is accepted as a guarantor of a higher moral Being, which of course he is not, but which only in him and nowhere else in the world finds something real that approximates to its own value. Personal love lives by faith in this highest that is within

the loved one, which despite its inadequacy love senses prophetically. Such love is ethical divination in the pre-eminent
sense of the word, not of course divination of a universal human
ideal, but of the Ideal of a particular individual. It sees the
perfect in imperfection, infinitude in the finite.

(b) LOVE, ITS DISTINCTIVE LIFE AND VALUE

Because it is the mirror and fulfilment of the loved one's
personal being, love for him creates an ethical situation of a
special kind, an intimate, absolutely reciprocal union between
two human beings. A third person requires again a new and
equally special commitment. Distributed among several, love
loses its personal character and approximates the more to
superficial sympathy existing among members of the same class.
And even when a man personally loves several individuals, his
love for each is distinctive, even individualized, reflecting the
individuality of its object. Hence every personal love tends to
an existence-for-itself, to isolation. There is an individualized
ethical existence-for-itself only between two. Neither more nor
less than two is consistent with its nature. One person for
himself is not "for himself"; several in a group are not what
they are, each to each; they are no longer strictly personalities.
One for one is the only form of existence-for-self.

There is a unique feature in the creation of this personal
situation. It widens the sphere of personality. Personality is
raised to a higher power by including within its compass and
counting as its own the personal Being of the loved one. Where
this widening is reciprocal, each of the two personalities is
re-enforced; there arises a new communal structure of an ethical
order, which is not contained in the two persons and which in
its significance and power can develop beyond both of them.
Herein the human ethos is seen to be eminently creative, and
creative of something literally beyond itself. For in its development beyond the two who love, the total relationship raises
their personal being, and confers upon them a dignity which

they do not have for themselves, but still never in such a way that the total structure is merged in either of them. The total situation leads a life of its own beyond that of the participants, and indeed with the full import of a really ethical existence of its own. Like everything actual, it has a moment of beginning in the temporal process; it develops in its own way from frail and perishable origins; it grows strong, reaches its prime, undergoes inner crises, transformations and conflicts; and likewise it can decline and die. In its own life it is conditioned by the personal ethos of the two who love; but as it can grow in power far beyond their combined wills and capacities and can even determine their destiny, there is a law of a higher order which rules in it, which is also individual but never coincides with that of the participating personalities.

The relationship consists not simply in the union of the empirical personalities, but at the same time in the higher union of two kinds of ideal ethos. And on this account the law of its life transcends the empirical being of the persons, because it issues from the axiological fusion of two purely valuational complexes with their respective preferential tendencies. This is what the one who loves never fully sees, although at times he may surmise it, namely, that it is precisely the ethical nature of himself and the other person which in his love is struggling for fulfilment, and that it is his own innermost nature especially which (not understood by him, strengthened by the support in the inward self of the one he loves) is striving to raise him above itself. Intelligible characters take stronger hold of one another than do the empirical persons. Thus in these a destiny is fulfilled which is greater than their actual ethical being—a destiny to the power of which they in their finiteness might very easily succumb.

Nevertheless just this destiny is the true revelation of their own infinitude. And this is the distinctive power of all love which enters deeply into one's personal life; it brings to light the otherwise hidden and neglected essence of one's individuality. That this revelation can be achieved only in a life of

another order than that of the empirical man, is because of the
gulf between him and the Ideal of himself.

(c) Love, its Strength and its Will as Values

The narrower moral value of love, its virtue, is distinct from
the objective value of its real life. Its virtue, like all moral value,
inheres in the disposition, the intention. Love is the absolutely
positive disposition as such; it is absolute affirmation, good-
will, devotion, constructive tendency, just as hate is denial,
overthrow, annihilation. Love that is personal is the same
affirmation in regard to personality.

Hereby effort enters as a factor into it, a factor which is
liable to be forgotten on account of the emotional strength
of love. Something of the moral strength, the efficacy and
productiveness of ἔρως reappears in it. Not as if personal
love must develop a special working energy, nor as if a will
must stand behind it—that would make of love something
planned and not genuine. A will accompanying it or behind it
could only be in contradiction to it. Love no more allows itself
to be forced than to be willed. It is unique, a primal tendency.
But it is precisely this which we have to consider.

There is of course a love that is weak in will, which may
still be strong emotionally, just as the converse is sometimes
the case. In the end a man can introduce into his love no more
volitional energy than is native to him. Nevertheless an element of will rightfully subsists in love. It has the tendency to
draw to itself and into its service a person's entire volitional
energy. And the stronger it is emotionally, the stronger is this
tendency.

In love the element of will does not consist in willing to
have the loved person for oneself. This tendency also is naturally
in it and a certain valuational emphasis is laid upon it, although
a subordinate one; it is akin to egoism and manifests itself
in the same way. That this is so is evident from the fact
that a love in which there is no will to possess does

not act convincingly, and is not accepted as entire by the loved one himself. But this is not the question which now concerns us.

In all personal love there is a second and more deeply rooted factor, which expresses only the positive trend, the kindness and devotion which place oneself at the service of the other— a tendency of the will, which is the reverse of the desire to possess and which even in renunciation can continue undiminished. Expressed in a formal way, it is a pure Being-for-thee on my part, irrespective of any Being-for-me on thy part, and stands in perceptible contrast and occasionally in acute conflict therewith.

The altruism of personal love is essentially different from that of brotherly love, which looks primarily to the empirical Being of another, to his welfare, happiness and the like. It is much more closely akin to the altruism of love of the remotest; like this, it looks to the pure ethos, the Ideal of man, except that here, the Ideal is the individual ideal of personality. And here again the distinctly marvellous, the metaphysical character of personal love manifests itself. To the loved one it is what his own will can never be to him, a will, a striving, a guidance, a creating directed toward his unfulfilled moral being, his personality as a value. No one can strive for the actualization of his own ethos as such, without running the risk of failure. But everyone can strive to fulfil—naturally not in his own person but in that of the loved one—the ethos which with the eye of love he beholds in the beloved; and there will not be the slightest danger that he will thereby mistake it or distort it. For it is not his own. Such a striving is of course limited in means, it can never be more than a favourable circumstance. But that is much. In fact it is a supremely real and decisive power in the life of the beloved, an actual leading up to his true moral being. No one who has experienced it will deny that genuine, deeply felt love has the power to transform him morally whom it is directed toward, to make of him what it sees and loves in him. Such influence is certainly not all-powerful, it encounters all the resistances of the empirical man, and often enough also a radical misunderstanding of its real trend. But in tendency it still persists. And everyone experiences it who has the good fortune to be surrounded by the genuine personal love of another.

One must not reduce this phenomenon to purely intellectualistic terms. It does not take place in the light of consciousness; only seldom does it force its way through to a rational surmising of its ethical significance. It remains obscure, borne by the emotions; and obtrusive consciousness can only embarrass it in its instinctive certainty of its own goal. In one who loves there can indeed be a happy sense of such a power, like the no less happy sense in the loved one of being led and exalted by it. To the one who loves it gives the triumphant consciousness of being for the beloved the highest which one person can be to another; and in the beloved, who feels this love resting upon him like a fulfilment, there is a thankfulness, without his knowing precisely wherein its high value for him consists. But neither of these is a knowledge of the metaphysical circumstance involved in the love. The loved one feels the power that upholds him; he feels that the loving glance penetrates his empirical being and points beyond it. Thus he is aware that for the one who loves him he has become transparent, but he himself cannot see what the other sees in him. He cannot follow with his sense of values, because he cannot cast his gaze upon and through himself. At best he can trustingly surrender and yield to the other's guidance. But he is in need of nothing more. For even this exalts him above himself; he feels also that which shames him for not being in reality as the other sees him. But instead of feeling that he is misunderstood he has rather a sense that he is known to a pre-eminent degree, and at the same time is forced to be what the other sees him to be.

These are of course only general circumlocutions which hint but imperfectly at the secret of the moral power of love. The peculiar metaphysical element in it—the deep trans-

cendence, the gliding over from man to man of valuational
insight and of creative power—remains untouched. It is fundamentally a different transcendence from that in brotherly love;
nor does it have its effect through outward conduct or the
visible work of love; and yet it is a moral deed, a genuine
creative activity. Indeed, in greatness and objective value,
what is accomplished by the other kinds of love cannot be
compared with its achievement. No longer is there here that
disparity between the intended value and the value of the
intention, which we noted in the case of every other virtue.
For the achievement of personal love is the moral Being of
the loved one. The one who loves causes this Being to rise
transformed into what it is in Idea and what it was to him
from the beginning. At least the tendency thereto exists in all
genuine personal love. And often enough also there is fulfilment in part.

(d) Beyond Happiness and Unhappiness

According to the ordinary conception, the emotional value of
love stands in the foreground of its nature. In this view thus
much is indisputable, that it is the most positive of all human
emotions; among life's manifold riches it possesses the highest
intrinsic value, it is the purest and most elevated joy, the
deepest happiness. To feel itself to be eternal, super-temporal,
is of its essence, despite its temporal, psychological, affective
growth and decline. Its meaning is eternal, just as the real
object which it beholds is an eternal one. And one who loves
feels its eternity immediately and convincingly as the better
part in himself. Every personal love is individual and unique,
as are its carrier and the object he beholds. Each love has its
own special ideal existence. And this is in fact eternal. How long
the empirical man is able to retain it is quite another question.
Nevertheless it is precisely the empirical man who loves. And
thus it happens that in his love the high sense of participation
in the eternal comes to him. At the same time, this improb-

able event, altogether incredible to one who does not love, is not a delusion but sober truth.

"Happiness" is a misleading term to describe this high emotion. And the popular conception, which can detect nothing but happiness in the emotional feeling of love, overlooks the essence of the matter. It is precisely happiness which is secondary in love. It always includes both suffering and joy. From the point of view of happiness its peculiar feature is that beyond a certain depth of emotion, pain and pleasure are matters of indifference to it, they become literally indistinguishable to it. The suffering of one who loves can even be happy, his happiness be painful. The specific emotional value of love falls on the further side of happiness and unhappiness. Its sense of inner exaltation rises above both of these—it is a feeling of another order with a different spiritual content, in which pleasure and pain with the incessant beat of their waves form only a subordinate factor. They are the empirical temporal accidents of a substance which, as the deeper emotional strain in him who loves, is the immediate presence of the participating Idea, the eternal value.

The proof of this remarkable phenomenon is to be found in unhappy love, as it is called. Where it is fated to meet one who loves superficially, in whose love the will to possess dominates, there undoubtedly the burden of misfortune, of privation, of resignation is preponderant. It is something altogether different for him who loves deeply and whose striving tends wholly toward the loved one. Although unreciprocated, his love remains the lofty emotion which it is in itself; in him it suffers no loss of value, it is unperturbed. This exalted sense is *toto cœlo* removed from self-indulgence in pain. It is simply the feeling of the autonomous value of love itself.

Certainly all personal love looks forward to a return of love. Indeed it can even awaken a response, so far at least as the loved one feels an enrichment of his being. But its emotional value by no means depends upon the response. Being loved is indisputably a value and is altogether unique; but the value of one's own love is not dependent upon it; in contrast thereto it is a "moral" value. The worth of the love which receives is not a condition of that which gives, but conversely. The emotional depth ther of one's own love does not wane because there is no return; it often grows the more; but it becomes a source of pain. For the loved one, on the other hand, the value of another's love is evidently enhanced in proportion to his own love. Not until he himself loves can be appreciate it. The proverbial bliss which a man experiences only in personal love is not that of being loved but of loving.

(e) DEPTH OF SOUL AND SPIRITUAL COMMUNION

It is the depth of the self's participation which corresponds to the sense of eternity and to the elevation beyond pleasure and pain. That precisely this feeling can on the one hand become a passion (and by no means merely on a sex basis) and on the other can flood a whole human life with vast serenity, is due to the fact that, deep below the threshold of consciousness, it touches, like soft light, the primal source of spiritual life.

If to this fact we relate the transcendent linking of man to man, we discover in it a characteristic contrast to every other kind of love, indeed to every other kind of virtue. Justice, for instance, joins person to person, but only surface with surface. Still more is this the case with the virtues of social converse. Brotherly love binds far more deeply; likewise love of the far distant and the dissemination of spiritual values, each after its own kind, but both obviously at certain points only. Personal love, however, unites forthwith innermost depth to innermost depth, overleaping the surfaces. It is quite possible for those who are bound in personal love to irritate each other superficially and to suffer disagreements and restraints of every kind. The remarkable thing is that this love can remain steadfast despite the conflicts. It can also suffer under them; into its emotional values the savour of pain can enter; indeed, this love can succumb to antagonisms, when it has not the strength to rise above them. But a characteristic feature of it is that even when it is oppressed by conflicts it does not settle them, but finds a way over them to an inward harmony. For love is capable of suffering, it can endure and bear; it is not rooted where conflicts have their root; it is embedded in a different stratum of our moral being.

Nor does it merely strike its roots into the spiritual source of personal life, but is able also to raise this into consciousness, or at least into the region of clear emotional discrimination. It even invests with speech the mysterious depth which else would remain for ever mute. Its speech is only imperfect language. But the language of love is not tied to words. Verbal expression does not embarrass it; it has a thousand languages, symbols, revelations. Body and soul must serve it with all their capacities. It makes for itself organs of insight, its resources are inexhaustible. From it there blossoms an understanding, of which a man who does not love knows nothing, a life of inward and profound communion. Without it a man would never discover his own innermost nature, he would pass it by with no suspicion of its existence. It is no fairy tale which the lover dreams, when to him there appears to open within him a depth hitherto closed and yet full of unimagined treasures. In very fact such a one unlocks his own being; what is higher and better in him, what was not understood, comes into its own and sways him. Indeed, it may well happen that his love outgrows his strength and follows another law (the law germane to love), one even different from that of his own personality. In that case from the unlocking of his nature ensues a painful up-rooting, a desolation. Even love as a value manifests here something like an inherent danger-point.

(f) Love as a Source of Knowledge

Love has a value of its own not only as a disposition, a striving and emotion, but, finally, also as a kind of cognition.

This element in it is the least recognized. Nothing seems

remoter from love than knowledge. It appears to take the beloved person as it sees him, or would like to see him; and for it that is enough. The popular saying declares that love is blind and this means: love is fortunate in its blindness, it has no need of seeing.

Still the whole series of valuational factors in it, mentioned above, presupposes a radical element of knowledge. How can love move to the ideal value of personality, even find its way to the real Being of the man, unless it somehow comprehends it? This comprehension is its presupposition. That it is an emotional understanding makes no difference. In this sense a cognitive element is always contained in love, and not only in the inferences from it. Anyone who means by knowledge only a thinking, reflective, rational consciousness of an object, must naturally find a contradiction in our contention. But that is an untenable idea of knowledge, which not even science—much less life and the ethical consciousness—would admit to be adequate. Still every understanding of values rests upon feeling. Hence the fundamental element of valuational knowledge is based on feeling. Plainly this must be true of personal love also. For it is an emotional hold upon values of its own kind.

In a certain sense the popular saying is right. Love is blind, in so far as it does not see what is before its eyes. More correctly stated: it sees what is not in front of its eyes, what is not really at hand. It sees through. Its glance is of the nature of divination. To it the ideal essence behind the actual man is the man proper. As regards personality, he who loves is the only one who sees; while he who is without love, is blind. That is why the just man is blind to personality and the loving man in his discernment of its essence is unjust. The former being loveless accepts only the actualized, the latter only the ideal personality. But also on this account the loving man must necessarily appear to the unloving to be blind; what the latter sees is exactly what the former does not see. The loving man in his way is always right as compared with the throng of the unloving—always of course only in regard to the one person whom he lovingly beholds. For every other person the knowing glance can only be that of one whose love is differently directed. Love's ability to know does not permit of being universalized. It is as individualized as its object—the ideal personality. But within these limits it is autonomous, it shows a conviction which is rightly regarded as infallible. The lover's proverbial unteachableness, which causes the man of experience to smile indulgently and shake his head, is exactly what betrays the utter seriousness of this phenomenon. Even where the facts justify the man of experience, the lover is ideally in the right. In fact no experience, not even his own, can teach him, so long as he really loves, that is, so long as he has intuitive insight into the ideal ethos of the loved one. For even his own experience is not an experience of the ideal but only of the actual personality. But his valuational insight holds good in reference to the ideal. And this he discerns, not empirically but aprioristically, through the empirical personality.

The problem of personality as a value has already led us to this paradox in the apriorism which recognizes and accepts the individual.[1] The cognitive factor in personal love coincides with such apriorism. For only the lover knows personality as a value. There is no way of understanding it, except through the insight of love. It discovers the ideal in the empirical. And as, by striving and leading, it actualizes for the first time the ideal ethos and within the limits of its power creates it in the loved one, it must first have understood the ethos and known it in contrast to the given empirical person. Here as everywhere else an anticipation of the ideal precedes its actualization. The constructive work of love follows after its discernment. All fulfilment together with all deep sense of fulfilment rests upon the penetrating knowledge of intuitive love.

It cannot be shown how empirical and aprioristic discernment supplement each other. The latter is conditioned by the presence of the empirical person, but in content stands con-

[1] Cf. Chapter XXXII (k), Vol. II.

trasted to it. The valuable element in it is seen in a state of unfulfilment, the ideal in the inadequate actual. A tendency towards fulfilment of course always exists in the actual personality. It shows the way to the gaze which is in search of the Ideal. But still it is not as if the one who loves saw two personalities, one disposed behind the other; he discerns the ideal immediately in the real, he sees it projected upon the latter, he sees the actual raised to the Ideal.

In this there is not only a truth, but also an error; for if he sees the actual man as if he were the ideal, he sees him under a false aspect. On this point the observer who is without love is by comparison right. But he is wrong in what he does not see, in the Ideal. To the lover this error may become an evil fate, a disappointment for life—just as much as, on its reverse side, the truth discerned may mean fulfilment for him and the loved one. The crisis depends upon how far he knows how to love the Ideal alone, how far he is able to unite the life of the Ideal with a sober view of the actual, that is, with actual life and the actual man. This combination need not be a compromise.

Of course no suffering he may undergo is too dear a price to pay for the highest degree of pure vision and participation. The whole art of love consists in retaining this high point of vision as a perspective and remaining under its spell. A life of love is a life spent in the knowledge of what is best worth knowing, a life of participation in the highest that is in man.

Thus personal love, like radiant virtue, gives an ultimate meaning to life; it is already fulfilment in germ, an uttermost value of selfhood, a bestowal of import upon human existence—useless, like every genuine self-subsistent value, but a splendour shed upon our path.

Section VIII

THE ORDER OF THE REALM
OF VALUES

THE LACK OF SYSTEMATIC STRUCTURE

(a) LIMITS OF OUR SURVEY

THE uniform character of the morally good has resolved itself
into a whole firmament of stars. If one examines it searchingly,
one involuntarily arrives at a kind of classification of values.

But the classification which is obtained in this way cannot
be accepted as complete or unambiguous in its arrangement.
In this it is characteristic of the stage which our investigation
has reached. We are at the beginning of our search, our procedure is still external, a gathering and putting together of
scattered details. We see ourselves resorting to accidental
points of contact which are supplied from history, and we can
add very little to what is acquired in this way. Nevertheless a
number of single values or small groups has been added,
although to the total problem such accession makes no perceptible difference.

The extent of the realm of values is greater not only than
our philosophic consciousness, but also than our primary
sense of values. We realize that on all sides we cannot see the
boundaries. In the direction of the simplest elements it became
clear that what seem to us final are not really so. And, in the
opposite direction, in regard to the most complex materials
the case is similar; in regard to personality we can never speak
of strictly single values. Of these there are indefinitely many,
but there are still more in the case of personal love, which in
every instance has a different character. In this stratum the
territory stretches out into a wide variety apparently without
bounds, the riches of which the philosophical consciousness can
surmise only in the abstract.

The two poles of the realm of values, that of the simplest
elements and that of the most complex materials, elude our

observation. They lie beyond the limits of what can be known. It is only in the intermediate section that we can move with some freedom. The maximum of knowledge is in the higher strata of the conditioning values, and in the lower and more general strata of the moral values. Accordingly one might expect that the "good," which here occupies the central position, must be most capable of being known. But almost the opposite is the case. The "good" is comprehensive as to contents, and presupposes the whole table of values, not only in its details, but in their reciprocal relationships. It also presupposes orderliness among values.

(b) Results Obtained Concerning the Scale of Values

The question arises: What do we know about these inner relationships, this orderliness? Can we learn anything from our incomplete survey?

Only within very modest limits can we answer in the affirmative. Very little order may be inferred. Where connections are clearly indicated, we cannot discover whether a relation revealed by some particular values recurs in the case of others or not. Even there we have no real insight into the law. At best we catch sight of a certain inherent order.

Here great expectations of discovering the system are radically disappointed. Our survey is inadequate even for a mere "theory concerning a tabulation of values." Likewise, even for a further analysis of the "good." If its content consists in aiming at the higher value,[1] the scale of values is presupposed in it. Upon detailed analysis much of the order of rank vanishes. But even here the gain is little, although the elaboration of the materials produces also a more exact discrimination of the valuational responses and predicates.[2] Nevertheless we must not fail to recognize that almost everywhere qualitative discrimination is in the foreground, and

---

[1] Cf. Chapter XIV (h), Vol. II.
[2] Cf. Chapter IV (c) and (d), Vol. II.

that discrimination of the relative grade lags far behind. Quality stands much nearer to the material differences. And it is only the material factors that present themselves for direct description, while the distinctive characteristics of the value remain a matter of feeling.

In contrast to the external criteria (for instance, Scheler's),[1] which indicate only the larger differences of rank, analysis also distinctly furnishes within the narrower class of moral values certain differences of grade. Thus, for example, brotherly love is evidently higher in value than justice, love for the remotest higher than brotherly love, and personal love (as it appears) higher than either. Likewise bravery stands higher than self-control, faith and fidelity higher than bravery, radiant virtue and personality again higher than these. But it is more difficult to say how, for example, truthfulness, wisdom and faith stand to one another in relative height; it is the same with the basic motives running through all the more special values, such as universality and individuality, likewise purity and fulness of life, pride and humility, and so on. It may be that these values stand on the same plane. But even this cannot be definitely known. The materials involved are too heterogeneous. We cannot bring them near enough together to decide.

In general it appears that the sense of preference indicates only within a certain material kinship the finer distinctions of grade. If the realm of values were a lineal, one-dimensional manifold, we could at all events establish the proximity of value to value once for all, and thereby make the differences of grade perceptible. But since there is evidently a co-ordinated variation, which at every grade extends as a horizontal level, the problem is much more difficult. The separate values never permit themselves to be torn from their special place in "valuational space." Just as the values which are separated vertically (in the order of height) cannot be brought together by any artifice—it might be done in the abstract, but then their specific

[1] Cf. Chapter IV (a) and (b), Vol. II.

character would be sacrificed,—so it is with those that are horizontally separated. The projection of all the materials upon a perfectly simple linear scale is easy to effect in the geometrical scheme which everyone involuntarily makes use of here. But it cannot be effected in the realm of values, because our actual emotional discrimination is bound fast to the material and axiological differences; and on all sides in several dimensions these arrange themselves about the scale of grades as about a line of reference.

We must leave undetermined, whether there be some other kind of procedure which would make such a projection possible, without eliminating the feeling for values; and this would depend upon retaining it, since the feeling for values is the only cognitive authority which could test the projection by the scale of heights. Yet it would always be possible that there might be an analysis especially directed to valuational grades, perhaps on the basis of a qualitative analysis of the materials. But evidently at the stage which investigation has reached, we are not capable of answering this question.

This is why in the present state of the problem the meaning of the good cannot be fathomed. And it is well to assume that here, in general, limits to insight are drawn, that is, that in the problem of the good we are confronted with a problem which can never be completely solved. But it would be entirely wrong to draw sceptical conclusions from this, or to give up analysis as a vain effort. The disappointment, which is always natural for the beginner when he sees the solution of a much-discussed problem suddenly removed to a remote distance, is only the disenchantment inevitable to the inexperienced. Before any investigation, he held the matter to be too simple. Analysis has just the merit of laying bare the great difficulty and complexity of the ethical problem at the very start. For the many cleavages in the realm of values are not self-evident. Descriptive analysis yields only the initial orientation in the realm of values. But starting with it, we can at least grapple with more urgent problems.

(c) Types of Regularity in the Table of Values

Uniformities are never disclosed at a first glance. In the beginning we find them only adumbrated. But where nothing is transparent, such adumbration may be most helpful.

We must naturally start from the fact that the table of values, like every diversified object, has its structural laws. Nothing else then is to be expected than that at least something of these will be somehow manifested in the values themselves. It is only a question whether our analysis penetrates sufficiently deep to strike upon them.

Now, in surveying the whole series of developed values, we can, without too great difficulty, discriminate among them laws of six different types of connection, which fall into three groups of two laws each. They are:—

1. Laws of Stratification
2. Laws of Foundation   } First Group
3. Laws of Opposition
4. Laws of Complementation   } Second Group
5. Laws of Valuational Height
6. Laws of Valuational Strength } Third Group

These essentially different types and groups of regularity, as such, can be seen with great distinctness. But the laws themselves are difficult to set forth, although one intuitively feels quite able to grasp them in many special cases. Nevertheless, amidst the general obscurity which surrounds the system of values, even to hold in mind the mere types of regularity is a help.

Besides, it is natural to look about in other departments of reality for analogous laws of systematization. Here the danger that the analogy will not fit is not great. What is not applicable is excluded by the mere fact that it is not applicable. Values do not allow any law to be forced upon them. And since we have in hand a certain foundation of values, this constitutes a natural criterion. In the realm of values there can be no law which would not at least be confirmed in the values visible at any time.

The realm of the categories offers itself as a region where the laws are possibly analogous. It is the universal system of the principles of Being. Now, as ethical Being retains the universal outlines of Being in general, while it acquires specific ones of its own, the relation of ontological to axiological principles remains fixed, as regards essential points. There is a relation of supplementation and continuation in all antithesis (for instance, in that of the Ought to real Existence), as both kinds of principle refer to the same actuality. Thus it comes about that much of the character of the categories can be recognized again in the values. In their lowest stratum, in the valuational contrasts, the categorial elements of value and the Ought appear themselves as valuational elements. Here we immediately detect the proximity of the ontological basis. It is not indeed the stratum of the transitional links—this cannot be shown; where one may assume it, it is unrecognizable; it falls into the *hiatus irrationalis* between the realm of the categories and that of values but, in the universal continuum of principles in general, the stratum of transition lies close to the structures which can be comprehended. It makes itself known in the prevalence of the ontological structure, as also in the paleness of the valuational quality. Here one can still trace what farther up in the realm of values fades into the background: that in a more extended sense values are as yet categories (principles of existence *sui generis*), and have in them a categorial arrangement, except that they are other categories than those of ontological reality.

The transference of the term, like all further mixture, is naturally a metaphysical venture as well as a kind of speculation in which one is not accustomed to engage. The matter at issue is only the strictness of the fundamental analogy amid the equally fundamental differences. From this point of view it is not only justifiable, but is also fruitful, to bring forward certain basic regularities of the realm of the categories into the table of values, and to test them at the same time in it. It may be anticipated that these regularities, where they ought in fact to apply, nevertheless will exist in essentially different form. But the changed form itself would be the instructive feature. At least it should be traced back to the peculiar axiological regularity.

In the following pages this is attempted within the different types of relationship. It does not come into question to the same degree for all the types. The first two and the last two of the above-mentioned relationships receive the most elucidation. But the difficulty there is this, that there can be no question anywhere as to a direct transference of a regularity. So long as the decision does not arise out of the valuational relationship, the possibility of such a transference is everywhere questionable.

CHAPTER XXXV (LX)

STRATIFICATION AND THE FOUNDATIONAL RELATION

(a) THE DIALECTICAL LAW OF COMBINATION

IF we look more closely, we see that the laws of the categories in general are adapted to the valuational relationships, but with restrictions and in a very different degree. The validity of some shows evident gaps. Others appear throughout to be confirmed, but they undergo an essential displacement; some gain an entirely new meaning. Hence it can be inferred that the orderliness ruling in the realm of values contains the categorial order, but is not restricted to the latter; it is more complex—conforming to the more complex categorial structure of values and to the Ought generally—and as such is constructed upon the categorial order and based upon it. One may therefore reckon upon a recurrence of the categorial laws, but not without a transformation.

What in the table of the categories immediately strikes every investigator—and not only in an absolute table which is the desideratum of all research, but also in most historical schemes —is the extraordinarily close union of the separate principles with one another. It is not possible to isolate them, without forfeiting their essence. This law, which Plato established in the *Sophist*, and which we might call the "dialectical law," may be formulated in this manner: there are no isolated categories, no existence for itself on the part of any one of them, but within every group or stratum there is a co-existence, a reciprocal conditionality, an interwovenness—the Platonic συμπλοκή. In the realm of the categories this law prevails almost universally. Here every principle has its inner essence at the same time beyond itself, in its every-sided connection; it is a distorted image of the whole system, and in this sense is itself a system. Hence it can also be discovered from the other co-ordinated members of the class.

In the realm of values there is evidently nothing analogous to this. Here it is not possible in any stratum to find the separate value directly from the others. There is indeed the implication. But it is much more elusive. It extends so far that, from some values which have been found, one sees that there must be still others co-ordinated with them; but where discernment (or the feeling) is lacking, the content cannot be estimated. And indeed the strength of the implication decreases with the height and the concrete complexity of the stratum. In that of the valuational opposites, and partly also in that of the conditioning values, it goes so far that discernment can be guided by the connecting threads at least up to the unseen values. But upwards from the "good" even that fails—even up to the few separate cases in which there is clearly present a relationship of another kind, a kind specifically axiological. The higher the valuational relationships are, so much the less dialectical they become. If it be granted that implication is a phenomenon specifically ontological, this assumption of its validity could be simply explained by the fact that the lower valuational strata stand nearer to the existential categories—as also that their quality as values is paler—that consequently in them the type of the categories comes more strongly to expression, while it fades away in the higher values. In the case of the moral values proper, the law of implication at all events plays only a subordinate rôle.

(b) The Implication of Disvalues and the Implication of Values

If a dialectic of the categories is already a daring conception, which has hitherto always led to speculative aberrations, so much the more so is a dialectic of values. Nevertheless it cannot be entirely abjured. It might be possible that with the advance of investigation there would be a place for it. But in any case it would be structurally different from that of the categories.

This is indicated by the circumstance that disvalues stand over against values, that they are counter-members, such as the realm of the categories does not know. An interlacing of disvalues must run parallel to the interlacing of values—or possibly not parallel, but according to a regularity of its own. That would give a doubled dialectic with a constant reciprocal polarity, whereby what is not discernible in the one series could very well be visible in the other. If we recall that many anti-values are far more comprehensible than their positive counter-members, that many values are definable only indirectly by way of their disvalues—a fact which we became practically acquainted with in our analysis—then it becomes clear that a dialectic of values would need to have a main support in one of disvalues. What exists unconnected in the values could very well be bound together in the disvalues. The Aristotelian method is one which in all naïveté makes use of this principle. Here the determination of a currently accepted value is arrived at by its position between two disvalues. Even the ever-recurring twofoldness of the disvalues in their attachment to the oneness of a value may cause us to reflect. So much at least is noticeable, that the relationship between values is different from that between disvalues, a fact which does not prejudice the fixed connection of the one with the other.

This, again, explains why the implication of values is more indefinite than that of the categories; it is more complex, because of the interweaving with the differently constructed implication of the disvalues. And, finally, in principle it is not otherwise possible. The absence of a fixed relation to reality allows a wider scope to co-existence: the valuational mode of being is merely an Ought-to-Be, it is necessity without the fulfilling conditions of possibility. Values can be united to one another according to a totally different principle; even harsh antinomic oppositions are not excluded here. For the two members never purport to be anything but an Ought-to-Be, which does not involve an existential contradiction. Only in the actual, in a situation, in a conflict of real life can a clash occur. It does not become actual until there is a move towards realization. What could not exist ontologically and under the categories, does exist in the valuational realm. But this question concerns another kind of regularity, which we are to consider later.[1]

(c) STRATIFICATION AND ITS LAWS

We have previously seen that the structure of valuational materials gives the widest scope to logical subsumption. Because the materials are made up of ontological factors, their law naturally obtrudes with them. But it does not affect the valuational character of the materials or their valuational height or their specific quality. And even in the relation of the materials themselves, where the laws of subsumption are exactly fulfilled, the weight does not rest upon them, but upon a series of other laws which accompany and mould the subsumptional relation. We may name them laws of stratification, after their fundamental character. In the categorial realm they play a conspicuous part, and even in the realm of values they are still dominant, although not without certain displacements. There are four laws: that of recurrence, of transformation, of novelty and of distance between strata. As they are the universal laws of the principles of stratification, and not at all special valuational laws, they may be stated here at the outset in their general categorial form.[2]

  1. The lower principles and their elements recur in the higher as their partial factors; thus they may enter into the foreground or the background of the higher structures, and accordingly be visible in them, or "vanish." In both cases they are pervading structural elements.

[1] Chapter XXXVI, Vol. II.
[2] Naturally only the general doctrine of categories can offer an explanation of these laws. Still, by their own import they may be clearly recognized.

2. In their recurrence these elements are not affected by the structure of the higher forms. They vary in many ways, according to the rôle which falls to them in the higher complex. Only their elemental essence remains the same.

3. The higher forms cannot be resolved into the various elements recurring in them. Together with the elementary stratification—which is only in the structure of the complex— they always manifest something specifically new, which is not contained in the elements. It is this novelty for the time being, which determines the prominence or seclusion of the elements, as well as the transformation of their significance.

4. The superimposition of the higher upon the lower principles does not advance in unbroken continuity but in strata, which are separated from one another by distinct intervals. As compared with the lower ones, each higher stratum shows a new feature common to it, while its union with them is preserved by the recurrence of the self-transforming elements.

The recurring elements constitute a cluster of divergent lines, which cut through the superimposed strata. They move in a dimension which lies at a right angle to the plane of the strata; at the same time, through their transformation the elements spread out over the width of the strata (divergence). In this way the stages in their modification are determined by the intervals between the strata as well as by the regional novelty. The four laws of stratification give in common the type of a connection which binds the strata "vertically" together, while the dialectical law of implication applies to the "horizontal" relation within the separate strata. Dialectical unification and the binding of the strata together stand, therefore, at right angles to each other, and only together constitute the multi-dimensional unity of the system, which for the realm of the categories is characteristic.

Thus arises a deep interpenetration of the two types of systematic unity. Ontologically the recurrence and the transformation extend not only to the elements but also to the implication; that is, the dialectical binding of principles itself reappears in a changed form in the higher strata. It is here complicated by the regional novelty of a higher implication, and from stratum to stratum produces ever new and firmer types of reciprocal dependence.

(d) THE LAWS OF STRATIFICATION, THE LIMITS OF THEIR VALIDITY

But in the realm of values this is the case only to a limited degree. Here we find not only the law of implication, but also the laws of stratification very considerably modified.

In general the law of recurrence retains its force. Yet, the higher the grade of the value, so much the more indefinite is it in form and so much the less binding in validity. The most general elements of value evidently recur pervasively, as may be easily seen in the pairs of contrasts of the first group (in Section II). It is most striking in the example of the individual and the collective unit, which as polar directions are decisive even up to the highest virtues, which are divided throughout into the more communal and the more individual. This holds good only in a limited way of the basic values which concretely condition the others. For the conditioning relation here introduces a new and differently articulated factor of stratification. But among the moral values recurrence is almost entirely lacking. The four basic values of course recur characteristically modified in many ways. The ethos of nobility, that of purity and that of fulness of life, are in evidence again and again in new garb. Likewise in the types of love we can follow a graded recurrence of certain basic elements (for example, that of solidarity); and finally in personality the whole series of general values is presupposed. But whether the law can here be pursued still farther is questionable.

It has its foundation in this, that here the two laws of transformation and of novelty come more into the foreground The peculiarity of the single virtues, and moreover of the valuational strata, evidently outweighs the relatively thin species of recurring elements. In regard to personality and personal love we may indeed find a higher significance in fidelity and faith than on the level of mere contract, upon which these values first occur. Likewise there is a lower (literal) and a higher (spiritual) meaning in truthfulness, bravery and other values besides. But the higher and more complex types of ethos are thereby characterized only quite externally; their proper essence is scarcely touched. That is to say, with values this essence inheres in the new factor to a quite different degree from that found in the categories. The specific peculiarity of the higher values, as compared with the character of the lower, is far more autonomous than that of the higher categories as compared with their categorial elements. The fissures between transformations are greater, the space between the strata is wider. This is especially noticeable in the vast interval between the moral values proper and the values of goods and of situations.

But even among the moral values themselves similar fissures appear; for example, between the whole complex of universal values (from justice up to radiant virtue) and the individual values (those of personality and personal love). With those of personality, where the recurrence of the universal values is clearly seen in the factor of the preferential trend, it is quite evident that the stratification of the elements falls completely into the background before the new factor. It is just this gap between the strata that can of course be filled up by the series of the type-values. But there can be no doubt that even for these, *mutatis mutandis* (from stratum to stratum), the same thing holds good. Finally, in personal love the universal elements, of faith, of fidelity, of altruism, of solidarity and so on, are raised up to a higher power and transformed into something new, something higher, in such a way that they almost vanish in comparison with the novelty of personal devotion.

(e) THE ABSORPTION OF THE CONDITIONING RELATION INTO STRATIFICATION

This laxity of the categorial laws in the realm of values evidently has other grounds than an actual failure of power. On the contrary, the laws of the gradational principles retain their force—as one sees in the fact that some of them even increase in power—only they do not now rule alone. Together with them other connectional laws come to the front, albeit laws of a more complex kind. Indeed the whole realm is more complicated in structure. But it is another question whether these unique, specifically axiological laws of connection can be discovered. And—in the present state of research—it must be, on the whole, answered in the negative.

Only at one point can we lay our finger on such a law as is not found in the realm of the categories. And this one instance, however isolated it stands in the refusal to be generalized, is of the greatest value for the philosophical understanding of the situation, because it in fact has to do with a gradational type of a more complex kind, a regularity of a higher and indeed purely axiological order. It is the relation of goods and situational values to moral values, a relation we continually met with as a conditioning relation, when we were considering the moral values.

The expression, a "conditioning relation," taken by itself, of course says very little. In a certain sense one may regard every basis as a condition and all stratification as a conditioning. In this wider sense one may find many kinds of conditioning in the table of values.[1] But these other kinds it shares with all systems of principles. It is different with the specific, complex mode of conditioning which prevails between situational and moral values.

The central position, which this relation assumes in the table of ethical values, we have been able to trace even down to the particular virtues. Everywhere the moral value adheres to an

[1] Cf. Chapter I (b), Vol. II.

intention directed towards a situational value; it is therefore conditioned by the situational value, but it reveals throughout a different character, which cannot be compared with that of the situation. Thus brotherly love aims at the well-being or happiness of one's neighbour, but is not itself a eudæmonistic value; the object of truthfulness is that another shall know the truth, but its own value does not consist in the value of this knowledge; it even has no axiological resemblance to it. In general, the values of intentions do not resemble in any way the values aimed at. And precisely herein lies the basic difference between the conditioning relation and stratification. In reference to what has been previously said concerning particular virtues, this difference may be summed up in the three following statements:—

1. In stratification the lower value reappears as an element in the higher; it is contained therein in a modified form, and cannot be removed from its substance. In the conditioning relation, on the other hand, it does not reappear, it does not enter as a constituent into the new material. The moral value no longer has in it anything of the situational value. The latter is neither transformed in it nor even merely completed by any new factor, but is simply presupposed in it, as its axiological condition. The content of the condition does not enter into the thing conditioned, but stands over against it. The irremovable difference between the carriers of the values is clearly seen to be this: the moral value inheres in the person, but the conditioning value remains inherent in the situation. Each is inseparable from its carrier. The valuational character of the situation does not at all reappear in that of the attitude directed toward it. The latter is indeed built upon it, but leaves it outside of itself. With its whole material it adds a higher storey to the building. For it the conditioning value is an external, not an internal, condition. Hence the peculiarly hovering position of the moral values above the situational values, as becomes perceptible in the two following factors.

2. In stratification, when the higher value is actualized, the

recurring lower element is necessarily actualized at the same time. In the conditioning relation, on the other hand, when the conditioned value is actualized, the conditioning value is not necessarily actualized with it. With regard to love, as such, it is not a question whether the service which it undertakes succeeds or not (whether the intended situation becomes actual), but only whether it was sincerely undertaken. Truthfulness is not morally less valuable, if the speaker is in error or if the hearer fails to grasp the truth. Moral value does not depend upon its success but exclusively upon the disposition, not upon the actualization of the desired object but exclusively upon the genuineness of its existence in the intention. Since the moral value of a person is already real in the mere intention, the conditioned value is actualized in the conditioning relation, although the conditioning value be not actualized. This might be stated formally as follows: The value of a moral disposition is indeed dependent upon the value of the object aimed at; but its actualization in the person depends in no wise upon his achievement of the object, but simply upon the object's being intended in his disposition.

3. Wherever there is a stratification of values, the matter of the higher value is not only conditioned by that of the lower, but even the grade of the higher is conditioned by the grade of the lower. The value of trust rises with the strength, venture and courage contained in it; that of radiant virtue grows with the fulness of life within it. But this dependence also does not reappear in the conditioning relation. The value of a just disposition is not less, where small possessions are involved, than where it is a matter of great ones; the value of brotherly love is the same, whether it has (or wills to have) great or small effects in the life of one's neighbour. Everywhere here the moral value rises or falls with the degree of commitment, as well as with the depth and genuineness of the intention, but not with the height of the value aimed at. We had the supreme example of this in the relation of brotherly love to love of the remotest.[1]

[1] Cf. Chapter XXX (i), Vol. II.

There the values aimed at are scarcely any longer commensurable in height; but in order of rank the values of the respective intentions stand close to each other. The reason is simply this: the values aimed at and those of the intention stand to each other in no assignable relation as regards their order of rank. The highest moral values may be based upon the lowest situational values, and conversely. In formal terms, the moral value is indeed dependent in general upon the existence of the situational value aimed at, but its axiological height is in no wise dependent upon the axiological height of the situational value. This type of independence very clearly shows the cleavage between the two types of value. Yet the presence in general of an intended situational value is a condition of the value of the intention. In all other details it is "unconditioned."

This conditioning relation stands by itself. There is nothing analogous in the realm of the categories. But even in the realm of ethical values there is no other relation of the same kind. At best one might find further down, between goods and situational values, a relation which always shares some features with it. At least situations that can be aimed at (such as the well-being of one's neighbour or his knowledge of the truth) are referred back to goods (for instance, the goods upon which well-being depends, or the objective truth the knowledge of which is to be conveyed). But here the reference is far simpler. It stands much nearer to categorial stratification and its regularity. Yet there is evidence here of the reappearance and transformation of the goods-value in the situational value, likewise of the dependence of the actualization and height of the conditioned value upon the actualization and height of the conditioning value. And finally we must consider that in their genus the values of situations and goods do not differ, that situations have the character of more complex goods. Neither the heterogeneity nor the distinctive "hovering" of moral values finds anything analogous here. It is a type of dependence which stands structurally between stratification and the conditioning relation. But it stands nearer to the former.

(f) The Relation between Ethical and Æsthetic Values

In passing, it may be mentioned here that we find the nearest analogy to the conditioning relation in a far distant and entirely different region of the realm of values—outside of all distinctively ethical problems as to value—namely, in the relation between certain æsthetic values and those of morality.

There is a series of æsthetic qualities (most evident in the domain of epic and dramatic poetry), which in subject-matter are bound to the ethical conduct of persons and presuppose the valuational diversities in such conduct, without being themselves merged therein or even being axiologically similar. Here are found the well-known values of the heroic, the tragic and the comic, the all-too-human lovable, the ironic and the naïve, among others, likewise the various values of the dramatic situation, the fore-shortening, exaggeration, suspense and relaxation, and so on. All such values and a throng of others akin to them manifest the same "hovering" over the moral values, as these manifest over the situational values, even if in an essentially distorted form.

They have as their presupposition the substance of the human ethos in all its concreteness and fulness of values and disvalues; they are therefore founded upon the moral values, and as much upon the universal virtues as upon the personal (down to the smallest idiosyncrasy). The ethical accent reverberates through them, just as the moral partisanship of the listener is throughout a factor in the dramatic effect. But as the dramatic effect is not contained in the partisanship, so the dramatic values are not contained in the conditioning moral values. The æsthetic value (for example, that of the tragic) is by no means dependent upon the degree to which the tragic hero actualizes moral values, indeed not even upon the moral height and quality of the ethos which inheres in his Ideal. In general the manifestation of the æsthetic value is relatively indifferent toward the actualization of the conditioning moral value; finally its specific quality and its height follow an entirely different law from that of the former. A highly significant tragic situation can be built upon human figures who are extremely insignificant. And nevertheless, if these figures were entirely deprived of their moral significance, the æsthetic value also of the situation would completely vanish, exactly as the moral value of honesty would vanish, if the goods-value of property were denied, to which the honesty is directed.

Here accordingly there is in fact present a similar conditioning relation, in which the stratum of æsthetic values appears to be in the same way suspended over that of the ethical values. Here also there is no proper recurrence, any more than a transformation, of the values; the moral values remain entirely outside of the relevant æsthetic values, and do not become a proper axiological constituent in them. Here accordingly there is no simple stratification. It is superseded by a more highly constructed, more complex conditioning relation.

The fact throws a strong light on the whole situation in the realm of values, in so far as one clearly sees how the moral values, together with their narrower system of stratification, constitute a compact body which on both sides, above as well as below, is shut off by a deep chasm, by a space of another kind than the interval between strata—one might say that on both sides it is shut off by a *hiatus irrationalis*. As to the isolation on the upper side, we must be cautious how we interpret it axiologically. For with æsthetic values, being "higher" is by no means a self-evident feature and upon closer analysis might easily prove to be false. Rather would it appear that in general no clear relationship exists between æsthetic and moral values as regards their respective scales of rank; and this seems to indicate a kind of incommensurability of the two scales. But this in no wise detracts from the conditioning relation which we have described. Much rather can we learn from it that it does not universally inhere in the essence of a conditioned value to be a higher value, and that there might be conditioning relations which prevail in some other axiological dimension than that of "height."

It is to be expected that a closer analysis of æsthetic values and an elaboration of their table—which has never yet been made—must needs throw further light upon the structure of the ethical table of values. We should not forget that moral values do not constitute the whole realm. They are merely nearest to life and actuality. This is why they have from of old forced themselves into the foreground of investigation.

(g) CONSEQUENCES

So far as can be seen to-day, it inheres in the essence of the complex conditioning relation that, wherever it occurs, there is a manifest hiatus in the stratification. Now the table of the more restricted moral values begins with such a conditioning relation. This is the reason why in ethics the valuational analysis cannot directly commence with the moral values, but must draw into its consideration the lower strata which are entrenched in front of them. The conditioning relation consists in a rigid, indissoluble connection, without prejudice to the peculiar hovering of the higher structures.

But because in this way a hiatus extends through the table of values that are normative for ethics—like a cleft which splits the whole from start to finish into two axiologically heterogeneous parts—this cleft forms the limit to the laws of stratification. They extend continuously to the highest conditioning values (even to those which adhere to a conscious subject and transform him into a person). But then they break off, to enter again above the hiatus, together with the newly-formed conditioning relation, which in part determines them. Thus we can understand that within the strata of the moral values they can occasionally be pursued a little farther, but no longer play a really dominant rôle. They are here outdone by another kind of dependence extending in the same dimension, and are forced into the background.

Thus it happens that here the law of recurrence seems to be encroached upon, while the law of novelty gains in importance; but transformation makes such considerable leaps forward that it can scarcely be recognized as such. For with the greatness of the modification the identity of the thing modified diminishes. Yet identity is the presupposition of the transformation. As it vanishes, the transformation becomes equivalent to the introduction of something new. Hence the seeming disparity between groups of ethical values and the width of the intervals between their strata.

OPPOSITIONAL RELATION AND THE SYNTHESIS OF VALUES

(a) FIVE TYPES OF AXIOLOGICAL CONTRAST

An entirely different type of regular connection is that of contrast. It stands nearer to implication than to stratification, but does not completely fall into that dimension, as is the case in the realm of the categories.

Valuational contrast is more complex than existential contrast. The new factor in the realm of values is the pervasive plus-minus relation, which is peculiar to them all. We know it as the polarity of value and disvalue. The opposition is by no means one of contradiction, as might be supposed, in distinction from the positive relation of value to value. Rather is the contrast contradictory between the valuable and the neutral, and between the neutral and disvalues. "Value-disvalue" is, on the contrary, a special polarity, characteristic only of the valuational realm. It co-exists with the positive contrast, as we learned from the lowest stratum where the positive contrast is the ruling principle, and then again in the higher strata where it continually recurs and often develops into a sharp antinomy.

In the positive contrast both members have their special disvalues over against themselves—but "over against" in a different dimension—although the conceptual expression for the disvalue as distinguished from the opposing value is by no means always at command. One need only recall the instructive instance of "inertia" as a value and "inertia" as a disvalue.[1] That the dimension of the positive contrasts, at least preponderantly, coincides with the breadth of the strata is seen in the majority of the pervasive antinomies; but that this is not

[1] Cf. Chapters VIII (b) and XI (c), Vol. II.

a fixed law is shown by such cases as that of justice and brotherly
love, or that of brotherly love and love of the remotest, where
the positive opposition evidently extends over the strata and
is shifted diagonally into the vertical dimension of height.

Hence it is not feasible to identify the value-disvalue dimension, which evidently stands at right angles to that of the
antinomic relation, with the vertical of stratification. Much
rather does one clearly see in it that in the table of values we
have to do with a higher multi-dimensionality which no longer
can be expressed in a plain three-dimensional scheme. And
it must be added that the elementary contrasts constitute
among themselves a kind of "valuational space" of several
dimensions,[1] and, finally, that, just as with these, so the disvalues are connected oppositionally, and together form a
system in contrast to the whole positive realm of value.

If one wished to bring into view the entire variety of oppositions, one would need in every individual case to have in
mind the following five types of contrast in their extremely
anomalous inter-connectedness:—

$$I \begin{cases} 1. \text{ Value-Neutrality} \\ 2. \text{ Disvalue-Neutrality} \end{cases}$$
$$II \quad 3. \text{ Value-Disvalue}$$
$$III \begin{cases} 4. \text{ Value-Value} \\ 5. \text{ Disvalue-Disvalue.} \end{cases}$$

It is easy to see that these five types fall into three heterogeneous groups. Only the first two (types 1 to 3) are common
to all values. The third group (types 4 and 5) does not recur
in all. Not every value has a positive contrasted value, but
every one has a disvalue and a neutral point. Likewise (but
it does not necessarily follow) not every disvalue has a contrasted disvalue, but of course has a value and an indifference
point. The first three types of contrast inhere in the very
essence of all valuational Being, the last two on the other hand

[1] Cf. Chapter VI (c), Vol. II.

only in the essence of special valuational structures. They are merely contrasts in the contents of the value.

(b) REDUCTION OF THE TABLE OF CONTRASTS

Now valuational neutrality has two meanings. On the one hand, it is that which in general stands outside of all valuational reference, anterior, as it were, to value and disvalue (like everything that is merely ontological); but on the other hand it is what stands ideally midway within the polarity of value and disvalue, therefore at the indifference-point in their continuum. In the first sense it does not at all belong to axiology, and therefore not to ethics, but to the much more general discussion of the relation between ontology and axiology. In the second sense, however, it is drawn into the basic correlation of value and disvalue and forms in it only a structural moment, in so far as every value-disvalue scale passes through an indifference-point. Hence, without going beyond any essentially axiological factor, we may omit for the present from our consideration the relation both of value and disvalue to neutrality, and devote our attention to the remaining three types of contrast.

The omission of course must not lead to a misunderstanding of the problem. For on one point neutrality retains a peculiar significance. It is involved in the problem concerning the order of rank. For values, like disvalues, differ widely from one another in the scale of grade, but over against them all the indifference-point is one and the same. It is the fixed point, in relation to which the distances of height first attain an absolute meaning. But a special chapter must be devoted to this matter.

What chiefly appertains to the regularity of the table of values is the determination of the relation between types 3 and 4, that is, between the essential contrast "value-disvalue," which is axiologically universal, and the positive contrast "value-value," which is not universal but is confined to definite structures. Upon the latter depends the riddle of valuational antinomy, the elucidation of which is an undisputed desideratum of research. Any light which falls upon this complicated question—and, as was shown, it extends even into the most vital moral conflicts—is of supreme importance for ethics. If an inner relation between the antinomies and the value-disvalue relation could be shown, much would thereby be gained towards an understanding of the situation.

(c) The Formal Relation between the Types of Contrast and their Reciprocity

Now it is easy, on the one hand, to see that absolutely no such relation can be directly discovered in the nature of these two

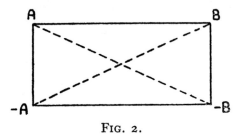

Fig. 2.

types of opposition. Both evidently lie in different dimensions—the value-disvalue relation in that of height, but the positive value-value relation principally in the horizontal dimension of the strata, and each plainly varies independently of the other.

On the other hand, a diagram of the relation can easily be constructed. So much at least can be taken in at a glance that there can be no question of complete indifference between the types of contrast. If, for instance, the values A and B stand to each other in positive antinomy, then each one has besides (in the other dimension) its relevant disvalue over against it; these may be represented diagrammatically by —A and —B. Then it is clear that the positive contrast of the values must recur in the disvalues, whether in strict analogy to the positive contrast or differently constituted. So the contrast between the two disvalues emerges as something indirectly involved in the contrast of the two values, that is, implied through the value-disvalue oppositions. In this way the fifth type is drawn into the relation between the two main types (3 and 4).

This is significant to the extent that the examples show that the relation between disvalues, which corresponds to an antinomy between value and value, is not at all antinomical and indeed need be scarcely oppositional. Purity and fulness of life stand in an antinomic relation; but impurity and moral poverty may quite well be compatible. Justice and brotherly love exclude each other at least in some essential respects; but injustice and lovelessness never bar each other out—merely in content are they different vices, but the same man in the same deed without the slightest inner conflict can manifest both.

Therefore, in the diagram (figure 2) only three of the four basic relations represented are in opposition (A to B, A to —A and B to —B), but the fourth (—A to —B) is not oppositional. This is so striking that from the relation between the disvalues one might expect light to be thrown upon the whole relational complex. The expectation, if possible, increases, when one further discovers that even the two diagonally placed connections A to —B and B to —A manifest no oppositional character at all. Brotherly love is entirely compatible with injustice, but justice also with lovelessness. Likewise purity does not conflict with moral poverty, but neither does fulness of life conflict with impurity. Here a value is compatible with a disvalue. And this is easy to comprehend: the disvalue stands in a doubled (a two-dimensional) contrast to the value; it is the negative antithesis to its positive counter-value—thus blunting the point of the antithetical relation.

(d) The Antithetic of Disvalues and the Theory of the μεσότης

One's expectation here is of course at first disappointed. Nothing issues directly from introducing the relation between disvalues—or at most this, that in general the reciprocal relationships between disvalues must be different from those between the values to which they belong; but even without the diagram this was no mystery.

Are there then no oppositions among disvalues? The question inevitably obtrudes itself here. For it is natural to set up the counter-test: what relation holds between the values in question (A and B) when their disvalues (−A and −B) are antinomic to each other?

This question assumes a very serious aspect if one sees it in the light of the wider problem. Over against the whole realm of values there stands a realm of disvalues, its counterpart, member for member, but in its inner dependencies not at all a true counterpart. Now, since the regularities of the realm of values are in part unknown, indeed in some points (in the antinomies which emerge) are directly enigmatic, so in reference to the complete polar connection of the two realms the thought suggests itself that from the co-ordination of the disvalues, and perhaps in contrast to it, that of the values could be inferred.

In their concrete materials there are contrasts enough among disvalues; miserliness and extravagance, cowardice and foolhardiness, wantonness and coldness, pretension and self-belittlement, precipitate anger and incapacity to feel righteous indignation. This type of contrast is familiar to us from Aristotle's doctrine of the virtues.[1] They are those ἄκρα, between which, as opposed "vices," a virtue is always installed as a μεσότης. Aristotle therefore was evidently on the way towards inferring the character of values from their relation to disvalues. Now here is the point at which through the unintended blending of two methodological perspectives the two-sided problem-complexes can throw light on each other: the Aristotelian theory of the μεσότης and the antinomic of values.

But what appeared illuminating and at the same time objectionable in the Aristotelian theory is precisely its central

[1] Cf. Chapter XXIII, Vol. II.

thesis, namely, that moral values are midway between two disvalues; as if the good were nothing but the commonplace average. Now the offensiveness was removed, by placing here two oppositional dimensions at right angles to each other, an ontological and an axiological.[1] The virtue is a mean only according to its existential determination (its matter); according to its value, on the other hand (κατὰ τὸ ἄριστον καὶ τὸ εὖ), it is the highest point (ἄκρον). This furnishes for the continuous transition from the one κακία to the other the curve of a parabola. But how is this diagram consistent with that of the contrasts (Fig. 2)? Plainly enough both dimensions reappear; the ontological one is horizontal; the axiological, vertical. Here —A and —B correspond to the Aristotelian ἄκρα (the ὑπερβολή and ἔλλειψις). But at the upper pole not one single value but two correspond to them. Each of the disvalues has its own opposed value. Aristotle therefore either had not grasped the whole valuational relationship or else in the square of the contrasts is concealed some error.

Now the latter is not really possible, as the cited diagram (Fig. 2) is a purely formal one, and in its structure is easily grasped. The examples of purity and fulness of life, justice and brotherly love, demonstrate besides that the twofoldness of the values A and B is in fact present, as can be seen in all cases of positive antitheses. But precisely here we strike upon the remarkable fact that the antithetic of the values corresponds to no antithetic of the disvalues. In agreement with this is the other fact that the antithetic of the values is by no means an all-pervasive phenomenon, but emerges at best only in single pairs of values. Hence the cases analysed by Aristotle are in fact different cases. The only question is: Wherein does the difference consist? Does only a single value really stand here over against the duality of the disvalues? Or, hidden behind the Aristotelian virtues, is there always a duality of antithetic-ally placed values, the synthesis of which constitutes the sought-for "virtue"?

[1] Cf. Diagram, Fig. 1, p. 256.

(e) The μεσότης as a Valuational Synthesis

At this point the enigma must be solved. It can be shown that the second of these alternatives is the true one: behind the Aristotelian virtues there are in fact two values always concealed, and these manifest a distinct oppositional character. The only difficulty is that language (and not only the German but also the Greek) has no labels for these values; one can only describe them. But one sees clearly that they are present, when one views the reputed unitary "virtue" in the twofold light of both the κακίαι, which are attached to it as opposites. This dual light dissolves the unity; there is another valuational element in the virtue; one value is over against one κακία, another over against the other.

Every individual example can teach this. In juxtaposition to σωφροσύνη stand ἀκολασία and ἀναισθησία; only in contrast to the former of these is it properly self-control; in contrast to the latter it is the fully developed capacity to react emotionally, to live in the affections. In contrast to δειλία bravery is spirited endurance, in contrast to θρασύτης it is deliberate foresight, cool presence of mind. Seen against ὀργιλότης πραότης is mildness, but seen against ἀοργησία it is the capacity to be righteously indignant. ἐλευθεριότης is liberality with regard to material values, and at the same time the capacity not to spend, the former in contrast to ἀνελευθερία, the latter to ἀσωτία. Αἰδώς is the capacity to be ashamed of oneself, and at the same time it is the limitation of shame, the latter as opposed to the conduct of the κατάπληξ, the former to that of the ἀναίσχυντος. Still clearer, if this be possible, is the relation in the case of the more complex virtues. Νέμεσις stands in contrast to φθόνος as unenvious delight in another's happiness, but in contrast to ἐπιχαιρεκακία as participation in undeserved calamity. Μεγαλοψυχία, finally, is perhaps the purest example of such a decomposition in its dual attitude to μικροψυχία and χαυνότης; in opposition to the former, it is justifiable moral pride, the power to stand alone; in opposition to the latter, the modest consciousness of the limitation of one's own moral being.[1]

It is characteristic of this state of the case that the terminology concerning the virtues is never quite correct in regard to the double bearing of the contrast and the duality of the valuational factors, since in the expressions chosen by Aristotle only one side of the depicted value is made clear, but the other, the opposed shade of meaning, is omitted. It must strike everyone who reads the *Nicomachean Ethics* that in the analysis of the virtues a second side of the virtue is indicated, which from the name of the virtue one would not expect. This proves sufficiently that the Aristotelian virtues are not so much μεσότητες as valuational syntheses. They are complex values, which never consist of one-sided enhancements of single valuational elements alone, but of inner organic combinations of two materially contrasted elements. These syntheses manifestly form more highly constructed values; they have the stratification of the lower in them, but it is a very specific stratification, namely, the unification of such elements as have a tendency to go to a one-sided extreme and to exclude each other. Here the thought is undoubtedly right, and at all events incomparably deeper than the superficial morality of the golden mean. It is the view that morality imposes upon man complex claims, which through an inner oppositional relationship of constituent values are raised high above the constituents themselves. Both sides of an alternative are always required of man at the same time. If he satisfies the demand of only one of the members of the twofold claim, he is morally of little worth. Not until there is a synthesis of the values in one and the same disposition of the man is there real virtue.

To anyone who has grasped the principle, this is easily made evident in each of the Aristotelian examples. Bravery is neither boldness alone nor cool foresight alone—for the prudence of the coward is as worthless as the daring of the foolhardy man—but solely a synthesis of both. Just as little

[1] Cf. Chapter XXIII (*b*)–(*f*); also Chapter XXIX (*c*), Vol. II.

can the apparent self-control of a person without passion pass for virtue (rather is there nothing in him which it would be worth while controlling); likewise with the passionateness of the uncontrolled; σωφροσύνη is simply the self-control of one who is overflowing with the fulness of life, an unmistakable synthesis of two heterogeneous elements.

In this way it is easy to complete the whole series of the examples given above. Everywhere the positive synthesis behind the μεσότης rises to the surface; everywhere the latter is only the outward form it assumes. On this point μεγαλοψυχία, the crown of the Aristotelian virtues, is especially instructive. Moral self-sufficiency is ridiculous and vain, when one's moral nature does not justify it; and the moral being of one who really has this virtue is lowered if he refuses to maintain it. Justifiable moral pride consists of a harmonious agreement between one's moral being and one's moral self-consciousness.

In this way a new meaning is given not only to the Aristotelian μεσότης, but also to the antithetic of values in general. It is shown to be untrue that the μεσότης is merely built upon the antithetic of disvalues. Actually it is also built upon an antithetic of values. That Aristotle did not see this, although it is his analyses which have proved it, is nothing against it; and herewith is solved the question previously raised: How is the formal diagram of the axiological contrasts (Fig. 2) consistent with the Aristotelian theory, according to which it is always only one value which corresponds to two disvalues? According to the diagram two values necessarily correspond to them, and indeed two values which are in positive opposition.

The solution is this. If in the μεσότης is concealed a synthesis, the synthesis presupposes the antithetic of the elements contained in it; as a fact, therefore, two values are always hidden in it. But this means that the previously given diagram of the parabola, which shows the culminating point of ἀρετή (Fig. 1, page 256) can be incorporated into a diagram of the contrasts (Fig. 2); the arrangement of the one is confirmed by that of the other (Fig. 3). Ἀρετή is the synthesis of the one-sided factors A and B (this is expressed only vaguely in the diagram by the position between A and B); now since A and B have their disvalues opposite them, ἀρετή is referred to the two disvalues as opposites.

Also in the two diagonal lines the diagram indicates the vanishing of opposition. The disvalue —A and the value B, likewise the disvalue —B and the value A, stand in a double (two-dimensional) opposition; the opposition is cancelled through opposition to it. In fact the examples exhibit not only the cancellation but even a close material kinship—a kinship so close that only a slight shade divides the disvalue from the value which is diagonally opposed to it. Thus, in the complex

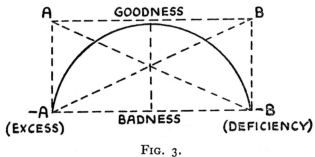

FIG. 3.

of σωφροσύνη, ἀναισθησία is in content so closely akin to a one-sided self-control that the ethics of the Stoics could confuse the two and recoin the disvalue as a value; ἀκολασία is just as closely allied to a one-sided development of the emotional life, and often enough this likeness has led to a rejection of the emotions. In the complex of bravery, imprudence is similarly akin to boldness, while cowardice resembles prudence. Still more annoying in practice is the difficulty, in the complex of μεγαλοψυχία, of distinguishing genuine pride from χαυνότης (unjustifiable self-esteem), and modest self-criticism from μικροψυχία. On this account the right ethical appraisement of pride as well as of humility has suffered. Fundamentally all such confusion rests upon obtuseness of insight into values, as well as upon ignorance of the basic structure of the oppositional combinations underlying all valuational syntheses.

(f) APPLICATION OF THE SYNTHETIC PRINCIPLE TO THE HIGHER MORAL VALUES

Thus far there is no conflict between the two views of valuational contrast—between the Aristotelian and the formal. But there are two things which are not in agreement.

First, the relation of A to B is different. Here the oppositional complex manifests an open antinomy (of course only in regard to some values, but these are the only ones which come under consideration); it is precisely here that the Aristotelian virtues, on the other hand, exhibit unity, a synthesis of values.

And, secondly, the relation of —A to —B is different. Here the *Nicomachean Ethics* throughout exhibits the antithetic of disvalues ($\dot{\upsilon}\pi\epsilon\rho\beta o\lambda\dot{\eta}$ and $\ddot{\epsilon}\lambda\lambda\epsilon\iota\psi\iota\varsigma$), while the formal complex on the other hand shows a cancellation of the antithetic, a thorough conciliation (for example, in the relation of love-lessness to injustice).

How are we to understand these two discrepancies?

The question is substantially the same as if we asked: How does it happen that brotherly love, truthfulness, fidelity, faith—that is, the entire series of the higher values—no longer manifest the character of syntheses? Is there then lacking in them the antithetic of the disvalues? And is this perhaps the reason why in them their antithetical character becomes more prominent and in some of them is most striking? Then it would have been right to expect that this character would somehow exist latent in the rest of the values, and must permit of being seen even there from some wisely chosen point of view. But the point of view would need to be that of the anti-thetical disvalues; from thence the blended elements could be seen even in the Aristotelian virtues. But a wider, most highly important consequence then follows: the higher values which are antinomic must be understood to be $\ddot{\alpha}\kappa\rho\alpha$, in which synthesis is lacking, and in the antithetic of which it must therefore needs be perceptible to feeling as an axiological postulate. The principle of the synthesis would thereby be carried over

into the higher values without a remainder, of course as a
principle still unfulfilled in our present-day morality, which
declares itself in valuational antinomies merely. The whole
table of moral values would then need to be so conceived that
in their lower elements the syntheses would be apprehended
by the emotional sense of values—namely, in such virtues as
the Aristotelian and others like them—but in the higher
elements the syntheses are still lacking, because our feeling
for values cannot discern them (whether at times only or not
at all). Then from the unitary principle of the table of values
it would be evident why in the lower values the antithetic has
vanished and can be reconstructed only by analysis, while in
the higher values the synthesis seems to be lacking and the
antithetic alone seems to rule.

Now, even if it cannot be proved, it can be stated with strong
hypothetical certainty that the fact is so, and that the principle
of synthesis constitutes a universal law of the ethical table.
The difference between the Aristotelian and the higher moral
values is in truth not an all-important one; one sees this, as
soon as one drops the habit of looking only for single values.
Even Aristotle could not apply his principle to the higher
virtues. In regard to justice the μεσότης is very questionable
(and on that account it was the centre of ancient polemics),
but in it the synthesis also seems to be weak. Both are quite
lacking in φιλία and the dianoetic virtues. If syntheses proper
do exist here, at all events they are not to be sought for within
the valuational structure of these virtues but outside of it, in
its relation to other valuational materials. On the other side
it is clear that the syntheses, as they are found in his "virtues,"
are not really completed in the consciousness of values, but
rather are discerned only as moral claims. Perhaps in
ἐλευθεριότης, σωφροσύνη, ἀνδρεία and some others it is completed in the consciousness of positive morals. On the other
hand, in μεγαλοψυχία one sees clearly how the philosopher
struggles, without being quite able, to grasp it positively. If
we think of this struggle in regard to synthesis as being carried

still a stage farther—even to the point where the sense of values cannot anticipate the unity of the antithetical elements, not to mention the concrete discernment of the unified moral disposition in idea, we stand exactly at the place where we find ourselves to-day in regard to higher valuational antinomies.

What is it exactly which we feel to be antinomic in the relationship of justice and brotherly love, of purity and fulness of life, indeed even of pride and humility? Precisely this, that our sense of values longs for a synthesis, searches for it, but cannot grasp it concretely. Of course it could very well be that these antitheses are "genuine antinomies," that is, cannot be resolved by any synthesis. One may be especially inclined to assume this in regard to purity and fulness of life. But that does not change the situation. The axiological demand for a synthesis as such still exists; it exists independently of the possibility of fulfilling it. It is simply due to the fact that in all actual cases of conflict the conduct of man cannot fail to be a unity. In an ideal moral disposition the idea of synthesis is, therefore, in the face of all existing antitheses, the necessary postulate of ethics. What is sought is precisely a unified ethos of purity and fulness of life, of justice and brotherly love, of pride and humility. Only this should be called "virtue" in the higher and stricter sense, since the one-sided values do not properly deserve the name—just as with Aristotle neither boldness nor prudence, neither penuriousness nor lavish expenditure, bear by themselves the name of ἀρετή, but only in their syntheses, ἀνδρεία and ἐλευθεριότης, both of which (each in its own grade) signify a superiority of an ideal disposition above the tyrannical one-sided ethos of the single valuational elements.

It is of course a very different and high-strung moral demand when one requires a similar superiority to such values as brotherly love and justice, which are both no less tyrannical but are far higher in the scale of values. Here real moral striving struggles only too hard for the one-sided value. How could it at the same time struggle also for a synthesis of these qualities? But this distinction is not one of principle: it is purely empirical, relative to the given stage of development in the actual moral existence. *Sub specie æternitatis*—and this means: from the point of view of the ideal realm of values—the distinction does not exist at all.

(g) The Tyranny of Values and its Restriction in the Synthesis

That the same thing applies to all cases of the antinomies in question, that everywhere the living sense of value spontaneously seeks for the synthesis and thereby indicates most clearly the direction in which philosophical reflection must look, is in need of no proof. It is a priori evident in the essence of the valuational antinomies. Whether in all cases the synthesis really exists, and whether, even when it does exist, it is discernible to the sense of values, is quite another question. The watchfulness of valuational feeling is independent of that, and with it the indication of the way to a philosophy of values.

At all events there are single antinomies which are of special interest for the construction of a table of values. Such preeminently is the antinomy between the values of personality and the universal values, which divides the whole of the moral realm into two layers. Closely observed, it is seen to consist of an innumerable variety of special oppositions—for each single universal value finds its limiting counterpart in a throng of values peculiar to personality—and all these opposites demand a special synthesis. But the universal type of these syntheses has at its foundation the double demand: on the one side, so to act as all ought to act; and on the other, within this type of action to have in all one's conduct a distinctive mark, which could not and should not be found in everyone's conduct.[1]

[1] Cf. Chapter XXXII, Vol. II, on the conversion of the categorical imperative.

Not less instructive is the opposition to almost all other virtues, especially to justice and brotherly love, into which love of the remotest sees itself drawn. Even behind this is concealed a great diversity of contrasts and, although of another kind, such contrasts pervade the whole of the table of ethical values. In this case the difference is that between the values of the present and those of the future. The synthesis would need to unite these two in one and the same disposition, as guiding points of view. How it should be brought about is just as much a question as with the other antinomies.

But with all the contrasts which can be directly established the abundance of moral diversity is not yet exhausted. There are many relationships besides, which have not the character of antinomies. If that ended the matter, the principle of synthesis would not be universal—even if it be only in the watchfulness of the valuational emotion. For its postulate is nothing but contrast.

But here two things must be considered. Contrast of values is by no means limited to the antinomies proper. These are only special cases where the contrast is intensified. There are conflicts, however, between all values, that is, in every concrete situation. This simply brings the material diversity with it. Now where it inheres in the structure of the situation that two different values, participating in it, cannot be satisfied at the same time, the decision can be only for one and must violate the other. If the two values lie in very different grades, the conflict of course is not a moral one; precedence is due to the higher (according to the law of the good). But if they are approximately equal, or even only comparable in height, the conflict exists. There are conflicts of this kind[1] which permeate the whole of human life. They place before a man the necessity of choosing. But on principle this means that in the concrete situation all material diversity of value can assume an antinomical character. And granted that just here fully satisfying syntheses would be perhaps least possible, the moral

[1] Cf. Chapter XXV (b), Vol. II, the instance of the "necessary lie."

requirement still holds, to search from case to case for the syntheses.

But, secondly, something of an oppositional character inheres in all moral values. One recognizes this immediately, if one takes the single values which are extreme in their one-sidedness, each in the strict rigour of its idea. To do so is not a theoretical experiment in abstraction. In practical life there is a sense of the inexorableness of single values. It can mount even to fanaticism. Every value—when once it has gained power over a person—has the tendency to set itself up as sole tyrant of the whole human ethos, and indeed at the expense of other values, even of such as are not inherently opposed to it. This tendency of course does not adhere to the values as such in their ideal sphere of existence, but to them as the determining or selective powers in human feeling; it is the tendency to crowd out other values from the range of emotional appraise-ment. Such tyranny shows itself plainly in the one-sided types of current morality, in the well-known intolerance of men (even men otherwise compliant) towards the customs of foreigners, but still more in the individual person's obsession by one single value. Thus there exists a fanaticism of justice (*fiat justitia pereat mundus*), which by no means attacks love merely, not to mention brotherly love, but all the higher values. Like-wise there is a fanaticism of brotherly love, which can become self-surrender, indeed even self-torture; it clashes not only with justice, but with most of the moral values, from the highest down to that healthy egoism which is necessary for life.[1] Even a fanaticism of love for the far distant is in itself possible, as we know—so far as theory is concerned—in Nietzsche's case. Not less dangerous is the fanaticism of truth-fulness and fidelity; the former is willing to betray friend and fatherland for the sake of an empty principle; the latter, blind to the most hazardous moral entanglements, clings to a person, a party, a principle through thick and thin, no matter what the consequences of an error once committed. The same holds

[1] Cf. Chapter VIII (*e*), Vol. I.

good of a one-sided extreme of modesty (self-belittlement), of humility (self-depreciation), of reserve (superciliousness), of pride (an inflammable sense of one's own dignity), and even of faith (an elated blissfulness of trust). All these values in their extreme degree are most dangerous. This is most evident in trust and faith. "Blind faith" is the greatest moral risk; whether one should exact it of any man is always a critical question of conscience.

In this sense it may be said that every moral value has a point in it, not indeed in itself but for men, where it becomes a danger; there is a limit beyond which its dominance in consciousness ceases to be of value. In it recurs an axiological motive, which we are well acquainted with from other spheres of value. Activity, suffering, freedom, foresight, predetermination are of value only within the limits within which a man has a carrying power equal to them.[1] It is the same with moral values, except that the line is drawn not by the carrying power of the person, but by the concrete manifoldness and reciprocal violability of the valuational materials. Here lies the danger line of values, in the relation between the narrow field of consciousness and the structure of the table of values itself. That even personal love has its danger line we have seen in our analysis of it.[2]

What Aristotle so strongly felt in the lower moral values, without being able to formulate it, was just this, that all valuational elements, taken in isolation, have in them a point beyond which they are dangerous, that they are tyrannical, and that for the true fulfilment of their meaning in their real carrier there is always a counter-weight. Because of this profoundly justified feeling, he assigned virtue to no one of these elements but to their synthesis. It is precisely in their syntheses that the danger in values is diminished, their tyranny in consciousness paralysed. In this matter Aristotle's procedure is a model for every further treatment of the problem of contrasts.

[1] Cf. Chapter XI (c)–(h), Vol. II.
[2] Cf. Chapter XXXIII (e), Vol. II.

For the further understanding of the table of values it is necessary to apply this point of view to the higher moral elements which we see still to be unconnected and without synthesis. The danger in the higher moral values, as well as their evidently tyrannical nature (although this is in many ways graduated), sufficiently proves that here also there is throughout an antithetic of disvalues, even if the quantitative diagram of the ὑπερβολή and ἔλλειψις should prove to be too narrow. That we see instead only the antithetic of values is due to the fact that we cannot discern the syntheses concretely, however much we grope for them with our sense of values. Here, also, only the syntheses would be virtues proper. Only a sense of justice which is at the same time loving, only a brotherly love which also considers the far distant, only a pride which would likewise be humble, could be valid as an ideal of moral conduct. But in so far as the antithetic of values, with its gradations, permeates the whole realm, it follows that in general no isolated values exist for themselves, that rather does every value reach true fulfilment only in its synthesis with others—and indeed finally only in Idea, only in its synthesis with all.

The law of συμπλοκή, from which we started in our discussion of the table of values, acquires in this way a new and far stricter meaning than it could derive from an analogy to the realm of the categories. The implication of values is universal; only it is different from that of the categorial dialectic, is of a new kind, is axiological: every single value first attains its own full character through its axiological counter-weight in the synthesis. Even in itself it is incomplete; it is even threatened in its valuational character, without its counter-weight. Whether this consists, as with the antinomies, in a single, specific counter-value, or as in other cases in a larger series of values, makes no great difference. The synthesis, the understanding of which is under question, may have any degree of complexity.

(h) The "Unity of Virtue." Outlook upon the Ideal System of Values

In pursuing this thought it is imperative that we turn our attention to an ideal synthesis of all moral values. So long as single values—however complex they may be in themselves— stand over against each other without being bound organically together, they must necessarily retain some element of danger in themselves. Since this danger destroys their value, they can be fulfilled only in a synthesis which destroys the force of the dangerous element.

Along this line ethics approaches again the old Stoic idea of a "unity of virtue." The Stoics taught that he who lacks one virtue lacks all; he who really has one possesses all. Accordingly he cannot be brave, wise or self-controlled who is not just. The error in this doctrine has often been denounced: the theory may very well be applicable to the ideal virtues, but not to the actual conduct of men, which is always only an approximation to the idea. The objection is right, but it is no objection. The Stoic is referring to the ideal virtue; he does not cede validity to compromises. This rigorism is of course as little tenable in practice as the fanaticism of the single virtues. Yet the universal synthesis of values is contained in the idea of a table of values. All that is said is this, that in the strict and absolute sense only the just man can be truly loving, only the proud truly humble, only the pure truly participant in the fulness of life. These paradoxes are right throughout, but of course only in idea. It would be wrong to contest the virtue of a living man, merely because the axiological counterpoise was lacking in him.

For anyone who is speculatively inclined, it is a tremendous temptation to follow up this outlook constructively, to forestall the gradual historical development of the valuational consciousness by a bold stroke, and to take by storm the whole starry realm of the moral values with the aid of a heaven-assailing dialectic. Such a dialectic, so it seems, would need only to start with the antinomies which are present to the sense of values and to pile on top of them synthesis on synthesis up to the highest and all-embracing synthesis, in which then the essence of the good must needs be fulfilled and must maintain a unity of meaning. This meaning would then no longer be lost in a preferential trend, the guide-posts to which were an open enigma, but would be identical with the unity of moral values in general, with their total, inter-articulated system.

Unfortunately, this seductive ideal is both practically and philosophically as good as worthless. To construct dialectical syntheses is of course not difficult. Although the "unity of virtue" were not reached, a few steps might be gained beyond the discerned values, and perhaps even a system of axiological stages might be indicated, to which the sought-for syntheses must belong. But the stage would be empty. Dialectical or any otherwise completed construction of values remains an idle play, so long as it does not succeed in causing our insight into values, and ultimately our primary sensing of them to accompany it upward to its own heights. Values must be felt and on the basis of feeling must be concretely discerned. There is no other way to secure their ideal self-existence. But the sensing of values has its own, quite differently articulated law of procedure, which allows the intrusion of no outside scheme of work. To it values, and consequently also their syntheses, always become accessible only in proportion to their own autonomous mode of advance, only in proportion to their own historical mellowing into new perspectives. On the other hand, no speculative impatience can prosper. All daring dreams here find their limit.

(i) THE ANTITHETIC OF VALUES, ITS REMOVAL TO THE DISVALUES

The partial transparency of the connectional laws prevailing in the table of values should not deceive the serious investigator. We never attain the "system of values," concretely understood, merely from its inner arrangement, even when we fully comprehend this. So far as we grasp it, it can only help our orientation amid the many discerned values, as well as our critical awareness of the limitation set to all human discernment of values.

But the vastness itself of the perspective causes no detriment. One may well say that only here—after analysis—does the whole scope of the problem unroll. This alone would be of decisive significance. But there is something more. The mere outlook upon the possibility of higher syntheses suffices to reflect a new and unique light upon the antinomic of values.

The Aristotelian virtues showed an antithetic of disvalues; this is lacking in the domain of the higher virtues. On the other hand, the antithetic of values, which had disappeared in the Aristotelian virtues, emerged here, that is, had not been cancelled but overlaid with syntheses and at the same time bound by them. If now this displacement of the whole structural form rests upon the problem elaborated above, that is, upon the fact that insight penetrates incomparably deeper into the total structure of the lower moral values than into that of the higher, it follows that, with advancing penetration of insight into the complex materials of the latter (in case it should be possible), the antithetic relation must more and more vanish from the realm of the actually discerned values, but must become conspicuous in the counter-realm of the disvalues. The oppositional relation itself must at the same time be transferred from the values to the disvalues, so that, the higher the grade, so much the more distinctly would be manifested on the part of the values a kind of superiority to the oppositional relation.

The one side of this double proposition, the tendency of values to synthesize, can be proved by the valuational sense itself. As against every oppositional relation, the search for synthesis is spontaneous and inheres in the essence of the valuational consciousness.

The other side is more difficult to prove. For, as we saw, —A and —B, in the higher strata, exhibit no antithetic proper.

Impurity is compatible with deficiency in fulness of life, injustice with lovelessness, and so on; may we assume that these disvalues intensify each other when their positive opposites are unified in syntheses? This question cannot be decided by the feeling for values; in order to decide it, one would need already to have the syntheses and, proceeding from them, to survey the entirely oppositional complexes—yet even the Aristotelian ἄκρα can be exhibited as opposed to each other only by the unity of the intermediate virtue.

From this, one can always infer something in anticipation. If, for example, there exists a unitary "virtue" which would bind justice and love together, then it would follow from this that a moral attitude which would be merely just, without being loving, must clash with a disposition which was only loving, without being just. The conflict would always be purely inward; it would not necessarily appear in external conduct. The question is only one of dispositional opposition, of contrast in quality of intention. The relation perhaps becomes clearer in the case of love of the nearest and love of the remotest. So long as these two remain discrepant, the mere absence of regard for one's neighbour harmonizes very well with absence of regard for the men of future times. But if one views the relation from the summit of an ideal synthesis, in which spiritual solicitude for the nearest would be blended with solicitude for the remotest, then, inwardly in one's dispositional commitment, the one-sided devotion of oneself to a neighbour (and to his immediate situation) is seen to be inconsistent with the equally one-sided devotion to the remotest (and to future humanity). The change in the relation is due to the fact that the disvalues themselves, which stand over against the fuller synthesis, show a character which is axiologically more positive. They absorb the antithetical factors into themselves, and it was to these that the contrast adhered. They also then are no longer absolute disvalues, but only elements of disvalues which adhere to a disposition in itself valuable but one-sided. Their matter, which beforehand existed in the duality of the values, is the same; only that now, seen from the point of view of the synthesis, the one-sidedness as such becomes conspicuous; and this is an anti-value. The one-sidedness of what is axiologically positive in them is the contrastedness, which breaks forth in them and appears as the antithesis of the more complex, and in this sense the higher, disvalues.

If, therefore, the removal of the antithetic of values to disvalues be rightly conceived, it follows that with adequate knowledge—in which all lower values would be seen united synthetically under higher ones—the whole table of values must be presented as free from antinomies. But this means nothing else than that in its ideal self-existence it must "be" without antinomies. But at the same time it is implied that the table of disvalues must "be" throughout antinomic. To the idea therefore of a "unity of virtue" there would correspond no "unity of disvirtue"—not even in idea. The perfect coward would not need at the same time to be completely uncontrolled and unjust. The Stoics were not acquainted with this counter-relation. In their absolutistic antithesis of the "wise man and the fool" is involved much rather the thesis that the moral disvalues also would all cling inseparably together. This thesis is fundamentally false, a purely abstract counter-thesis constructed to match the "unity of virtue." Badnesses, vices, shortcomings not only do not draw one another after them, but the many which are contrasted in content reciprocally exclude one another.

Hence, corresponding to the ideal unity of the realm of values, there would be an ideal oppositionality and disunity of the realm of disvalues.

(k) The Question as to the Genuineness of the Valuational Antinomies

Whether this is really a fact is nevertheless doubtful. We do not know whether the chain of syntheses which leads to the "unity of virtue" subsists in the realm of values in itself or not. That it can be constructed in thought proves nothing—after all, what is there which cannot be constructed in thought? It would need to be discerned, felt.

Valuational feeling looks out undisturbed for syntheses, where only antinomies are indicated. But this expectant attention does not prove that syntheses can be found. Nothing can be found in the realm of values which is not there. And what is there we cannot know, if inspection as a concrete fulfilment and confirmation does not follow constructive thought, or the yearning watchfulness of feeling. If, for instance, every given opposition to the over-arching synthesis were really certain, and if all antinomic were really transferred to the disvalues, it would need to follow immediately that no antinomies among the positive values were genuine. For antinomies which can be resolved are not genuine; the resolution of them (their synthesis) proves that their incompatibility was not originally native to them, that they arose much rather from some peculiarity in the observer.

There are some instances of antinomy, of which the genuineness can be detected almost in the feeling itself. Perhaps that of purity and fulness of life is of this kind. Here even watchfulness itself feels its helplessness. It were possible that upon closer analysis more of such cases would be forthcoming. But at least with all antinomies it remains questionable whether their syntheses exist in the realm of values. Now what would be the consequence if all (or even only some) of the antinomies of values should be genuine? Would that mean that there is nothing in their syntheses, and that all anticipation of them by the sense of values is in vain?

To assert this would in the end be just as daring. In fact we still know so little about the laws of the antithetic of values that we cannot draw such inferences—even hypothetical ones —either positive or negative. Still it would be in itself conceivable that the antinomies somehow were retained within the syntheses, that the latter therefore signified no suspension or dissolution of the oppositions at all, but only an embracing or bridging over. Then the genuineness of the antinomies would remain within the syntheses themselves, and in spite of them. It is not possible to judge here according to the analogy of the categorial antinomies. Even structurally these are differently constituted; in them there are no negative counter-members, to which the opposition could be transferred.

In a certain sense it may hold good of those syntheses of the Aristotelian virtues which we know and discern concretely, that in them is retained the opposition of the component values —for example, spirited boldness and cold-blooded foresight in bravery, self-esteem and self-criticism in μεγαλοψυχία. Why should not the same apply to the higher syntheses, which are not yet discernible?

If the synthesis is not really a resolution but only a covering up of the antithetical elements, one will not be able to deny the possibility of such an issue, at least on principle. But what this means, and how the relation, at the same time antinomic and synthetic, is constituted in the higher values, is a further question, which here only needed to be touched upon. Whether there exist ways and means of treating it must for the moment remain unconsidered.

THE COMPLEMENTARY RELATIONSHIP

(a) VALUES, THE RECIPROCAL FULFILMENT OF THEIR MEANING

FINALLY, there is linked to the oppositional relationship a second one, of a different kind but lying in the same dimension: the complementary relationship.

We see it in trust and trustworthiness (or sincerity), faith and fidelity, personality and personal love. But if one pursues the differentiation of moral values a step further than has been done in our analysis of them, one finds many more such: for example, honourableness and bestowing of honour, worthiness and esteem, right to honour and veneration, merit and joyful recognition, heroism and admiration, kindness and gratitude, capacity for happiness and unenvious delight in another's good fortune, radiant virtue and generosity in acceptance (the capacity to appreciate). Indeed even in justice is concealed a complementary relationship; just conduct is rightly regardful only towards him who is justly disposed, at least it presupposes the claim and the credit of such a disposition, in as much as every objectively just relation is necessarily reciprocal. This is especially evident in all community of interests and of work, particularly in every (even personal) form of communal life. In a lesser degree the same relationship recurs in the types of love; love is indeed not dependent upon return of love, does not derive its value therefrom; but yet it arouses a kind of expectancy of a return of love. And in personal intimacy it becomes a really strong complementary relationship, that is, a reciprocal understanding and fulfilment.

In the majority of these cases the relation between the moral value of the one person and adequate valuational response on the part of the other is fundamental. What could not be seen in the earlier discussion of valuational response,[1] here becomes

[1] Cf. Chapter IV (c), Vol. II.

plain: In all such response a unique axiological note is present, and indeed one that is different from the value which is responded to. In the adequate response there is a note with a positive value, in the inadequate response the note is a disvalue. And where these are expressed in the concrete relation toward the carrier of the fundamental value, moral value and moral disvalue are immediately present in them.

This moral element in the response goes further than one might think at first glance. For example, it is met with even in bravery. Bravery presupposes the pre-eminent value of fatherland, race, State, political freedom, life and the welfare of neighbour and loved one—that is, of such goods as those for the sake of which the surrender of life, health and personal success is worth while. Without this presupposition bravery is senseless, a gamble with danger. But this means that, when genuine, it is already a valuational response, a response in action.

In life there are many such responses through action. Wherever anyone commits himself to any cause, the presupposition is in the same way the sense of the value of that for which the commitment occurs. But in this extension is seen the complementary relationship throughout the whole diversity of ethical situations and values, although it receives complete expression in the real equality of both the related values only in particular cases (as in that of trust and reliability). And there is always this peculiarity in it, that the one value requires the other, demands it, has fulfilment of meaning in it—but without its own worth thereby becoming dependent, that is, without its losing itself in its complementary value. Thus the trust bestowed upon one who is unreliable or the fidelity shown to one who is suspicious is still of moral worth; it lacks only the axiological completion of its meaning in the adequate disposition of another.

(b) Extension of the Relationship to the Lower Values

There is no such reciprocity in the realm of the categories. There all correlations are a plain, a necessary involution, a permanent co-existence of counterparts. Of this there is nothing in the realm of values. Only the values themselves involve one another; but this implication does not extend to the actual world. It is only an ideal relation of the materials and their valuational qualities, only an Ought-relation: where the value A emerges, there the value B also ought to occur. This complementary relation therefore is specifically axiological. Where trust is shown, he to whom it is shown ought to be worthy of it, and vice versâ. But simply on that account it is by no means so in actual life.

Now, ordinarily, the complementary relation is not limited to the moral values. It extends farther down to those that condition other values. Indeed it is here still more apparent, more suggestive; it is simpler, even if less significant. The world of goods is evidently quite permeated with it. Thus material goods are complementary to certain biological values, upon which the capacity of the person to enjoy goods (to appraise them) depends; for example, physical comfort, health; but complementary not less to the communal good of legal status, which renders possible the use and enjoyment of material goods. The converse holds true in the same degree: the bodily capacity to enjoy and the protection of property have meaning only for one who is in possession of material goods. This is of great significance for the common life; the interest of the particular individual in the legal relation and in public order is conditioned by a certain grade of material possession. A deficient appreciation of the State and of law on the part of a proletarian (that is, of one who has really nothing to lose) is merely a manifestation of the lack of the complementary relationship.

In general the whole situation in the sphere of goods is this, that individual goods, taken by themselves, are well-nigh meaningless and are scarcely to be called "goods"; that is, in their strict valuational quality they suffer damage, and their value is fulfilled only in their reciprocal supplementation. Not until a certain degree of many-sided fulfilment is reached do the separate goods attain their full value. But this means that their axiological tendency presses peremptorily towards a universal synthesis of goods-values.

Still more strictly does this apply to the foundational values which adhere to the subject and which together constitute personality.[1] Here the case is such that the lower value always finds its full meaning only in the higher, the value of mere living in the value of consciousness; this again in activity, suffering, strength and so on, while the higher has only its material foundation in the lower. Thus far the complementary relationship would here be only one-sided. But it also appears to be two-sided, for example, between activity and strength, strength and freedom, freedom and foresight, foresight and purposive action. Activity without strength is impotent, strength without activity is inert; strength without freedom is mere naturalistic power, freedom without strength is fruitless yearning; freedom without foresight is blind arbitrariness, foresight without freedom is the consciousness of being buffeted by accident; purposive action without foresight is a dangerous power in the hand of the mentally blind, foresight without purposive action is unbearable knowledge of the unavoidable.

Here again it is evident that only synthesis brings the single values to fulfilment—in as much as in personality, as such, this entire group of values forms an inextricable texture. But there are other syntheses than those of the Aristotelian virtues, and those in which the sense of values looks out upon a higher stage. For the values, which in personality constitute a complex synthesis, stand in no antithetical relation; they form much rather a rising series, in which simply the higher value always contains the complex of the lower ones and adds to it a new valuational factor.

The synthesis here has no inner obstacles to overcome. It fulfills itself unchecked.

[1] Cf. Chapter XI, Vol. II.

(c) Independent of Stratification and of the Conditioning Relation

The complementary relationship therefore pertains to the same concrete manifoldness of values—in its entire extension —to which the remaining relations pertain. The question thus arises, in what relation does it stand to these? As an orderliness *sui generis* it is throughout embedded in the remaining order of the table of values. But how does it fit into the otherwise determined relations?

Over against universal stratification the complementary relationship is evidently independent. As a dimension it even cuts through the strata. In the higher values, extensions in content appear, which in the lower ones were not at all in evidence or were only presupposed. These correlations—for it is these which are in question—are in the higher values incomparably richer and more complex than in the lower. They therefore do not belong to what reappears and is transformed in the stratification but to what constitutes the novelty of the higher. As this complementary relationship permeates all strata, we have one of the grounds why in general in the realm of values the novelty of the single values—as also the regional novelty of whole strata—has a decided preponderance over recurrence.[1]

More positive is the connection with the conditioning relation. This, as we saw, extends through the stratification of the values like a chasm, by which the moral values are radically divided from those which are situational. Every moral value presupposes its conditioning situation. But how is it with two moral values which stand in complementary relation to each other? Are they conditioned separately by different situations or, in common, by one and the same?

This question is easy to answer. They are evidently conditioned in common. Take a relationship like merit and recognition, or heroism and admiration. Moral merit and

[1] Cf. Chapter XXXV (*d*), Vol. II.

heroism are based upon the value of the situation, perhaps the commonweal or spiritual goods, for which the commitment of the person occurs; but precisely upon this the moral recognition and admiration are also founded. And indeed here also in the conditioning relation the complete heterogeneity of the conditioned value is preserved over against that which conditions it. The latter does not reappear in the former as a valuational element, nor need it be realized at the same time. As heroism which fails of its object is still heroism, it deserves the same admiration as though it had been successful. Likewise the conditioning relation is equally independent of the rank of the situational value. Kindness and gratitude evidently refer to the same situation in which the kindness is performed, or at least attempted; but genuine thankfulness does not consider the greatness of the gift, but only the greatness of the kindness; it is a response to this, not to the gift. Exactly in the same way trustfulness and reliability are based upon one and the same objective value of the situation or goods; truthfulness and faith in another's word, on the same value of the knowledge of truth. Everywhere the two factors in the complementary relationship are perfectly independent of the rank and success of the conditioned value.

But here we have a different function of the conditioning relation from what is found elsewhere. In a certain sense it may be said that any two complementary values are reciprocally conditioning and conditioned. In so far as the meaning of the one is only fulfilled in the other and without the other would be floating in the air, this is perfectly clear. In itself, according to its idea, heroism is something worthy of admiration, kindness of gratitude, just as fidelity and truthfulness are worthy of trust and faith. Conversely, admiration attaches only to heroism, gratitude to kindness, trust and faith to fidelity and truthfulness. Here then is a reciprocal conditioning. And this is what constitutes the eminently positive character of the complementary relationship. Indeed the relation extends even to the disvalues. Not only does the unreliable man deserve distrust, but also the

THE COMPLEMENTARY RELATIONSHIP

distrustful man deserves to be deceived. It is just as fair that the unkind man should win no thanks as that the unthankful man should receive no kindness. The unheroic man is as little worthy of being the object of admiration as a man incapable of admiring (whether because he be envious or generally insensitive to human greatness) is worthy of being the object of heroic sacrifice.

In the complementary relationship then there is concealed a reciprocal conditioning relation; but the former does not merge into the latter, and the latter is not a very strict conditioning. There is nothing here like the connection between situational and moral values, where the latter rest upon the former as genuine axiological pre-conditions and stand and fall with them (as the value of honesty stands or falls with that of property). Moreover, trust remains valuable, even when bestowed upon someone who is unworthy of it; reliability, although no one trusts himself to it. Except that without the response there is not a complete fulfilment or actualization. Here then the conditioning relation is not something constituent in the value, but only something which carries it out and brings it to completion. To speak more exactly, the conditioning does not affect the moral value itself, but only its subjoined goods-value.[1] Every moral value of a person is at the same time an indirect goods-value for other persons; reliability for the one who must rely upon others; trustfulness for the one who is thrown upon the good faith of others; kindness for him who receives it; gratitude for him who deserves it. The fact that virtues are goods has nothing to do with the conditioning values of goods and situations, which are the presupposition of moral values. Goods and situational values are the common condition for both the values which are complementary. The goods-value of a gift does not enter into the attitude of thankfulness towards kindness, but the goods-value of kindness conditions the thankfulness. For the man who is trusted, the goods-value of trustfulness is totally different from the goods-value of what is entrusted

[1] Cf. Chapter XV (c), Vol. I.

to him; the good, which a friend with his personal love is to the friend, cannot be at all compared with the goods which the love may bring.

In the fact that virtues are goods for someone—and they are the highest kind of goods—is rooted the reciprocal dependence of the complementary moral values. And just on this account the moral value as such is unaffected thereby; the complementary values do not properly condition each other, but each depends upon the goods-value of the other. What a man's moral value is for someone else, we may speak of as the fulfilment of its meaning. All the moral value of a person deserves to be appreciated and responded to as a good by those to whom it comes as a good. And if they participate in what is deserved, its fulfilment is thereby actualized.

(*d*) CONNECTION WITH THE OPPOSITIONAL RELATION

The connection with the relation of opposites is again different. The complementary relationship is on the same plane with it. The connection is therefore closer. The opposites also show that they are founded upon the same situational value, for example, justice and brotherly love upon the same goods-values, with which they deal. Except that the correlation itself is fundamentally different. With justice, discrepancy dominates; with brotherly love, reciprocal benefit.

But now the question arises: how far in this respect is there a real difference here? Do not the valuational opposites on their part also press towards synthesis? Do not the Aristotelian virtues show that even the opposed values require each other, and indeed exactly in the sense of completion, of appreciation, of fulfilment? But is it then not the case, that the complementary and the oppositional relation are at bottom one and the same?

Is the difference perhaps only one of degree? It would seem so, from the fact that in the lower stages of the complementary relationship (as with freedom and foresight, foresight and purposive activity) exactly the same synthetic structure appears as in the lower virtues, that is, in the elements which combine in them. But against this view stands the fact that in the complementary relationship there are no opposites at all, but only the correspondence of the one value to the other, and therefore in the case of the moral values not a demand that the attitude of one and the same person shall harmonize two values. All that is demanded is rather this, that to every moral attitude of the one person shall correspond a given attitude on the part of the other. This corresponding attitude of the other person is itself indeed quite differently formed from that of the first, but it is in no way in contrast. In the sphere of the moral values the complementary law is a law of adequate reciprocity in human behaviour, in so far, namely, as the required reciprocity signifies neither similarity of disposition nor opposition, but an organic interpenetration of heterogeneous conduct on the part of different persons.

(e) THE INTER-PERSONAL SYNTHESIS OF VALUES

In the lower strata it is more likely that an approximation of the two relations could be found. But even here any proper contrast of complementary values is lacking. At least the kind of synthesis strikingly resembles that which we became acquainted with in the Aristotelian virtues. Similarly goods gain in value through one another, just as boldness does through foresight, self-esteem through self-criticism.

It is otherwise in the domain of the moral values. Here we can no longer speak in this sense of synthesis of the complementary values, for the opposed values are in another person. The carriers are not the same. The complementary relationship here does not consist in the completion of one and the same complex attitude, but in one person's moral completion through the moral value of another. For since moral conduct is conduct towards persons, every value in it has a claim upon a specifically reacting attitude of another person, upon an axiologically adapted reaction, which on this account bears a specific valuational quality. Now if the other person reacts in this way, that is a moral value, but at the same time a fulfilment of one's own value. In other words, there is established in the reciprocity of the two persons an ethically real structure of a higher order, which as a union of two dispositions bears a unique, a higher and more complex value, a value which cannot be resolved into its constituents.

This can be felt most clearly in trust between man and man, where the trust and the trustworthiness complete each other. More elementary but not less perceptible is it in two-sided justice, although here the specific difference fades away. It is deepest in the relation of love, where the special life and worth of the mutuality that has been formed are strikingly plastic.[1]

Such communion in the inter-personal relation of two human beings is the categorial form of complementary relationship. The higher value which appears in it is the specific synthesis characteristic of these values and is required by them. It is a synthesis of a new kind, fundamentally different from that towards which the contrasts tended. It is never fulfilled in the conduct of one person. It is an inter-personal synthesis. It embraces in its unity not only two values, but also two carriers of values. And as it forms out of the values one value, so also it forms out of the carriers one carrier; and as the one value is the higher, so the one carrier is the more able to carry the values.

Inter-personal synthesis differs from that of contrasts also in its simple transparency. Here there is no seeking or struggling for the synthesis, on the part of the sense of values. The factors unite without coercion, without obstacle. Indeed to anyone who is morally unspoiled, it is a matter of course, a necessity, to react in all conduct within the complementary relationship and thus directly to establish the inter-personal synthesis. The sense of values is here in a much more favourable position than towards valuational contrasts; it is confronted with no conflict at all, at least not with a moral one, in which value stands against value. For only a definite kind of conduct is encountered and

[1] Cf. Chapter XXXIII (b), Vol. II.

no other comes in question. Conflict, on the other hand, begins only when a reaction is required against an opposed disposition, that is, when through the opposition conflict is already present.

If one interprets the complementary relationship from the point of view of the inter-personal synthesis, one can entertain no doubt that, as compared with the oppositional relation, it signifies something entirely new, that in it a fundamental relation, pressing towards a different synthesis, is in command. It is throughout a positive relation, to which all discrepancy is alien, and it is more complex than that of contrasts; for the syntheses which inhere in its trend fulfil themselves independently of the oppositional syntheses, and they do this in the pure discernment of values as well as in their actualization in life.

This latter point is of immeasurable significance in all moral life. Man's life moves from moment to moment in reaction, in reciprocity and within inter-personal situations; if now the establishment of complementary syntheses depended upon the establishment of oppositional syntheses—which for the higher values we not only cannot establish but cannot even conceive concretely in idea—then human conduct would be in a very sorry plight indeed. It is the difference and the independence of the two relationships which give scope within ethical reality to the complementary relationship, as against the eternally unfulfilled meaning of oppositional synthesis.

At the same time the former increases in general significance. As the complementary relation penetrates the whole table of moral values with its regularity, it forces its way into all the relations of life; and as it, together with the contrasts but independently of them and unaffected by the antithetic, permeates all materials, so its formative and unifying tendency among men runs through all relations, regardless of conflicts and their responsible solutions, engendering good by good, awakening virtue by virtue, through the persuasiveness of response to values and through its transformation into living disposition and deed.

THE GRADE AND THE STRENGTH OF VALUES

(a) GRADATION AND STRATIFICATION

FROM the beginning of our analysis of values we have had before us the problem of the order of gradation, and we were able to follow it through the stages of its development. The importance of its bearing upon ethics became continually more evident; but on the whole the prospect of solving the problem diminished. Not only the general criteria of grade showed themselves to be inadequate, as clues to the order of rank,[1] but even the general view of the table of values, which discloses quite other refinements of difference in grade, cannot suffice here.[2] There still remains the possibility that the co-ordinations of the table, so far as they are evident, may throw light on the problems.

Here one naturally thinks at first of the laws of stratification. For strictly speaking there is in stratification a kind of order of rank. The only question is whether it is the specific order of rank which we mean, when we speak of higher and lower values. Taken in its universality, this question must be answered in the negative. Stratification only gives the differences in the degree of complexity in the material, and this is not identical with valuational height. There are values of the most complex structure, which in height stand lower than those of simpler structure. Such, for example, are all the goods-values attaching to virtues; they not only presuppose but in themselves contain the virtues as materials; yet in height they are subordinate, because they are not moral values at all. Within every larger group, for example, within the moral values, it may hold true that the height increases with the grade of stratification. But precisely here the stratification itself breaks up, the novelty

[1] Cf. Chapter IV (b), Vol. II.   [2] Cf. Chapter XXXIV (b), Vol. II.

of the single values overbears the recurrence and transformation in such a way that the perduring elements retreat into the background. There are also specific cases which contradict the parallelism of the two relations; thus the value of noble-mindedness, in spite of its relatively elemental simplicity, transcends in height most of the more special virtues; and, conversely, the whole of the narrower group of social virtues undoubtedly is to be placed in order of rank below the great swarm of simpler virtues (such as justice, self-control, bravery). The hope, therefore, of a radical explanation of the order of rank by means of the laws of stratification proves delusive.

The conditioning relation, on the other hand, might prove more adequate as a clue, if it were something that bound all strata of values together. Here it is evident that a conditioned value is always the higher. But precisely such conditionality does not always prevail. Within the wider ethical realm it characterizes only one stage: the relation of goods and situations to the moral values. And just at this stage there is no need of orientation, because the marked difference of rank is given with the most evident clearness by the sense of value.

(b) HEIGHT AND SYNTHESIS

The relation of contrast first brings us a step forward. With the Aristotelian virtues it became clear that in every antithetic the synthesis is higher than the factors which are united in it. This provides a sort of regularity, according to which in general all synthesis is a valuational advancement. Indeed we may perhaps add: the more complex the synthesis, the more antinomical the elements united in it, and the more firm the fusion, so much the higher does it stand in the order of rank.

This does not contradict what was said concerning stratification; complexity in stratification is not the same as in a synthesis of opposed elements. Degree of stratification is an unresisted complexity, while a synthesis of opposites is a conquest over opposing values. It is the latter, upon which the peculiar valuational element depends, which assists essentially in determining the order of rank. For a harmonious equipoise of moral qualities in an ideal situation would naturally be of absolute value.

Here we have a distinguishing mark which is universal and applies to all moral values. Nor can it be denied that the valuational sense, with its laws of preference, on the whole follows this distinctive mark. We discriminate exactly the higher syntheses of opposites, so far as we can discern them concretely, as the "higher values," in which at last the lower values attain fulfilment.

Indeed, even beyond this limit, the searching watchfulness of the sense of value for the synthesis which still fails us and is not yet discernible reveals the like tendency towards an order of gradation. Of all general marks distinctive of height this is the most suggestive; in it at least there is a conceivable relation of law between the structure and the height of values.

Still, even from it we cannot construct a comprehensive theory as to height; and not only because the syntheses of opposites in great part are not given in our discernment, but for another reason. This reason is contained in the fact that the order of rank does not simply concern the principle of valuational height, but involves in itself a second decisive factor: valuational strength, or weight.

(c) The Fundamental Categorial Law and its Corollaries

If height and strength coincided, our calculation would be a very simple matter. That this is not the case, we have already seen in another connection.[1] Our object now is to go to the root of their relation, so far as this is possible for theoretical generality.

Here the law of height and of strength proves to be far more general than one would have surmised from the table of values —certainly from the ethical table alone. It is a fundamental categorial law, which prevails ontologically in all ideal and

[1] Cf. Chapter III (e), Vol. II.

real Being and thence extends over the realm of values; but in this extension it gains a new meaning. It is therefore necessary here once more, as it was with the laws of stratification, to look to the realm of categories, and to ask in how far its laws recur in the domain of values and are transformed or replaced by a new kind of regularity.

There are three laws which here come in question. In content they link up with the laws of stratification, but unlike these latter they do not concern the structure of the categorial edifice, but the dynamic type of dependence. They are laws of dependence. The first, that of strength, is the basic law of the categories. The two others may be regarded as its corollaries, although in comparison with it they have a content of their own. They form only the reverse sides of one and the same relationship and therefore can be brought into one single formula. Both are here cited rather for the sake of clearness and comprehensiveness of view. For they reflect a light upon the basic law. Upon this more than anything else depends the solution of our problem. The question concerns its validity for the table of values.

1. The law of Strength: higher principles are dependent upon the lower, but the converse is not true. Hence the higher principle is always the more conditioned, the more dependent and in this sense the weaker. But the more unconditioned, the more elementary and in this sense the stronger principle is always the lower one. In the abstract, the inversion of this relationship is quite conceivable, but is never to be seen in the reality of principles.

2. The Law of Material: every lower principle is only raw material for the higher which is raised upon it. Now since the lower is the stronger, the dependence of the weaker upon it goes only so far as the scope of the higher formation is limited by the definiteness and peculiarity of the material.

3. The Law of Freedom: compared with the lower every higher principle is a new formation which is raised upon it. As such it has unlimited scope above the lower (the material

and the stronger) fixity. This means that in spite of dependence upon the lower principle the higher is free, as against the lower.

How these laws can be proved we cannot discuss here.[1] Their relation to the laws of stratification is, however, clear. It could not be simply inferred. But, for anyone who knows in general the import of categorial dependence, there is here a perfectly evident relation of reciprocal conditionality between the laws of stratification and the laws of dependence.

The first of these laws, by virtue of its dominating position, is the basic law of the categories in general. In our criticism of universal teleologism and metaphysical personalism we have already become acquainted with its significance.[2] In another connection we shall meet with it again, when considering the problem of freedom.[3] Without citing any examples of it, its content and the content of its consequences are easily noted, so far as the laws of stratification apply. The more simple principles reappear in the higher ones, as building stones, as material. Hence the higher structure cannot, for all its transformation, annul or change the lower; the lower has the wider range of validity, it continues to be binding even in the higher combination. And no higher law can avail against its validity, but can only bring it within the new formation. The novelty in the latter is its freedom as against the lower order; thus in the law of freedom the stratification of the new form is found to be fully established.

The law of material and the law of freedom together therefore stand against the law of strength, limiting it. They restrict it. Their purport is that, in the scale of structures, superior strength extends only to the sphere of the lower principles as factors within the more complex forms, that it means only complete fulfilment and indestructibility of the lower, but not domination. Hence the autonomy of the higher is not infringed by the material upon which it depends. The pecularity of the finalistic

---

[1] This is the task of the general doctrine of the categories.
[2] Cf. Chapter XXI (c) and Chapter XXV (c), Vol. I.
[3] Cf. Chapter VI (b) and Chapter VII (c), Vol. III.

nexus is that it is not at all causal, but presupposes the universal validity of the law of cause and effect; upon this it is dependent as upon a *conditio sine qua non*, but in its own essence it is independent. In spite of its dependence the weaker principle is "free" as regards the stronger. We found the same relation between the subject and the person; the latter can subsist only in a subject, in this sense is dependent upon it, but is itself nevertheless not a subject but something essentially different. Wherefore the superior height of the weaker is preserved by the superior strength of the lower. In the latter it finds its categorial condition, in the former its freedom.

(d) THE LAW OF STRENGTH

As in the categorial realm the laws of dependence are linked to those of stratification, it is clearly evident that they can be valid in the valuational realm only so far as stratification is concerned. A second condition of their validity is the identity of structural complexity and valuational height. Just at this point stratification is connected with order of rank.

Neither condition is completely fulfilled. The laws of stratification hold among values, but so many more complex structures are built over them, that they are almost concealed from view. Yet height of value means something quite different from structural complexity of materials; and although on the whole the higher values are the more complex, still this must not be taken as a universal rule.

Therefore the law of strength does not apply strictly in the same sense to the table of values. Not only is valuational height different from categorial height, but valuational strength does not coincide with categorial strength. In the ontological domain there is no analogue of these; these are specifically axiological and cannot even be expressed in existential terminology. The indirect proportion of height and strength, which prevails among the categories, is either relaxed or disarranged, as was to be expected.

The twofold law of material and freedom is more favourably placed in the table of values. As the elements retreat into the background, the freedom of the higher form has greater scope, but the form has only a material character. And this holds good not only for the stratification of the materials and their values, but also for the more complex connections which prevail among them, for the conditioning, the oppositional and the complementary relations, as well as for the connection of the two latter with the syntheses which fulfil them. As compared with the conditioning values, the conditioned are always axiologically the higher; likewise syntheses as compared with antithetical and complementary correlates.

But when the corollaries of the basic law of the categories agree, nothing else is possible than that the law itself should correspond within certain limits. The only question is, within what limits? An answer is close at hand: within the limits within which the laws of stratification hold good. Still, this restriction is inexact; it would be too wide for the sphere of the moral values, in as much as recurrence and transformation retreat here too far, while the relation of height and strength makes itself very perceptible. The second factor, which in part determines the transference of the law to the table of values, is therefore decisive: the new meaning of height and strength in the realm of values.

What height is must already have been made sufficiently clear in our analysis of values. But what is the significance of valuational strength? If the basic law can be said to hold at all among values, it must inhere in the unconditionality of Ought-to-Be, in its elementariness, in its fundamental character. But wherein does one recognize this character? In what form is strength presented to the sense of values?

A clear answer can be given. If the clue to height is the assenting sense, as it expresses itself in specific responses and predicates (approval, acceptance, respect, admiration, enthusiasm), so the clue to strength lies in the negative, the rejecting sense, as it asserts itself wherever values are violated. Strength is distinguishable by the corresponding disvalues. The rejecting sense also has its specific responses and predicates. They are reactions to disvalues. And these show an independent scale of intensification (disapproval, contempt, horror, disgust and the like), which is by no means a simple reflection of the scale of positive responses. The variability of strength, which is independent of height, is attached to the independence of the negative scale.

That this independence is justified, instances of it will easily convince one. Heroism deserves admiration, but the absence of it is neither despicable nor horrifying, but is at most to be bewailed as a human weakness; conversely, trustworthiness is merely commendable, but breach of trust is despicable, revolting. The more grievous disvalues do not correspond to the highest values. The examples lead us to infer the converse.

This fact is proof of the peculiar autonomous character of strength as compared with height. Evidence of strength is found in the seriousness of the offence against a value, while height is known by the meritoriousness of fulfilment (wherein the merit is to be understood not in any subjective sense, but purely as taking part in the actualization). Now the basic categorial law, carried over into the table of values, substantiates this—and it is the wholly new meaning which it acquires in the realm of values:—in the fulfilment of a value the merit increases, not directly in proportion to the grievousness of violating it, but indirectly. When the higher value is violated, the transgression is less, not more serious; but when the stronger value is fulfilled, the meritoriousness is not greater but less. This fact can be gathered into a formula in which the meaning of the basic law, when transported into the axiological realm, is clearly given:

The higher value is always the more conditioned, the more dependent and in this sense the weaker; its fulfilment is conceivable only in so far as it is raised upon the fulfilment of the lower values. But the more unconditioned, the more elementary, and in this sense the stronger value is always the lower; it is only a base for the moral life, not a fulfilment of its meaning.

This is equivalent to saying: the most grievous transgressions are those against the lowest values, but the greatest moral desert attaches to the highest values.

Whether this law holds good throughout the entire table is questionable. It can be easily shown that it does not pass beyond the dividing line between goods-values and those of the virtues. It has no meaning to say that the violation of goods-values weighs heavier than that of moral values, which, however, must be so according to the law, since the latter are evidently higher (just because of the sphere they are in) than the former. For goods are only valuable "for" someone; with the goods the person also is affected. One cannot destroy goods without immediately injuring persons also. It is precisely the moral values which are built upon goods-values of every kind— according to the law of the conditioning relation—and these moral values are concerned with man's control of goods. Hence here the higher is plainly injured with the lower value; with property, for example, justice; with the happiness of one's neighbour, brotherly love.

Therefore we cannot properly say that the law does not fit here. But conversely—because the fate of the higher goods is involved in that of the lower—it is evident that here the law becomes empty of content. This is explicable, since exactly in this point simple gradation (which the law of strength follows) is abrogated and is replaced by the far more complex relation of conditioning and conditioned. But we saw that this relation prevails only at the dividing line between the two domains; elsewhere scope is granted to stratification. It must therefore be assumed that within both domains the law of strength can be valid.

But it must be proved separately for each of the two classes.

(e) THE MEANING OF SUPERIOR STRENGTH IN THE SPHERE OF GOODS-VALUES

Now in the sphere of goods-values it is clear that a loss of material goods is in general a more serious matter than a loss of spiritual goods. The former are undoubtedly more fundamental, more essential to life. A threat to life and limb is the gravest threat; but mere life is not on that account the highest good. Material possessions weigh more heavily upon one than spiritual; and a violation of them is morally more grievous (it is dishonest, dishonourable). The destruction of one's happiness and pleasure is felt the more keenly, the more elementary its nature, while the height of the value rises and falls according to an entirely different standard. Æsthetic is far higher than material pleasure. A happiness in personally harmonious converse is far higher than that of outward social status. And yet man strives much more for the latter, so long as he does not have it (or thinks he has not sufficiently attained it), than for the former.

Just here in the lower sphere of values one sees plainly how strength takes an independent position by the side of height and asserts itself, without encroaching upon height as such. The lower value is not of more worth. Superiority of height signifies superior value. But the lower value is more fundamental, it is recognized as more unconditional, because its fulfilment—if not always in the single case, still in general—is the condition for the fulfilment of the higher. The fulfilment of the lower takes precedence, because with its violation the fulfilment of the higher is endangered. The man who is hungry or suffering in body loses his sense for spiritual enjoyments. In a community where the legal order is overthrown spiritual goods also (to which law does not directly extend) go to ruin. The legal order and the social security of the individual's material existence have an Ought-to-Be which is more unconditional than the more valuable goods, the achievement of which gives meaning to existence and to public order. The more elementary value has a prior claim.

Here we can at the same time see how with values superiority and inferiority have a different meaning from that which they have with the categories. If the degree of complexity and the stratification were the decisive factors, the lower goods would need to be contained in the higher as elements. But evidently this is not the case. The material goods are by no means contained in the spiritual as constituents. Æsthetic enjoyment in itself has nothing to do with outward possessions or with bodily well-being. It is marked by a detachment which is more than mere difference. And yet if one disregards the individual case and surveys the whole, the dependence of the higher upon the lower cannot be denied. But it is not that the one contains the other, but that the fulfilment of the one conditions the fulfilment of the other. Fulfilment, however, is actuality. The question is not concerning a relation between value and value, but between one valuational actuality and another. This is an ontological, in the last resort a categorial relation, which in no way coincides with the axiological connection among valuational qualities.

In this secondary, ontological relation stratification recurs. Here also it is concealed behind the gradation of height which dominates the sense of values. But since actualization is itself valuable and destruction is contrary to value, it reacts from its place in the background upon the valuational relation, and introduces into the table a second gradation along with that of height.

It is not the higher value itself which depends upon the lower, but its actualization which depends upon that of the lower. It is not the material as an element which is contained in the material, its quality in the quality of the value, but rather its actualization as a condition. Thus, concealed behind the order of rank, stratification with all its laws returns as an ontological relation of values and sets up strength in opposition to height.

(f) Strength and Height in the Sphere of the Moral Values

This same double relation recurs among the moral values, because here every single one is based upon a definite goods-value (or a group of such values). Indeed the height of the conditioned value need not be proportionate to that of the one on which it is based; but a certain proportion subsists between the strength of the one and the strength of the other. That murder, theft and all real "crimes" are felt to be the most grievous moral transgressions, is due to this, that the justice which they violate is based upon the most elementary of goods-values (life, property and the like). Justice is the virtue which protects these goods—the goods which support every actualization of values. Hence the unique moral import of justice. This import, however, does not attach to its height, but to its strength.

If we compare the highest moral values, for instance radiant virtue or personal love, with justice, the twofold relationship becomes immediately evident. A neglect of radiant virtue and love exposes no one to radical danger; a person who is incapable of them is not on that account a bad man; his conduct threatens no one, it merely lacks the higher moral content. Even in the realm of virtue the lower value is more elemental, basic, and therefore requires prior and unconditional actualization. Not until it is fulfilled, is the fulfilment of the higher values rational. Even here ontological stratification and actualization are disclosed to view in the superior strength of the lower values.

In this it can be clearly seen that only the lowest moral values, as claims imposed upon man, can assume the form of commandments, at least of reasonable commandments. And it is doubly characteristic that the more elementary these are, the more negative they are; they appear as prohibitions (thou shalt not steal, not murder, not commit adultery, not bear false witness and so on). This proves that it is not the height of the values that is involved, but the seriousness of the disvalues of transgression. Only brotherly love can be commanded, and that not in the strict sense; but personal love cannot be commanded at all.

Equally characteristic is the inner misplacement when a person, who partakes of a higher moral value, dispenses with the lower, when, as it were, one who loves is suspicious and is unworthy of trust, when a wise man lacks self-control, a humble man is not honourable, a proud man is cruel, an imparter of spiritual values is cowardly. No one truly believes in the virtue of this sort of virtuous person, and rightly so. It bears the stamp of unreality, although it is evident that in itself no contradiction inheres in such a one-sided moral disposition. The misplacement is deeper down. The higher virtue is unreasonable, hollow, not sterling; it has no basis in a lower value, as it should have even if the materials have nothing to do with each other. Genuine morality is built from below up. Its essence is not the ideal self-existence of values, but their actualization in life. Only upon the actualization of the lower does the actualization of a higher value rest solidly.

Hence the lower moral value is throughout the "stronger." But here also superiority of strength does not mean superiority of value, but only greater elementariness, priority of condition as a basis, within the entire realm of actual moral conduct. The lower value touches a wider circle of values in general; with its violation much more of the moral order and the moral life collapses than with the violation of a higher value. Its commandment is more unconditional, is fraught with greater import. On the other hand, the higher value has a narrower field of activity; contains less palpable substance, its existence for itself is more pronounced. It stands and falls for itself alone. When it suffers injury it injures little else, only what stands above it in order of rank. The basis beneath it remains intact. This becomes most evident in extreme cases, like that of the dispensing of spiritual value, which is altogether "useless" and has nothing further dependent upon it. It is similar with love of the remotest, personal love and all the values of individual personality.

How far the indirect relation of height and strength prevails throughout the domain of the moral values, we can see best by comparing a series of values, which most unmistakably rise in order of rank, with the attributes of the corresponding disvalues. To the rising line of valuational grades—for instance, of justice, truthfulness, brotherly love, blind faith, love of the remotest, the imparting of spiritual values—corresponds an equally unmistakably descending line of valuational strengths. Namely, dishonesty (theft, for instance) is a "crime" (while not stealing is far from being meritorious); a lie is not a crime, but is surely a stain upon one's honour; lovelessness does not affect one's honour, but is morally of poor quality; not to be capable of blind faith cannot even be called poor in quality, at most it is a moral weakness; but one who is not capable of great enthusiasm for ideas and of sacrifice for the future of mankind cannot even be said to be morally weak, he simply lacks moral greatness; finally, one who is no imparter of spiritual values may, for all that, still possess moral greatness and moral strength; all that is lacking in him is the ultimate height above all great aims, the glory shed over life, which is seldom attained.

(g) The Twofold Aspect of Morality

If one glances along any one such line of ascent in height and of descent in strength, the inference is unavoidable that throughout the realm of values two equally important orders of gradation hold sway and that two opposed laws of preference correspond to them.

It is here proved to be untrue that there exists only one line of precedence, that of height. There exists a second, that of strength. It is wholly different from the other; it tends in the opposite direction. It gives preference not to the higher, but to the lower values. And for the essence of morality this preference is just as decisive as that for the higher. It is simply a preference of a different kind. It refers not to the actualization of values, but to the avoidance of disvalues. In a certain sense one may say that the order of rank in values is itself twofold—or is two-sided and has two meanings. For since ascent in strength is in the opposite direction to ascent in height, the orderly sequence as such remains one throughout. But it is bi-polar, and both poles contend for mastery. But the kind of mastery of the one is essentially different from that of the other. The lower values have their unique import in relation to the higher, while these possess their superiority in the conferring of meaning upon life and in its fulfilment. For the meaning of the moral life is no more to be found in the lower values than its foundations are to be found in the higher. Thus it comes about that two kinds of mastery can co-exist in one ordered sequence.

Morality, however, does not subsist in values as such. Values have their ideal self-existence, independently of their actualization. But morality is their actualization in man, hence actual man's relation to them. And this relation, corresponding to the double meaning of ordered gradation, is twofold with a twofold Ought, a twofold requirement: not to violate the lower values and at the same time to actualize the higher. Corresponding to this is the fact, reflected in every system of current morality, that there always exist lower values which are actualized in a quite different degree from the higher. To them adhere the prohibitory demand and its characteristic claim to priority.

Irrespective of this, however, one can divide all values into those which exhibit the negative and those which exhibit the positive requirement. Among those of the first kind purity is pre-eminent; its whole content is negative.[1] Equally to this belongs justice with its whole series of "prohibitions"; self-control also as an inner check and restraint; it is the same with modesty, reserve, deference, humility. Indeed even in brotherly love, besides its positively creative tendency, there is a strain of negation, in so far as it finds its occasion in another's need. These virtues predominantly represent the preference for strength in morality. Preference for height is represented by the

[1] Cf. Chapter XVII (a), Vol. II, on the avoidance of evil.

virtues of the second class—they are not only the higher moral values, but some of them exist in every stratum; of course the higher in the scale we go, the more abundant we find them. Of this kind are the general basic values of nobility and fulness of experience, the former always aiming at the axiologically highest, the latter exclusively and positively directed towards attainable values. The same tendency is to be seen in bravery, wisdom, fidelity, faith (especially when blind) and the higher types of love.

Morality shows a double face—its symbol is the head of Janus. In it the Ought sets up a backward-looking claim and at the same time one that is forward-looking—not temporally backward and forward, but axiologically. If the elementary values had an absolutely secure position in life, if a man of serious mind could always be absolutely certain even of himself —in the sense, for instance, of perfect self-control, honesty, modesty—he could be exempted from the watchful glance backward upon the interests of the lower values and look solely forwards to the higher values, which lie before him waiting for fulfilment. But no man is so. With man no claim, however elementary, ever becomes a law of nature (to use Kant's expression); in regard to it he always retains the freedom of the For and Against; he must always be alert against relapse. Along the entire line everything of moral value is at every moment exposed to danger, of course in infinitely varying degrees. This is why the prohibitive command and with it preference for the strength of the lower values extend upward to the highest stages of human morality.

(h) The Antinomy in the Nature of the Good

In this way the meaning of the good shifts. There is no need to retract anything from what we observed in our analysis of the good. It still remains the "teleology of the higher value."[1] But this is only one-half of its nature, its positive side. It corresponds

[1] Cf. Chapter XIV (h), Vol. II.

to the law of preference for the higher. But opposed to that stands the law of preference for the stronger. This is the reverse side of the good, which looks to the security of its foundations.

The one order of rank is two-sided, and a special stress falls at each pole. But since the good is involved in this arrangement of grade, it is the same with the double law of preference which prevails in it. It claims validity in two directions. And as these are opposed to each other, we here encounter a fundamental antinomy, which is rooted in the essence of the good as the comprehensive basic value: the unconditional preference for the higher is restricted by an equally unconditional preference for the more fundamental values.

As we saw, the more special moral values take cognizance of this duality. And from here we can survey the dual classification of current moralities; while some are clearly related to the stronger values, preferring the avoidance of the more grievous transgressions, others are related to the higher, preferring the actualization of ideals which are richer in content. All morality of justice, of self-control, of renunciation, of purity, is of the first type; all morality of bravery, wisdom, fulness of experience, of fidelity, love, or moral greatness, is of the second. The one-sidedness of the one is as humanly finite as that of the other. Each is only half of morality. Not until the two preferential trends are joined in a synthesis, could a system be called moral in the full sense of the word.

The general antinomy of valuational preference between higher and lower is found in all the antinomies which subsist preponderantly between values of equal or almost equal rank. Its dimension intersects them. We could correctly call it the fundamental ethical antinomy.

(i) THE SYNTHESIS OF THE TWO TRENDS OF PREFERENCE, AS AN IDEAL

Whether finite human perception can ever resolve this antinomy cannot be known in anticipation. But what can be distinctly seen is this, that the sense of value is alert to find a synthesis of the two preferential trends and distinctly points to it in the value of the "good," which, although not concretely discerned as one, is sought for in its unity. It is here as with the higher virtues which can be anticipated by the sense of values as required syntheses, but cannot be directly known in the unity of a concrete ideal.

On the other hand, it is not difficult to conceive—by having a formal diagram without the contents filled in—how in general the synthesis will result. If the preference is not to values but away from disvalues, one could then say: it is a non-teleology of the lower disvalues. But in itself this is not really opposed to a positive teleology of the higher values. Rather does it appear as a continuation of the same basic trend.

To express it positively, the synthesis between preference for strength and preference for height proves nothing but this, that morality in the full and genuine sense has to do always and at the same time with the entire gradational ladder of moral values, that the lower ones are never a matter of indifference from the point of view of the higher, while these can never be dispensed with for the sake of the more fundamental. If one remembers how very prone our narrow and humanly finite consciousness is to one-sidedness on this point, how unstable our equipoise is at this dividing line, one sees that this requirement is eminently practical and positive; and especially so for anyone who yearns for the highest; for with him the rudimentary foundations are most endangered.

Security against transgression of an elementary kind is never guaranteed in the fulfilment of higher claims—not more at all events than the latter is guaranteed in the former. Genuine morality must build from below up and work incessantly at the foundation; and this the more strenuously, the higher it builds; for the foundation has so much the more to carry. But its meaning can never be exhausted in this work; its meaning is in the superstructure.

The synthesis of preferences in the essence of the good has

no purport except the demand for solidity, from below up, in so far as it is the condition of all genuine moral elevation. And even here again it is clear that the antinomy as well as the idea of the synthesis refers not to the relation among values themselves but to their actualization. For the lower values as such do not antagonize the higher; it is only the preference for their actualization which clashes with the preference for the actualization of the higher. Rather does the synthesis attest that in one and the same ethical disposition the fulfilment of the higher is conditioned by the fulfilment of the lower. Who wills the height must first will the conditions.

This may be stated more concretely. A moral life is perverted, if it is related only to the highest values and neglects the lower, as if it were possible to actualize the former while they float in the air and have no foundation. But poverty-stricken is a moral life, which with all its purposes is imprisoned in the lower values and spends itself upon them. A morality which culminates in self-control and justice easily becomes pharisaical; it exhausts itself in safeguards against crime and the lowest baseness; it makes even the spiritual freedom which it acquires, empty. But that morality is dangerous which provides scope only for personality and fosters it only; it devastates the ground on which personalities grow. The fulfilment of the meaning of humanity is never to be found in the foundations of human life; but the possibility of actualizing that meaning is never attached to its positive contents alone. Its aims should be placed so high that man can only just discern them, but its foundations should be laid as firmly as ever they can be laid.

Many are the errors and aberrations which miss this synthesis. The majority of the current moralities and philosophical theories have not escaped them. The radical one-sidedness of the preferential trend joins with every one-sidedness that shows itself in the discerned material. The new morality, which comes forward with the claim that it is a higher morality, only too easily throws away the "lower" in the gross—an error which will avenge itself, even if the new really be higher. It does not see that it is demolishing its own foundation.

Thus it befell Nietzsche in regard to Christian morality. He rightly saw that love of the far distant is the higher moral value. Yet he was at the same time wrong; for brotherly love is the "stronger" value. The mistake of Christianity is the belief that the fulfilment of the moral life depends upon brotherly love alone. Nietzsche's mistake is to suppose that love of the far distant is possible without a basis in brotherly love, that its aims are in themselves sufficient. Only in their synthesis is to be found the reciprocal content of both ideals. But to discern the synthesis is a task of far greater magnitude than to attach oneself to the one side and despise the other.

On this point the ethics of early Christianity was wiser in its attitude towards the ancient morality of justice, which to it rightly appeared poverty-stricken; it was wiser in its intention "not to destroy but to fulfil." Fulfilment is the meaning of all progress in the moral life. Destruction of the old undermines the new at its inception. In fact synthesis is always required. And it is difficult to discover. Even the narrowness of our vision of values sets a limit to our discernment of it. That is why the moral life of man, viewed historically, makes so little progress, despite all the intensity and all the earnestness of human yearning and solicitude.

The secret of human progress is that advance must be along the whole line, and not by fragments, that the trend towards the highest must be accompanied by a trend towards the most elementary. Every other progress is only a semblance. It surrenders on one side what it wins on the other.

VALUE AND VALUATIONAL INDIFFERENCE

(a) VARIOUS ALTITUDES OF THE SCALES BUT THE SAME ZERO-POINT

IN formulating the table of opposites[1] we waived the question of valuational indifference and its dual relation to value and disvalue. But in so far as every single scale contains a neutral point, this is evidently involved in the fundamental axiological relation. And, on the other hand, in as much as neutrality indicates the attitude of real existence to the whole realm of valuational gradations, there is a problem here as to the limits of gradation. Hence our investigation cannot entirely ignore it. It requires a special exposition. And this becomes so much the more important, since, as we indicated when we waived it aside, the gradation of values stands in a very definite relation to neutrality.

In addition to all the limitations of our discernment of values, what makes their gradation so difficult to grasp objectively, is the circumstance that so far as we can see there is no fixed point of reference in the scale. The same of course holds true of the ordered rank of disvalues, of the gradation of their gravity, which marks their downward descent.

But according to their position in "valuational space" their order of rank falls under the polar dimension of value and disvalue. Yet in this there is the fixed point to which all that is of value or contrary to it is related, the indifference-point. It is the absolute zero of dimensional elevation. To it corresponds—throughout the whole extent of the realm—a single average level, at which without distinction of material or qualitative difference value and disvalue separate.

This level of neutrality therefore is the same for all materially

[1] Cf. Chapter XXXVI (b), Vol. II.

different scales, that is, for the scales of every single value and its corresponding disvalue. These scales all cut the indifference-level. But as they, with their very different ranges, also combine very different grades one with another, so their position as regards the indifference-point is also necessarily very different. But in so far as the position of the neutral point is fixed and absolute for all, this means that in their "absolute" height they differ.

There are scales of values, in which the positive pole is only a little above the indifference-point but in which the negative pole is far below it; and there are others, in which the positive pole is raised to a considerable height above neutrality, while the negative lies close to it. Of the first kind are manifestly the scales of the lowest values; of the second, those of the highest.

Herein is confirmed the axiological law, that the lowest values are the strongest, while the weakest are the highest. "Strength" shows itself in the low grade of the anti-value, that is, in the gravity of a violation against the corresponding value. It is this relation of height and strength in their almost indirectly proportional position, which finds visible expression in the schematic relation of all scales to the level of the zero point.

(b) The Relation of the Heights of the Values and the Depths of the Anti-Values to the Indifference-Point

Anyone who turns to the analysis of values without first considering this fact, naturally expects that in every scale the indifference-point must lie midway, that value and anti-value must always stand equidistant from it, that therefore, for example, the vice of lack of self-control and the virtue of self-control, or the badness of an unloving heart and the goodness of loving-kindness, would be axiologically of the same magnitude, only on opposite sides of the indifference-point.

This is evidently a mistake. And indeed not only because magnitude is here only figurative and moreover can be measured only with difficulty, but because the whole conception is wrong. For either the ranges of all scales are of equal magnitude, or they are not. Now, in the former case, all values must needs stand equally high above, but all anti-values equally deep below the zero-point. In the latter case, however, the correspondingly deeper-lying anti-value must correspond to the higher-lying value; this would mean that the higher values would be at the same time the stronger, and the lower would be the weaker. Each of these views is evidently false. The first contradicts the clear differentiation in the sensing of values as to their height (for example, in the gradation of responses both to values and anti-values), but the second contradicts the law of strength, which affirms the exact opposite.

All this is changed, as soon as one surrenders the prejudice as to the midway point. Indifference is not necessarily midway in the single scales. Rather is it to be found now nearer to the value, now to the disvalue, according to the rank of the value. It may of course lie midway also; and there is a series of values of average grade, in the scales of which this applies approximately (for instance, in those of bravery and cowardice, or of humility and pride); here the value and disvalue manifest approximately the same strongly-marked axiological character.

The diversity in the position of the indifference-point in the various scales by no means indicates a fluctuation of the point itself. Rather does this remain fixed, as at one level, while the scales, for their part, assume extremely various heights from this level—which fact again exactly corresponds with the diverse grades. Thus it comes about, that precisely the constant relation of the scale to valuational indifference confirms the law of strength. According to this law the lower-lying (more grievous) disvalue must not correspond to the higher value; but to the higher value the higher-lying (less grievous) disvalue corresponds.

This is what can be very easily understood in the relation of every scale to the one indifference-point. Indeed one also understands that, if all scales were also of the same range between value and disvalue, the indirect proportionality of height to strength would be quite mathematically exact. That there are valuational relations where this is not precisely the case, is easily explained by the diversity in the range between value and disvalue. This explanation is of the greatest importance for the understanding of the relation of height to strength, since from it ensues that, even in the apparent exceptions, the law of strength is not suspended, but is strictly carried out. It is, however, involved with another uniformity, the exact structure of which we do not know, a uniformity which concerns the variation of the span between value and disvalue in the different scales.

If at this point one compares the rising group of values mentioned in the preceding chapter, one sees in the attached responses an illustration of gradational displacement of the entire scale. Dishonesty (stealing, for example) is criminal; honesty, on the other hand, attains only to the height of what is merely approved, that is, it almost coincides with the indifference-point, rising above it only to the lowest degree. Lying is dishonourable, but not criminal; but sincerity deserves a far more positive recognition. An unloving disposition is by no means dishonourable, still it is morally of no value, while neighbourly love compels respect. An incapacity to feel implicit trust is only a certain weakness, but implicit trust is something worthy of esteem. Indifference to the destiny and future of mankind can scarcely be called a vice, it is simply evidence of a lack of moral greatness; universal love, on the other hand, because of the vastness of the self-subjection involved in it, is something directly heroic and merits admiration. Finally, the absence of the virtue which dispenses spiritual values is manifestly no moral delinquency, but its presence influences others like a kind of moral perfection.

If we compare the last two scales with the first, we clearly see the extreme positions towards valuational indifference reversed. With honesty almost the whole scale lies below the zero-point, the value scarcely rises above it; with universal love and radiant virtue almost the whole scale lies above indifference, the corresponding disvalue scarcely below it. The intermediate values show an evident rise, a progressive advance of the values themselves as well as of the disvalues. The latter approach nearer to the level of indifference, the values move farther from it.

Here one can accordingly reduce the law of strength to a definite formula: with the height of the value the absolute grade of the whole scale moves against the indifference-point, likewise also—and indeed in the same way—the grade of the disvalue. In the case of the higher values the whole scale lies more above, in the case of the lower more below the indifference-point. Hence with the lower values the anti-value is far below it; with the higher, the anti-value is near to the indifference-point. Since the depth of the anti-value is a measure of the grievousness of transgression, but since in the grievousness of the transgression is seen the strength of the value, it follows universally and on principle from this diagram that the lower values are the stronger, a fact which heretofore could be seen only inductively from particular values.

(c) The Absolutely Indifferent and the Absolutely Valuable

Finally it should be observed that, besides the common zero-point of the scales, there exists a second manifestation of valuational indifference, which at the same time is a limiting phenomenon of the table of values.

A survey of values proves beyond all doubt that increasing height indicates also an increase of the valuational quality itself; but a decreasing height shows a diminution of quality. This is not at all a self-evident fact. The opposite could just as well be true. Still the lower value is the stronger; and, as such, it will be felt immediately in the grievousness of the violation of it. But, for the sense of value, it is significant that the characteristics of the strongest become less marked, while those of the highest are discriminated with the greatest sensitiveness.

The most elementary values, where they are actualized, are taken for granted—thus life, health, welfare, especially whatever is necessary for daily needs; and even beyond these, ordinary but not necessary possessions, in so far as one is accustomed to them as necessities. We first become properly aware of the value of such goods, when we are in need of them. What we in this way become aware of is therefore by no means the height of their value but its strength, that is, the seriousness of the anti-value, of the lack of the value, of the need, the deprivation, the danger. Indirectly, then, the value of such goods is felt with painful acuteness. Through anxiety its neutral colour is changed into a vivid hue. But these colours are not properly its own. If one only considers whether for the sake of such goods life would be worth living, their borrowed vividness fades away. In the realm of positive moral values it is the same as regards those which are the strongest (such as justice and self-control).

But everywhere here, with goods as with virtues, the valuational quality, despite its paleness, is nevertheless felt directly. This is otherwise only when one goes a step further towards the most elementary factors which we can comprehend, towards the "most general pairs of valuational opposites."[1] Here the immediate sensing of value is at the limit of its power of discrimination; to make any one of these values perceptible there is need of a complex survey of the axiological situation as a whole. This became most evident in the case of the modal contrasts.[2]

And yet even these values are not the final ones, not properly the ultimate elements. They are only the last discernible ones in this direction. That beyond them exist further elements, can scarcely be doubted; it is simply that their distinctive quality can no longer be discriminated; they approach the indifference-point. If one further bears in mind that precisely in this direction,

[1] Cf. Chapters VI–IX, Vol. II.   [2] Chapter VII, Vol. II.

beyond the elements which are given in irreducible plurality, man's valuational vision goes on seeking a first and simple unity and that such a unity necessarily must lie beyond the range of our sense of values, the thought naturally arises that this irrational limiting point of the realm must at the same time be itself the limit of valuational character, that is, that there is no value beyond, but that there must be an absolute indifference—a merely categorial unitary termination to all values.[1] As there exists a variety of categorial determinations (laws, structures and so on) which stretch far into the realm of values, there is nothing especially daring in this metaphysical inference.

Naturally on this point nothing definite can be said. In the realm of values (as we see it to-day) nothing is more obscure than the existence of an elementary unity entrenched behind all plurality. But it is precisely the total perspective of values in their diversity, so far as the diversity can be surveyed, which brings this thought home to one. For the diminution downwards of discernible quality is beyond all doubt. Moreover, an absolute limit to value in this direction—if it exists—must necessarily itself be the limit of what is of value. But that is the absolutely indifferent. The ideal "beginning" of the realm of values lies at the level of the axiological zero.

Thus arises further a new perspective as to the total arrangement of the table of values. If it be granted that its ideal "beginning" is not a value, how is its exfoliation and final consummation to be understood? Evidently it must culminate in a value of which the axiological character constitutes the absolute counter-pole to its beginning—therefore in something universally valuable, something absolute in the sense of embracing all values. That we can concretely discern such a value as little as we can discern absolute valuational neutrality, has become sufficiently clear from our analysis of the higher values. But at the same time from our analysis it became clear that the whole diversity of values—both where it shows contrasts and where it shows complementary relationship—presses urgently

[1] Cf. Chapter V (c), Vol. II.

towards valuational syntheses, to which the perpetual watching on the part of the sense of values is itself an eloquent witness. Thus far the thought of a highest synthesis of all values is no play of idle fancy. A supreme value, understood in this sense, would in truth be the exact counterpart to the absolute indifference of the beginning. As in the latter all quality disappears, so in the absolutely valuable—that is, in the extreme augmentation of valuational character—all material difference must needs vanish. For here all valuational materials would be united. Here would be the maximum in content as in value; there the minimum.

(d) THE BEGINNING AND END OF THE REALM OF VALUES

If one draws into this perspective the law of grade in the scales of values, according to which the higher-lying (the lesser) disvalue corresponds to the higher value, one sees that in the "beginning" of valuational diversity, the positive pole of the scale falls at the indifference-level and the negative must have lain at the lowest point below; that is, it must have been the heaviest disvalue, the absolute anti-value, in which every valuable constituent is annihilated. In the "end" of the realm of values, however, which is its fulfilment, when the positive pole of the scale lies at the highest point, the negative pole must at the same time take the highest position possible for a disvalue; that is, it must fall at just the same level of indifference at which in the "beginning" the positive pole lay.

Thus, then, would of course arise an exact symmetry throughout the whole arrangement. The positive-negative scale of the highest value would lie wholly above the indifference-point; that of the lowest, entirely beneath. The disvalue of the former would, in axiological height, coincide with the value of the latter. Neither the extreme difference in material nor the fundamental opposition of value and anti-value would necessarily be in contradiction to the identity in gradation.

The disvalue reappears projected into the zero-point. It is retained in the evanescence of distance.

But between the beginning and the end would lie the whole manifold realm of values. We know neither the lower nor the higher boundary of the realm, and all speculations concerning it (even those here suggested) remain conjectural. Even as regards the variety of materials and their order of gradation we know only a middle section. But in this section is at least clearly discernible the displacement of the scales, the extremes of which must constitute the lower and the upper boundaries.

GLOSSARY OF GREEK TERMS AND PHRASES

ἀγαθόν	the good; goodness
ἀγάπη	love of one's neighbour; brotherly love
ἀγάπησις	affection; friendliness
ἀγροικία	boorishness; rusticity
ἀγροῖκος	boorish; countrified
ἀδικεῖν	doing wrong
ἀδικεῖσθαι	suffering wrong or injustice
αἰδήμων	one who feels ashamed
αἰδώς	sense of shame
ἀκολασία	licentiousness; intemperance
ἄκρον, ἄκρα	extreme(s)
ἀκρότης	extreme
ἀλαζονεία	boasting; imposture; pretence
ἀληθεύειν	sincere demeanour
ἀναισθησία	apathy; dullness; stupidity
ἀναίσχυντος	shameless; impudent
ἀναξίως	undeservedly
ἀνδρεία	manliness; courage
ἀνελευθερία	penuriousness; stinginess
ἀνθρώπινον	human
ἀνώνυμος	nameless; without a name
ἀξιοῦν ἑαυτόν	self-appreciation
ἀοργησία	lack of passion; incapacity for righteous anger
ἀπειροκαλία	lack of taste
ἄρεσκος	complaisant; obsequious
ἀρετή	goodness; excellence; virtue
ἄριστον	the best
ἀσοφία	folly; stupidity
ἀστεῖον	urbane
ἀσωτία	squandering; profligacy
αὐτάρκεια	self-sufficiency; independence
ἀφιλοτιμία	lack of ambition
βαναυσία	vulgar display; vulgarity
βωμολοχία	frivolity; ribaldry
βωμολόχος	frivolous; ribald
γέννησις	engendering
δειλία	cowardice; timidity
δικαιοσύνη	justice; righteousness
δύσκολος	unapproachable; difficult to deal with

ἐγκράτεια	self-mastery; self-control
εἰρωνεία	self-depreciation; dissimulation
ἐλευθεριότης	liberality
ἔλλειψις	deficiency; defect; omission
ἕν	The One
ἐν μέσῳ	midway; intermediate
ἔνδεια	lack; want
ἕξις, ἕξεις	habit(s); attitude(s)
ἐπαινεῖται	commendable
ἐπαινετόν	praiseworthy
ἐπιδεξιότης	cleverness; pleasing intellectuality
ἐπιθυμία	striving; desire; yearning
ἐπιμέλεια	diligence; attention; care
ἐπιχαιρεκακία	delight in others' misfortune; malignity
ἐπονείδιστον	disgraceful
ἐραστής	lover
ἔρως	love; desire
εὖ	good
εὐδαιμονία	appreciative participation of success; happiness
εὐτραπελία	urbanity; pleasing liveliness
εὐτυχία	favourable circumstances or destiny; success; prosperity
ἡμαρτημένον	defective; faulty
θαυμαστόν	admirable
θρασύτης	foolhardiness; audacity
κάθαρσις	purification; cleansing
κακία, κακίαι	evil(s); vice(s)
κακόν	bad
καλοκἀγαθία	nobleness; steadfast goodness
καλόν	beautiful
καταπλήξ	intimidated
κατὰ τὸ ἄριστον καὶ τὸ εὖ	concerning the best and the good
κρατεῖν	rulership
κύησις	conception; pregnancy
κόσμος ἀρετῶν	a world of excellences
λόγος	universal reason
μακαριστόν	superb
μεγαλοπρέπεια	magnificence
μεγαλοψυχία	magnanimity
μεγαλόψυχος	magnanimous; high-minded

μεγάλων ἑαυτὸν ἀξιῶν ἄξιος ὤν	deeming oneself worthy of great things
μηδὲν ἄγαν	nothing in excess
μερισμός	individuation; division
μεσότης	mean; "golden mean"; medium
μεσότητες	mean; intermediate
μεταμέλεια	regret; repentance
μετάνοια	afterthought; backward look
μίασμα	defilement; pollution
μικροπρέπεια	meanness; shabbiness
μικροψυχία	self-depreciation; self-disparagement; mean-spiritedness
μισητόν	hateful
νέμεσις	justifiable participation in what befalls others
νεμεσητικός	one who wishes to give everyone his due
ὀργιλότης	violent temper; irascibility
οὐσία	essence; essential quality
πάθος	passive state; passivity
περὶ τί	what is concerned
περὶ τιμάς	concerning honour
πραότης	mildness; equability
πρόνοια	prevision; foresight
πρὸς ἕτερον	concerning others
πρῶτον κινοῦν	primal agent; "first mover"; source of activity
σοφία	wisdom
συμπάθεια	community of feeling
συμπλοκή	combination; interwovenness; interlacing
σωφροσύνη	self-control; moderation
σώφρων	sane; prudent
τὰ καλὰ καὶ ἄκαρπα	the ornamental and the unprofitable
τί ἦν εἶναι	existence in thought or in idea
τιμὴ μεγάλη	great honour
τιμητόν	worthy of honour
τὸ παρὰ φύσιν	that which is contrary to Nature
ὑπερβολή	excess; extravagance
φθόνος	envy; malice; ill-will
φιλητόν	lovable; worthy of love

φιλία	friendship; "love of a friend"
φιλοτιμία	ambition; love of honour
φόβος ἀδοξίας	fear of contempt
χαυνότης	arrogance; conceit; vanity
χρήματα	possessions; material goods
ψεκτόν	blameworthy

INDEX FOR VOLUMES I-III